New Approaches
to Preventing Suicide

A Manual for Practitioners

Edited by David Duffy and Tony Ryan

Jessica Kingsley Publishers
London and Philadelphia

Box 2.2 is reproduced from Gask, L. and Morris, R. (2003) 'Assessment and immediate management of people at risk of harming themselves.' *Psychiatry 2*, 7, 10, by kind permission of The
Medicine Publishing Company Ltd. Table 2.1 is reproduced from www.nelmh.org by permission
of the National Electronic Library for Mental Health. Figure 9.1 is reproduced from *Mental Health
in a Multi-ethnic Society*, edited by Suman Fernando (1995) by permission of Routledge. Box 2.1 is
Crown copyright material, reproduced by permission of the Controller of HMSO.

The right of the contributors to be identified as authors of this work
has been asserted by them in accordance with the Copyright, Designs
and Patents Act 1988.

First published in 2004
by Jessica Kingsley Publishers
116 Pentonville Road
London N1 9JB, UK
and
400 Market Street, Suite 400
Philadelphia, PA 19106, USA

www.jkp.com

Copyright © Jessica Kingsley Publishers 2004
Second impression 2005

Library of Congress Cataloging in Publication Data
New approaches to preventing suicide : a manual for practitioners / edited by David Duffy & Tony
Ryan ; foreword by Louis Appleby.
    p. cm.
Includes bibliographical references and index.
ISBN 1-84310-221-8 (pbk.)
    1. Suicide--England--Prevention. 2. Suicide--Prevention. I. Duffy, David, 1951- II. Ryan, Tony,
1958–
HV6548.G7N48 2004
362.28'7--dc22
                                                    2004007492

British Library Cataloguing in Publication Data
A CIP catalogue record for this book is available from the British Library

ISBN-13: 978 1 84310 221 2
ISBN-10: 1 84310 221 8

Printed and Bound in Great Britain by
Athenaeum Press, Gateshead, Tyne and Wear

for Chris Duffy
and
Maggie Ryan

Contents

List of Tables

List of Figures

Foreword

Suicide is a major problem and its prevention is a worldwide priority. In recent years, significant steps have been taken to reduce the incidence of suicide. Prevention initiatives have been launched in the USA, Canada, Australia and other countries, including England, where the National Institute for Mental Health in England (NIMHE) is co-ordinating the implementation of a National Suicide Prevention Strategy.

Suicide is a complex, multifactorial phenomenon. There is no single way of preventing it. Population approaches such as the reduction of access to suicidal methods need to be combined with attention to particular high-risk social groups, with engagement with the media to ensure the appropriate portrayal and reporting of suicide and with the promotion of good mental health. Research needs to continue into effective preventive interventions and initiatives need to be co-ordinated across society to include not just health and social services but education, the workplace, voluntary organisations and the criminal justice system.

However, such large scale national efforts will not be effective unless people are equipped to play their part. The objective of this book is to help people, whether they are professionals from such backgrounds as medicine, nursing and social work or whether they work in other capacities with those at risk, to increase their understanding of suicide prevention. A wide range of imaginative perspectives from health and social services, the criminal justice system, service users, voluntary organisations and the legal profession has been brought together to provide fresh insights into how suicide can be prevented in practice and how education and training can make a difference. I commend this book to the individual practitioner, to service managers, to educationalists and to all who come into contact with those at risk.

Professor Louis Appleby
National Director for Mental Health in England

Chapter 1

Introduction

David Duffy and Tony Ryan

According to the World Health Organization (WHO), around one million people worldwide currently die from suicide each year and 10 to 20 times more attempt suicide. This represents an average of one death every 40 seconds and one attempt every 3 seconds (WHO 1999). In England alone, approximately 5000 people die by suicide annually (Department of Health (DoH) 2002). Although suicide rates fluctuate, in recent years there has been a relentless rise in the number of young people who die by suicide, especially young men, for whom suicide has become the leading cause of death (DoH 2002). Along with these deaths there are very large numbers of people, estimated to be as many as 142,000 (Hawton and Catalan 1987), who are admitted annually to Accident and Emergency (A&E) departments because they have harmed themselves non-fatally. Even these numbers will be less than the actual total of people who self-harm, since many will not be in receipt of any form of health care afterwards. Among admissions to A&E departments for non-fatal self-harm, the majority involve self-poisoning. Between 10 and 15 per cent tend to be cases of self-injury, with most of these involving cutting (Hawton and Catalan 1987). Many admissions are of people who have harmed themselves previously and whose problem has therefore not been successfully addressed. Some of these people will eventually go on to die by suicide (Hawton and Fagg 1988).

In response to the alarming scale of the problem, the British Government has identified a reduction in the rate of suicide by 20 per cent by the year 2010 as a measure by which it is prepared to be judged (DoH 1999, 2002). The first ever National Suicide Prevention Strategy for England (DoH 2002) was developed to promote a co-ordinated approach to meeting this target.

Clearly, if a significant reduction in the suicide rate is to be achieved, major efforts will need to be made across the whole of society. While suicide prevention is undoubtedly a priority for mental health services, suicides by people in contact with these services only make up around one quarter of all suicides. Not only the rest of the health service, but social services, the education system, business, the criminal justice system, the voluntary sector and individual citizens will all need to be engaged in responding appropriately to the needs of people at risk and in seeking to prevent people becoming suicidal.

This book is an attempt to contribute to this work. Offering a wide variety of up-to-date perspectives on suicide prevention, it aims to be as practical and helpful as possible to those engaged directly or indirectly with people at risk, whether they are professionals, voluntary workers, service managers, service commissioners or educationalists.

The foundation for preventing suicide in practice is effective risk assessment. Chapter 2 of the book therefore begins with evidence-based guidance by Dr Jayne Cooper and Dr Navneet Kapur on how best to detect suicide risk. The authors argue that the role of suicide risk assessment is not one of attempting accurate predictions about future behaviour. Rather, in seeking to integrate current knowledge about risk factors based upon epidemiological studies with knowledge of the person's individual characteristics, effective risk assessment can assist us to make informed, safer decisions about how people can be supported.

Health care workers have an opportunity to prevent suicide across the whole range of care settings, and in the following four chapters practitioners from primary care, A&E, the mental health in-patient environment and from community settings have offered practical examples of how to go about this.

In Chapter 3 on primary care Dr Barry Lewis, a GP with considerable interest and expertise in mental health, highlights the role of this sector in the prevention of suicide. Suicide is an infrequent event when seen at general practitioner level. GP practices may go a number of years without having someone on their list die by suicide and GPs may go through long periods in their careers without being affected by the death of one of their patients in this way. A consequence of this is that suicide and its prevention can be viewed as less important in comparison to other areas and conditions that they work with. Barry not only highlights the ways in which GP practices can work to prevent suicide and the training that can improve practice in this area, he also stresses the impact that these events can have on professionals and how practices might learn from such events.

Allied to primary care within the health care system is the Accident and Emergency department (A&E) in its function of serving whole populations. A&E can be a significant point of contact with those who are considering suicide, particularly with many of the social groups who are at statistically high risk for suicide. In Chapter 4 Alison Pearsall and Dr Tony Ryan describe how the role of A&E has become more sophisticated in relation to people with mental health problems, especially to those among the general population who are not known to specialist mental health services. The collaboration of mental health liaison services with A&E and other general hospital services can provide a powerful method for the delivery of suicide prevention interventions. For many the A&E department may be the most accessible form of support when they seek help, whether for psychological problems or because of physical factors which might be compounding or masking underlying suicide ideation.

A number of people in the care of acute mental health in-patient units die by suicide each year. It is true that mental health service users in general are one of the highest risk groups for suicide, yet – as individual incident investigations continue to show – some of these deaths are preventable. In Chapter 5 Nick Bowles explains one perspective on suicidality in in-patient settings, linking it to the pressures of the social environment on some mental health units and offering lessons from his experience in implementing the 'refocusing' approach in a variety of mental health Trusts.

People with mental health problems tend to benefit from care delivered in less restrictive settings that seek to empower them to manage their own mental health. In Chapter 6, Nigel Crompton and Peter Walmsley review community-based suicide prevention. They argue that communication is crucial to the management of suicidal behaviour, and they discuss the nature of communication and effective care co-ordination. They consider how contracting can aid in the management of the suicidal person in the community, and explain their view that the central focus of any effort to prevent suicide in the community should be to empower the person to ensure their own suicide prevention by building self-worth, inspiring hope, decreasing helplessness and teaching stress reduction.

There are a number of groups within society at particular risk of suicide. There is no doubt that young men are the highest risk group of all. Not long ago men over 75 were the highest risk group, yet today the under 25s have overtaken them by some distance. Given this alarming trend, Mike Smith notes in Chapter 7 that young men are ironically not often considered to be at such a high level of risk by their families, the media and mental health professionals. His chapter considers the reasons why young men are killing themselves at such a rate and offers a number of practical recommendations for what can be done about it.

Prisoners form another high-risk group for suicide. In Chapter 8 Jo Paton and Dr Jo Borrill note that, while 94 per cent of prisoners who die by suicide are male, women prisoners actually take their own lives at the same rate as do men. Prisoners are known to be a vulnerable population, at increased risk of suicide before they even enter the prison gates, while the prison environment and the experience of custody bring their own risk factors. This chapter argues that close attention needs to be paid to such issues as the type of prison, the type of regime and the particular stage of the prisoner's custody – for example, remand and unsentenced prisoners are at most risk. A holistic approach is needed to address suicide risk in this population.

Hári Sewell makes the case in Chapter 9 that the surprising fact with regard to suicides of people from Black and minority ethnic groups (BME) is that there are not more of them. His chapter addresses some of the complex issues that arise in trying to understand the needs of people from BME groups in relation to suicide prevention. There are no formulaic answers to working effectively with individuals and communities from BME groups. However, the method of finding the answer is simple. Services need to hear and act upon the particular needs of BME groups.

While this book is primarily concerned with suicide and suicide prevention, non-fatal self-harm is very much more common than suicide, and is also significant as a precursor to actual suicide. Many people who self-harm do so through overdoses, which is responsible for many thousands of admissions to A&E departments each year. Some of these acts of self-harm are unsuccessful suicide attempts while others are expressions of distress without the intention to actually die. 'Self-injury' is a term which refers to the infliction of damage to the body, often by self-cutting, though also by other means such as burning, in order to relieve unbearable feelings of tension, to regain a feeling of control in difficult circumstances, or for many other and varied reasons. Many people who self-injure do so without any contact with health or social services. However, self-injury in a care setting often raises complex challenges, prompted by the personal reactions of staff, the duty of care, and the person's wish to retain autonomy in their choice of behaviour. Two chapters focus on these issues. David Hewitt, a solicitor, explains the legal background in Chapter 10, showing how duty of care should be interpreted, and provides a constructive way forward for the development of what could legally be accepted as a 'clinical consensus' in regard to reasonable practice. Complementing the legal approach, in

Chapter 11 Christine Hogg, a mental health nurse and lecturer, engages in a dialogue with Clare Shaw, a service user with personal experience of self-injury. The dialogue explores self-injury in terms of its meaning for the person who self-injures and considers what actions can be helpful to the person, offering constructive suggestions for responding appropriately to self-injury.

Suicide among children and early adolescents is a rare event. However, its incidence increases significantly among those in their later teens and it continues to rise until the early twenties. In Chapter 12, on this high-risk group, Dr Gemma Trainor explores important aspects of both completed and attempted suicides in young people and considers a range of treatment options. She notes that adolescents who repeatedly self-harm are likely to be at higher risk of completing suicide due to adverse mental health and psychosocial difficulties. At the same time, they may be difficult to engage in conventional treatment programmes. A comprehensive service for these young people therefore needs to involve a variety of therapies and new and more creative ways of working.

The National Confidential Inquiry into Suicide and Homicide by People with Mental Illness is one of three confidential enquiries in England and Wales that were set up with funding from the Department of Health in order to investigate adverse outcomes under health services. Jo Robinson and Harriet Bickley describe in Chapter 13 the contribution of the Confidential Inquiry in preventing suicide. They explain the background and aims of the Inquiry, its methodology, and the implications of the Inquiry data for the understanding of suicide in England and Wales, and discuss how data from the Inquiry is used at a national level, some of its key findings and recommendations and its role in the development of national policy. Their chapter then considers how the Inquiry data can be used locally for audit purposes and service development. They conclude with a summary of new developments for the Inquiry.

When suicides or suicide attempts occur, one of the positive steps that can be taken by any services that were involved is to review what happened in order to learn for the future. One effective way of doing this is to carry out an audit. In Chapter 14, Dr Lester Sireling emphasises that an audit is not an attempt to cast blame. Nonetheless, undertaking an audit of this form of death involves particular challenges. The chapter reviews ways in which these challenges can be met and shows how suicide audit can identify service gaps and populations at high risk within a service.

Another approach to learning from suicides and serious incidents is Root Cause Analysis. This approach is explained in detail in Chapter 15 by

Kathryn Hill, Dr Sally Adams and Suzette Woodward, who, like Lester Sireling, emphasise that investigations should be undertaken in a spirit which is open and fair, non-blaming but accountable. Investigations should focus on the system rather than the individual, ensuring that lessons can be learnt and solutions implemented.

The National Suicide Prevention Strategy for England (DoH 2002) recommends that all mental health staff who work with people at risk of suicide should receive training in risk management every three years. Such training is often developed in house, or is undertaken on short courses or as part of professional education, and there is as yet no agreed understanding of what should be expected of risk management training. Jenny Droughton, Dr Linda Gask, Dr Clare Dixon and Gill Green provide an account of the STORM project, an exemplar of an effective, evidence-based training programme, in Chapter 16. They explain the background to the project, noting the particular importance of addressing attitudinal change to tackle negative beliefs about suicide and negative attitudes towards the suicidal. The authors provide an account of how the training is being implemented in a range of settings and, importantly, how the impact of STORM on actual practice is being evaluated.

In Chapter 17, Professor Richard Ramsay addresses suicide prevention training from two perspectives. One looks at the relevance of an international guideline for Nations to use in formulating and implementing national suicide prevention strategies. The other looks at the use of social research and development methods to develop suicide intervention training for community and potentially international dissemination. The Applied Suicide Intervention Skills Training (ASIST) program developed in Canada is presented as an international dissemination example.

Suicide is a devastating event for 'survivors', a term which usually connotes those bereaved as family or friends. However, staff who have cared for people who go on to take their own lives are also very much affected. Victoria Pallin describes the ways in which suicide impacts on mental health staff in Chapter 18, and notes that they may not only feel alone and unsupported but also traumatised and blamed. She offers a systematic approach to thinking about staff support after a suicide, with innovative suggestions for all those involved.

Since their foundation 50 years ago, the Samaritans have played a notable role in responding to the needs of the suicidal. While they are popularly associated with contact by telephone, in fact they have for long engaged with suicide prevention in many other ways, for example in working with the media to promote more appropriate reporting and portrayal of suicide.

The Samaritans are continuing to undertake a range of proactive initiatives to reach out to people, and Sarah Nelson and Simon Armson describe a number of these initiatives in Chapter 19, all based on the premise that by encouraging people to share difficult feelings fewer will take their own lives.

PAPYRUS is a national charity originally founded by parents who had been bereaved by suicide. Members include professionals from many different fields and others who are interested in the prevention of suicide. In Chapter 20 Tony Cox, Anne Parry and Anna Brown describe the contribution which PAPYRUS makes to suicide prevention, working across boundaries to support and disseminate preventive initiatives and identifying gaps in service provision which it seeks to help to bridge. Given the vulnerability of young people, the emphasis of PAPYRUS on the young is of particular importance.

While mental health services have an important role to play in suicide prevention, it is nonetheless true that two thirds of suicides are by people who are not in contact with such services. It is vital therefore that the whole of society is engaged in the process of preventing suicide, and in Chapter 21 Jude Stansfield and Pippa Sargent describe a 'whole system' approach to mental health promotion within the community, including building protective factors and reducing social, environmental and economic risk factors.

Finally, Rowan Purdy provides a collection of wide-ranging good practice exemplars and useful references to assist anyone engaged in the vital work of preventing suicide.

Altogether, we hope that this collection of diverse and practical materials will provide a useful resource for anyone who is concerned with the prevention of suicide.

References

Department of Health (1999) *Saving Lives: Our Healthier Nation.* London: The Stationery Office.

Department of Health (2002) *The National Suicide Prevention Strategy for England.* London: The Stationery Office.

Hawton, K. and Catalan, J. (1987) *Attempted Suicide: A Practical Guide to its Nature and Management.* Second edition. Oxford: Oxford University Press.

Hawton, K. and Fagg, J. (1988) 'Suicide, and other causes of death, following attempted suicide.' *British Journal of Psychiatry 152*, 359–366.

World Health Organization (1999) *Figures and Facts About Suicide.* Geneva: WHO.

Chapter 2

Assessing Suicide Risk

Jayne Cooper and Navneet Kapur

Introduction

Assessing risk is part of everyday practice. For example, professionals working in mental health often need to assess the risk of harm to others, risk of harm to self, or the relative risks and benefits of a particular form of treatment (Kapur 2000).

Suicide risk assessment is an inexact science. The problems in applying risk factors to identify suicide are formidable. Known characteristics describe vulnerable groups rather than individuals. The features of risk vary between groups, while circumstances in an individual can change over time, making them more or less vulnerable. Further, the known characteristics identified for suicides from previous research are largely based on various groups of individuals who have died by suicide, irrespective of what psychiatric treatment they may have received (Hawton 1987). Prediction models of suicidality have consistently demonstrated high false positives, that is, patients identified as high risk who do not subsequently commit suicide (NHS Centre for Reviews and Dissemination 1998). High false negatives (patients identified as low risk who subsequently commit suicide) would be unacceptable in clinical practice. As clinicians the aim should not necessarily be to predict suicide but simply to assess risk in a reliable and consistent way.

Even though we cannot always predict suicide with certainty, important risk factors have been identified that increase the likelihood of suicide. The National Confidential Inquiry into Suicide and Homicide by People with Mental Illness found that nearly one quarter of people who died by suicide in England and Wales had been in contact with mental health services in the year before death (Appleby *et al.* 2001).

Psychological autopsy research studies (Barraclough *et al.* 1974; Appleby *et al.* 1999) indicate that a substantial minority who commit suicide have been in recent contact with primary care services prior to death. However, many have had no recent contact with the health services. These findings highlight the role for mental health, primary care, social and voluntary services in the recognition and effective treatment of suicidal patients. Assessing suicide risk involves knowledge of what makes an individual more vulnerable to suicide (see Box 2.1), knowledge of factors that make suicide less likely and being able to obtain reliable information. In this chapter we will discuss the concept of risk as well as considering the practical aspects of assessing risk.

Box 2.1: Risk factors for suicide

- Loneliness (social isolation)
- Male
- Alcohol/drug misuse
- Other psychiatric disorders, particularly depression
- History of previous self-harm (particularly if avoided discovery)
- History of psychiatric treatment
- Family history of psychiatric disorder (previous self-harm, depression, alcohol/drug misuse)
- Hopelessness
- High suicidal intent:
  - choice of violent method of suicide (e.g. hanging, shotgun)
  - access to means of suicide
  - plans for death (e.g. will changes, family farewells)
- Lower social class
- Unemployment
- Personality disorder (particularly co-morbidity with other psychiatric disorders)

- Physical problems, e.g. cardio-vascular, peptic ulcer, particularly in elderly males
- Life events:
  - ° bereavement and loss (last two years)
  - ° financial problems
  - ° legal problems/recent forensic history
  - ° abuse past or present (sexual, physical or emotional)
  - ° relationship problems
  - ° loss of parents through separation or death during childhood
  - ° exposure to suicidal behaviour

What is risk?

Risk is simply the probability or likelihood of a particular event occurring. Risk tends to be expressed in binary terms, that is, 'high risk' or 'low risk', although this classification tends to create an artificial paradigm, as risk exists within a sliding rule of these two extremes. Risk is dynamic, not static. It varies between populations and across age ranges. Even for an individual, identified risks can increase or decrease over time, and the nature of the risks may change (Snowden 1997). This has important implications for risk assessment, which may be no more than a 'snapshot' of a situation.

Expressing risk

The degree of risk can be expressed in several ways. A clinical classification might simply use the categories high and low risk, although these might be extended in order to provide a guideline for subsequent action (see Box 2.2). Additionally it might be useful to distinguish between acute risk, chronic high risk and chronic high risk with acute exacerbation. Acute risk is time limited. Chronic high risk involves long-standing multiple suicide attempts and so these people are always at elevated risk. Acute exacerbation of this state occurs when there is a marked re-emergence of symptomatology.

Box 2.2: Categories of risk

Use the following categories as guidelines to help determine level of risk.

Low risk

- Fleeting thoughts of suicide which are soon dismissed
- No plan
- Mild or mental illness – no or few symptoms of depression
- No alcohol/drug abuse
- Stable psychological situation

Action for low risk

- No follow up required because of suicide risk
- Defuse emotional distress as far as possible
- Screen for evidence of mental disorder – if present arrange for treatment, usually through GP

Medium risk

- Fleeting thoughts of suicide
- No plan
- Some evidence of mental disorder
- Some evidence of drug/alcohol abuse
- Unstable psychological situation but no immediate/impending crisis
- Infrequent dangerous behaviour

Action for medium risk

- Defuse emotional distress as far as possible
- Follow up required in 74 hours–1 week
- Once safety obtained, requires a full assessment of mental health, psychosocial problems and crisis prevention strategies

Medium high risk

- Frequent/fixed suicidal ideas
- May have considered different methods but no specific plan/immediate intent
- Significant mental illness
- Unstable psychological situation with impending crisis

Action for medium high risk

- Defuse emotional distress as far as possible
- Remove/restrict lethal means of suicide
- Follow up required next day
- Once safety obtained, requires a full assessment of mental health, psychosocial problems and crisis prevention strategies

Very high risk

- Definite plan of suicide
- Access to means of suicide
- Significant mental illness
- Significant drug/alcohol misuse
- Unstable psychological situation with impending crisis
- Escalating dangerous/Russian Roulette behaviour

Action for very high risk

- Immediate attempt to assure safety after interview – 24-hour support and follow up
- Remove/restrict lethal means of suicide
- Defuse emotional crisis
- Once safety obtained, requires a full assessment of mental health, psychosocial problems and crisis prevention strategies

Gask and Morriss 2003

Other measures of risk that can be calculated from epidemiological studies include *attributable risk* (the disease rate in persons exposed to the risk factor of interest minus the disease rate in unexposed persons) and *relative risk* (the ratio of disease rate in exposed persons to those not exposed). Attributable risk is the measure of association that is most relevant for making decisions about individuals, but relative risks are more generally available because they can be estimated from a wider range of study designs. Relative risks can be misleading. For example, the relative risk of suicide in the year following self-harm is 1 in 100 (Hawton and Fagg 1988). This seems impressive, but because suicide is a rare outcome it means that if self-harm is used as a basis on which to predict future suicide, the prediction will be correct less than 1 per cent of the time. The *population attributable risk* is the rate of disease (or outcome of interest) in the population minus the rate that would apply if all of the population were unexposed. It measures the potential impact of control measures in a population. For example, it has been calculated that if there were full employment in the UK, the suicide rate would drop by 11 per cent (Lewis, Hawton and Jones 1997).

Evaluating risks and making decisions

Much of clinical practice involves the evaluation and balancing of the risks of different courses of action. 'Decision analysis' was originally developed in the business world and is an explicit quantitative approach to examining difficult decisions. Its aim is to enable clinicians to make the best decision for individuals or groups of patients (Hatcher 1995). Decision analysis involves assigning a probability to each potential clinical outcome. These probabilities represent the clinician's 'best guess' about how likely a particular outcome is, and are based on clinical features and data from relevant clinical studies. However, the use of decision analysis to evaluate risks in psychiatry has its problems – the evidence to guide us in certain situations simply does not exist.

Quantifying risk

Research would suggest that we are not terribly proficient when it comes to quantifying and predicting risk. It could be argued that we might be better off simply assuming no one will have the (generally rare) outcome of interest, in which case we will be right more often than not (Grubin 1997). Central to the task of improving the risk assessment skills of clinicians has been the debate regarding the relative merits of actuarial and clinical methods of risk evaluation.

Actuarial approaches to risk

Statisticians use the term actuarial to refer to mathematical techniques they use to set insurance premiums and pension schemes. In the psychiatric risk assessment literature the term has been used to describe any mathematical means of combining information (Buchanan 1999).

The use of actuarial methods in psychiatry is limited, first, because the outcomes we are interested in are rare and second, because most of our assessment tools are less than perfect. This means that the *positive predictive value* of actuarial assessments (the proportion of individuals identified as high risk who are actually high risk) is often disappointingly low, and many patients would need to be treated to prevent one adverse outcome. There are other problems with actuarial techniques (Grubin 1997). These include a lack of flexibility and poor generalisability across patient groups and over time, as risk factors may change between different cohorts. Actuarial approaches also fail to take into account the individual circumstances of the patient and to provide an explanation of the behaviour.

Clinical approaches to risk

Some view the clinical method of risk assessment as merely an informal and unsystematic version of actuarial approaches. It has been argued that, like actuarial tables, clinicians either allocate patients to reference classes or assign weights to variables and combine these weights mathematically, but that they simply do this much less well.

Clinical risk assessment is defined as a person specific assessment, which takes into account past behaviour and the context in which this behaviour occurred (Vinestock 1996). It refers to a 'balanced summary of prediction derived from knowledge of the individual, the present circumstances and what is known of the disorder from which he [or she] is suffering' (Department of Health and Home Office 1994). Central to this approach is a detailed understanding of the person's underlying mental state and psychopathology. The risks in each individual case need to be identified and then assessed in terms of frequency and severity. The assessment process should be multidisciplinary and information needs to be obtained from all available sources (Snowden 1997).

Clinical approaches undoubtedly have their drawbacks. When clinicians are asked to predict adverse outcomes they almost invariably over-predict. This is probably because of the current risk-averse climate in mental health services.

Clinical risk assessment has failed to prevent disasters in mental health services because of (Lipsedge 1995):

- failure to lend sufficient weight to reports by carers and members of the public about disturbed behaviour
- undue emphasis on the civil liberties of patients
- failure properly to implement the Mental Health Act
- tendency to take a cross-sectional rather than a long-term view of risk
- failure to share information in the best interests of the patient.

Practical risk assessment

A sensible approach to risk assessment involves using our knowledge of risk factors from epidemiological studies as well as our knowledge of the patient's individual characteristics in order to inform our clinical decisions (see Box 2.1). It may be that the role of risk assessment is not about making an accurate prediction but about making informed, defensible decisions (Grounds 1995). Moore (1995) suggests a framework that can be applied to most risk assessments in psychiatry, including:

- defining the behaviour to be predicted
- distinguishing between the probability and the cost of the behaviour
- being aware of the possible sources of error in the assessment
- taking into account the influence of both internal and external factors on the behaviour
- checking that all the necessary information has been gathered
- predicting factors likely to increase or decrease future risk
- identifying when other professionals or agencies need to be involved
- planning key interventions.

The assessor needs to be aware of the possible sources of error in the assessment, arising from the patient, the assessor themselves or the context of the assessment. The interaction of internal factors (e.g. attitudes, drives, needs, controls) should be considered. For example, risk assessment is influenced by gender; men tend to downplay risk compared to women (Ryan 1998). A check needs to be made of whether all necessary information has been gathered. If it has not, what additional information is needed and where might it be obtained? A longitudinal perspective should be adopted, with some prediction of the factors and circumstances likely to increase or decrease future risk. Key interventions should be planned and a decision made about whether to involve other professional groups.

Sometimes the realities of clinical practice mean we do not have as much time as we would wish to make clinical decisions. We often have to act in less than ideal circumstances with less than comprehensive information. Three questions might help us to triage the risk decisions (Taylor 1995): What is the seriousness of the risk? What is the imminence of the risk? What is the probability of the risk becoming actual?

Interview techniques

Information collected at interview should be reliable and accurate if it is going to be useful to the assessment process. It has already been suggested that sources of information should be multidisciplinary where possible, but corroborative evidence from relatives may also be useful. Skills of the interviewer include adopting an appropriate manner (genuine, warm, respectful, professional); demonstrating empathy (acknowledging feelings and problems); observation; clarifying, reflecting, summarising; probing (feeling and events); and asking clear concise questions (avoid directive and double questions).

Questions should initially be open in order to elicit cues, for example:

- What brought you to the emergency department/surgery/clinic?
- What has been the main problem?
- Could you tell me how you've been feeling in the past three weeks?

Follow up with more closed and directive questions/statements, for example:

- How many days in the last week have you felt depressed?
- Have you had thoughts of ending your life?

Guidance on history taking

1. Ask simple questions – pick up on non-verbal cues (e.g. behaviour that may be indicative of mental illness) and verbal

cues (key words or phrases that require exploring). Follow up with probing questions and clarify ambiguities. Summarise what has been said so that the interviewer can correct any misconceptions or factual inconsistencies. This also demonstrates to the interviewee that they are being listened to.

2. Control the interview – as the practitioner it is important to appear competent, that you are there to extract the relevant information.

3. Be aware of cultural differences – for example, a person whose religious beliefs sanction against suicide may be less willing to admit to suicidal ideation.

4. Introduce yourself and explain the parameters of the interview, i.e. that you need to find out about their problems in order to try to address them.

5. Ask open questions initially.

6. Cone down – from the general to the specific.

7. Early stage – check that they have discussed all their problems (note possibility of social problems).

8. Mental state symptoms – try not to ask leading questions but be non-directive, for example, 'What time of night is it difficult to sleep?'

9. Precipitants to current crisis – determine what happened in the last few months and in the previous few days, what were they thinking about at the time of crisis? Has the situation been resolved?

10. Assessing risk – what is the likelihood that they will get into the same circumstances or mental state again, through, e.g. alcohol use, relationship problems? If not sure, ask the opinion of relatives – is there a safer environment to go home to, i.e. somewhere else or someone else that they could stay with who is willing to help and is acceptable to the client.

Factors which make suicide more likely

The following have been suggested as factors that increase the short-term risk of completed suicide in the suicidal individual (Gask and Morriss 2003):

- access to means of suicide
- plans for death (e.g. will changes, family farewells)
- recent escalation of:
  - ° deliberate self-harm
  - ° maladaptive behaviour (e.g. drug/alcohol abuse)
  - ° help-seeking behaviour (e.g. visiting GP, A&E etc.)
- current symptoms of mental disorder
- likelihood of further bad news – 'the last straw'
- a self-imposed deadline passes without the good news the person hoped for
- expressed intention to carry out suicide.

A caveat to this is the 'smiling depressive', i.e. a sudden calmness after disturbed behaviour, without evidence of a resolution of problems.

Risk factors for suicide

A number of socio-demographic and clinical factors contribute to individual risk of suicide (see Box 2.1). Suicide is more common in males than females, with men aged 25–34 being at highest risk. Approximately half of suicides have a history of self-harm (Foster, Gillespie and McClelland 1997) and this proportion increases to two thirds in younger age groups (Appleby *et al.* 1999). Adverse life events can trigger suicidal behaviour in vulnerable individuals. These stressors include interpersonal difficulties and legal problems. One quarter of suicides were known to be in contact with mental health services in the year before death, although 10–15 per cent of all suicides occur in the four weeks after discharge from psychiatric hospital (Appleby *et al.* 2001). Although certain professional occupational groups are at increased risk of suicide – doctors, farmers, vets, dentists and pharmacists – they make up only a small percentage of all suicides and an influencing factor is their access to potentially lethal means of suicide (shotguns and poisons).

Factors relating to high-risk groups

Table 2.1: High risk groups: increase of suicide risk	
High risk group	*Estimated magnitude of increased risk*
Males compared to females	x 2–3
Current or ex-psychiatric patients	x 10
4 weeks following discharge from psychiatric hospital	x 100–200
People who have deliberately self-harmed in the past	x 10–30
Alcoholics	x 5–20
Drug misusers	x 10–20
Family history of suicide	Not known
Serious physical illness/handicap	Not known
Prisoners	x 9–10
Offenders serving non-custodial sentences	x 8–13
Doctors	x 2
Farmers	x 2
Unemployed	x 2–3
Divorced people	x 2–5
People on low incomes (social class IV/V)	x 4

National Electronic Library for Mental Health

Psychiatric illness
Retrospective psychological autopsy studies indicate the presence of a high rate of psychiatric disorders at the time of suicide (Appleby *et al.* 1999; Foster *et al.* 1997).

Affective disorder
Follow up studies on patients with affective disorder calculated that 15 per cent will die by suicide, which equates to a 30-fold increased risk compared to the general population (Guze and Robins 1970). Symptoms which distinguished suicides with depression from depressed patients who did not commit suicide were insomnia, impaired memory and self-neglect (Barraclough and Pallis 1975). Other factors include delusional ideas,

single status, living alone and a history of deliberate self-harm. Hopelessness, specific suicidal ideas and plans also increase risk in depressed patients (Beck *et al.* 1985).

Schizophrenia

The estimated prevalence of suicide among individuals with schizophrenia is 10 per cent (Miles 1977), the risk being highest during the early years of the illness. One in five suicides aged under 35 were found retrospectively to have a probable diagnosis of schizophrenia (Appleby *et al.* 1999). A history of previous suicide attempts has been shown to be a factor most strongly related to suicide. Females have been shown to have a raised risk for suicide among the unmarried, divorced or widowed and among those living alone, whereas in males increased risk was found among those with a history of alcohol abuse (Allebeck *et al.* 1987). Other important features include fears of mental disintegration, suicidal threats and hopelessness (Drake *et al.* 1984).

Alcohol and drug disorders

Around 15 per cent of alcoholics will subsequently commit suicide and the risk of suicide among drug addicts has been estimated to be 20 times that of the general population. As many as 33 per cent of suicides in the under 35s have a primary diagnosis of alcohol/substance misuse (Appleby *et al.* 1999). Co-morbidity with depression is common (Foster *et al.* 1997). Other features that distinguish alcoholic suicides from surviving alcoholics include poor physical health, poor work record and previous deliberate self-harm.

Personality disorder

Factors increasing suicide risk in these patients include the presence of co-morbid mood or addiction disorders, severity of childhood sexual abuse, degree of antisocial or impulsive characteristics and a history of irregular psychiatric care discharges. Complicating suicide risk management in this population, suicide gestures without lethal intent are common and suicide threats may be presented in a manipulative manner. Hospitalisation may be counter-productive and regressive in some personality disordered patients. Prognosis may improve if the patient survives the disruptive early period into their fourth and fifth decades.

Young suicide

Parental separation or divorce and impaired parent–child relationships (including poor family communication styles), and extremes of high and low parental expectations and control are important risk factors in suicide in the young. Co-morbidity of psychiatric disorders is common, such as depression and personality disorders. Other contributory factors include family psychiatric history, abuse and legal difficulties.

Case studies

Some of the principles of the assessment of suicidal risk may best be illustrated using case studies.

Presentation to Emergency Department following deliberate self-harm

---

Case study 2.1

Initial information

Male, late 20s, attending emergency department in a dishevelled state, smelling strongly of alcohol. Appears to have self-presented, seems confused and is bleeding profusely from a self-inflicted wound to wrist. Patient has a number of scars on wrists and forearms and is loud, aggressive, unco-operative and is refusing treatment.

What should be done?

- Persuade him to accept immediate life saving medical treatment.
- Keep him in the department.

What do you do next? (What can you do?)

Use common law to keep him in the department due to his incapacity.

Test of incapacity:

1. Can he understand what is being said?
2. Can he retain the information?
3. Can he weigh the pros and cons?

Patient is intoxicated and not able to make a rational decision therefore detain under common law. Contact psychiatric services to assess for capacity. If a mental health liaison team can be contacted they may assist with keeping him in the department and help with restraint if necessary.

What do you do if he leaves?

- Patient unable to give full history, but even on current information appears at least at moderate risk of suicide and therefore should be actively followed up.
- Contact police – give as many details as available.
- Contact community mental health team and GP.

Completed suicides

The names and some details have been altered to protect the identity of individuals, otherwise these are genuine cases.

Case study 2.2

Initial information

A young woman, aged 17, brought into casualty with her mother. States she took 10 paracetamol tablets less than 2 hours previously.

Discuss what further information is required re background

Did not want to die, remorseful, impulsive act in a crisis situation, since resolved.

What further information is required concerning her psychological status?

No previous psychiatric history and no symptoms of depression. Mother is accompanying patient and is supportive. The patient is willing to accept help from her GP.

Discuss appropriate management

Assessed as low risk of suicide and can be discharged back to her GP. Not really needing psychological assessment by a mental health specialist, although may benefit from discussing coping mechanisms with counsellor attached to GP service.

Case study 2.3

A 27-year-old white male had a history of self-harm behaviour in response to relationship difficulties with his girlfriend – the most recent episode being three months before death. He had been referred to a local psychiatric day hospital some years previously but failed to continue with treatment as he felt it was unsuitable. He had a forensic history related to excessive alcohol intake and 'following the crowd'. No personality disorder was diagnosed but there was evidence of histrionic personality difficulties with dissocial and dependant traits. He had been binge drinking for the past 10 years, which, on occasions, had resulted in violent behaviour. Despite being employed, he had mounting financial worries in the year before his death by suicide. He broke up with girlfriend three months before death due to drinking and violent behaviour and moved out of the house. A stormy relationship with his girlfriend continued, however, but again broke down following an argument two weeks before his death. He agreed to attend Alcoholics Anonymous but became despondent due to realisation of his alcohol problem, and shortly afterwards hanged himself.

Risk factors

Despite its brevity this vignette highlights a number of risk variables presented earlier. This was a young white male with a history of alcohol problems, including an escalation of alcohol intake. He had a history of self-injurious behaviour and had received psychiatric treatment, although non-compliant. Relationship and financial problems were associated with his alcohol abuse. A recent change in accommodation meant he lived alone. His relationship difficulties and sense of hopelessness stemming from the recognition of his alcohol problems appear to have acted as triggers to suicide. It is difficult to know how this suicide might have been averted as he was no longer in touch with the psychiatric services and did not contact his GP. However, this case emphasises the increasing role of voluntary organisations in managing mental health and the need for adequate assessment procedures for their clientele.

Case study 2.4

A white male aged 25, whose background history included a physically aggressive alcoholic father. His parents separated when he was 11 and he lived with his mother initially, then his father. He was known to social services due to difficult behaviour and truanting from school. He was often in trouble with police. His numerous attempts at self-harm from adolescence onwards were described as impulsive attempts.

Numerous admissions to psychiatric hospital over the past ten years, mainly for alcohol withdrawal, anxiety (diagnosed agoraphobic) and difficulty sleeping. Also diagnosed as borderline personality disorder with anxious personality disorder, traits of impulsivity, dependence and paranoid ideation. There had been a recent escalation of problems with a number of admissions to a psychiatric ward in the last year. Described hearing voices associated with alcohol intake saying 'kill self' or 'kill ex-girlfriend' and could hear music in his head. (On his penultimate admission he was discharged in his absence as he broke a contract of alcohol use while an in-patient.)

Recent life events included relationship breakdown with longstanding girlfriend and son in the year before death. Two months prior to death, he saw her with another boyfriend, which upset him. He had previously moved into hostel accommodation due to the split from his girlfriend. His key worker, with whom he had a good relationship, had left the area one month before his death. He continued drinking due to anxiety and possibly panic attacks and continued to experience alcoholic hallucinations. In the week prior to death he contacted the psychiatric services complaining of feeling 'depressed and not sleeping'. He was admitted to in-patient psychiatric ward but was discharged three days later and was dead within the week.

Risk Factors

This person could be described as chronic high risk with acute exacerbation. He had a number of background risk factors including a past history of abuse, father an alcoholic, separation from parents due to divorce, a history of self-harm and alcohol abuse with a co-morbid diagnosis of anxiety and personality disorder. He had a number of disruptive life experiences including relationship breakdown with two significant figures (girlfriend and key worker) and moving house and consequently living alone. His alcohol intake had escalated and caused him increasing problems. He was psychotic and suicidal. He died at a time known to be a high-risk period (24 per cent of suicides occur within three months of discharge from in-patient care) (Appleby et al. 2001). This case demonstrates the importance of expertise in alcohol and drug treatment among mental health professionals in a general psychiatric hospital setting.

Conclusion

Assessing risk is an important part of clinical practice. Suicide risk is difficult to predict, although research has provided us with important clues. The use of a combination of clinical techniques and knowledge of epidemiological risk factors might best be employed in order to inform risk management.

References

Allebeck, P., Varla, A., Kristjansson, E. and Wistedt, B. (1987) 'Risk factors for suicide among patients with schizophrenia.' *Acta Psychiatrica Scandinavica 76*, 4, 414–419.

Appleby, L., Cooper, J., Amos, T. and Faragher, B. (1999) 'Psychological autopsy study of suicides by people aged under 35.' *British Journal of Psychiatry 175*, 168–174.

Appleby, L., Shaw, J., Sherratt, J., Amos, T., Robinson, J., McDonnell, R. *et al.* (2001) *Safety First: National Confidential Inquiry into Suicide and Homicide by People with Mental Illness.* London: Department of Health.

Barraclough, B., Bunch, J., Nelson, B. and Sainsbury, P. (1974) 'A hundred cases of suicide: Clinical aspects.' *British Journal of Psychiatry 125*, 355–373.

Barraclough, B. and Pallis, D.J. (1975) 'Depression followed by suicide: A comparison of depressed suicides with living depressives.' *Psychological Medicine 5*, 55–61.

Beck, A.T., Steer, R., Kovacs, M. and Garrison, B. (1985) 'Hopelessness and eventual suicide: A 10 year prospective study of patients hospitalised with suicidal ideation.' *American Journal of Psychiatry 145*, 559–563.

Buchanan, A. (1999) 'Risk and dangerousness.' *Psychological Medicine 29*, 465–473.

Department of Health and Home Office (1994) *Report of the Department of Health and Home Office Working Group on Psychopathic Disorder.* London: Department of Health and Home Office.

Drake, R.E., Gates, C., Cotton, P.G. and Whitaker, A. (1984) 'Suicide among schizophrenics: Who is at risk?' *Journal of Nervous and Mental Disease 172*, 613–617.

Foster, T., Gillespie, K. and McClelland, R. (1997) 'Mental disorders and suicide in Northern Ireland.' *British Journal of Psychiatry 170*, 447–452.

Gask, L. and Morriss, R. (2003) 'Assessment and immediate management of people at risk of harming themselves.' *Psychiatry 2*, 8–12.

Grounds, A. (1995) 'Risk assessment and management in clinical context.' In J. Crichton (ed.) *Psychiatric Patient Violence – Risk and Response.* London: Duckworth.

Grubin, D. (1997) 'Predictors of risk in serious sex offenders.' *British Journal of Psychiatry 170* (suppl. 32), 17–21.

Guze, S.B. and Robins, E. (1970) 'Suicide among primary affective disorders.' *British Journal of Psychiatry 117*, 437–438.

Hatcher, S. (1995) 'Decision analysis in psychiatry.' *British Journal of Psychiatry 166*, 184–190

Hawton, K. (1987) 'Assessment of suicide risk.' *British Journal of Psychiatry 150*, 145–153.

Hawton, K. and Fagg, J. (1988) 'Suicide and other causes of death, following attempted suicide.' *British Journal of Psychiatry 152*, 359–366.

Kapur, N. (2000) 'Evaluating risks.' *Advances in Psychiatric Treatment 6*, 399–406.

Lewis, G., Hawton, K. and Jones, P. (1997) 'Strategies for preventing suicide.' *British Journal of Psychiatry 171*, 351–354.

Lipsedge, M. (1995) 'Clinical risk management in psychiatry.' In C. Vincent (ed.) *Clinical Risk Management*. London: BMJ Publishing.

Miles, C.P. (1977) 'Conditions predisposing to suicide: A review.' *Journal of Nervous and Mental Disease 164*, 231–246.

Moore, B. (1995) *Risk Assessment: A Practictioners' Guide to Predicting Harmful Behaviour*. London: Whiting and Birch.

NHS Centre for Reviews and Dissemination (1998) 'Deliberate self-harm.' *Effective Health Care Bulletin v*, vi, 1–12.

Ryan, T. (1998) 'Perceived risks associated with mental illness: Beyond homicide and suicide.' *Social Science and Medicine 46*, 2, 287–297.

Snowden, P. (1997) 'Practical aspects of clinical risk assessment and management.' *British Journal of Psychiatry 32*, 2–4.

Taylor, P.J. (1995) 'Schizophrenia and the Risk of Violence.' In S.R. Hirsch and D.R. Weinberger (eds) *Schizophrenia*. Oxford: Blackwell Science.

Vinestock, M.D. (1996) 'Risk assessment. "A word to the wise".' *Advances in Psychiatric Treatment 2*, 3–10.

Further Reading

Royal College of Psychiatrists (1994) *The General Hospital Management of Adult Deliberate Self-harm: A Consensus Statement on Standards for Service Provision. Council Report No. 32.* London: Royal College of Psychiatrists. (A consensus statement produced by experts in the field regarding the management of self-harm. Currently being updated, but existing version available for download from www.rcpsych.ac.uk/publications/cr/index.htm)

Chapter 3

Primary Care

Barry Lewis

Introduction

Suicide is a devastating event for all concerned. This may be obvious when considering the close family and friends but the implications for the health and social care team are not always considered. Receiving news of the event is often dramatic (press or A&E report), unexpected and produces mixed emotions of sorrow, anger and guilt. Forty per cent of people who commit suicide will have seen a health or social care worker within three months of the event (Appleby *et al.* 1999). Consultations with a GP have often taken place within two weeks of the event (Appleby *et al.* 1999). The natural reaction of the clinical and social teams is, therefore, 'could we have done more in terms of recognition and prevention?' This chapter will consider the risk factors that can be recognised by team members, the clinical and organisational skills needed to improve recognition and act upon the information gathered, and learning exercises that will, we hope, enable the development of effective suicide prevention strategies in primary care.

Incidence

The National Confidential Inquiry into Suicide (Appleby *et al.* 1999) was notified of nearly 21,000 suicides or probable suicides in the 4 years from 1996 to 2000. This gives an average annual suicide rate of 10 per 100,000 people. Primary care will therefore have 1 per 10,000 per year and only 1 every 4 or 5 years for an 'average' GP. Practices with high numbers of severely mentally ill patients, those serving areas of high deprivation or social isolation and those with transient populations, reflecting many of the risk factors outlined in this and other chapters, will have a higher incidence.

Seventy-five per cent of the suicides notified to the National Confidential Inquiry were male, the highest male to female ratio being in the 25–34 age band. The average age of suicides was 41, with a range from 13 to 95.

Suicide method is of interest in terms of awareness of risk and prevention of the act. Three methods accounted for 71 per cent: hanging was the most common, self-poisoning by overdose and carbon monoxide (car exhaust) poisoning the next most frequent methods. The sex ratios reflect violence in men, with hanging commonest in men and overdose in women.

Deliberate self-harm (DSH) merits specific mention in terms of incidence. On average, 1180 suicides per year occur within one year of an episode of DSH. A GP with a list size of approximately 2000 would expect 4–6 patients per year to be referred to hospital after deliberate self-harm. An unknown number of 'minor' incidents will have occurred, many under the influence of alcohol or other drugs, which do not reach hospital admission but may be presented to GPs by the patient or a relative or friend. The previous predominance of females in this group is steadily reducing, with a current 1.3:1.0 female to male ratio. It is still an act of the 'young': usually a person under 24, unemployed and often 'unwell' due to physical or mental health (including substance misuse) problems.

Risk assessment in primary care

The following quotes can be used as clear pointers for the direction primary care professionals can take in tackling risk assessment and reduction in the populations they serve:

- Primary Care staff should be able to assess and manage depression, including the risk of suicide.

- Mental Health staff should be competent to assess suicide risk among those at greatest risk.

- Training in risk assessment and management is a priority for both services and should be updated every 3 years.

(Department of Health 1999, Standard 7)

The major role of the GP in the prevention of suicidal behaviour is in the detection and treatment of depression and in the aftercare of DSH patients. (Houston *et al.* 2003)

The assessment of suicide risk may be approached in the same way as the assessment of serious consequences due to underlying physical health problems. This is by the combination of *organisational risk awareness* and *indi-*

vidual risk assessment. An example would be the risk of acute myocardial infarction: the practice will have registers of patients with significant risk factors such as hypertension, smoking status and raised cholesterol together with accurate records of individuals' screening results; the individual consulting with a GP or practice nurse will have their blood pressure and cholesterol control considered along with acute stressors that could precipitate an 'event'. This dual approach of at risk population awareness and individual assessment when applied to suicide prevention affords a structured format for the practice to apply, and within which audit can be performed.

Population risk factors for suicide include:

- male <24 or >65

- in touch with mental health services

- during the year following DSH

- involved with criminal justice system

- specific high-risk occupations.

This creates a picture that reflects current patterns of suicide, particularly high risk categories. The young severely disturbed male in contact with mental health services due to severe mental illness or substance abuse is at high risk of violent self-harm or suicide. The older, isolated, male from a high-risk occupation such as farming or medicine may not be perceived in the same light but can, in reality, carry a similar level of risk; the common factor for both groups is often the presence of depressive illness. Communication between mental health teams and primary health care teams (PHCT) is vital for the accurate recognition of risk and effective management where the risk is perceived to be high. Most clinicians within each of these teams are dependent on accurate records for them to be able to perform individual risk assessments.

From an organisational point of view this leads to a set of prerequisites for good practice in the management of risk for the practice population:

- an up-to-date register of patients in contact with mental health services, especially those with a Care Plan Approach (CPA)

- a system for alerting clinicians of the discharge from hospital of patients who have deliberately self-harmed

- consistent electronic or paper recording of mental health diagnoses, especially depressive illness

- up-to-date summaries (paper or electronic) that record mental health diagnoses as well as physical illnesses, especially previous depression or self-harm
- a clear method by which mental health teams and primary care teams can alert each other to perceived risk and record this in the relevant records
- accurate recording and monitoring of repeat prescriptions for all drugs, especially where higher risk is noted.

The 'Threshold Approach'

Mathews and Paxton's (2001) model demonstrates the interaction of personal risk and protective factors that produce a 'threshold' for suicidal behaviour in an individual. The model acts as a bridge between the organisational areas considered above and the interpersonal communication and clinical skills needed during one-to-one interviews.

Areas of risk assessment include:

- long-term predisposing factors: identify those in the high-risk groups
- short-term risk factors: may predict when someone may act
- precipitating risk factors: recent life events; access to means; these allow assessment of immediate risk
- protective factors: long or short term, that can offset risk.

Analysing these factors in more detail allows them to slot into organisational and individual clinical skill areas as follows.

Long-term factors
Genes/biology

- a family history of suicide
- a family history of major depression
- a family history of alcohol or drug abuse

These factors require accurate and consistent record keeping processes.

Personality

- all or nothing thinking
- rigid thinking

- excessive perfectionism, with high standards that cause distress to self or others
- hopelessness, extreme pessimism about the future
- impulsivity
- low self-esteem and feelings of worthlessness
- poor problem-solving skills

These are assessments made in one-to-one interview.

Short-term factors
Environmental

- loss – bereavement, separation, divorce, unemployment
- age – under 24 or over 65

Entering life 'events' in electronic records is becoming a prerequisite of high standard record maintenance.

Psychiatry

- depression – illness satisfying the criteria for major depression (ICD 10 F32# -)
- substance misuse including alcohol
- schizophrenia
- less frequently associated with personality disorder, obsessive-compulsive disorder and panic disorder

Accurate diagnostic coding is a requirement for both clinicians and administrative staff.

Precipitating factors
These are events which may 'tip the balance' when a person is at risk:

- imprisonment or threat of it
- interpersonal problems, especially humiliating events
- reminders of recent loss, especially bereavement
- work or school problems
- unwanted pregnancy.

Information from other agencies, outside the primary care team, needs clear handling and recording mechanisms so that it is available to the clinician 'when needed'.

Protective factors

Reducing the acute risk factors are protective factors, as are:

- hopefulness
- receiving mental health care and support
- being responsible for children
- strong social and family supports.

Estimating risk

The degree of risk is the sum of long term factors, short term factors and precipitation factors, less any protective factors (Mathews and Paxton 2001).

Deliberate self-harm

DSH merits special consideration because it is an area where primary care intervention can significantly alter risk. Careful management of depressive illness falls into the same category but DSH is usually presented to the PHCT by contact from secondary services, therefore requiring the integrated handling of information already described.

Formal psychiatric disorder is uncommon (5–8% of patients require in-patient psychiatric care), social and 'life event' problems predominate. DSH is often spontaneous, usually only being considered in the hour before the act. At the time up to 35 per cent of patients claim they wished to die, however, the circumstances and later assessment suggest few have serious suicidal intent. Despite this the statistical link between DSH and subsequent suicide requires follow up and mental health assessment by the primary care team. A format for this assessment can follow these areas listed below.

- events that preceded the act
- degree of suicidal intent
- current problems
- current psychiatric disorder
- family history

- previous episodes of DSH
- risk of repetition
- suicide risk (see below)
- coping supports and resources
- type of help available and whether this would be accepted.

Suicide after an episode of DSH occurs in approximately 1 per cent within one year of the act of self-harm, a risk 100 times greater than that of the general population. The risk is greatest where the characteristics of self-harm overlap with those of true suicide intent. These are:

- self-harm performed in isolation
- event timed to avoid being interrupted
- preparing for the act, both in the means (e.g. tablet saving) and aftermath (e.g. making a will)
- telling others about the intention to self-harm; this usually implies preparation of several hours rather than impulsive acts
- leaving a note
- failure to alert others during or after the act.

Apart from patients with serious psychiatric disorder requiring detailed specialist assessment, primary care professionals are the principal providers of follow-up and intervention. A significant proportion (30%+) will be suitable for and benefit from problem solving interventions. Brief problem solving can be delivered by GPs or practice-based counsellors and is aimed at enabling the patient to develop practical solutions to the social or emotional problems that precipitated the self-harm. Psychotropic medication is only occasionally required, should be considered only where depressive illness is clearly diagnosed, and requires careful monitoring and repeat prescribing precautions.

Risk management

For the clinician to effectively assess and manage risk with the individual patient it is necessary for his or her organisation to have:

- accurate, up-to-date, clinical records
- risk recognition and telephone skills

- clear diagnostic coding and prescribing information
- information from outside agencies.

The clinician also needs the following:

- knowledge
  - specific mental health/risk factors
  - safe prescribing policies
  - service provision
- skills
  - interview and listening skills
  - diagnostic
  - specific therapeutic interventions
- attitude
  - 'care'
  - non-judgemental attitude (especially for DSH)
  - team 'worker'.

Managing risk is intricately woven with risk assessment, as the techniques for managing the individual at risk depend on an effective assessment of the level of risk. A hierarchy of approaches allows the clinician to plan interventions and choose, with the patient, from a range of options the intervention that is most appropriate at the time.

Low risk

- Follow usual contact and structured follow-up arrangements.
- Follow a patient-centred counselling approach to encourage shared responsibility for safety.
- Get further advice from colleagues or outside agencies.

Medium risk

- Involve the patient in using past coping mechanisms to ensure safety in the current situation.
- Assess the current support system, discuss how this will be used and consider contact with them yourself if the patient agrees.
- Early follow-up, especially around weekends, by appointment or telephone.
- Contact other professionals for direct intervention, bring forward existing appointments with other professionals.

High risk

- Urgent specialist referral, either secondary care or community mental health professional.

- Immediate intervention, 999 or consultant psychiatrist, with possible use of the Mental Health Act.

Improving prevention in primary care

Suicide is, fortunately, a rare event encountered by primary care teams. The starting point for consideration of training or system changes is often an event itself. By analysing such a 'significant event' in a structured way the feelings of the PHCT can be expressed in a supportive environment while plans for organisational change or skill development can be formulated.

Significant Event Audit

Pringle and colleagues (1995) developed a format for structured analysis with four possible outcomes:

- no change is necessary

- immediate change is needed

- further exploration or education (research, audit, skill development)

- celebration of good practice.

To be a true audit agreed changes or developments should be re-assessed after a set time to ensure effective change has been achieved. The format for Significant Event Audit can be modified to the situation being considered as long as basic prerequisites are honoured. These are:

- All members of the PHCT and relevant others associated with the practice are invited.

- A clear initial statement of events and list of all involved is provided.

- An opportunity to consider the emotions generated by the event is clearly demarcated early in the process.

- A set of probing 'questions' are agreed against which analysis, generation of a broad range of ideas and clear plans may be set.

- Follow-up timescales are agreed for audit/review meetings/education.

- A copy of the process is held in the practice for personal and practice development planning.

How this can work in practice may be demonstrated by using an anonymised, but real, case.

Case study 3.1

Jack was a 57-year-old warehouseman. He had been consulting his own GP for several months about his depressive illness. A significant factor in this was his excessive use of alcohol, taken in 'binges', which resulted in problems at both work and home. As well as regular attendance at the surgery Jack was intermittently attending counselling sessions at the local Alcohol and Drugs Service where he had been referred by his GP. His family and his employers were aware of his condition. There was a strong family history of depressive illness but not of deliberate self-harm or suicide. Jack had not made previous attempts on his life. Two lengthy periods off work (four to six weeks) had required medical certification and reports to his employers. On the day of his death Jack attended work under the influence of alcohol, was sent home with a final written warning from his employers, and died by suicide by hanging on the way back to his house.

The analysis process:

- All PHCT members (clinical and administrative) attend, along with 'relevant' professionals outside the immediate team.
- *What happened?* Someone gives a clear resume of the 'case' and events as they relate to the practice.
- *Who is affected?* A list of the clinicians involved, the administrative staff who dealt with the patient, family members and others is created.
- *How do people feel?* An opportunity is provided for all those directly involved to express their feelings about the situation and what they hope to gain from the analysis process.

The analysis can then be structured to cover the areas outlined as administrative and clinical responsibilities and interventions discussed that would improve the response of the practice should a similar situation occur. Using Jack's suicide as an example, analysis can be linked to interventions as shown in Table 3.1.

Table 3.4 A structured approach to learning lessons after a suicide

Question	Analysis	Outcome	Training/ Intervention
Clinical records	Clear history of depression Clear history of alcohol use No formal risk assessment entered	Celebrate Explore	What suicide risk recording tools exist?
Prescribing	Safe Appropriate Monitored	Celebrate	None specifically needed
External service information	Record of referral No return letter	Explore	Meet with counselling services to discuss information transfer
'What if...'? Jack had called that day?	No appointments No protocol for this type of call	Immediate action	Develop call handling protocol
Risk recognition	Depression monitored well No repeat prescribing Referral for counselling	Celebrate Does that clinician have learning needs?	Personal learning needs explored and plan to meet them
Skills	Jack requested same GP Reports from Jack's family No risk noted at last consultation	Explore risk assessment skills	Interview and risk assessment training
Attitudes	Non-judgemental referral letter	Celebrate Explore behaviour change skills	Interview skills training for behaviour change

Using the template above gives both celebration of aspects done well and a set of clear educational and organisational tasks for the team to address. These need to be 'timetabled' so that those requiring immediate attention actually receive this and are not 'sidelined' for the more interesting aspects.

By prioritising call handling protocols the administrative staff are immediately engaged in promoting safe care that may avert a future similar event without criticising individuals. Record keeping was celebrated but could easily have formed the basis of a general discussion of risk recording tools in current GP computer software.

For the clinician(s) involved specific areas of skill development can be identified that can then be incorporated into personal or practice development plans. By an open analysis of the whole case the clinician(s)' skills and care are praised while the learning needs are identified, which should give encouragement and clear focus to the educational process.

Examples of practice-based training sessions

Call handling protocol development

- In groups of four or five, led by a clinician, administrative staff draw up an 'essential questions' list.

- As a large group the lists are shared and a final format agreed.

- In small groups an 'ideal management process' is developed.

- Back as a large group this is debated so that, by the end, anyone taking a call of this nature is clear about 'what to do + who to speak to + timing'.

Developing the skills

- A script needs to be developed by a clinician (GP/community psychiatric nurse (CPN)/counsellor).

- A mock telephone call role-play involving caller (clinician), receptionist and an observer is acted out.

- The observer gives the receptionist feedback on the way the call was handled from both the protocol adherence and personal skills aspects.

- All three discuss the 'best features' of how the call was handled and, in particular, specific phrases that were helpful in assessing the situation or calming the caller.

- The 'best phrases' are shared between the groups and the process repeated with roles reversed to allow all participants the opportunity to practise call handling.

Collating information

- Any recent correspondence relating to DSH or CPA allocation is brought to the group (administrative staff + clinician).

- How this is identified is important as in most groups it is based on personal knowledge/memory of an individual rather than a systematic search.

- In small groups the best way to record, file and bring the information to the attention of a clinician is debated.

- As a large group the ideas are shared and the most effective and practical method agreed.

- The system is then applied to the correspondence originally brought in to see if the system is more effective and whether it would improve safety.

- A chain of responsibility is then agreed so that the system does not collapse if an individual is on leave or absent for other reasons.

Asking about suicide (for clinicians)

This type of exercise requires a skilled facilitator able to manage role-play situations and clinicians willing to role-play with colleagues or professionals from other specialities. An initial discussion is usually necessary to allow participants to share their anxieties about asking searching questions about suicidal ideas.

- A scenario is agreed, preferably based on a participant's 'real' case.

- The person bringing the case takes the role of the patient.

- Another clinician agrees to conduct the interview and practise the questions outlined below.

- The patient role-player responds based on their knowledge of the patient.

- The group comment on the process, the role-players on how they felt asking the questions and responding to them.

Questions to ask:

- Do you feel low or hopeless?
- Do you feel desperate?

- Do you feel unable to face each day?
- Is life a burden?
- Do you sometimes feel life isn't worth living? Do you feel that now?
- Have you thought of harming yourself or committing suicide?
- Do you have a plan of how you would do it?

These questions are best asked as a part of the overall assessment of a patient suspected or already diagnosed as suffering from a depressive illness or having self-harmed.

The diagnostic features of depressive illness need to be understood by everyone involved and it can be helpful to reiterate them at the start of this type of educational session. They are:

- low or sad mood
- loss of interest or pleasure (anhedonia).

At least four of the following associated symptoms should have been present for at lease two weeks:

- disturbed sleep (early morning waking or initial insomnia)
- disturbed appetite (increase or decrease)
- feelings of guilt or low self-esteem or loss of self-confidence
- hopelessness
- decreased libido
- diurnal mood variation
- poor concentration
- fatigue or decreased energy
- suicidal thoughts
- altered speech pattern (agitated or retarded).

Other training exercises for clinicians are described in detail in Chapter 16 on the STORM project. Exercises in the recognition and management of depression are widely available, either as training packs with video examples or case scenarios to be worked through individually or as group exercises.

Conclusion

Even though suicide is a rare event in primary care its effects are devastating enough for it to merit both preventative action and detailed analysis when it occurs. Approaching mental health interventions in the same way as physical health interventions gives a structured format for all the members of the primary health care team to work with, both in changing their organisation and developing personal skills.

References

Appleby, L., Shaw, J., Amos, T., McDonnell, R., Bickley, H., Kiernan, K., Davies, S., Harris, C., McCann, K. and Parsons, R. (1999) *Safer Services: Report of the National Confidential Inquiry into Suicide and Homicide by People with Mental Illness.* London: Stationery Office.

Department of Health (1999) *National Service Framework for Mental Health.* London: Department of Health.

Houston, K., Haw, C., Townsend, E. and Hawton, K. (2003) 'General Practitioner contacts with patients before and after deliberate self harm.' *British Journal of General Practice 53,* 365–370.

Mathews, S. and Paxton, R. (2001) *Suicide Risk: A Guide for Primary Care and Mental Health Staff.* Newcastle: Newcastle, North Tyneside and Northumberland Mental Health Trust.

Pringle, M., Bradley, C.P., Carmichael, C.M., Wallis, H. and Moore, A. (1995) *Significant Event Auditing. Occasional Paper 70.* London: Royal College of General Practitioners.

Chapter 4

A&E and Mental Health Liaison

Alison Pearsall and Tony Ryan

Introduction

This chapter will discuss the nature and role of A&E and how its general service can support suicide prevention. The role of specialist mental health liaison services based in A&E will also be highlighted before examining ways in which both the general A&E and liaison services can work with high-risk groups who present to the department.

Accident and Emergency (A&E)

A&E is the rapid access point to the National Health Service (NHS) and its range of services, providing services for all forms of injury, illness and conditions. A&E can offer various forms of quick and easy-to-conduct assessments, deliver interventions, provide information and signpost to other services. Culturally A&E is the place that most people think of when they experience some form of crisis, whether this is physical or psychological. Given the high volume of people that go through A&E there will inevitably be some for whom interventions to prevent suicide will be appropriate, particularly high-risk groups for suicide who may also be significant users of A&E, for example people who self-harm and young men who often do not use primary care services.

Most A&E services operate over the 24-hour period and are staffed at the front line by medical and nursing staff. Other professionals who may be involved directly or indirectly in A&E services include social workers, radiographers, phlebotomists, administration and ancillary staff. Additionally, the past two decades have seen a growth in mental health professionals providing a service in A&E, either based there or on call to the department.

The A&E department also acts as the gateway to a wider range of other health care services. Medical, surgical and orthopaedic services can be accessed through A&E, all of which may be required after an episode of self-harm, in addition to other support services such as X-ray and haematology.

From a mental health perspective A&E can often provide a gateway to mental illness in-patient beds, particularly out of office hours through psychiatrists based in or on call to A&E or through A&E liaison teams, depending on local arrangements.

A&E, mental illness and self-harm

Traditionally A&E departments have found it very challenging to respond to people with mental health needs. Partly this has been down to a lack of specific expertise in A&E prior to the development of mental health liaison services and other forms of psychiatric input to A&E. Morgan and Coleman (2000) found that having a mental health liaison service based in an A&E department increased the number of referrals by general A&E staff for psychosocial interventions following acts of self-harm. This subsequently reduced the number of re-presentations over the following year. Furthermore, Gunnell et al. (2002) found that a significant number of people who present at A&E for self-harm go on to consult their GP within the next month, thereby highlighting the access and signposting role that A&E can play within the care pathway for people at risk of suicide.

Hickey and colleagues (2001) compared outcomes for people who had self-harmed and presented at an A&E department. A significant percentage (58.9%) of those attending out of hours had not received a psychiatric assessment. Those who were not assessed had exhibited more disruptive behaviour than those assessed and were significantly more likely to re-present for self-harm over the following 12 months than those given a mental health assessment.

A&E medical staff might be the first and only line of risk assessment for suicide and therefore have a key role on its prevention. Dennis et al. (1997) found that risk assessment by A&E medical staff of people who self-harmed overlooked suicide intent in 30 per cent of cases and rarely explored alcohol or substance misuse. The self-harming population shares some of the known risk factors with suicide: for example, male gender, social class V, unemployment, a previous psychiatric history and substance misuse (Hawton and Van Heeringen 2002). However, self-harm is more common in women and younger age groups. There has been an increase in the number of suicides among young men that also coincides with an increase in hospital admissions for self-harm among this population.

One of the major issues that staff face within the A&E department is that of providing a service to people who intentionally harm themselves. While it may seem logical to assume that people who harm themselves have a mental illness this is not necessarily the case. Many people who present with self-harm will have no formal mental health diagnosis although they are likely to be experiencing psychological distress and social problems (Ellis and Lewis 1997). Consequently, approaches to working with groups at high risk of suicide are not necessarily the sole preserve of mental health specialists within A&E.

Some people who harm themselves do so with no intention whatsoever of dying (see Chapter 11). Paradoxically some people do this in order to manage the risk of suicide (Ryan 2000). Furthermore, it is an effective way of coping with the significant levels of psychological distress they are currently experiencing, which if not released in the form of self-harm may well escalate to the point of suicidality. Nevertheless, one of the most important factors in the history of people who have died by suicide is that of previous self-harm. Differentiating between the two issues can be very difficult and in some cases the person may feel ambivalent to such as a degree that the risk of suicide is dynamic and constantly changing throughout the risk period. For these reasons the Royal College of Psychiatrists (RCP) and the British Association for Accident and Emergency Medicine (RCP 1996) recommended the establishment of multidisciplinary mental health liaison services in all A&E departments to support staff in responding to mental health needs.

A&E has also been affected by the negative attitudes of non-mental health specialists towards a client group that can be at their most difficult when they are in crisis and particularly when they repeatedly self-harm. Crowley (2000) found that A&E staff with no formal mental health training held negative attitudes about mental health issues and that this was in part reinforced by the short-term nature of most A&E work by comparison to the perceived longer-term needs of people with mental health needs. Perego (1999) reported that general A&E staff felt unskilled and unconfident in dealing with mental health issues and also felt largely unsupported by mental health services. Consequently, many mental health liaison teams include delivering psycho-education to their A&E colleagues as part of the function of the team (Johnson and Thornicroft 1995). The National Institute for Clinical Excellence has highlighted a significant need for training A&E staff in order to improve their understanding of self-harm and their support to people at such high risk (National Collaborating Centre for Mental Health 2003).

A&E liaison services

In addition to providing consultation, assessment and brief interventions at the point of contact liaison services now provide a gateway into primary care and secondary mental health services, signpost patients to non-mental health services and provide training and support to A&E staff (Johnson and Thornicroft 1995).

Liaison services vary widely in terms of the range of services offered, hours of operation, levels of resource and skill mix. In some areas single practitioners work in the A&E department during office hours. Individual practitioners working in this way have reported feeling isolated and unsupported, however, despite this they provide a valuable service to people, particularly following self-harm or attempted suicide. Other areas have comprehensive services comprising full multidisciplinary teams, including medical staff, nurses, social workers and psychologists who provide 24-hour cover, biopsychosocial assessments and short-term interventions and therapy (for a review see Callaghan *et al.* 2003).

Risk assessment in A&E

While mental illness is a significant factor associated with suicide only about a quarter of all people who die by suicide have been in touch with mental health services in the year prior to death (Appleby, Shaw *et al.* 1999). Consequently, assessment needs to include psychosocial assessment and assessment of risk not just for people with a known history of mental illness but all high-risk groups (see the Good Practice Guidelines box following).

An individual's risk of suicide can fluctuate over very short periods of time. Suicidal ideation can also be expressed in numerous ways. What might appear to be ambivalence or be dismissed as 'attention seeking' may actually be part of a process of rehearsal where the person is checking out reactions by friends, relatives and others to their possible death. This may serve as an indicator that life is too difficult and that the person requires support to continue to live. Although expressions of suicidal ideation in relation to suicidal behaviour are not wholly reliable it is worth noting that many people who complete suicide have experienced ideation and that their intentions and actions can be reinforced by such thinking (Van Heeringen 2001).

Good practice guidelines for professionals involved with people contemplating suicide

Do:

- take any expression of wanting to die seriously
- when a person expresses a wish to die believe them and accept the pain they feel
- ask if they are feeling suicidal.

Three main indicators of risk:

- a current suicide plan
- a previous history of suicidal or self-harming behaviour
- the resources to die by suicide (access to means).

Aim to:

- prevent a suicide attempt, not just to delay it
- encourage and enhance the thoughts of the person that suggest they wish to live
- assist the person to find alternative solutions to their problems, which may seem overwhelming
- at a minimum, stop the person dying today, with the hope or intention of reducing or eliminating the desire to die tomorrow.

The six steps of intervention:

1. Engagement – establish a relationship based on trust.
2. Identification – establish suicidal intent, risk factors and risk behaviours.
3. Inquiry – ask the person to describe how they got to the point where they wanted to take their life.
4. Estimation – estimate the probability of them dying by suicide.
5. Formal planning and management – agree a specific, short-term plan with the person to at least temporarily continue life.
6. Implementing – deliver the commitments agreed with the person in the management plan.

In addition to transient factors such as ideation, there are differences in vulnerability to suicide between individuals because of specific risk factors that relate to sub-groups of the population that place some at greater risk than others. For example, people with a history of self-harm, mental health problems, alcohol or drug misuse and homelessness are all associated with an increased risk of suicide as is simply being a young man (Appleby, Dennehy *et al.* 1999; Department of Health (DoH) 2002); King 2001.

Working with high-risk groups through A&E

As highlighted earlier there are a number of specific groups that present a high risk for suicide (DoH 2002). The A&E department can play an important role in preventing suicides by such people and deliver interventions that can complement other services and strategies.

Homeless people

Homeless people are often excluded from primary care services because of the nature of their social circumstances and, unlike other groups who may choose not to use services, A&E may be their only legitimate gateway into support services.

Homeless people may have significant physical, psychological and social needs that have been neglected due to the difficulties in accessing and maintaining appropriate care and treatment. In addition, they often face stigma and discrimination in the health, social care and public arenas, particularly if their appearance indicates self-neglect. It is important to provide a comprehensive physical and psychological assessment and arrange effective care at the point of contact, as homeless people may have difficulties in attending follow up appointments.

Case study 4.1

Jack has been brought to A&E by staff from the soup run who have known him for several years. He is intoxicated and probably alcohol-dependent. The workers who have brought Jack say that he seems very depressed and they suspect that he may have serious physical health problems as he has a severe cough that has not improved in the past month. Jack suspects that he has lung cancer and believes that he does not have long to live, even though this has never been investigated.

Issues to consider
- What are the suicide risk factors associated with Jack?
- What information sources should be considered in undertaking a risk assessment?
- What interventions can be delivered by the general A&E team?
- Are there any interventions that should be delivered by the liaison staff rather than the A&E team; if so, what are these?

Good practice
It is important to consider evidence of suicide risk alongside the specific risk factors. Jack has a number of high-risk factors for suicide, in particular his gender and alcohol dependency.

Jack seems concerned about his physical health. People who are homeless and dependent on substances are known to be at increased risk of physical illness. Help to access ongoing appropriate medical assessment and intervention would be important now that Jack has presented and may also aid any future therapeutic engagement with him.

The A&E team is ideally placed to deliver a comprehensive and flexible service for Jack. His chest condition can be examined and diagnosed, along with a psychosocial assessment and alcohol screening. The inter-relationship between mind and body must be captured within any interventions, e.g. if Jack feels physically ill, he may drink to combat the discomfort, which then results in him feeling low and lethargic; because he is inactive his chest condition worsens, so he drinks more, becomes more depressed and so on. The availability of effective simultaneously delivered medical and mental health care at the same location can be appealing and hugely successful.

Older people

The mental health needs of older people often only become obvious when a physical condition has developed and warrants active hospital investigation. High numbers of older people present to A&E of their own volition or on the advice of their GP or family members (Cook 1999). Assessments of mental health and possible suicide risk may be compounded by complications such as confusion arising from severe constipation caused by the side effects of medications.

Loneliness, bereavement, loss of purpose and role, lack of stimulation, physical ill-health, social isolation and declining capabilities are all factors that should be assessed as indicators of suicide risk in older people. Risks are greater among older men, who do not access health care as effectively as older women, and who are statistically at greater risk of suicide than older women (Appleby *et al.* 2001). The absence of belonging, combined with loss and loneliness, gives rise to significant suicide risk. The interplay between the physical and mental health needs of older people means that this group can benefit most from joint assessment and interventions by general A&E and mental health liaison staff.

Case study 4.2

Waseem is a 73-year-old man who has presented in A&E complaining of blurred vision.

The triage nurse cannot identify any immediate cause for Waseem's condition. However, she has established that he finds it difficult to sleep at present and recently lost his wife to cancer after 46 years of marriage. Waseem is adamant that he is coping well although his clothing is loose and ill-fitting and he appears to be somewhat dehydrated.

Waseem avoids initial attempts to assess his mental health and appears not to want to burden staff with his problems as he regards the A&E department as a place for physical health care.

Issues to consider

- What information should the triage nurse gain in order to best assess any suicide risk?
- What options are open to the nurse if Waseem remains evasive about his feelings?
- Which staff might be best suited to working with Waseem during his contact with A&E?
- What aftercare options can be put in place to support Waseem?

Good practice

Initially it is important to establish whether Waseem lives by himself. He may be reluctant to provide this information, recognising that people are concerned about his ability to live independently. It would be useful to know when Waseem's wife died, how long she had been ill and whether Waseem had received support as a carer.

Sleep disturbance can be a significant issue for people who are depressed and can increase any suicide risk. It is important to establish if Waseem has difficulty getting to sleep, wakes early or there are any changes in his sleep pattern since his wife died.

Waseem has voluntarily expressed concern about his vision, therefore it is important to investigate this for him. Alongside addressing Waseem's vision difficulties a wealth of information about his sleep, diet, drinking, loneliness, bereavement, etc. could be explored. Despite any concerns for Waseem's ability to cope on his own it is important to ensure that interventions do not reduce his sense of self-worth and personal control. Waseem may fear admission to a nursing home if seen to be unable to cope, therefore it would be important to reassure him that support can be provided to help him to continue to live independently.

Women experiencing domestic violence

Women who experience domestic violence may be at increased risk of suicide at such times but may present solely for treatment to physical injuries. Apart from the physical damage that victims of domestic violence endure they also experience greater levels of mental ill health than women who do not suffer domestic abuse (Roberts *et al.* 1998). Women with severe mental illnesses have also been identified as more likely to suffer domestic abuse than women with no such illnesses (Coverdale and Turbott 2000).

Engaging women victims in any ongoing health care is a considerable challenge for A&E and mental health staff alike. The non-attendance rate for women is significant, due to a number of issues including control from the abuser, childcare responsibilities, guilt and continued concealment of the abuse (Phillips and Rakusen 1989). When women attend A&E it is usually for treatment of potentially serious injuries although this could mask abuse issues and associated risk of suicide. It is important for staff, if suspicious, to sensitively question and clarify the reasons behind the physical injuries and explore any suicidal thoughts or feelings. In providing information about support services, such as local safe houses and counselling services, A&E staff can play an important role in suicide prevention as well as responding to the abuse issue.

Case study 4.3

Shirley is well known to the A&E department staff and has a history of self-harm and alcohol misuse. Several A&E staff believe that this has been used as a ploy to gain a bed on a medical ward in the past and she has been admitted many times as a result of self-harm before discharging herself the following day when sober.

Shirley has presented at 10 pm with a suspected broken nose and has a number of minor cuts and grazes on her arms and face and smells strongly of alcohol. She was found wandering the streets and brought to A&E by a police officer, who informs staff that Shirley is known to be involved in a violent relationship as she has been called to the house three times in the past month to deal with disputes.

Issues to consider

- Are women with suspicious injuries routinely asked about possible domestic violence?
- Are there any systems to record the prevalence of domestic violence within local information technology provision?
- Are staff aware of the local domestic violence support services?
- Would staff be equipped to deal with a victim/survivor of domestic violence who presented to the service requesting help?
- What education and supervision structures are in place to support staff in working with domestic violence?

Good practice

Domestic violence and suicide intent are both issues that professionals find difficult to ask about. Victims/survivors may find it hard to talk about violence due to feeling ashamed or embarrassed; they may fear repercussions from the perpetrator or that children may be taken away. With sensitive inquiry, victims/survivors will often discuss issues, listen to options and make informed choices. It may take more than one attempt for a victim/survivor to successfully leave a perpetrator due to lack of confidence, restricted options and concern for the children.

Shirley may be hoping for an opportunity to tell someone whom she feels she could trust, therefore establishing a rapport with her is essential. It is important for A&E departments to convey zero tolerance to domestic violence, by having poster campaigns, leaflets and business-size helpline information cards that women in particular could pick up easily for future reference.

When women attend A&E with their partner and domestic violence is suspected it is important to sensitively separate the two in order to probe the issue. Most women will not speak up with their partner present and will go to great lengths to conceal the abuse. During any physical examination older and untreated injuries may provide clues or proof of abuse. A mental health assessment may be needed as depression, anxiety and substance misuse among victims/survivors of domestic violence is known to be high. Professionals should not automatically presume the person will leave their abuser immediately and should never convey disappointment or annoyance if they decide to return as this could jeopardise any future relationship they have with the woman.

Alcohol and substance misuse

Alcohol-related deaths in England and Wales are estimated to be between 5000 and 40,000 per year, which is considerably higher than those caused by other drugs (DoH 2001). Both alcohol and other substances are likely to be linked to even greater numbers of deaths but go unrecorded. Alcohol and substances such as amphetamines and cocaine can increase impulsivity in people. People with a dependency on alcohol or other substances can also experience depression during initial periods of abstinence and have also been identified to be at increased suicide risk (Merrill *et al.* 1992).

Case study 4.4

Ronnie has presented in A&E at 2 am seeking help. He has a disturbing past comprising of physical, emotional and sexual abuse as both a child and adolescent at the hands of his parents and older siblings.

Ronnie states that he began drinking at 14 as it 'dulled the pain, made me forget'. During his young adult life alcohol played a major part in his coping strategy: 'it was my only true friend'. Ronnie sometimes became so frustrated at his inability to put his experiences behind him that he would bang his head into walls, punch doors and cut himself with broken glass and knives as 'it relieved the emotional pressure and stopped my head exploding'.

Ronnie was recently released from prison after serving a sentence for involvement in a pub brawl. He states he was sexually assaulted while in prison, which led to extreme drinking and illicit drug use upon his release. He says he 'wants to die as there is no point in living, life is a living hell and who wants to live in hell, it's bad enough to go there when you're dead, but hell on earth is something else'.

The member of staff who has completed an initial assessment believes 'people like this are just attention seeking and preventing us doing our real job'.

Issues to consider

- What are the risk factors that are present in this case?
- How immediate a risk does Ronnie present?
- How can the A&E and mental health liaison teams work jointly to support Ronnie?
- How might such support needs be addressed in a way that ensures staff objectivity and reduces suicide risk?
- How can Ronnie be involved in any plans to manage the identified risk?

- How can A&E and mental health services exchange information, skills and knowledge for the benefit of Ronnie, and one another?
- What are the training and support needs for the staff member who has done the assessment?

Good practice

People who have a history of self-harm are at greater lifetime risk of suicide than the general population (Owens and House 1994) and this is increased by alcohol dependency (Appleby et al. 1997). Alcohol can dampen both physical and psychological pain effectively in the short term, but also reduces inhibitions and increases impulsivity.

It is important to note any changes in behaviour to determine actual suicide risk in those who are known to self-harm, e.g. someone who usually self-harms by laceration to cope with life then presents with an overdose. The change in behaviour requires exploration as this may be indicative of a suicide attempt rather than an act of coping through self-harm.

Low self-esteem and hopelessness are important factors to identify and it would be beneficial to talk with Ronnie about his life and whether continuing to live is painful. Ronnie will have substantial information about his risks, for example the times of the day when he feels more inclined to self-harm, has thoughts of death or the situations that increase his negative thoughts. Ronnie may also benefit from using a telephone helpline at the time of a crisis and this can reduce the risk of impulsivity.

Mental health and A&E staff are ideally placed to participate in joint training which would maximise knowledge by participants sharing expertise, experience and varying perspectives on issues such as alcohol misuse and sexual abuse. Case presentations can be of benefit to devise management strategies to support staff in dealing positively and effectively with people such as Ronnie who have complex needs.

Black and minority ethnic people (BME) / asylum seekers

As with homeless people asylum seekers may not be registered for primary care services or know how to go about the process. Some people from BME groups and asylum seekers may find that language barriers, stigma and social isolation prevent access to many mainstream services. See Chapter 9 for a more detailed discussion of the issues relating to people from Black and minority ethnic groups.

Young men

Men who find it difficult to ask for help are more likely to die by suicide than women (Van Heeringen 2001). Traditionally, young men are poor help seekers of primary care and other health and social care services. However, for many A&E may be their main contact point for NHS services, albeit often seeking help for physical conditions or alcohol/substance misuse related accidents or problems. Many young men will use A&E as an alternative to primary care due to its accessibility and direct access nature. How any initial contact is built upon may be crucial in targeting this group. See Chapter 7 for a more detailed discussion of the issues relating to young men.

Summary

A&E is a critical point in the health and social care system where suicide prevention interventions can be made effectively. Such interventions are not necessarily the sole preserve of mental health staff. For a wide range of reasons the A&E department may be the first or only place that many people at risk of suicide can turn to in order to seek help. The advent of mental health liaison teams has increased opportunities for A&E departments to more effectively recognise suicide risk and deliver appropriate interventions. Such teams should be located within every A&E department in the country, as the Royal College of Psychiatrists suggested in 1996, if we are to maximise the use of this location for suicide prevention interventions. At the time of writing no national policy directive exists to ensure this occurs. Given the high use of A&E by many high-risk groups, for many people the A&E department may represent the best chance to make effective suicide prevention interventions.

References

Appleby, L. Shaw, J. and Amos, T. (1997) 'National Confidential Inquiry into Suicide and Homicide by People with Mental Illness.' *British Journal of Psychiatry 161*, 101–102.

Appleby, L., Dennehy, J.A., Thomas, C.S., Faragher, E.B. and Lewis, G. (1999) 'Aftercare and clinical characteristics of people with mental illness who commit suicide: A case-control study.' *Lancet 353*, 9162, 1397–1400.

Appleby, L., Shaw, J., Amos, T., McDonnell, R., Bickley, H., Kiernan, K., Davies, S., Harris, C., McCann, K. and Parsons, R. (1999) *Safer Services: Report of the National Confidential Inquiry into Suicide and Homicide by People with Mental Illness.* London: Stationery Office.

Appleby, L., Shaw, J., Sherratt, J., Robinson, J., Amos, T., McDonnell, R., Bickley, H., Hunt, I.M., Kiernan, K., Wren, J., McCann, K., Parsons, R., Burns, J., Davies, S. and Harris, C.

(2001) *Safety First, Report of the National Confidential Inquiry into Suicide and Homicide by People with Mental Illness*. London: Stationery Office.

Callaghan, P., Eales, S., Coates, T. and Bowers, L. (2003) 'A review of research on the structure, process and outcome of liaison mental health services.' *Journal of Psychiatric and Mental Health Nursing 10*, 2, 155–165.

Cook, J. (1999) 'Self harm, with serious intent: A review of the literature on non-fatal deliberate self-harm.' *Mental Health Care 3*, 2, 57–59.

Coverdale, J.H. and Turbott, S.H. (2000) 'Sexual and physical abuse of chronically ill psychiatric outpatients compared with a matched sample of medical outpatients.' *Journal of Nervous and Mental Disease 188*, 7, 440–445.

Crowley, J.J. (2000) 'A clash of cultures: A&E and mental health.' *Accident and Emergency Nursing 8*, 1, 2–8.

Dennis, M., Beach, M., Evans, P.A., Winston, A. and Friedman, T. (1997) 'An examination of the accident and emergency management of deliberate self harm.' *Journal of Accident and Emergency Medicine 14*, 5, 311–315.

Department of Health (2001) *Statistical Bulletin: Statistics on Alcohol – England 1978 Onwards*. London: HMSO.

Department of Health (2002) *National Suicide Prevention Strategy for England*. London: Department of Health.

Ellis, D. and Lewis, S. (1997) 'Psychiatric presentation to an A&E department.' *Psychiatric Bulletin 21*, 10, 627–630.

Gunnell, D., Bennewith, O., Peters, T.J., Stocks, N. and Sharp, D.J. (2002) 'Do patients who self-harm consult their general practitioner soon after hospital discharge? A cohort study.' *Social Psychiatry and Psychiatric Epidemiology 37*, 12, 599–602.

Hawton, K. and Van Heeringen, K. (eds) (2002) *The International Handbook of Suicide and Attempted Suicide*. London: John Wiley & Sons.

Hickey, L., Hawton, K., Fagg, J. and Weitzel, H. (2001) 'Self-harm patients who leave the accident and emergency department without a psychiatric assessment: A neglected population at risk of suicide.' *Journal of Psychosomatic Research 50*, 2, 87–93.

Johnson, S. and Thornicroft, G. (1995) 'Emergency psychiatric services in England and Wales.' *British Medical Journal 311*, 287–288.

King, E.A. (2001) 'The Wessex Suicide Audit 1988–1993: A study of 1457 suicides without a recent psychiatric contact.' *International Journal of Psychiatry in Clinical Practice 5*, 97–104.

Merrill, J., Milner, G., Owens, J. and Vale, A. (1992) 'Alcohol and suicide.' *British Journal of Addiction 87*, 83–89.

Morgan, V. and Coleman, M. (2000) 'An evaluation of the implementation of a liaison service in an A&E department.' *Journal of Psychiatric and Mental Health Nursing 7*, 5, 391–397.

National Collaborating Centre for Mental Health (2003) *Self-Harm: Short-term Physical and Psychological Management and Secondary Prevention of Intentional Self-harm in Primary and Secondary Care. Draft for First Consultation*. London: National Institute for Clinical Excellence.

Owens, D. and House, A. (1994) 'General hospital services for deliberate self-harm.' *Journal of Royal College of Physicians 28*, 370–371.

Perego, M. (1999) 'Why A&E nurses feel inadequate in managing patients who deliberately self-harm.' *Emergency Nurse 6*, 9, 24–28.

Phillips, A. and Rakusen, J. (1989) *The New Our Bodies Ourselves: A Health Book for Women.* The Boston Women's Health Book Collective. Harmondsworth: Penguin Books.

Roberts, G.L., Williams, G.M., Lawrence, J.M. and Raphael, B. (1998) 'How does domestic violence affect women's mental health?' *Women and Health 28*, 1, 117–129.

Royal College of Psychiatrists (1996) *Psychiatric Services to Accident and Emergency Departments: Report of a Joint Working Party of Royal College of Psychiatrists and the British Association for Accident and Emergency Medicine. Council Report 43.* London: Royal College of Psychiatrists.

Ryan, T. (2000) 'Exploring the risk management strategies of mental health service users.' *Health, Risk and Society 2*, 3, 267–282.

Van Heeringen, K. (2001) *Understanding Suicidal Behaviour: The Suicidal Process Approach to Research, Treatment and Prevention.* London: John Wiley & Sons Limited.

Chapter 5

Mental Health In-patient Settings

Nick Bowles

Introduction

People harm themselves and die by suicide for many reasons; many are distressed, lonely, frightened or angry, others simply can see no other way out of their difficulties. Some of these people may spend a period of time in acute wards, where mental health professionals must provide an environment in which people can come to terms with their feelings and co-create a sense that there are more options available than just to end one's life. However, many acute wards are not able to deliver care of this nature and a number of such people die by suicide each year (see Chapter 13).

Suicidality on acute mental health wards

The available evidence (e.g. Sainsbury Centre for Mental Health (SCMH) 1998) suggests that in-patients on acute mental health wards may receive an impoverished and substandard service from admission to discharge. The admission process tends to be poorly expedited; inadequate time is spent on 'induction' despite the crisis that admission represents in many people's lives and only limited information is available. while on the ward patients commonly report feeling unsafe, fearing abuse and violence which in some cases is all too real. Opportunities to leave the ward, even to have some fresh air, may not be freely available.

Deprivation of privacy, especially among those formally observed, is commonplace. This affects the most disturbed clients and falls short of the 'highly specific and sophisticated...professional care' (Barker and Cutcliffe 2000, p.19) such patients require. This creates an environment in which 'anti-therapeutic interpersonal tensions' (SCMH 1998, p.42) can emerge, eroding the 'traditional focus of nursing', i.e. engagement with people in care (Barker and Cutcliffe 2000, p.19).

Patients may receive little more than custodial care, with treatment intended to meet only their most pressing and immediate needs. Many do not have access to a daily programme of purposeful activities so that many patients are bored and unsupported for long periods. Patients are commonly uninvolved in their plan of care (or discharge planning), they feel they do not have a say on their care or any influence on the environment in which they are living (see Case study 5.1).

Case study 5.1: Adopting customer service ideas for an acute ward on the Wedgwood Unit, Bury St Edmunds

At the Wedgwood Unit in Bury St Edmunds the staff wanted to get the message across that they are approachable. They achieved this in a number of ways, but one of the most simple and striking was to professionally print pictures of the staff onto attractive, eye-catching posters supported by text written by patients, to encourage current patients to approach staff and talk about their experiences. These are displayed prominently in the ward living areas, at entry and exit points or near small seating areas, usually tucked into a corner with just a couple of chairs.

These displays may be regarded by some as unnecessary or superfluous. However, they are absolutely necessary for those patients and relatives who do not know whether they can approach staff or exactly what they can expect from the staff, i.e. what they can talk about, especially in the first few days of an admission. These simple posters underline the fundamental values of the Wedgwood staff and their belief in the importance of approachability and 'psychological availability'.

Patients may therefore be effectively disengaged from staff on acute wards, may experience a lack of support and feel misunderstood and uncared for. Further, some patients express their distress in ways which make them unpopular with staff and fellow patients, leading to (usually covert) rejection by the ward community. This phenomenon, known as 'malignant alienation' (Morgan 1979), has been studied in detail in relation to mental health nurses (Duffy 2003a; 2003b) and shown to be responsible for an increase in suicidality.

It is possible that some staff have grown to tolerate, even accept, this inappropriate environment over time. Nonetheless, in some of the wards I have visited, staff members have commented that they are at their best when they are 'fire fighting' a crisis; they really pull together as a team. However, sadly the rest of the time they are less clear on what they should do and how they should manage their time. Consequently, nurse–patient relationships have been characterised as 'passing' (Higgins, Hurst and Wistow 1999) for many in-patients, as a result of the reactive concentration of nursing resources on managing crisis and 'short-lived episodes' (Higgins *et al.* 1999), such as patients who require formal observation.

As the other half of this interpersonal dynamic, the staff within acute wards also face high levels of strain from a variety of sources including a noisy, chaotic and unsafe environment, in which they are often the boundary keepers, a role which can feel uncomfortably close to being jailers. Staff are often unable to deliver the skills for which they are employed and in which they trained, and face instead a mountain of paperwork, much of it performance managed (e.g. Care Plan Approach and risk management paperwork). while no one would suggest that we scrap these (and other) structures to co-ordinate and guide care, the time they take from a relatively small number of staff, almost always qualified nurses, surely deserves critical scrutiny, as the alternative is that wards run at certain times of the week on skeleton staff because the most highly trained staff are engaged in paperwork.

Also many staff do not receive appropriate or meaningful clinical or line management supervision and their freedom to pursue education and training is all too often compromised by a lack of staffing and short-term duty rostering that prevents forward planning for booked study leave.

Overall, it seems that the emotional climate within acute psychiatric wards is not in keeping with that which most people would recognise as suitable, or even necessary, for the restoration of mental health and the development of new answers to the existential questions faced by suicidal patients. Instead of the safe, calm, quiet, structured, orderly, democratic, valuing, understanding and approachable climate they require, patients and staff face high levels of strain within acute wards and experience a negative polarisation across the service user/staff divide.

Changing the emotional and psychological climate on acute wards

In late 1998 the team on Oakburn Ward in Bradford believed that the practice of formal observation undermined the potential for nurses to develop satisfying, supportive relationships with the entire in-patient group. Hence, Bradford staff sought to reduce formal observations and replace 'control' oriented interventions with 'care' interventions. The results were improved patient care with reduced risk and reduced incidents of self-harm and improved staff satisfaction (Bowles and Dodds 2001; Dodds and Bowles 2001). See Case study 5.2 below.

Case study 5.2: Managing for engagement on Oakburn Ward, Bradford (refocusing)

On Oakburn Ward, the importance of daily one-to-one interaction with all patients is demonstrated by a system of delegating and managing this 'meaningful engagement'. The ward manager or shift co-ordinator develops a role allocation schedule that requires each member of staff to engage with around three patients each day. Based on the Bradford approach, meaningful engagement is operationally defined with the following guidelines.

- The engagement is a delegated and performance managed expectation.

- Staff must advise patients who their one-to-one worker is for that day – in some settings this is done in the morning patient–staff meeting.

- Qualified and unqualified staff must use care plans to guide their interaction; where possible qualified nurses will take care plans into the interaction and complete them collaboratively with the patient.

- The engagement does not 'count' unless it is written up as a 'one-to-one' and highlighted as such in the care plan (by the use of a coloured marker in the margin).

- Every patient must receive at least a daily one-to-one; some patients will be seen more than this depending on their needs and their 'safety plan'; every patient must receive at least three one-to-ones with a qualified nurse, one of which is a formal review of the week prior to a ward round.

In summary, the nursing team know that their priority activity on each shift is to ensure that they have delivered this meaningful engagement, i.e. one-to-one time is a priority over the secondary but all too often occurring paperwork, meetings, etc. When completed and documented staff record that they have completed their one-to-one. This system is easily audited and enables the ward manager to ensure that all patients are seen daily and that each member of staff is meeting this minimum standard. while it is possible to criticise this approach on the basis that it does not specify the content of the one-to-one or which therapeutic approach to use, this level of specificity is unnecessary. It is clearly a matter of judgement for the senior staff to determine whether their staff have the necessary skills and if not, they will reflect this in their delegation and make such skills the focus for supervision, support and possibly training.

This simple approach has been used in a number of sites, and it is not uncommon for patients who have grown familiar with this system to approach staff at the start of the day to enquire as to who their one-to-one worker is for the day. For this reason, some wards display the list of workers in a public area and others (for example the Meadowbrook Unit, Bolton, Salford and Trafford Mental Health NHS Trust) will announce who each patient's worker is in daily community meetings.

Although a small proportion of patients may be unable or unwilling to make use of a one-to-one session, interviews conducted with patients on Oakburn indicated that the one-to-one time was very positively regarded by patients.

This case study highlights the way that positive leadership, effective management and audit combine to remind staff and patients of the key priorities for staff time. In Shelton Hospital, Shrewsbury, where this system was adopted, refocusing data showed that, despite the demands of an acute ward, the staff in 'refocusing' areas were delivering a one-to-one on a daily basis. Unsurprisingly, the use of formal observations fell significantly during this period.

These themes were further examined by Sunderland (in a discussion between us that we published jointly, see Bowles *et al.* 2002). She argued that people who are suicidal make health care workers (and their managers) feel they have to 'do' something, and usually placing patients on observation is this something. Sunderland challenges the notion that observations and engagement are synonymous, arguing that while observations enable physical proximity between nurse and patient, meaningful interpersonal interaction or emotional closeness rarely follows. As an alternative

Sunderland described a practice she called 'containment', characterised by interpersonal engagement which did not prevent the expression of distress but sought to develop ways and means of managing the distress without the person's self-control or responsibility being stripped from them. She describes it as:

> the process of containing the patient's feelings…being receptive to what the patient is experiencing, being able to bear and think constructively about these feelings. When we can do this, the next step is to use the understanding we have gained about the nature of the patient's feelings or anxieties and communicate this to the patient…it is 'containing' for patients to have the things they experience named and understood (Bowles *et al.* 2002, p.259)

Being contained in this way may be an important learning process for patients, albeit at times uncomfortable as many have had years of experience in acute settings where their distress was reacted to, rather than understood, hence people may seek the expected, routinised response from staff (which will commonly include formal observations), leaving staff and patient stuck in a cycle of action; reaction; action.

There is no doubt that containment *is* skilful practice, but I wonder if these skills are not possessed by the majority of direct care workers: the ability to listen and make sense of experience while managing the internal ambiguity and stress that catharsis can generate. I believe that most health professionals are capable of doing this – some may require training and all will benefit from supervision – but that for this practice to be possible, staff need a work environment in which practice of this nature is both expected and supported (through meaningful handovers, care plans, policy documents, multiprofessional treatment planning, supportive management, etc.). In the following case study, the approach taken by acute ward staff in Bury St Edmunds is described. They opted as a service to employ solution-focused techniques to guide their 'containment' and collaboration with suicidal patients.

Case study 5.3: Containment through solution-focused conversation in Wedgwood Unit, Bury St Edmunds

Meaningful engagement with patients on a daily basis is emotionally taxing and makes demands on the skills of even the most highly trained staff. Consequently, staff avoidance may be predicted, perhaps camouflaged behind 'busyness' or note-writing. Through delegation and audit (as discussed above in Case study 5.2) such avoidance may be minimised but these actions do little to ensure that engagements are meaningful and do not make demands on staff that they are unprepared to handle, particularly unqualified staff. The answers must include supervision and training for meaningful engagement.

The Wedgwood Unit in Bury St Edmunds opted to train every member of direct care staff in 'solution-focused conversation' skills to address this need. Over a period of two weeks, every member of staff participated in one of three two-day workshops, delivered on-site. Unqualified and qualified staff from all disciplines trained together. Three months later, it was evident that solution-focused skills were being used across the Unit in one-to-one sessions, informal contact and also in groups. Patient satisfaction was increased and the quality of one-to-one engagement was regarded very positively by senior staff, who noted that case note entries were sharper, more focused and more patient centred. Significantly, the level of staff comfort with fulfilling one-to-ones was higher. The solution-focused approach (De Shazer 1985; Hawkes, Wilgosh and Marsh 1993) shares many similarities with the 'recovery' model (Repper 2001) and Phil Barker's Tidal Model (Barker 2002) in that it establishes the patient's own priorities and sources of motivation, the patient's view on how they would like their life to change and enables goal setting and planning in a collaborative relationship. With supervision it may be used safely by all grades of staff. It is an ideal tool for staff wanting to co-write care plans with patients (a recommendation made by the Department of Health in their Acute Policy Guidance, DoH 2002).

At the Wedgwood Unit, worker–patient interactions on a one-to-one and group basis, note-taking and staff supervision are solution oriented, i.e. they consider strengths and resilience factors and are future focused. One of the ward managers described how solution-focused approaches provided tools that the staff have been using to good effect with people who are at risk of harming themselves. He commented that staff gently challenge negative thinking, speech and behaviour, they use numerical scaling in their conversations (rating degrees of risk on a numbered continuum) and in collaborative care plans to introduce the possibility of change and reinforce present coping behaviours, including those things the patient or others around them are doing to maintain their safety. Consequently, he argued that patients are safer, they are more engaged with their workers and experience respectful, collaborative relationships; in short he said patients' time in hospital is more meaningful.

The Wedgwood team exemplify the importance of the whole team working together to engage patients, even (or especially) those who are very distressed or who have a negative outlook or expectational set (or 'frame of mind'). Training and leadership are also clearly important but the fact that such engagement is part of the Wedgwood culture remains the predominant learning point in this case study.

The Wedgwood team are practising 'containment'. Patients treated in the manner described in the case study are likely to experience a sense that their distress is 'containable' and that talking about their hopelessness and their intention to harm themselves does not automatically lead to a loss of responsibility, self-control, privacy, etc. Conversely, if the feeling generated in the staff team is anxiety, fear of self-injury and/or suicide, or even anger towards the patient, then it is probable that these feelings will be transmitted to the patient overtly through practices such as 'observations' and less obviously through social means. However, as Sunderland reminds us (Bowles *et al.* 2002) when these feelings are 'expressed, understood and named but not acted upon the patient may experience a release from the normal cycle of unbearable feelings and self-destructive action'. Teams who don't manage to break this cycle pitch themselves and the patients with whom they work into a negative cycle of distress that they meet with a ritualistic control reaction; consequently the staff may feel they do little more than observe patients, who may form the view that in such environments their silence is less likely to trigger a reaction from staff that they find aversive than is discussing their intention to die by suicide. Little wonder then that some in-patients who exhibit very few or no risk factors will succeed in their suicide attempts.

The principles of containment and meaningful engagement resonated with the values and the experience of the Bradford staff who sought to replace observations with more meaningful care. The pioneering work conducted in Bradford led to the development of the 'refocusing' approach; this was highlighted in Department of Health (2002) guidance and has since been developed, tested, evaluated and applied in a number of other settings.

However, in these other settings, while observation use *is* a focus for evaluation, it is not the principal target for practice development. It is more accurate to say that the practice of observations may be expected to reduce over time in refocusing wards as a consequence of other interventions, including environmental management (to reduce noise, ambient stress, perception of risk), one-to-one engagement, collaborative safety planning, high visibility nursing throughout the day and strategies intended to maintain personal control and personal responsibility even for very poorly patients. This was particularly notable in Bolton, where between 2001 and 2003 on two wards (one an open acute ward, the other a Psychiatric Intensive Care Unit (PICU)) observations were rarely used and more recently in Shelton Hospital, Shewsbury, where observation use has tumbled over the seven months that staff have been providing daily meaningful one-to-one engagements. Hence, refocusing is not concerned with merely stopping observations, but is a package of interventions that are intended to change the emotional and psychological climate on acute wards, improve meaningful engagement and remove some of the obstacles to effective care for all members of the ward community.

Having visited many acute wards in the UK and overseas over the last five years I suggest that there are some, if not many, who are mired in the ritualised cycle of knee-jerk reaction described above. In these wards staff often feel powerless to change their way of working and a sense of reactive fire-fighting pervades their everyday working lives. These wards are dangerous places for suicidal patients. Refocusing is an approach to practice development that seeks to reverse the loss of therapeutic values that afflict this sector. Clearly, it is not only refocusing sites that are delivering high standards of care, nor would I argue that refocusing is intended *primarily* to reduce the risk of suicide on in-patient wards. However I contend that some of the principles outlined below are likely to resonate with acute ward staff and if applied are likely to generate positive outcomes. In the following section I describe the refocusing approach.

What is refocusing?

At its heart the refocusing approach contends that the purpose of acute wards and the therapeutic values of the staff have become blurred over the last 10 to 15 years. Gijbels (1995) argued that staff have the skills to work with patients but are frequently unable to use them because of the competing demands upon their time. Over the years, this lack of opportunity has combined with a lost sense of the primacy and importance of interpersonal engagement within a working environment that is stressful, and a managerial environment which is risk averse, defensive and often more concerned with paperwork than people-work. Consequently, lack of purpose, low expectations and a reduced level of staff commitment to interpersonal engagement and collaborative care can be both predicted and observed.

Refocusing is intended to re-establish the purpose of acute care within the whole multidisciplinary team and reinvigorate the staff with the belief that they can deliver meaningful care and consequently expect more of themselves and of the people with whom they work. Refocusing holds that the prime reason staff are unable to deliver effective and safe care, perhaps even the 'containment' described above, is the high level of work strain they face. The job strain model of Karasek and Theorell (1990) posits that where job strain is high, the quality and quantity of the work provided by staff falls, to the point where staff exhibit behaviours associated with burn-out and are at increased risk of serious illness.

Job strain is greatest when staff face:

1.   High workload and high levels of demand, i.e. staff may report working very hard, working fast or not having sufficient time to get the job done. This is likely to be particularly relevant when the work demands are not regarded as intrinsically valuable or worthwhile.

2.   Low personal control or decision latitude in meeting those demands, i.e. they are not able to use their own judgement and skills or their decision-making ability is undervalued.

3.   Inadequate social support in the workplace: this includes the informal peer-to-peer 'climate' but also includes formal arrangements such as supervision, team meetings, effective policies and management attention that is collaborative, positive and engaged.

Karasek and Theorell (1990) have established that workers are at greatest risk when all three factors are present; they call this 'isostrain', a noxious level of demand which has been shown to lead to deteriorating work performance, increased sickness and, in the worst cases, stress-related illness (Cheng et al. 2001; Kivimäki et al. 2002).

In acute psychiatry, it is often evident on a daily basis that nursing staff and care assistants face high demands in each of these three areas. Consequently they are likely to be facing stresses which over time may prove to be intolerable, may lead to poor performance and place the member of staff at high risk of developing a stress-related illness. Hence, 'isostrain' is likely to be a reality for much of their working week. However, this model also applies to patients, as they face the same noisy and chaotic environment, have reduced personal control and support, limited engagement, poor privacy, lack of cleanliness, poor levels of information and limited structure and activity within their day.

Clearly, practice changes that are intended to reduce strain for staff *and* patients are likely to be of the greatest value; the interpersonal dynamics examined above require that practice change must include challenging the social world of acute wards, raising expectations and firming the ward purpose, clarifying values and reinforcing boundaries on all. However, in addition to these steps, in order to reduce strain on staff and patients practice changes, refocusing aims to increase personal control and decision-making latitude, reduce the onerous demands that the environment makes upon the individual and increase the level of support provided, in all cases for staff and patients.

Refocusing has been applied in ten sites across the UK. The results from each site look promising: changes include increased leadership, improved multiprofessional working, greater patient involvement, significant changes to practice including structured activity, more meaningful engagement, reduced environmental stress and noise, reduced violence and aggression (for example in Bolton one ward reported a drop in incidents of over 80% over a 12-month period), improved induction on admission, raised patient satisfaction and increased staff supervision (see Case study 5.4).

Case study 5.4: Supervision that works

In Maple House, a PICU in Bolton, one of many practice development targets achieved between 2001 and 2003 (when along with three other wards in Bolton they won the National Institute for Mental Health England Positive Practice Award for modernisation) was to deliver consistent, regular and effective staff supervision. This was managed on a cascade basis that enabled every member of staff to receive supervision monthly. Care delivery, documentation and team working were highlighted in the supervision process and records. This simple but well organised management strategy turned almost every member of qualified staff into a 'leader', with a responsibility to ensure compliance with team standards, and to support and develop their colleagues. Now established, a supervision culture exists on Maple House, again supported by simple but rigorous audit mechanisms to ensure that each staff member is supported and that their individual contribution to the life of the ward is tangibly recognised. As well as providing support and coaching, well organised supervision reduces the prevalence of a common phenomenon within large teams, known as 'social loafing', which put simply is the tendency of a worker to reduce their work output as the individual contribution they make becomes less visible.

The most important element is the value staff and patients place on meaningful engagement. If refocusing were to be boiled down to one thing it would be meaningful engagement, or 'the gift of time' from a friendly professional as Jackson and Stevenson (1998) characterised it. Such engagement aims to help people in distress to make sense of their experience and to find new ways of managing their distress and returning to, possibly even achieving mastery of, their lives. In some settings, it is likely that staff do not know how to do this, or are unsupported in their practice or therapeutic values, in others, this awareness has led to specific training for all staff who engage with patients regularly (see Case study 5.5). Clearly, meaningful engagement must be managed, supported and prioritised, and if necessary supported with training. In each of the refocusing sites this is an 'early win' in the change process and a priority, along with regular audit to remind staff that this is a priority.

Case Study 5.5: Therapy and support in Eastbourne/Community education in Bolton

Meaningful engagement does not just mean one-to-one contact; a range of social and therapeutic activities is an essential part of treatment plans in acute psychiatry for everyone, in particular for those people who are withdrawn, experiencing reduced volition and reduced self-esteem. In the Department of Psychiatry at Eastbourne a multi-professional team provides a programme every day with a range of activities both therapeutic and social. They provide physical activity every day including weekends, including salsa dancing and Tai Chi.

In Bolton, on K1, K2 and K3 wards activities are managed by nursing staff, sometimes supported by Occupational Therapist staff. These nurses are relieved of the more mundane activities on the ward that otherwise dominate the working day; they are also protected from being moved to other wards to cover staff shortages. A consistent, reliable programme of activities is offered and is well used, rendering the ward quieter, calmer and more manageable for the staff who remain on the general ward area. On K2 ward staff have secured the involvement of community education staff who deliver activities and training on the ward, which patients can continue after leaving hospital, in some cases up to a City and Guilds award.

Conclusion

Many people who experience a desire to end their lives do not act upon it, or are 'unsuccessful' but do not repeat their attempt. These people somehow find ways to continue to endure the daily stresses and strains of life, to wrestle with the things which drove them to consider suicide and choose to engage with life.

Mental health staff working in acute wards are often the last people who have the chance to work with suicidal people, the last line of defence, one of the remaining sources of hope available to patients in an acutely distressed state. This has got to be one of the most important tasks that any person can face. It is certainly one of the most demanding and rewarding aspects of mental health practice.

However, there can be little doubt that acute wards sometimes fail to provide an environment in which staff may engage with patients to the degree that their journey to recovery is positively influenced, little doubt also that acute wards are stressful places in which to work, sometimes as a consequence of the negative dynamics that emerge in response to the distressed, hopeless or suicidal. Yet there is also evidence from refocusing wards and many others to show that acute wards can be therapeutic, can challenge outmoded practices and can provide truly collaborative care for those people who are so distressed that they wish to end their relationship not just with the rest of the world but also with themselves.

The challenge the staff in these exemplar areas have met is to deliver good risk management and increased safety for staff and patients, not only through addressing risks in the physical environment such as access to lethal means (see Chapter 13) but also through high levels of engagement, structure and collaboration with patients. As the Department of Health (2002) makes clear, many acute ward teams in England have yet to meet this challenge and, until they do, the cycle of distress and ritualised reaction will continue with all the risks and negative outcomes this implies.

References

Barker, P. (2002) 'The Tidal Model: The healing potential of metaphor within the patient's narrative.' *Journal of Psychosocial Nursing 40*, 7, 42–50.

Barker, P. and Cutcliffe, J. (2000) 'Hoping against hope.' *OpenMind* Jan/Feb, 18–19.

Bowles, N. and Dodds, P. (2001) 'An eye for an eye.' *OpenMind* March/April, 7–9.

Bowles, N., Dodds, P., Hackney, D., Sunderland, C. and Thomas, P. (2002) 'Engagement and observation: A discussion paper.' *Journal of Psychiatric and Mental Health Nursing 9*, 255–260.

Cheng, Y., Kawachi, I., Coakley, E.H., Schwartz, J. and Colditz, G. (2001) 'Association between psychosocial work characteristics and health functioning in American women: A prospective study.' *British Medical Journal 320*, 1432–1436.

De Shazer, S. (1985) *Keys to Solution in Brief Therapy.* New York: WW Norton.

Department of Health (2002) *The Mental Health Policy Implementation Guide.* London: Department of Health.

Dodds, P. and Bowles, N. (2001) 'Dismantling formal observations and refocusing nursing activity in acute inpatient psychiatry: A case study.' *Journal of Psychiatric and Mental Health Nursing 8*, 3, 183–188.

Duffy, D. (2003a) 'Exploring suicide risk and the therapeutic relationship: A case study approach.' *Nursing Times Research 8*, 3, 185–199.

Duffy, D. (2003b) 'The Therapeutic Relationships of Mental Health Nurses and Suicidal Mental Health Patients.' University of Manchester. Unpublished PhD thesis.

Gijbels, H. (1995) 'Mental health nursing skills in an acute admission environment: Perceptions of mental health nurses and other mental health professionals.' *Journal of Advanced Nursing 21*, 3, 460–465.

Hawkes, D., Wilgosh, R. and Marsh, I. (1993) 'Explaining solution focused therapy.' *Nursing Standard 7*, 33, 31–34.

Higgins, R., Hurst, K. and Wistow, G. (1999) 'Nursing acute psychiatric patients: A quantitative and qualitative study.' *Journal of Advanced Nursing 29*, 52–63.

Jackson, S. and Stevenson, C. (1998) 'The gift of time from the friendly professional.' *Nursing Standard 12*, 51, 31–33.

Karasek, R.A. and Theorell, T. (1990) *Healthy Work.* New York: Basic Books.

Kivimäki, M., Leino-Arjas, P., Luukkonen, R., Riihimäki, H., Vahtera, J. and Kirjonen, J. (2002) 'Work stress and risk of cardiovascular mortality: A prospective cohort study of industrial employees.' *British Medical Journal 325*, 857.

Morgan, H.G. (1979) *Death Wishes? The Understanding and Management of Deliberate Self-harm.* London: Wiley.

Repper, J. (2001) 'Adjusting the focus of mental health nursing: Incorporating users' views on recovery.' *Journal of Mental Health 9*, 6, 575–587.

Sainsbury Centre for Mental Health (1998) *Acute Problems: A Survey of the Quality of Care in Acute Psychiatric Wards.* London: SCMH.

Chapter 6

Community Mental Health Services

Nigel Crompton and Peter Walmsley

Introduction

Increasingly mental health service provision in the UK has a community focus, a trend that started with the introduction of more effective psychotropic medications in the 1950s and continues in the current drive towards the establishment of assertive outreach teams and crisis resolution/home treatment teams as part of the Mental Health Policy Implementation Guide (Department of Health (DoH) 2001).

Commissioners and providers of services along with practitioners are striving to discover alternatives to hospital admission for individuals in mental health crisis. Wherever possible patients benefit from care delivered in less restrictive settings that do not ghettoise people in mental health institutions but empower individuals to manage their own mental health. We look briefly at the literature around community based suicide prevention and establish the nature of suicidality and aspects of good practice, including risk management, which we illustrate with some case examples. Crucial to the management of suicidal behaviour is communication and we discuss the nature of communication and effective care co-ordination between all parties. Finally, we look at how contracting can aid the management of the suicidal individual in the community.

Background literature

Research into suicide prevention is difficult as it is almost impossible to say when we have successfully prevented a suicide. We only tend to know when we have failed. Fortunately, albeit tragic, suicide is rare at 1 in 10,000 of the UK population and subsequently the numbers required to provide statistical power to demonstrate effectiveness of interventions is prohibitively high. Research has tended to concentrate on the nature of suicide and we have a range of demographic facts and figures pertaining to this important public health issue (Hawton and Fagg 1988; Hawton, Fagg and Simkin 1997). The intervention studies that have taken place have tended to focus on populations who have presented with non-fatal self-harm as these individuals demonstrate far greater propensity to go on to commit a successful suicide than the next person in the population (Buglass and Horton 1974).

Rudd and Joiner (2001) undertook a review of such intervention studies and discovered in a comprehensive search that there were only 25 randomised or controlled studies targeting suicide. Three were pharmacological studies (all over 20 years old) and the 22 remaining studies included supportive case management, follow-up letters and phone calls to those refusing treatment, home visits and intensive tracking, brief medical (non-psychiatric) hospitalisation and improved access to emergency services. Six were essentially procedural, rather than therapeutic, interventions. Fifty per cent were described as positive (i.e. were deemed to have reduced subsequent suicidal behaviour) and included intensive three-month case management by volunteers (Termansen and Bywater 1975), follow-up home visits by a community mental health nurse (Van Heeringen, Jannes and Buylaert 1995) and improved access to emergency services (Morgan, Jones and Owen 1993). Of the negative studies Motto (1976) found follow-up letters and telephone calls had no effect over a four-year period. Similarly, Litman and Wold (1976) found telephone calls, home visits and befriending had no effect and, not surprisingly, Waterhouse and Platt (1990) found an average 17-hour medical in-patient stay post attempt had no effect on subsequent behaviour.

It must be noted that even those with positive findings had a number of methodological drawbacks including high attrition rates and limited follow-up times, and some excluded high-risk groups, such as multiple attempters (Van Heeringen *et al.* 1995; Morgan *et al.* 1993). However, there are some good practice guidelines that can be drawn from this work.

Good practice guidelines

- Intensive follow up, case management, telephone contacts, letters or home visits may improve treatment compliance for low-risk groups.
- Improved access to emergency services with a clearly defined crisis plan, can reduce suicidal behaviour.

Eleven of the 16 treatment studies employed some form of cognitive behavioural intervention. Of the 11, 10 were short-term interventions of less than 6 months treatment. Of these, 10 incorporated problem solving and 7 reported positive findings: some in reducing suicidal ideation (Joiner, Rudd and Rajab 1998; Libermann and Eckman 1981; Salkovskis, Atha and Storer 1990); some in reducing suicide related symptomatology such as depression (Lerner and Clum 1990; Libermann and Eckman 1981; Salkovskis *et al.* 1990), hopelessness (Lerner and Clum 1990; Patsiokis and Clum 1985) and loneliness (Lerner and Clum 1990). Most studies did not demonstrate a sustained reduction in suicidal attempts, except McLeavey *et al.* (1994), but this study, again, excluded high-risk groups and had a small sample group. Of the longer-term studies Linehan *et al.* (1991) utilising dialectical behavioural therapy with a long-term (two-year) intervention reported a reduction in subsequent attempts but no effect on related aspects of depression, hopelessness or suicidal ideation.

The extent of evidence is therefore limited and we are in the very early days of establishing effective interventions in the treatment of suicidal individuals. The best we can do it seems is speculate from the limited evidence that we do have. Rudd and Joiner (2001), however, felt that there were conclusions that could be drawn from their review and these give us some limited good practice guidelines.

Good practice guidelines

- Intensive long-term treatment following an attempt is most appropriate for high-risk individuals.

- Short-term cognitive behavioural therapy (CBT) based interventions utilising problem solving are proven to reduce suicidal ideation, depression and hopelessness for up to one year.

- Reducing future suicide attempts requires long-term treatment targeting emotional regulation, poor distress tolerance, anger management, interpersonal effectiveness and self-esteem.

- High-risk suicidal patients can be treated safely and effectively within the community.

The National Confidential Inquiry gives us a significant piece of work that puts meat on the bone of the demographic facts and figures that we already know but has also come up with some surprises (see Chapter 13). We have learned that 16 per cent of all suicides where the person was a user of mental health services, occurred while they were psychiatric in-patients and a further 23 per cent had only recently been discharged from hospital (DoH 1999a). These were alarming figures that gave birth to a wide range of recommendations, many of which have been encompassed in the National Suicide Prevention Strategy (DoH 2002). Most look at practical prevention matters such as eliminating non-collapsible bed rails, reducing prescription sizes and ensuring more frequent follow up. These are all important and sensible precautions. It is arguable that the greater figures for those receiving in-patient care is due to the fact that such services cater for those of the highest suicidal risk. Interestingly, there is perhaps another lesson to learn. These figures debatably introduce a significant new risk factor for completed suicide; that of in-patient care or indeed any intervention where the locus of control is taken from the individual in crisis (see Duffy 2003). To examine this further we need to examine the nature of suicidal thinking.

The nature of suicidal thinking

There are many factors to be considered as part of suicidal thinking and there is no simple way of defining a 'set' of suicidal thoughts. Beck *et al.* (1979) felt that the motivation toward suicide varied between the need to escape and the need to communicate. Where escape was prime then hopelessness was the key factor and where communication was prime then intervention needed to identify what was being communicated to whom.

We do know, however, that there are a range of factors that commonly emerge as being part of the repertoire of suicidal thinking, such as low self-esteem/low self-worth, helplessness (a concept of not being in control) and poor distress tolerance which is manifested in greater impulsivity. There is little evidence as yet to say what works but there is some degree of consensus about the cognitive and behavioural risk factors central to suicidal risk. These factors inform the therapeutic process.

The lesson to be learned

Interventions that are restrictive or do not empower individuals in suicidal crisis can inadvertently re-affirm or confirm such negative belief patterns. Gutheil (1990) noted that 'experienced clinicians are aware that psychiatric hospitalisation presents some clear risks, including regression, fostering dependency, loss of time from work or studies, and severe stigma' (p.335). We potentially increase people's perceptions of low self-worth by removing them from the community in which, they may feel, they have no place. By adopting over-controlling methods of dealing with their crisis we take the reins of control and, again, reinforce the notion of helplessness that they possess. By placing somebody in temporary asylum we remove them from the stresses of reality but in so doing strip them of the ability to learn to deal with these stresses. Community and home-based interventions, when appropriately employed, can avoid these dangers. Not only this, but by empowering individuals to deal with the nature of their suicidal thoughts and feelings through focused community interventions, we engender a deleterious impact on hopelessness; the determining factor in any completed suicide. This suggests a necessity to embark upon positive risk taking as a therapeutic norm. This is not to say that there is no place for in-patient care as one part of an overall suicide prevention plan, that is produced collaboratively with the client, in order to enhance their notion that they are in control of their care. It is perhaps judicious to be mindful that 'an overly restrictive environment can be as destructive as an overly permissive one' but also that when a patient is 'dangerously suicidal, hospitalisation and close supervision are clearly indicated' (VandeCreek and Knapp 1983, p.277).

Community management

In order to provide sound community management of the suicidal individual several issues need to be considered. These include:

- balancing risk factors along a continuum of maintaining the individual's safety to empowering that person to be a collaborator in their recovery
- developing and maintaining a therapeutic relationship
- establishing appropriate support through good communication and negotiation.

Case study 6.1

Susan (34) has been referred by her GP to the community team with a 10-year history of persistent low mood, recent loss of self-worth and feelings of hopelessness following the breakdown of her 8-year marriage. Susan has no job and is left with two young children, Jennifer (7) and James (5). While she has notions of loss regarding her relationship, her overwhelming thoughts are about how she can face a future without her husband and whether she can cope alone. Common in suicidal ideation is a fear of facing an undesirable future. Not surprisingly, Susan has had thoughts of self-harm and occasional thoughts of suicide.

Questions for consideration

1. What options are there for Susan's care management?
2. What focus should any interventions take?
3. What might be the protective factors?
4. What considerations need to be taken in balancing risks?

In Case study 6.1 the first step would be to arrange assessment at home for Susan aiming to make urgent contact and negotiate a convenient time for assessment. Home assessment has a number of benefits. It allows the clinician to gain a better understanding of the person as they usually might be, as opposed to in the false environment of the psychiatric clinic. It better facilitates a normalising approach to Susan's experiences and, perhaps most importantly, gives Susan a greater sense of control over the situation. This is an important practical first step to mitigating hopelessness.

Many patients present to community mental health teams (CMHTs) following emergency treatment at an A&E department. In this case Susan would be assessed by the mental health practitioner in the department in an A&E liaison team which may include mental health nurses, social workers, psychiatrists or perhaps a junior doctor on call. Susan might have been given a psychiatric out-patient appointment at the local mental health hospital which may be some weeks away, or alternatively, admission to a psychiatric hospital. However, another option would be to follow Susan up at home the same or next day. Ideally two staff, at least one of whom would be a woman, would go to assess Susan at home. This not only allows for a better understanding of her experience, but also ensures staff safety. Although the GP may describe no risks to health care staff many health workers are assaulted on home visits (Lindow and McGeorge 2001).

A further alternative may be to give Susan an appointment within 48 hours at a crisis clinic. Such clinics may operate at out of hours GP centres, crisis houses or other facilities depending on local resources. In this way Susan's needs can be managed at the primary care level but with the option to be brought rapidly into specialist mental health services dependent upon ongoing risk assessment. In Southport it has been discovered that such clinics based in an out of hours GP centre have a 13 per cent DNA (did not attend) rate compared with over 40 per cent at the local mental health unit (Holmes and Walmsley 2003).

Questions for consideration

1. Why might a primary care clinic be more attractive to clients than a mental health out-patient department?

2. What beneficial effect may this have on managing suicidal behaviour?

3. What are the important factors to be elicited in the initial assessment?

4. What risks may there be in these options and how might they be managed?

It is important to determine the reason for suicide. Susan has undertaken a thought process and come up with a solution: that of suicide. We cannot be so arrogant as to dismiss this solution out of hand. It is a solution and in the initial visit(s) we need to explore how Susan came to this. We recognise that it is an option but need to assist Susan to move to a point where she can see other options. This is a period of exploration and it is important not to intervene too soon. We need to establish that we are starting a process where suicide is not the *solution to end all problems but the problem that ends all solutions*. We recognise that suicide is an option but once taken there is no going back. This is a period of negotiation with the service user where we persuade them that while we can recognise they have come to one decision, together we can explore other options. What we are asking them for is time to do this. We may use anti-suicide contracts to do this (see later).

Case study 6.2

John is a 33-year-old man with a history of recurrent depression with episodes of psychosis. He has lived with his mother, Pamela, for the past 18 months. Before this John was in a relationship with Pauline which lasted for four years. They have a daughter, Bethany, who lives with her mother. John now has monthly access to Bethany, supervised with his mother. John has a community mental health nurse who is his CPA co-ordinator. He is subject to Section 117 of the Mental Health Act (1983) previously having been an in-patient detained on section 3 for 21 weeks. Two years ago John attempted to asphyxiate himself while in his car on the local beach. A passer-by had phoned the emergency services and provided first aid. John spent time on the in-patient unit and had been detained under section as he had not consented to admission.

John's community nurse has been off work due to long-term sickness. His case was covered by another member of the CMHT but John found it difficult to cover old ground with a different member of staff. In addition John had been asked for more money for his daughter which had upset him. Over a couple of days he found himself increasingly distressed at the thought of financial burdens and guilt that his relationship had ended.

On Tuesday evening John found it difficult to sleep and made three lacerations to his wrist and one to his neck. His mother heard a noise, found him and telephoned an ambulance. John was seen at A&E by the mental health liaison team and, with the agreement of his temporary CPA co-ordinator and his mother, a care plan was immediately put into effect with numerous daily visits.

Questions for consideration

1. What might be the effect of John's previous experiences of mental health services on the treatment plan?

2. What might need to be in place to ensure John's safety?

3. Who needs to be involved?

As we have seen, people have legitimate reasons for suicide. It is up to practitioners to help them widen the scope of alternatives and to offer legitimate reasons for living. John might tell us: 'I'm a burden on my mother and she'd be better off without me.'

We need not deny that burden. There is little mileage in challenging a firmly held belief. But we might explore it further: 'If I were to ask your mother "which do you prefer, that your son, John, dies thus relieving you of this burden, or that he collaborates with a treatment plan that ensures his recovery?" what do you think she would say?'

John might reply that he is unable to go through with such a plan: 'Well, that's an entirely different issue, let's discuss that.'

Problem solving can be a useful tool in supporting people who are suicidal. In the cases of Susan and John they have arrived at suicide as a solution to seemingly intractable problems. The perception of being unable to problem solve is a key feature in the development of hopelessness and helplessness which can be fundamental to suicidal ideation. We need to help the suicidal person to view hopelessness as symptomatic of their circumstances and guide them to see that other interpretations and actions are possible and achievable. First, we should encourage John to identify the reasons for living and for dying. Ask him to list these and then, together, critically appraise each of those reasons. The aim is to reinforce the reasons for living and correct distortions in the reasons for dying. In engendering a problem solving approach we need to ensure that problems are dealt with systematically and solutions not arrived at and acted on impulsively.

Problem solving approaches

1.   First, define the problem.

2.   Brainstorm as many alternative solutions as possible. Encourage free thinking. It does not matter how ridiculous some of the solutions seem, this promotes creative thinking.

3.   Decide on the best solution by weighing up the advantages and disadvantages of each in turn.

4.   Go ahead with the chosen solution. If the chosen solution is one that would result in a harmful outcome the practitioner must intervene to encourage further appraisal or more directive action.

5.   Check out the results of the chosen solution. If it is not desirable return to the first point above.

In problem solving with individuals it is often wise to start with problems that may not be the most severe. Start off with achievable goals and move up to the bigger issues. This is important in building self-esteem, which is another factor in suicidal thinking.

Risk management strategies for community teams

There are a number of strategies that should be in place for the community management of suicidal individuals.

- Frequency of home visits or clinic appointments should be increased.

- There should be plans in place for non-attendances. Do not wait until it happens.

- Liaise with the person's GP to ensure that either relatively non-toxic anti-depressants are prescribed or that anti-depressants are prescribed more frequently in smaller quantities.

- Ensure that the individual along with their carers know how to contact services at all times.

- Establish with the individual when suicidal ideas become most prominent (this may be related to a time of day, specific thoughts or types of incident) and agree a crisis plan to deal with these events which initially places the control in the hands of the individual, but ultimately involves a plan for contacting services.

- Consider removing access to means of suicide or making it more difficult. It is important that this is balanced with not taking control, and wherever possible, the impetus for this should come from the individual themselves.

- Consider an anti-suicide contract with the person.

It is important that clinicians do not neglect the risk assessment because there is absence of explicit suicidal threat. Clinicians are less likely to be found liable if the worst happens where they asked about their patients'

Good practice guidelines

- Always ask about suicidal risk and clearly document the response.

- Risk assessment should be multi-disciplinary wherever possible.

- Consultation should be sought and documented.

- In the eyes of the court, if it is not written down, it did not happen.

thoughts, intent and plans in respect of suicide, received an affirmative response and then implemented a plan, than if they had never asked about risk at all.

Clinicians will be protected by the law when they establish a coherent treatment plan and have undertaken a thorough risk assessment. This is because they are demonstrating their professional judgement in assessing and balancing the therapeutic risks of working with the suicidal person in the community setting.

Contracting

There is no evidence to suggest that anti-suicide contracts are effective in reducing suicide but they are an important demonstration of a users' commitment to treatment, from both legal and therapeutic perspectives. Traditionally contracts have focused on what the patient *will not do*, i.e. attempt suicide, self-harm, etc., but such *negative* contracts are not necessarily useful in empowering an individual to be an active part in their suicide prevention plan. It is preferable to have *positive* statements of what the patient *will do*. This does not need be a separate document but can form part of the care plan. Examples of positive anti-suicide contract statements include:

- 'I agree that I will work with (clinician or team) to accept and take an active part in my treatment plan.'

- 'I agree that should I make any plans to harm myself that I will contact the mental health team (or the clinician or general practitioner or community mental health nurse, etc.) to discuss how I feel.'

- 'I agree that I will delay any decision to die by suicide until I have engaged in a treatment plan that looks at other options.'

All of the above are just suggestions. It is important that these are not a series of statements given to the patient to agree to but are collaboratively arrived at. Note that the common theme is that these are all positive statements of what the patient *will do* and not negative statements of what they *will not do*. Our aim is to empower, not to take control.

Communication and effective care co-ordination

It seems that every Inquiry into a serious untoward incident in mental health care reads the same. Blame is often attributed to poor communication and people falling through 'the net of care'. It is for this reason that the

Care Programme Approach and Effective Care Co-ordination in mental health services has been developed, which should now be firmly embedded within practice (DoH 1999b). Community management of suicidality depends heavily on good communication. Poor communication can sometimes happen because we are protecting an individual's confidentiality or because we hold uni-disciplinary notes such as nursing and medical notes separately.

It is essential in community management of this client group that we know:

1.   Who are the significant people in the person's life?

2.   How they impact on their suicidal beliefs either positively or negatively.

3.   What significant others are prepared to do to support the team.

4.   What are they not prepared to do? (They may feel responsible for the person being at home and not feel that this is safe; this needs to be explored openly.)

It is important that all care-givers are unified in the approach taken, or at the very least that differences in opinion are heard. This can either be achieved through regular multi-disciplinary reviews or taking the time to contact those involved, or potentially involved, to elicit views and share information. General practitioners have little time, often seeing 20 patients in one morning surgery, and can rarely can attend meetings, so rely on the information gleaned by other professionals. If out of hours or crisis services are involved in the care plan then it is imperative that GPs are made aware of the actual care plan so that continuity of approach can be ensured. Recording of information and its subsequent dissemination are often seen as chores that impact upon clinical time. In an age where we live with multimedia communications, where almost everybody carries at least one form of communication device with them at any time (portable internets, mobile telephones, pagers) there is no excuse.

Factors in community treatment for known clients

Community teams, in order to treat effectively clients like John or Susan, need to have the following:

- good communication systems with the wider community services including statutory, voluntary sector and primary care

- crisis plans that involve the service user, carer, relatives and care co-ordinator, and make it clear what is expected of each in a 'crisis'
- a system of supervision in place; both regularly planned and as required
- the ability to provide urgent assessment and treatment in the least restrictive environment
- accessibility 24/7 or have links to teams that are
- the ability to provide intensive home support until the crisis is resolved (in John's case this could involve visits twice daily or even more frequently)
- the ability to provide support to relatives or carers, including children
- the ability to monitor risk and alter care packages daily, referring on to others as needed.

Support following a suicide

Suicide can be viewed as an outcome (albeit unwanted) of specialist mental health services and we need to develop effective supporting strategies for all of the individuals involved (see Chapter 18). When a suicide occurs protocols should be in place providing timely support to relatives, carers and the staff team.

Great sensitivity should be given to supporting relatives. It is good practice to hold leaflets with relevant information for the family, such as where to get the death certificate, or where to receive counselling and support. CMHTs should become expert in delivering support to all individuals affected by suicide, including relatives and staff.

Summary

We have seen that there is little evidence for clinically effective interventions for working with suicidal patients in the community, although some limited evidence suggests that community management is possible and may even be preferable to in-patient care. What we do have, however, is good practice guidelines for working with patients who are known to mental health care. Good suicide prevention with known patients in the community is an extension of good mental health practice:

- Suicidal thoughts and life threatening behaviour should be assessed with every patient.

- Clinical notes should record these thoughts and behaviours.

- A brief, but formal, consultation should be undertaken every time a decision has to be made.

- Consultation and supervision should be documented.

- All parties should be connected up including families and carers (both formal and informal).

- Emergency/crisis provision should be in place and all concerned know how to contact relevant services (e.g. crisis cards, emergency numbers, etc).

- Most importantly, practitioners should empower the person to ensure their own suicide prevention by building self-worth, inspiring hope and decreasing helplessness by giving back the reins of control and by teaching stress reducing ways of managing emotions.

We stated earlier that it is often difficult to know when we have successfully prevented a suicide, however, where practitioners have operated in accordance with these good practice guidelines, they probably have done so despite the lack of hard evidence.

References

Beck, A.T., Rush, A.J., Shaw, B.F. and Emery, G. (1979) *Cognitive Therapy of Depression.* New York: Guildford Press.

Buglass, D. and Horton, J. (1974) 'A scale for predicting subsequent suicidal behaviour.' *British Journal of Psychiatry 124,* 573–578.

Department of Health (1999a) *Safer Services: National Confidential Inquiry into Suicide and Homicide by People with a Mental Illness.* London: HMSO.

Department of Health (1999b) *Effective Care Co-ordination in Mental Health Services: Modernising the Care Programme Approach.* London: HMSO.

Department of Health (2001) *Mental Health Policy Implementation Guide.* London: HMSO.

Department of Health (2002) *National Suicide Prevention Strategy for England.* London: HMSO.

Duffy, D. (2003) 'Exploring suicide risk and the therapeutic relationship: A case study approach.' *Nursing Times Research 8,* 3, 185–199.

Gutheil, T.G. (1990) 'Argument for the defendent-expert opinion: Death in hindsight.' In R.I. Simon (ed) *Review of Clinical Psychiatry and the Law.* Washington DC: American Psychiatric Association.

Hawton, K. and Fagg, J. (1988) 'Suicide, and other causes of death, following attempted suicide.' *British Journal of Psychiatry 152,* 359–366.

Hawton, K., Fagg, J. and Simkin, S. (1997) 'Trends in deliberate self-harm in Oxford, 1985–1995. Implications for clinical services and the prevention of suicide.' *British Journal of Psychiatry 171*, 556–560.

Holmes, W. and Walmsley, P. (2003) *GP On Call Clinic Review*. Unpublished internal report for CARDS Team. May 2003 (available from Peter Walmsley, see Contributor details).

Joiner, T.E., Rudd, M.D. and Rajab, M.H. (1998) 'Agreement between self and clinician rated suicidal symptoms in a clinical sample of young adults.' *Journal of Consulting and Clinical Psychology 5*, 396–399.

Lerner, M. and Clum, G. (1990) 'Treatment of suicidal ideators: A problem solving approach.' *Behaviour Therapy 21*, 403– 411.

Libermann, R. and Eckman, T. (1981) 'Behaviour Therapy versus insight oriented therapy for repeated suicide attempters.' *Archives of General Psychiatry 38*, 1126–1130.

Lindow, L. and McGeorge, M. (2001) *National Taskforce on Violence against Social Care Staff: Research Review on Violence against Staff in Mental Health In-patient and Community Settings.* London: HMSO.

Linehan, M., Armstrong, H., Suarez, A., Allmon, D. and Heard, H. (1991) 'Cognitive Behavioural treatment of chronically parasuicidal borderline patients.' *Archives of General Psychiatry 48*, 1060–1064.

Litman, R. and Wold, C. (1976) 'Beyond crisis intervention.' In E. Schneidmann (ed) *Suicidology: Contemporary Developments.* New York: Grune and Stratton.

McLeavey, B.C., Daly, R.J., Ludgate, J.W. and Murray, C.M. (1994) 'Interpersonal problem solving skills training in the treatment of self-poisoning patients.' *Suicide and Life Threatening Behaviour 24*, 382–394.

Morgan, H., Jones, E. and Owen, J. (1993) 'Secondary prevention of non-fatal deliberate self-harm: The green card study.' *British Journal of Psychiatry 163*, 111–112.

Motto, J. (1976) 'Suicide prevention for high-risk persons who refuse treatment.' *Suicide and Life Threatening Behaviour 6*, 4, 223–230.

Patsiokis, A. and Clum, G. (1985) Effects of psychotherapeutic strategies in the treatment of suicide attempters. *Psychotherapy 22*, 2, 281–290.

Rudd, D. and Joiner, T. (2001) *Treating Suicidal Behaviour: An Effective Time Limited Approach.* New York: Guildford.

Salkovskis, P., Atha, C. and Storer, D. (1990) 'Cognitive-behavioural problem solving in the treatment of patients who repeatedly attempt suicide: A controlled trial.' *British Journal of Psychiatry 157*, 871–876.

Termansen, P. and Bywater, C. (1975) 'S.A.F.E.R.: A follow-up service for attempted suicide in Vancouver.' *Canadian Psychiatric Association Journal 20*, 29–34.

VandeCreek, L. and Knapp, S. (1983) 'Malpractice risks with suicidal patients.' *Psychotherapy: Theory, Research and Practice 20*, 3, 274–280.

Van Heeringen, K., Jannes, S. and Buylaert, W. (1995) 'The management of non-compliance with referral to out-patient care among attempted suicide patients: A controlled intervention study.' *Psychological Medicine 25*, 963–970.

Waterhouse, J. and Platt, S. (1990) 'General hospital admission in the management of parasuicide: A randomised control trial.' *British Journal of Psychiatry 156*, 236–242.

Recommended reading

Kleespies, P. (ed) (1998) *Emergencies in Mental Health Practice.* New York: Guildford.

Linehan, M. (1993) *Cognitive-behavioural Treatment of Borderline Personality Disorder.* New York: Guildford.

Rudd, D. and Joiner, T. (2001) *Treating Suicidal Behaviour: An Effective Time Limited Approach.* New York: Guildford.

Williams, J. and Wells, J. (1989) 'Suicidal patients.' In J. Scott, J. Williams and A. Beck (eds) *Cognitive Therapy in Clinical Practice.* London: Routledge.

Chapter 7

Young Men

Mike Smith

Without the possibility of suicide I would have killed myself a long time ago!

Cioran (1996)

Seventy-five per cent of all completed suicides are men (Office for National Statistics (ONS) 1996). Indeed risk indicator number one, and one often overlooked for suicide, is clearly gender (ONS 1996). Within male suicides, however, the picture has changed from one where the over 75s are the high-risk group to one where the under 25s have considerably overtaken them in the suicide stakes (World Health Organization (WHO) 2002). Suicide is the biggest killer of young men in the UK. One in four of all UK suicides are young men under 25 years of age (ONS 1996; Registrar General for Scotland 1996). Young men, however, are not often considered to be at such a high level of risk by their families, the media and mental health professionals. This chapter will aim to consider the reasons why young men kill themselves at such an alarming rate and also what we can do about it.

The nature of the problem

Suicide is recognised as a major source of mortality in Western European countries and accounts for more premature deaths than homicide, war and civil unrest worldwide (WHO 2002). Suicide, for young men, is consistently in the top three causes of death throughout the region (WHO 2002). Although one may regard these figures in themselves to be shocking, it is the growth in suicide rates among young men that most alarms policy makers. This growth should also alarm the general public. However, very few people are aware of the figures and, apart from notable exceptions, little media interest has been shown in publicising the nature of the problem to general society.

The fact that I separate the two groups – policy makers and the public – highlights a major problem that young men face. The problem is that, if suicide does not directly affect us, or our family, then we do not recognise it as our problem. The great British fiction writer Douglas Adams described this phenomenon as the SEP ('somebody else's problem') phenomenon and it is evident in young men's suicide.

Suicide rates vary from publication to publication, whether research or policy documents, consequently for the purpose of this chapter I will focus upon the World Health Organization published figures for the UK and Ireland region (WHO 1997). These figures are more widely accepted as a reliable source of information than those figures produced by smaller and perhaps more politically influenced projects. WHO figures are also comparable regionally and internationally. Young men are defined as those who are aged under 25 when they die by suicide.

Suicide statistics in the UK and Ireland

In 1997 there were 5993 suicides in the UK, and 433 suicides in the Republic of Ireland (Central Statistics Office 1997). This amounts to one suicide every 82 minutes in the UK and Ireland. Seventy-five per cent of these suicides are by males. This figure is consistent across the years 1990–1997, and 869 of these suicides were by young people – more than 2 per day. Suicide accounts for 18 per cent of all deaths of young people (WHO 1997), which places it in the top three killers of young people overall. It is important to acknowledge at this point that this percentage only reflect deaths that are actually recorded as being by suicide and some speculate that the figure may be much higher as many suicides may be recorded as open verdicts (Charlton *et al.* 1992). Actual suicide rates vary in estimation from 4 to 10 times greater than the recorded suicide rates. Unfortunately it is unlikely that we will ever know the true rate of suicides among young men.

Perhaps more alarming than the increasing growth rate of suicide among young men is the growth of suicide and attempted suicide by young people (ONS 2003a). There are at least two suicides every day by young people under the age of 25 in the United Kingdom and Ireland. The rate of suicide among young men (15–24 years) in the UK and Ireland has increased dramatically since the 1970s. National statistics showed a downturn from 1993, but the rate rose once again in 1997 to 17 per 100,000, compared with a general suicide rate of 13 per 100,000 (ONS 1996, 2002).

The significant upward trend in young male suicide is even more pronounced in the Republic of Ireland, which has seen a 200 per cent increase between 1987 and 1997 (Central Statistics Office 1997).

Suicide attempts

Attempted suicide among young men and young women has also been increasing during the 1990s. It is estimated that there are approximately 19,000 suicide attempts by adolescents every year in the UK (Hawton and Van Heeringen 2002), which is more than one every 30 minutes. Young women aged between 15 and 19 years are still the most likely to attempt (as opposed to complete) suicide, usually by overdose (ONS 2002). However, the rate among young men has nearly tripled since 1985 (Brook and Griffiths 2003; ONS 2003b), but presentations at hospital for self-harm may be wrongly recorded as a suicide attempt.

The difference between suicide and self-harm

Professionals, including many mental health professionals, often confuse self-harm with suicide attempts and some use the terms interchangeably and wrongly (Favazza and Rosenthal 1993). Self-harm, as a diagnostic feature, is without the direct intent to end life (American Psychiatric Association 1994), whereas in definitions of suicide there needs to be a deliberate and direct intent to end life.

People who self-harm are statistically more likely to go on to kill themselves by suicide (Appleby *et al.* 1999; Royal College of Psychiatrists (RCP) 2003), but they are more at risk from accidental death following an episode of self-harm. A number of narratives (Lefevre 1996; Spandler 2001) have suggested that people who self-harm who go on to become suicidal attempt suicide by a different method, i.e. someone who cuts their wrists to self-harm may attempt suicide by hanging, so change of method may be an indicator that the person who self-harms is becoming suicidal.

In order to help young men appropriately mental health services need to assist them to be clear about the intent of their actions: is it an attempt at suicide or is it self-harm? The reasons people confuse the two are complex and historical, but we must recognise that the two are often confused by services and policy makers. It is not then surprising that our clients are baffled by the language used to describe their experiences. To differentiate between the two concepts, one has to explore them in depth with the suicidal young man. Many mental health professionals are ill prepared and lack confidence in exploring these concepts, fearing that they will make the person do something drastic. There is no evidence whatsoever that talking to a suicidal person, or indeed a self-harming person, makes them act upon their desires; however, it will aid them to come to some decisions about their future.

Although self-injury and self-harm are taxonomically without conscious or direct intent to die, there are statistical links between self-harm and suicide. For instance, people who self-injure have been identified as being at higher risk of eventual death by suicide (RCP 2003). The RCP found in a long-term study between 1978 and 1997 of people presenting at hospital for self-injury, that 2.6 per cent had died by the end of the study. This was far higher among men (4.8%) than women (1.8%).

Good practice guidelines

- Self-injury is classified as having no direct suicidal intent (APA 1994).

- Many clients are unclear of their own motivations.

- Practitioners should attempt to help clients to separate their suicide and self-harm motivations.

- 'Do you do this to feel better or to end all your feelings?' can be a helpful starting point.

- Some people who are self-harming may become suicidal as well.

Why do young men commit suicide?

Several thousand articles and books have been written about the cause and prevention of suicide. For the purpose of understanding, and not research, there are essentially five reasons, listed below, why people generally attempt suicide. There is no evidence that young men are any different, but one must ask whether these motivations are more prevalent among young men than the general population and if so, why? Understanding these reasons can help to assess the risk of suicide and understand how to help.

- *Change*: Suicide is a way to change how the person feels or what is happening in their life or at a given moment.

- *Choice*: Suicide is a way to assert or make a choice during circumstances in which there are no choices or when important choices are being taken away. It is often a final way to assert the only choice the person feels they have open to them.

- *Control*: The suicidal act is an attempt to stop the person's behaviour, to control events or to effect some change in others.

- *Self-punishment*: Suicidal behaviour can be a means to relieve guilt or punish the person for their actions.

- *Punish others*: The suicidal act is intended to inflict harm or punishment on others.

Factors linked to suicide and attempted suicide in young men
Alcohol and drug abuse

Substance abuse is thought to be a highly significant factor in young men's suicide (WHO 1999). Alcohol and drugs affect thinking and reasoning ability and can act as depressants. They decrease inhibitions, increasing the likelihood of a depressed young person making a suicide attempt. American research has shown that one in three adolescents who attempt suicide is intoxicated at the time of an attempt (Brent, Perper and Allman 1987).

Families

In general, adolescent suicide attempters appear to grow up in families with more turmoil than other groups of adolescents, coming more often from broken homes (due to death or divorce), homes where there is parental unemployment, mental illness, or addiction (Harrington and Dyer 1993).

Physical and sexual abuse

Young people who suffer, or have suffered abuse in the past, are often at increased risk of suicide or deliberate self-harm (Browne and Finklehor 1986; Shapiro 1987).

Custody

Within the prison population as a whole, young prisoners represent the largest group of at-risk individuals, particularly those under 21s who make up a substantial proportion of the remand population (Home Office 2003). In 1998, 21 per cent of prison suicides were by people under 21 (Home Office 1999).

The policy framework

There are a number of coordinated strands in public policy aimed at reducing suicide among high-risk populations that include young men.

National Service Framework for Mental Health

The National Service Framework for Mental Health (NSF) was launched in 1999 (Department of Health (DoH) 1999a). This document outlines the action necessary in order to meet the target in *Saving Lives: Our Healthier Nation* (DoH 1999b) of reducing the suicide rate by at least one fifth by 2010. The standard in the NSF that refers to preventing suicide, rather than younger people's suicides, is standard seven.

The NSF outlines the actions to be taken in order to meet standard seven, 'Preventing suicide' (DoH 1999a, p.76). It states that local health and social care communities should prevent suicides by:

- promoting mental health for all, working with individuals and communities
- delivering high quality primary mental health care
- ensuring that anyone with a mental health problem can contact local services via the primary care team, a help-line or an A&E department
- ensuring that individuals with severe and enduring mental illness have a care plan which meets their specific needs, including access to services round the clock
- providing safe hospital accommodation for individuals who need it
- enabling individuals caring for someone with severe mental illness to receive the support which they need to continue to care.

And in addition:

- supporting local prison staff in preventing suicides among prisoners
- ensuring that staff are competent to assess the risk of suicide among individuals at greatest risk
- developing local systems for suicide audit to learn lessons and take any necessary action (see Chapter 14).

National Suicide Prevention Strategy

In 2002 the first National Suicide Prevention Strategy for England (DoH 2002), was launched following a detailed consultation with a variety of stakeholders. England became one of the few countries worldwide to develop a strategy to prevent suicide.

It sets out a programme of activity to reduce suicide based on six goals. Key measures for young men in the suicide prevention strategy include reducing the suicide risk of men under 35 who are most likely to take their own lives, for example by improving the treatment of alcohol and drug misuse among young men who self-harm. Young men are of course identified as one of the high-risk groups.

Child and Adolescent Mental Health Services (CAMHS)

Between 1999 and 2003 the UK government invested £250 million in the development of CAMHS (Hansard 2003). This money is targeted to assist health and local authorities meet new joint objectives to improve child and adolescent mental health services. The funding also continued support for a range of innovative projects, to encourage local authority investment in services for young people with mental health problems.

Initiatives to reduce suicide among young men

Many local initiatives are supported through direct commissioning and through joint finance arrangements. Most provision targeted at younger people, however, is being delivered outside conventional mental health services and has much closer links to health promotion approaches. There are examples of this work discussed elsewhere in this book, for example see Chapters 20 and 21.

Many traditional approaches to suicide prevention, especially among young men, treat it as an impulsive act, one not thoroughly thought through. Although this may account for some suicides among young men it does not explain them all. In order to prevent young men from dying by suicide at today's extraordinary rates we must show a deeper understanding of why young men choose to die, and also why they choose to stay alive, in order that we can build upon those positive steps people do take to stay alive.

Helping the suicidal young person

Many suicides of young men are felt to be characterised by an impulsive personality (Garrison *et al.* 1993; Platt 2000), often coupled with substance use that increases this pre-morbid impulsivity. However numerous suicides do not fit this category and many appear to be well thought through. The case examples given below reflect both impulsive and planned suicides.

Case study 7.1

Peter is a 19-year-old man who has been receiving treatment for amphetamine abuse for two years and for addiction to crack cocaine for three months.

Peter was permanently excluded from a school at the age of 15 for setting fire to a storeroom and subsequently refused to go to school for the last six months of his school life. He was noticed by his parents to be smoking cannabis at all times of the day while at home and also suspected to be inhaling solvents.

Since this time Peter has had increasing contact with Youth Offending Teams for theft, shoplifting and vehicle theft. He is currently on bail for a number of criminal offences. Six months ago his parents threw him out of the family home for stealing from his sister and for being aggressive towards them; he has had no contact with them since this time.

In the last six months Peter has been living on friends' floors and occasionally living rough, he is still using crack cocaine daily and is shoplifting to pay for it. He has been referred to a mental health team because his probation officer believes he may be depressed. He disclosed to him that he had been sexually abused at the age of 13 by another older boy at school and now feels very depressed that this abuse has led him into his current lifestyle. Peter feels he has no one to rely upon, all his friends are trying to break their ties with him, his girlfriend finished with him last week because he was 'using too many drugs' and he presented at A&E last night having reported that he overdosed on seven paracetamol tablets.

Peter has been told to wait for an appointment to see a mental health worker who will help him with his depression; meanwhile the duty psychiatrist he saw the previous night has commenced him on antidepressant medication. Peter says that the only source of help and sympathetic listening is the church that is currently offering him accommodation but he feels bad about taking the paracetamol because he has let down the minister who has been 'so good to him'. Peter expresses regret that he is only now 'finding God'.

Questions for consideration

1. Consider what appear to be critical indicators that Peter may be about to attempt to die by suicide.

2. What may have prevented him from attempting to die by suicide so far?

3. What has changed recently that suggests Peter may be at increased risk of suicide?

4. What can you do to minimise the risks you have identified and/or to maximise the protection available to prevent Peter from suicide?

Risk factors

Specific risk factors as they relate to different groups can often be difficult for practitioners to remember, but there are many key indicators that Peter displays or reports. What you must try to remember is that the hierarchy and importance of risk factors is often debated but there is a consensus that generally the more the person has, and the more important they are in the life of the person, the greater the overall risk for the person of suicide.

Peter is at risk of a number of things: self-harm, suicide, neglect, further offending and accidental death.

Peter is in the high-risk age group, is the appropriate gender, living alone with little social support, homeless, has a recent history of suspected suicide attempts that appears to be escalating, is using substances that increase impulsivity, and has an apparent impulsive history with a picture of increasing drug use.

Peter has not been offered any immediate help or hope when he is seeking it, through his disclosures he may be contemplating suicide. Peter's girlfriend has ended their relationship and his drug use may be less controlled. He is alone and feeling increasingly hopeless. He may also be feeling a sense of burden to his friends and the people offering him help.

Protective factors

Peter feels responsible for the feelings of the minister helping him. This is, however, a fragile and inconsistent protection that you may not want to rely strongly upon. Similarly, Peter says he is becoming religious but this also must be checked out, as again this is only a recent rather than an apparently consistent theme in Peter's life. Peter reports having some friends that he has been staying with.

Outcome

Peter returned to the A&E department again the next night having taken 10 paracetamol and with superficial marks to his neck from a piece of electric flex. He said he had used the flex to hang himself from a branch, the branch was not thick enough and he fell down a railway embankment and narrowly missed getting hit by a train that had terrified him.

Peter was felt to be clinically depressed by the A&E mental health liaison staff and an immediate risk of further suicide attempts. He had no obvious psychiatric history and would not agree to any in-patient psychiatric care that was being considered. Because the area he lived in had a system of 'sponsor homes' (a service where actively suicidal people who cannot stay at home alone are placed with a volunteer family for a short period of time as an alternative to acute hospital admission), he was immediately matched to a sponsor home provider who had developed supportive relationships with similar young men in the past. He stayed in the sponsor home for 11 days, in which time he continued his antidepressants, began seeing a mental health worker for counselling and resolved to do something about his drug habit, which he recognised was both depressing him and making him impulsive. The mental health worker helped him to get an emergency assessment by the local drugs team.

Good practice guidelines

- Peter was helped promptly and was allocated to a worker quickly.

- Immediate practical help was given with his drug use and social circumstance.

- Peter was listened to and his objections to in-patient care were considered, respected and followed.

- Protection was maintained in the form of someone to stay with him.

- A number of local resources to help suicidal people were available and utilised.

Case study 7.2

Li is a 23-year-old PhD chemistry student at the local university. He is living in student flats and has a few fellow student friends who, like him, are also of Hong Kong Chinese origin. He is referred to your team for urgent assessment by the campus GP who believes that he is clinically depressed and requires specialist assessment and treatment.

Li completed his two previous degrees in New York (USA) and Liege (Belgium). His girlfriend is a Belgian national and has recently returned home leaving him alone. He feels that she intends to end their relationship. Li has a history of two previous episodes of depression and has attempted suicide once in Belgium 18 months ago, following an argument with his girlfriend when he then drank a caustic substance he obtained from college. He says that he had been depressed for some time, but on that occasion had not been thinking about suicide. However, he says he 'just decided to end it all'.

Li regrets his prior attempt and the long lasting physical damage it caused (he has breathing difficulty, scarring to his lips/face and tracheotomy marks where he was ventilated in intensive care) and reports that he feels stupid for doing this, however he still feels very depressed. Li feels he is a failure. His older brother is a professor of chemistry in New York and his older sister runs her own computer hardware research company in California and he feels he will not be able to complete his PhD as the work is too hard for him.

When you see Li he is in tears saying that he is ashamed of his suicide attempts and is desperate to stop his family from finding out about them. He says he cannot see any future for himself as he believes he is a failure at college, a failed lover and a poor son; he believes that he is a failure at everything including suicide. Li admits to contemplating suicide but does not think he is able to do it. He is stockpiling the chemical means for suicide but he says this just gives him reassurance, saying that he has no immediate plans and has not made any attempts to avoid detection. Indeed, he points out that he is actively seeking help.

Li is prepared to accept help but wishes to remain at home because he has been invited to an end of term party tonight.

Questions for consideration

1. What can you do to help Li? Write down an outline plan of support and treatment.

2. How great a risk do you feel that Li is to himself? Make a judgement from the information you have. On a continuum of

suicide say where you think he is. If you have a risk assessment tool use it; it should highlight the presence and number of major risk factors.

3. What measures do you need to take to manage the risk with Li?

Good practice guidelines

- If you rely on others (e.g. Li's friends) let them know you are relying on them.

- Validate what you are told with independent parties.

- Make a judgement from the information about the risk and document this.

- Look for objective information.

- Ensure a risk management plan reflects what you assess as the risks.

- Aim to minimise risk and maximise protection.

- It is not just a matter of suicidal thoughts being present that is a risk, rather it is the pervasiveness and incidence of them in Li's life.

- Seriousness of previous attempts is an important predictor of further attempts.

EXERCISE 7.1

Using Li or Peter as an example, write a risk management plan using the following process.

- Carry out a risk assessment.

- Identify individual, situational and systemic risks and protection for the person.

- Develop a management plan for all risks that minimises the risks where possible or maximises protection for the person.

- Consider how you will communicate the plan.

- Identify for yourself, where necessary, responsibilities and accountabilities to each team or worker involved.
- Consider how and when you will review this plan.
- How will you involve Peter or Li in the risk assessment and plan to manage this?
- Consider how you record your work and what actions you take to immediately reduce the risk to your client.
- Consider what advice you should leave with Peter or Li's carers/friends.

Ask yourself the following questions:

- How do you currently manage the risk of suicide with young men?
- Are you confident of your skills in this area?
- How will you improve your skills?
- Do you have the knowledge that you need to help young men?
- Are you aware of the human factors that complicate and bias risk assessments?

Crisis advice to leave with the suicidal young man and his family and friends

1. Suicidal thoughts, feelings and behaviour should not be ignored or minimised.

2. Contact a crisis intervention professional or qualified health care professional if you, or someone you know, may be suicidal or if there is a sudden change in the mental state of a suicidal person. If you are in any doubt contact them anyway for reassurance.

3. Recognising the signs of suicide risk will help you know when to seek help.

4. Many people think about suicide when they are desperate, however, if you do more than think about it fleetingly then you should consider seeking help.

5. Making plans and preparations for suicide is a reliable sign that you should seek help from others.

6. Find somewhere or someone with whom you feel safe, while you seek help.

7. If you are feeling suicidal, or know someone who may be suicidal, the best choice is to seek competent help; it is very difficult to deal with your feelings alone when you are desperate.

8. Asking a friend or family member if they are suicidal, and doing so in a caring and confidential manner, does not cause or encourage people to become suicidal.

9. It is not a sign of weakness or madness to seek help for desperate feelings.

10. Reducing stress in your life and resolving any conflicts in a positive manner is helpful.

11. Communicating support, hope and confidence will help if you are supporting a suicidal person.

12. Dealing with practical problems, immediately where you can, helps the suicidal person choose to live.

13. Evaluation and treatment for known or suspected drug and alcohol misuse is a critical part of prevention and treatment of suicide for young men; people are much more likely to attempt suicide if intoxicated.

14. When the risk of suicide becomes imminent, it is appropriate to get immediate professional assistance, if in doubt call and ask.

References

American Psychiatric Association (1994) *Diagnostic and Statistical Manual of Mental Disorders*, 4th edn. Washington, DC: APA.

Appleby, L., Shaw, J., Amos, T., McDonnell, R., Bickley, H., Kiernan, K., Davies, S., Harris, C., McCann, K. and Parsons, R. (1999) *Safer Services: Report of the National Confidential Inquiry into Suicide and Homicide by People with Mental Illness.* London: Stationery Office.

Brent, D., Perper, J. and Allman, C. (1987) 'Alcohol, firearms, and suicide among youth: temporal trends in Allegheny County, Pennsylvania, 1960 to 1983.' *Journal of the American Medical Association 257*, 24, 3369–3372.

Brook, A. and Griffiths, C. (2003) 'Trends in the mortality of young adults aged 15–44 in England and Wales 1961–2001.' *Health Statistics Quarterly 19*, 22–31.

Browne, A. and Finklehor, D. (1986) 'Impact of child sexual abuse: A review of the research.' *Psychology Bulletin 99*, 1.

Central Statistics Office (1997) *National Statistics.* Cork: CSO.

Charlton, J., Kelly, S., Dunnell, K., Evans, B., Jenkins, R. and Wallis, R. (1992) 'Trends in suicide deaths in England and Wales.' *Population Trends 69*, 10–16.

Cioran, E.M. (1996) *On the Heights of Despair.* Chicago: University of Chicago Press.

Department of Health (1999a) *National Service Framework for Mental Health.* London: DoH.

Department of Health (1999b) *Saving Lives: Our Healthier Nation.* London: DoH.

Department of Health (2002) *The National Suicide Prevention Strategy for England.* London: The Stationery Office.

Favazza, A. and Rosenthal, R. (1993) 'Diagnostic issues in self mutilation.' *Hospital and Community Psychiatry 44*, 2, 134–140.

Garrison C., McKeown, R., Valois, R. and Vincent, M. (1993) 'Aggression, substance use, and suicidal behaviors in high school students.' *American Journal of Public Health 83*, 2, 179–183.

Hansard (2003) *Written answers for 15th July 2003, The UK Parliament.* London: Hansard.

Harrington, R.C. and Dyer, E. (1993) 'Suicide and attempted suicide in adolescents'. *Current Opinion in Psychiatry 6*, 467–469.

Hawton, K. and Van Heeringen, K. (eds) (2002) *The International Handbook of Suicide and Attempted Suicide.* London: John Wiley & Sons.

Home Office (1999) *Prison Statistics England and Wales 1998.* London: Office for National Statistics.

Home Office (2003) *Prison Statistics England and Wales 2002.* London: Office for National Statistics.

Lefevre, S. (1996) *Killing Me Softly, Self-Harm – Survival Not Suicide.* Gloucester: Handsell.

Office for National Statistics (1996) *Mortality Statistics.* London: ONS.

Office for National Statistics (2002) *Mortality Statistics.* London: ONS.

Office for National Statistics (2003a) *Death Rates from Suicide Among Men: By Age.* London: ONS.

Office for National Statistics (2003b) *Death Rates from Suicide by Gender and Age 1971–1998.* London: ONS.

Platt, S. (2000) *The Sorrows of Young Men: Exploring Their Increasing Risk of Suicide.* Edinburgh: Edinburgh University, Centre for Theology and Public Issues.

Royal College of Psychiatrists (2003) *Significant Risk Of Suicide After Deliberate Self-Harm Persists Long Term.* Press release 1 June. London: Royal College of Psychiatrists.

Registrar General for Scotland (1996) *Annual Report.* Edinburgh: Registrar General for Scotland.

Shapiro, S. (1987) 'Self mutilation and blame in incest victims.' *American Journal of Psychotherapy 41*, 1, 46–54.

Spandler, H. (2001) *Who's Hurting Who? Young People, Self-Harm and Suicide.* Gloucester: Handsell.

World Health Organisation (1997) *International Suicide Statistics.* Geneva: WHO.

World Health Organization (1999) *Figures and Facts About Suicide.* Geneva: WHO.

World Health Organization (2002) *The World Report on Violence and Health.* Geneva: WHO.

Chapter 8

Prisons

Jo Paton and Jo Borrill

Introduction

Prisoners are recognised as a high-risk group in the Department of Health's Suicide Prevention Strategy. In this chapter we explore how knowledge of prisons and prisoners can help practitioners adapt their suicide prevention practice to the prison setting. When quoting figures we refer to *self-inflicted deaths* (all deaths which result from the individual's own actions) to prevent confusion with the narrower *suicide* verdict in the Coroner's Court, which requires clear evidence of suicidal intent.

In the calendar year 2002 there were 94 self-inflicted deaths in custody, corresponding to an annual rate of 133 per 100,000 prisoners. This is higher than the suicide rate for the general population, but similar to (or even lower than) suicide rates for offenders under community supervision (Sattar 2001). Ninety-four per cent of prisoners who kill themselves are male, but this reflects the higher male prison population. Women in prison kill themselves at approximately the same rate as do men, in contrast with the community where the rate is significantly higher for men than women.

Suicide prevention in prison needs to address two challenges:

- The prison environment and the experience of custody bring their own risk factors.

- Prisoners are known to be a vulnerable population, at increased risk of suicide before they even enter the prison gates.

The following sections will address each challenge in turn, looking first at the risks and then at actions to be taken.

The prison environment and the experience of custody

Rates of self-inflicted death vary according to the type of prison and its characteristics. Self-inflicted deaths are most common in 'local' prisons, which have a very high turnover and are disproportionately affected by the rising prison population (local prisons take prisoners direct from the courts). It is also worth noting that the majority of self-inflicted deaths occur among prisoners who are on normal wing locations rather than on health care and occur in single cells.

Equally important is the regime and general quality of life in a particular prison, for example the amount of time prisoners are locked up, and the availability of work, education or other activities. Prisons with lower rates of purposeful activity for prisoners appear to have higher rates of self-inflicted deaths, irrespective of type of prison.

Third, there are times or stages of custody which pose particular risks. These include the first hours, days and month of custody, periods following significant court appearances or changes in status and the period following release.

Prevention in the early days of custody

Just under half of all self-inflicted deaths occur within a month of the prisoner arriving at that establishment, with a third occurring in the first seven days. The majority of prisoners who fall into that category are those who are on remand or awaiting sentence who are held in 'local' prisons. Remand and unsentenced prisoners are consistently more likely to kill themselves than sentenced prisoners who usually move on, post sentence, to 'training' or 'open' prisons.

Prisoners who harmed themselves early in custody explained why:

'It was my first night in prison, I'd lost everything – my home, my job, my family.'

'I felt upset and depressed at being in prison again... It was as if I'd never left.'

'I was withdrawing. I felt depressed, angry, confused, tired. I wanted to sleep at any cost.'

'The first night was the worst... It kicks you in the head when you first come in.'

The area where prisoners first arrive in the jail is known as reception. In a busy local prison, reception is an exceptionally pressured environment, with large numbers of prisoners arriving from court at one time, often late in the evening. As a nurse, you may be involved in administering the health care screen, which includes a screen of suicide risk, on reception. Following reception, prisoners are located for the night, usually on an ordinary wing, sometimes if they are acutely ill in the health care centre. In the period immediately following reception, prisons run an induction programme. More thorough assessments of health, educational and other needs take place at this time.

The Prison Service is currently encouraging local prisons to develop dedicated 'first night centres', where specially selected officers work with extended shift times, and 'dedicated detoxification units'. Progress is hampered by the recent rapid increases in prison population.

Actions you can take to reduce the risk of suicide in the early days

- Familiarise yourself with the routine and the resources available for prisoners. Prisoners should be allowed a telephone call home and ideally should receive a first night pack containing a phone card, food, tobacco and reading material.

- Reassure prisoners and direct them to sources of support in the prison, such as an 'Insiders' scheme. ('Insiders' are prisoners who work in reception or induction wings, giving new prisoners information packs, answering queries about prison life, and providing a friendly face. Insiders may refer on to staff any concerns they have about a prisoner, including indications of suicide or self-harm risk.)

- Make sure that prisoners who go straight from reception to the health care centre do not miss out on their induction as a result.

- Maintain and use your listening skills, despite the pressure of time.

Prevention on the wings
'Healthy prisons' have been described as places where:
- the weakest prisoners feel safe
- all prisoners are treated with respect as individuals

- all prisoners are busily occupied, expected to improve themselves and given the opportunity to do so
- all prisoners can strengthen links with their families and prepare for release.

(Her Majesty's Chief Inspector of Prisons 1999)

'Wing-based nursing' is being introduced into prisons and so practitioners are increasingly working on wings, as well as or instead of in separate health care centres.

Actions you can take to improve the quality of life for prisoners

- Build relationships with prison officers and other staff.
- Demonstrate respectful and caring attitudes towards prisoners.
- Challenge inappropriate attitudes if you see them.
- Support and advise staff in how best to manage individual prisoner-patients.
- Advocate improved access to activities, education, work or opportunities for family contact, where necessary.
- If you have concerns about a particular area of the prison, ask the Suicide Prevention Team Leader (a prison governor) to monitor incidents of assault and self-harm in that area. He or she can then ask the unit manager to investigate and take appropriate action. (Every establishment has a Suicide Prevention Team and an anti-bullying strategy and some have designated staff, working as Suicide Prevention Coordinators, or anti-bullying coordinators.)

It is important to listen to officers as well as to try to influence and advise them, especially if you are new to prison work. Officers do not fit any one stereotype, their attitudes towards prisoners vary and you will meet many caring and highly skilled officers.

Prevention prior to release

Surprisingly, more prisoners kill themselves in the year following release than they do in prison (Shaw *et al.* 2003). Twenty-three per cent of those who kill themselves after release do so in the first week and 40 per cent in the first month. (These deaths are *in addition* to the large number who die from accidental drug overdoses soon after release.)

Work to help prisoners return to life 'on the out' is largely led by discipline staff under the banners of 'resettlement' and 'sentence planning' with drug education provided mainly by specialist drug workers.

Actions you can take

- Share information (with prisoner permission) with resettlement and other staff.

- Ensure that patients who are subject to the Care Programme Approach have a place to live and support and treatment when they are released.

Reducing access to means

The majority of prisoners who kill themselves do so through hanging or strangulation, using bedding or clothing, commonly attached to ligature points on windows, doors or furniture in their cells. The prison service has therefore developed 'safer' cells, which have fixed furniture and are free of ligatures points, for example windows without bars. Depending upon resources, all cells in high-risk areas (such as first night, detoxification, health care, segregation) may be of safer design or a small number of safer cells may be available for use by prisoners identified as at higher risk. Most deaths occur in single cells, or when the prisoner is alone in a double cell. It is therefore common to locate a prisoner who is at high risk of suicide in a double cell, so that the other prisoner can provide companionship and also be a restraining presence.

Health practitioners (usually doctors or mental health nurses) may be asked to decide, in consultation with other staff, which prisoners should be placed in safer cells, which personal possessions (such as shoelaces or belts) should be removed from a prisoner and whether a prisoner should remain in a single cell or be 'doubled up'. Decisions such as these are difficult to make and it is important that practitioners do not make them alone.

Actions you can take

- Ensure that placing a prisoner in a 'safer cell' never replaces attempts to talk to them about the problems that led to the suicidal crisis in the first place.

- If personal belongings or clothes are to be removed from a prisoner, explain that this is temporary and for their own safety.

Research shows that having things removed is less upsetting if explained properly.

- If a prisoner is to be put in a double cell, make sure that the cellmate is chosen carefully. If possible consult with the prisoner about this, and avoid placing them with a cellmate who is very young, highly vulnerable or who might encourage them to self-harm.

- Do not rely totally on the presence of the other prisoner to prevent a suicide attempt. Ensure that the prisoner is not left alone when his or her cellmate is absent.

Nurses may also be involved in observing prisoners who are at high risk of suicide and determining the frequency of observations. Those who are most determined to kill themselves are often located on the health care centre and subject to a 'constant watch'. It is important to use observation as an opportunity to talk and listen to the prisoner, not simply to watch.

Where a patient is on constant watch, you should:

- familiarise yourself with the individual's history and overall plan of care

- show that you care about the prisoner. If they are uncommunicative, initiate conversation and convey a willingness to listen

- find out how the prisoner would like to pass the time and facilitate this, for example, music, television, drawing

- explain to the prisoner why they are under observation, how long it will be maintained and what may happen

- seek the prisoner's permission to inform their nearest relative and solicitor about the situation. If the prisoner is on remand, the solicitor needs to know in order to enable speedy representation to be made to the court.

(More detailed guidance for nurses on observing patients at risk can be found in Paton and Jenkins 2002.)

First aid and resuscitation

The prison environment provides an unusual opportunity for preventing suicide attempts from succeeding. Although over 90 per cent of prisoners who kill themselves die by 'hanging', for every prisoner who dies, another attempts suicide but is found, resuscitated and survives. The cause of death in most 'hangings' is asphyxiation from a ligature round the neck attached to a ligature point (such as window bars) that is not high enough to allow death to be instant. Death may take several minutes, allowing time for re-suscitation, oxygenation and heart massage, as required. Speedy, coordinated action following an attempt can and does save lives.

Actions you can take

- Ensure you are fully aware of current procedures in your jail.
- Know how to speedily access equipment and check that is in working order.
- Keep your first aid training up to date.

The experience of custody – triggers

The experience of being in prison brings particular stresses and events that can trigger a suicide attempt in someone who may or may not have been identified as at risk. Examples include:

- setbacks in the prisoner's custodial 'career', for example refusal of parole or bail, return from failed licence, failure to progress to a prison with a lower level of security
- court appearances and outcomes, especially receiving a custodial sentence that is unexpected or long
- wing debts, threats and bullying (21% of prisoners who killed themselves in 1999–2000 had been bullied in prison)
- disciplinary procedures, especially if perceived as unfair
- transfer or change of location
- relationship problems or disappointments, e.g. a distressing visit or letter
- a suicide by another prisoner
- concerns about children being taken into care or losing custody. This form of bereavement can act as a particular trigger for female prisoners. There are specialised voluntary organisations working in this area (see Paton and Jenkins 2002 for details).

Actions you can take

- Ask prisoners who are in these situations about their mood and thoughts, and tell them about help available within the prison.

- Be aware that risk changes over time. Risk assessment is ongoing and does not end when the initial reception health screen has been completed.

- Ensure that your prison's visitor centre has leaflets for the family and friends of prisoners telling them how to contact staff if they are concerned that their loved one is suicidal.

Individuals at special risk

We can identify people at special risk by looking at the individual and social characteristics of those who have killed themselves in the past. Research has also examined the characteristics of those prisoners who have reported attempting or thinking about suicide (Meltzer *et al.* 1999). Knowledge of risk factors is important in order to assess the risk of suicide in a particular individual and to take action to reduce the risk in a high-risk group. The key individual risk factors are summarised below.

Previous self injury or attempted suicide

Forty-four per cent of female remand prisoners and 27 per cent of male remand prisoners have previously attempted suicide at some time.

Mental disorder

Fifty-seven per cent of prisoners who died in 1999 and 2000 had symptoms of psychiatric disturbance on reception (Shaw *et al.* 2003). Prisoners who attempted suicide had significantly higher levels of clinical depression, anxiety and psychosis than other prisoners, particularly multiple mental health problems, including personality disorders.

Alcohol and drug dependence and withdrawal

Dependence upon alcohol and on stimulants, alone or in combination with opiates, seems to be particularly associated with suicide attempts in prisoners. Prisoners addicted to crack cocaine are particularly vulnerable to suicidal feelings during withdrawal. Because there is no substitute medication available, many prisoners do not declare their use on reception and complete their withdrawal alone and unsupported on ordinary location.

History of adverse life events

Prisoners who report attempting suicide are particularly likely to have had disrupted early lives, experiences of abuse, and bereavements. Rates of physical and sexual abuse are highest in female prisoners who attempt or complete suicide but are also very high in men.

Offence

Remand prisoners are more likely to kill themselves than sentenced prisoners. Among sentenced prisoners, those serving long sentences, particularly life sentences, are at high risk. Prisoners charged or convicted with a violent offence, including rape, are disproportionately likely to kill themselves. A study of lifers who killed themselves revealed two risk groups:

1. Prisoners who had killed a family member or close friend, who were suicidal from their arrival in prison, sometimes talking of death as a way of being reunited with their victim.

2. Prisoners who were unsuccessful in obtaining parole or progressing towards release.

Social support

Prisoners who kill themselves or attempt suicide are particularly likely to be socially isolated, inside and outside prison. Forty-two per cent of prisoners who killed themselves in 1999–2000 were not receiving visits from anyone prior to their deaths. As one prisoner who recovered from a suicide attempt said: 'I haven't really got that many people out there'.

EXERCISE 8.1

Consider the risk factors above and how these apply to the (anonymous) example below of a prisoner who killed himself. What might have been done to prevent his death?

Jason was a young man of 18, whose father was a violent alcoholic and whose mother had a history of depression and attempted suicide. He was in and out of care as a child, had a family history of serious mental illness, was dyslexic and was bullied at school, which he left aged 13. Prior to jail he had had a substantial heroin and crack cocaine habit for at least two years and his ability to manage anger was assessed as poor. He had two children of his own, one of whom had been adopted. He was serving a long sentence (more than five years) for robbery and possession of a weapon. He was receiving psychiatric treatment and heard voices telling him to kill himself. Not long before his death, he had been transferred to another prison and received a visit from his mother which upset him. At the time of death, he was on an ordinary wing, in a double cell, but his 'pad mate' was absent at the time.

Assessing and managing prisoners at risk of suicide: taking a holistic approach

The key principles of assessing and addressing risk are the same inside prison as outside (see Chapter 2). A useful model is to consider five domains:

1. *Pre-disposing factors* that make the prisoner vulnerable (previous history of self-harm, mental disorder, substance dependence, previous adverse life events).

2. *Protective factors* that make suicide less likely (e.g. confiding relationships with family or friends).

3. *Current problems* that are triggering current distress (see above).

4. *Environmental risk factors* including staffing levels, the physical environment, means to suicide and the regime (see above).

5. *Immediate risk factors* – how the prisoner feels now, feelings of hopelessness, wishes to be dead, specific plans for suicide.

In assessing *immediate* suicide risk, the fifth domain is the most important. All prison health care staff need the core skills of assessing and managing risk, helping prisoners to manage crises, and solving problems. A prison-specific version of STORM (Skills Training on Risk Management) has been commissioned from Manchester University and is described elsewhere in this book.

In assessing *overall* risk, you need to consider all the factors together. For example, someone who is withdrawing from a combination of opiates and crack is at higher risk if alone on ordinary location than in a dedicated area with higher staffing levels and cell design that allows observation.

Reducing the overall risk also requires you to take action in all the domains. For example, in the case described above, 'Jason' required good mental health care, effective help with his substance dependence, social support, and help for his other social problems. Finally, he would have been safer if there had been a higher level of staff support and he had not been left alone.

Most action to reduce risk in people who have a history of self-harm, or who have a mental disorder or who are dependent on drugs and/or alcohol is similar whether the individual is in prison or outside. These issues are addressed in other chapters in this book.

Accessing social support (a protective factor) for your patients is usually much harder in prison than outside. Most prisons now have 'Listeners' who are prisoners trained by the Samaritans to provide confidential support to their peers. It is important though to help prisoners make and maintain contact with the source of social support they prefer. While some prisoners report that they have found talking to Listeners invaluable, others prefer to seek help from other prisoners/friends, or from staff who may be able to address their practical problems. It is essential to be aware of the resources in your prison, including peer support schemes and voluntary organisations.

Finally, helping prisoners make or keep contact with their families and friends outside the prison can be of great importance. Reducing suicide risk may just mean helping a young prisoner contact his/her mother or partner. Be aware, though, that many prisoners have difficult relationships with their families and/or partners, with women particularly likely to be in abusive relationships. What are known in prisons as 'bad visits' can trigger a suicide attempt.

Taking a holistic approach will involve staff from a variety of disciplines, including prison officers. As a result, a core element of good practice in suicide prevention in prison is participation in the prison service's multi-disciplinary care planning system. This system (known as the F2052SH) is currently undergoing review but the core elements of assessment and a multi-disciplinary care plan will remain.

Practise what you have learned – material for reflection

The following anonymous case studies are adapted from real-life interviews with prisoners. Read each case study and then spend some time thinking about the questions which follow. When you have jotted down your ideas or answers to both the case studies, go to the responses and follow-up section below.

Case study 8.1

Sheena is 20. She is currently in prison on remand for drug-related offences, and is hoping to be sent to a drug rehabilitation unit. She asked to be moved from a young offender wing, which she found too 'childish', and is currently in a single cell on an adult wing. She has a history of depression and self-injury from an early age, mainly cutting, but recently attempted to strangle herself. Staff are aware that she misses her mother, who died three years ago from a heroin overdose. As a child she was placed in care, in secure accommodation, for being 'rebellious'. Last month she was placed on segregation for being rude to a governor, where she also attempted suicide.

You are working on the wing and staff mention that Sheena is 'difficult'. You decide to go and have a talk with her.

Questions for consideration

1. What would you want to ask Sheena about, regarding her recent suicide attempt?
2. Why might some staff think Sheena is difficult?
3. What strategies might you discuss with wing staff for reducing Sheena's risk of suicide?

Case study 8.2

David is 50 years old. He had never been in prison until he was remanded in custody for this offence. He cut his wrists on the night he was returned to prison from court, having been convicted of murdering a friend in a domestic dispute. He was in a single cell on ordinary location. David has a long history of depression and suicide attempts outside prison, starting in childhood; he links this to the experience of being abused. He plans to appeal against his conviction and is currently working as a prison cleaner. He talks about the importance of keeping busy.

You are about to start working on reception/induction and you want to know how to avoid further incidents of this kind.

Questions for consideration

1. Why do you think staff failed to identify David as at risk of suicide on his arrival back from court?
2. What could they have done to help him cope with his sentence?
3. What help do you think he needs now?

Case studies: Responses and follow-up

Case study 8.1

Question 1

- To understand Sheena's suicide attempt you would want to ask her how she was feeling at the time it happened and what she was thinking about. You might need to ask for further details, such as whether there were any specific triggers or events.

- You would find out that:

    ° she had been feeling quite depressed and had missed some of her medication

    ° she grieves for her mother and at the time of the suicide attempt felt that this was a way of being reunited with her

    ° she was worried about her impending court case and had nothing to distract her from these worries.

- You would also want to ask her how she was feeling now. You would find that she is still self-harming and intermittently thinking about suicide.

- You would then want to ask her what could be done to help her now (see Question 3).

Question 2

- Staff may find her difficult because she makes demands on their time, by asking for things or by needing first aid when she injures herself. Prisoners like Sheena who frequently self-injure are often viewed by staff as 'manipulative'.

- Sheena has lodged a number of complaints, for example about her missing medication, which are valid but may stretch the patience of staff who feel they do not have time to do everything.

- You could help staff work more effectively with Sheena by explaining that self-harm is never just manipulation. Even though prisoners may injure themselves to bring about change this is understandable in an environment where they have no other power. Sheena's self-injury also reflects her difficulties in coping with unresolved grief.

Question 3

- The first step is for staff to take the initiative in talking and listening to Sheena, to find out what her needs are. It is important that they do this regularly, *not* just when she has self-harmed or attempted suicide, to show that self-harm is not the only way to get help. The fact that on two occasions she has moved from self-harm to attempted suicide emphasises the need to take every self-harm act seriously.

- When Sheena was asked what could be done to prevent her from attempting suicide again she suggested.

  - ° activities such as colouring books to fill her time and distract her from thinking about death

  - ° being allowed to have her friend in with her if she feels suicidal, even if it is at inconvenient times such as the middle of the night. It is recommended that suicidal prisoners should be in double cells whenever possible so staff should consider ways of ensuring she has peer support.

Follow-up

After the interview this information was passed on, with Sheena's consent. The staff agreed that she could be relocated into a dormitory with her friend. (Sheena preferred to talk to her friend rather than to a Listener.) The suicide prevention coordinator noted the importance of regular medication in her F2052SH and also obtained colouring books for her cell.

Case study 8.2

Question 1

- Ideally staff in reception should have known that prisoners convicted of murder or other violent offences have a higher than average risk of killing themselves, and that prisoners with a change of status (from remand to sentenced) and those receiving a longer sentence than expected are particularly vulnerable. However because David had been in the prison for almost a year on remand and had been going in and out to court during the previous week the staff on reception may not have identified him as a priority for their attention.

- David says that he is not surprised they did not identify him as a suicide risk from his demeanour as he was 'laughing and joking' with staff. He was in a state of shock and feeling all right until a few hours later when the situation hit him. He emphasised that everyone who returns from court with a conviction should be treated as vulnerable, regardless of how they appear.

Question 2

- Staff could have been more proactive in supporting David during the difficult first 24 hours after conviction, which is known to be a time of high risk. Instead of being placed in a cell on his own he should have been assigned a cellmate or Listener to talk to.

- If the prison had had an Insiders scheme in place, this could have been another source of peer support, and Insiders can also refer any concerns about suicide risk to staff. The key point is that David was in a state of delayed shock and did not feel able to ask for help; staff therefore need to work on the assumption that anyone who has just been given a life sentence, or an unexpected guilty verdict, is vulnerable.

Question 3

- David says that he needs to keep busy. At present he is appealing against his sentence and that is giving him something to focus on and keep hopeful about. However staff will need to be aware that if the appeal is not successful he could be at risk again.
- Staff need to draw up a care plan, including working with him to find out which other activities help him cope; for example getting a job, attending education, going to the gym, can all help but it will depend on what the individual finds useful.
- Staff could ask David if he would like contact details of agencies which offer support to adult victims of child abuse.
- David reported a history of depression. Health care staff should gather information about his former treatment and assess his current mental state.

Follow-up

David now has a job in the prison and is also a trained Listener. He has found a sense of self-worth through helping other men who are also in prison for the first time. However he still feels upset about the sentence he received and he may need careful monitoring if the appeal is unsuccessful.

References

Her Majesty's Chief Inspector of Prisons (1999) *Suicide is Everyone's Concern: a Thematic Review by HM Chief Inspector of Prisons for England and Wales.* London: HMSO.

Meltzer, H., Jenkins, R., Singleton, N., Charlton, J. and Yar, M. (1999) *Non-Fatal Suicidal Behaviour Among Prisoners.* London: Office for National Statistics.

Paton, J. and Jenkins, R. (eds) (2002) *Mental Health Primary Care in Prison.* London: Royal Society of Medicine. Website: www.prisonmentalhealth.org

Sattar, G. (2001) *Rates and Causes of Death Among Prisoners and Offenders Under Community Supervision.* London: Home Office Research Study no. 231.

Shaw, J., Baker, D., Hunt, I. and Appleby, L. (2003) *Safer Prisons: a Report from the National Confidential Inquiry.* London: Department of Health.

Further reading and resources

Prison Health: www.hmprisonservice.gov.uk for details of prison nurse training and prison detoxification clinical nurse specialists.

Safer Custody Group: for information on safer cell design standards, peer support programmes, training packages for prison staff on suicide prevention and understanding self-injury, booklets for staff on understanding self-injury, leaflets for visitors' centres. Contact: Anna Sedenu, Safer Custody Group, tel: 020 7217 2011, email: anna.sedenuSCG@hmps.gsi.gov.uk

Singleton, N., Meltzer, H., Gatward, R., Coid, J. and Deasy, D. (1998) *Psychiatric Morbidity of Prisoners in England and Wales*. London: Office for National Statistics.

Towl, G., Snow, L. and McHugh, M. (eds) (2000) *Suicide in Prisons*. London: British Psychological Society.

Chapter 9

Black and Minority Ethnic Groups

Hári Sewell

Introduction

The surprising fact with regard to suicides of people from Black and minority ethnic groups (BME) is that there are not more of them. This chapter tackles some of the complex issues that arise in trying to understand the particular needs of people from BME groups in relation to suicide prevention.

Terminology

Perhaps the first complexity to be considered is the term itself. Much discourse on race and health recognises the inadequacies of the terms 'minority ethnic group' or 'BME' (e.g. Modood *et al.* 1997). Every human being has an ethnic identity. In most environments one ethnic group forms the majority and all other groups are in the minority. The term 'BME' has however become synonymous with disadvantaged groups; a recognition of the reality that in the Western world the majority (i.e. White people) are usually more advantaged.

The term does however mask the fact that the cluster of individual ethnic groups referred to as 'BME' often bear few cultural, linguistic or religious similarities. This is illustrated when the Japanese are compared with West Africans. Simply put, 'minority ethnic groups' does not define a homogeneous group.

Many studies into suicides in BME groups, particularly in the USA, have focused on single minority ethnic groups. This is based on the recognition that patterns and trends *across* ethnic groups will be related more to social and economic factors than to culture or ethnicity (Health Education Authority (HEA) 1994). Effective work across BME groups will demand a focus on the one uniting factor: *social exclusion*, covering racism and other forms of discrimination.

Policy

The *National Suicide Prevention Strategy for England* (Department of Health (DoH) 2002) highlights the findings from research: poor socioeconomic status is contributory to increased suicide risk. The *Five-Year Report of the National Confidential Inquiry into Suicide and Homicide by People with Mental Illness* (DoH 2001) illustrates a spectrum of risk factors, particularly in relation to people who are in contact with mental health services.

Table 9.1 shows socioeconomic risk factors associated with suicides and an indication of whether, for each, these are raised in the case of people from BME groups. The table indicates a snowballing effect from an accumulation of risk factors in BME groups. Certain groups, such as African Caribbeans, have been subject to more research than others. This influences the types of deductions that can confidently be made. Some BME groups report that isolation, poor housing and language barriers are factors that limit access to mental health services and support intended to minimise risk of suicide.

Minority ethnic groups, suicide prevention and culture

Too much to be knowledgeable about

As illustrated earlier, the term BME does not refer to a heterogeneous group of people. The variations between groups are great and there are too many groups for practitioners to become fully knowledgeable about all of them.

Readers will be interested in some findings from studies that have looked at differences in suicide by BME groups. Studies have found, for example, that suicides by BME people are more often violent and that they are more likely to be unemployed. Suicides of Black Caribbean patients were considered to have been most preventable, with hindsight (Hunt *et al.* 2003). Caribbean people in the over 35 age group were found to be four times less likely to commit suicide than their White counterparts (McKenzie, Van Os *et al.* 2003). A similar pattern was found in Swedish studies which showed that the children of immigrants were more likely to commit suicide than the immigrants themselves. Religiosity is thought of as a factor in reducing the risk of suicide and is considered as contributing to the differentials across age and generations (McKenzie, Serfaty and Crawford 2003). Research by Raleigh and Balarajan (1992) into suicide by

Table 9.1: Socioeconomic risk factors associated with suicides

Suicide risk factor	Raised or diminished in BME?	Notes [1]
Diagnosis of schizophrenia	Yes, in some groups	Evidence for increased rates of diagnosis for African Caribbeans; high rates for Irish, Bangladeshi
History of violence	Yes, in some groups	Significant over-representation of African Caribbeans and African in secure and high security settings; increasing numbers of Irish and Bangladeshi
Personality disorder	Unclear, some evidence of low rates of diagnosis	Limited research, though that which is available indicates under-representation of BME groups
Substance misuse	Yes, in some groups	Under-representation in support services
Unemployed	Yes, in some groups	High rates of unemployment in Bangladeshi, African Caribbean and Pakistani groups; high unemployment among refugees and asylum seekers
Lone parents	Yes, in some groups	High reporting of lone parenting among African Caribbean groups
Non-compliance with treatment	Yes, in some groups	Disproportionate levels of disengagement by various BME, leading to high representation in assertive outreach services; disproportionate experience of Mental Health Act detentions
Missed final appointment with services	Yes, in some groups	As above
Homelessness	Yes, in some groups	African Caribbean, African and refugee groups are disproportionately represented; under-representation in support services.
Occupations: farming, nursing, medicine	Partially	High numbers of Asian doctors and BME nurses in some localities and in some settings; though numbers were declining others are being recruited from South Africa, Nigeria and the Far East making this picture more complex

1. See National Institute for Mental Health (England) 2002

self-burning generated much interest in the over-representation of Asian young women among those who commit suicide by this method. The research relied upon recognising Asian-sounding surnames because coroners' courts did not collect ethnic data at the time. Changes to this practice are being considered following publication of the National Suicide Prevention Strategy, though there are some credible reasons for the current arrangements. For example, following a purist approach, *ethnic group* must be self assigned. The lack of credible ethnic data has complicated analysis of the research. The important issue at stake here however is the need for services to understand pressures that drive some young Asian women to such a painful death, marked with such an anger and protestation.

There is much detail to grasp. It is important, however, for practitioners to have some understanding of working across cultural groups, irrespective of whether they have a detailed knowledge of each BME group and their specific suicide risks.

The following case study demonstrates however that having cultural understanding is essential in suicide prevention.

Case study 9.1

Lennox is a 26-year-old man. He is Black British, born of Jamaican parents. Lennox was diagnosed as suffering from bipolar affective disorder during his first ever admission. Following discharge, Lennox was asked by his parents not to return to his flat but to stay with them. The CPA care coordinator, Victor, visited weekly for the first month and became concerned by the number of visitors to the house. During the 45-minute visits a steady stream of family friends, relatives and people from church arrived, often bringing food. Some people from church stayed to pray. Lennox's parents said that they preferred to pray rather than to give their son his medication.

Victor became concerned that Lennox was not being given a chance to get well and advised the parents to prevent too many visitors. A week after Victor's conversation with Lennox's parents they reported that they no longer allowed visitors, apart from Lennox's girlfriend, Kate. After a while Kate felt embarrassed when the family kept asking her why she did not bring proper Caribbean food. Kate was White.

Victor found that the home visits were less stressful without the bustle in the house. He did however feel that Lennox seemed to be more subdued. Kate had stopped visiting after six weeks but the care coordinator was unaware. Lennox stopped getting out of bed.

Upon arrival for a visit Victor discovered that Lennox was not at his parents' house. He had decided to return to his flat. Lennox's parents reported that he stated that he wanted to find his girlfriend because at least she would be able to stay.

When Victor visited the flat he gained no reply. Lennox was found hanging inside his wardrobe.

Questions for consideration

1. What were the key risk factors that Victor appeared to have missed?

2. How might his assessment of risk have been improved?

3. What other actions or referrals might have been warranted?

The case illustrates how a worker can fail to pick up on risk factors. Knowledge of cultural practices and perspectives could have informed a more proactive approach.

Several factors could have been considered and acted upon:

- Family and friends rallying round at times of family crisis is seen as a fundamental aspect of many Caribbean cultures.

- The act of bringing food is an important way of caring in Caribbean cultures.

- The parents' decision to stop virtually all visits could have been an extreme attempt to be compliant with the care coordinator.

- The dynamic between Lennox's parents and Kate, his White girlfriend.

- The reasons why Kate had stopped visiting.

- The fact that Lennox's parents were religious and said that they preferred not to give him his medication.

- The possibility that Lennox may have had residual religious beliefs and the impact this may have had on his willingness to express suicidal ideas.

- The supportive role friends and family provided for Lennox's parents, as carers.

- Kate was not able to stay over at Lennox's parents' house because of family values and their religion. The impact of this on Lennox was not considered.

By its very nature much of 'culture' is unspoken. It is important for practitioners to explore with service users and their families the meaning of their actions. This is particularly important as no single practitioner will know about every culture they are likely to come across in their work.

A little learning is a dangerous thing

There are clearly benefits in having some knowledge of different cultures. The acquisition of cultural knowledge does however bring its own risks. The complexities in cultures are sometimes overlooked in order to present information in a simple and digestible form. In localities where there are several minority groups, it is difficult for a practitioner to have an understanding of all cultures. And of course the greatest risk is that the little knowledge gained of a culture will then be applied to service users, without consideration for individual identities shaped by family, regional differences, socialisation and individual psychology. There are clear risks in working with limited acquired cultural knowledge (LACK).

It is important not to lose sight of the fact that each person is unique. In response to the question 'What do Black young men want?' a worker was told by a specialist BME worker:

> Well, all the guys I work with say they really want their own place, doesn't have to be plush, just their own pad; they would like some money in their pockets so they can go to the pictures if that's what they choose. They would like a partner – someone they can chill with. Most of the guys would like a job or a bit of training. That's it really. Find a way to sort those things and you'll be on the right track.

Basic human need must not be eclipsed by the pursuit of some superior cultural knowledge.

EXERCISE 9.1

Identify a service user from a BME background with whom you have been working for at least two years and negotiate agreement for you to undertake this exercise.

Write down from memory the life story of this BME service user. In your description you should cover as much as you can about:

- early hopes and dreams
- what they wanted to be when they grew up
- what made them feel most loved and respected

- their interests
- their greatest source of dissatisfaction
- what their ethnic identity means to them
- how they feel that their ethnic identity affects their lives; and
- what they wish to achieve in the next three to six months.

Consider the gap between their aspirations (either those they hold currently or those they had as a child) and their current experience.

After you have completed the exercise reflect on how easy or difficult it was to remember the details. Ask yourself why.

Practitioners must be able to relate at a basic human level with people of all ethnic backgrounds. Failure to relate to this humanness leads to poorer engagement with BME agroups and therefore greater risk of disengagement. Two categories of problems arise from a failure to engage:

- increased risk of actual suicides by individuals from BME groups
- reduced impact across and within BME groups of initiatives to reduce suicides.

An approach to suicide prevention in BME groups must address these two dimensions.

Barriers to suicide prevention with BME individuals and communities

Care packages biased towards physical treatments

Missed final appointments are a risk factor in suicides. Studies over many years, including the recent *Breaking the Circles of Fear* (Sainsbury Centre for Mental Health (SCMH) 2002) have shown that people from minority ethnic groups find the use of drug treatments threatening. Satisfaction among BME services is lower than that for their White counterparts (Parkman *et al.* 1997; Sandamas and Hogman 2000; Wilson 1997). Perceptions are commonplace among BME groups that services are dangerous for Black people.

Suicide prevention strategies are likely to be less effective when there is undue focus on interventions that alienate service users.

Actions of professionals informed by stereotypes

Much is written about the relative proportion of diagnosis for depression and psychosis in certain BME groups. Fernando (1991) writes about the perception of psychiatrists such as Carothers in the 1950s that Africans do not suffer from depression due to a lack of purposefulness to their lives. Cartwright in the 1800s developed the diagnosis of *drapetomania* for slaves on plantations – the disease of running away. Modern mental health services are still plagued with the legacies of such racist perceptions.

- Studies have shown probable increased 'false positives' in the assessment of the risk of violence in people of African and African Caribbean backgrounds (Fernando, Ndegwa and Wilson 1998).

- Stereotypical views persist that Asian families will 'look after their own'.

- Some professionals routinely consider that claims of social exclusion and racism are exaggerated, i.e. that BME service users often have a 'chip on their shoulder'.

These stereotypical perceptions potentially lead to inappropriate interventions (e.g. disproportionate use of methods of control). This contributes to a cycle of disproportionate 'non-compliance' and ultimately disengagement by BME service users. A key function of mental health services in suicide prevention is the follow-up on patients within seven days of discharge. Any practice that contributes to disengagement increases the likelihood of suicide.

Restricted aspirations for people from BME groups

Another barrier to effective suicide prevention is the restricted aspirations that mental health services sometimes have for people from some BME groups. Professionals become desensitised to the gravity of the BME experience in society and in mental health services.

When front line staff and managers hear repeated accounts of social exclusion or read reports such as *Breaking the Circles of Fear* and still carry on doing the same things in the same way, it indicates that caring professions are losing the ability to care. The loss of trust that this generates affects communities as well as individuals. Suicide prevention strategies lose their impact in this context.

Failure of professionals to address culture, language and religion

Risks increase when practitioners fail to respond to cultural factors. This was demonstrated by Case study 9.1. Language, religion and faith are often key. Sometimes culture and religion are so bound together that it is difficult to disentangle the two. For example, much of what is discussed in relation to BME groups, and in particular Asian women, relates to the influence of religion on lifestyles and culture:

- During fasting some members of religious groups (including Christians) may not take anything by mouth during daylight, including oral medication.

- Some religious and cultural beliefs interpret mental illness as spirit possession.

- Some religious groups see actions of the faith community either as the primary intervention for addressing mental distress, or at least to play a part alongside medicine.

- Restaurant trade and other shift workers sometimes develop sub-cultures and may opt out of using statutory services due to alternative waking and working hours. This will include factory workers but also BME staff workers in health and social care, over-represented in employment that includes night work.

- All major religions deem suicide to be against their teachings. Those who adhere to the faith or religion may be more reluctant than others to articulate suicidal ideas.

Failure of professionals to recognise the effects of social exclusion and to take remedial action to address these

Failure to acknowledge the effects of racism in people's lives is racist in itself. Good practice is built on an awareness of the social context within which people live. This social perspective is part of the strength that social work and social care brings to mental health. Hence the National Service Framework service models requiring social workers to be part of teams. Some organisations (such as Camden and Islington Mental Health and Social Care Trust) have an executive director for social care, with a clear lead at board level on social inclusion. Table 9.1 earlier in this chapter demonstrates the clear link between socioeconomic factors and risk of suicide.

EXERCISE 9.2

This exercise is designed to challenge clinical teams to adopt a 'social interventionist' model of care.

As a team/service identify the last occasion when you advocated specifically on behalf of BME service users for improvements in external services. You may have challenged statutory partners because of the variations in the way that they provide services. These variations have potentially had a negative impact on your ability to deliver fair and equitable services. This may include actions of the police, or a GP's referral patterns. Inequitable patterns in allocations by the housing department may mean that your team's ability to provide support to service users from BME groups is undermined. (For example, disproportionately high numbers of BME service users on an estate with an open illicit drugs market.)

Once you have identified the intervention with an external partner, consider the following:

- When did you do this?

- Why at that point in the life of your team?

- What exactly did you do?

- How effective was the intervention in changing practice in your partner organisation?

It may be that as a team/service you have not been prompted to broaden your focus from clinical work into social interventions. If so, what does this suggest to you about:

- the understanding of the individuals in your team regarding obstacles to their work with BME groups; and

- management's ability to think systemically about making improvements in the lives of BME service users?

Suicide prevention with BME communities

Ensuring that initiatives to reduce suicides as outlined in the national strategy have an equitable impact across ethnic groups

One of the few ways that a service can determine whether its performance is equitable is if it is measured by ethnicity. This will be in relation to what it does (actions taken) and what it achieves (in terms of reducing suicides).

Clinical psychologist Sue Holland (1995) has written extensively on the subject of 'moving from private symptoms to public action'. She uses the diagram shown in Figure 9.1 to explain why and how services must monitor performance and set targets.

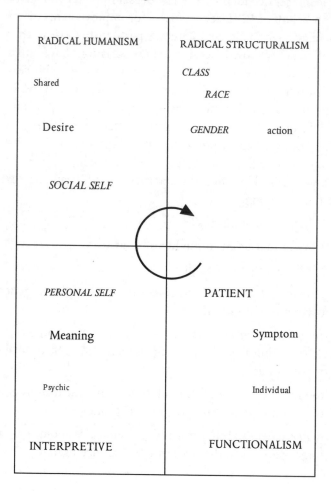

Figure 9.1 Actioning service targets and performance (Holland 1995)

The *Functionalism* paradigm in the first quadrant (following the direction of the arrow) is a model of intervention that focuses on the symptoms rather than the individual. The main aim of any work is not to establish a relationship in order to get to the root of the problems but rather to control or remove symptoms of mental illness.

The *Interpretive* paradigm moves beyond being symptom-focused and tries to enable individuals to understand what is happening to them. This is not solely in a biomedical sense but socially too. This may be in relation to their domestic situation or discrimination in society. This 'search for meaning' is initially likely to be in the one-to-one context of a worker/service user relationship.

Radical Humanism sees a move away from a focus on individuals and their attempt to understand and change themselves. This perspective develops from an interaction of individuals who are able to identify some commonality in their experiences. This leads to a recognition that factors other than their own individual biology, psychology and experience may be contributing to the pattern that they identify. This brings strength and support and potentially a realisation of systematic or structural injustice. This leads to the fourth paradigm.

Radical Structuralism aims to remove the disadvantages built into systems and structures in the social world that *disproportionately* affect particular groups of people. Having recognised that patterns exist, explanations for these are sought. This may lead to a range of analysis. Included in this will be a consideration of the direct or indirect role of policy and practice in affecting outcomes.

Case study 9.2

Anna is a 42-year-old Chinese woman from Hong Kong. She speaks mainly Cantonese and suffers from feelings of depression. She seldom visits her NHS GP as she relies upon her husband, Ken, to interpret. Ken owns a restaurant and works long hours, returning home at 2.30 am. He usually arrives home having enjoyed several alcoholic drinks to unwind. He heads back to the restaurant at 10.30 am to prepare for the lunch time trade. This pattern, combined with Ken's irritability, has contributed to Anna's feelings of depression. Anna arrived in this country as a teacher and feels frustrated in this secluded lifestyle, living on the outskirts of a middle England city.

She consults her GP, Dr Maddox, with her Chinese friend Sylvia, after she discloses that she feels so depressed she would like to be dead. Sylvia cajoles her friend into going to the surgery and acts as interpreter. Dr Maddox listens and prescribes antidepressants. Though Sylvia speaks English very well she has a strong accent. Dr Maddox found it 'hard work' listening and was pleased to be able to help in a clear cut way by prescribing antidepressants.

Sylvia notices a leaflet for a Health Liaison Worker for the Chinese community and makes contact. After a few sessions the Health Liaison Worker, Yuan, makes a referral to a psychologist. The psychologist is able to help Anna reflect on the things in her life that contribute to her depression. Together they consider areas of her life that she could change, perhaps with support. Yuan also mentions that a Chinese Women's Group is run in the locality. Anna attends as a break from the usual routine. There, she discovers that many of the women are in similar situations, though not all as depressed. With the help of Yuan they campaign for more information in Cantonese and more interpreters. They also appeal for more flexible hours of operation so that workers in the restaurant business are able to access health and social care services more readily; perhaps between 4 and 7 pm, when there is a lull in the activities in the restaurants. Managers in the service are provided with facts and figures on service uptake by Chinese people. Based on numbers in the population service use is very low. This evidence acts as a catalyst for providing small levels of funding for additional Health Liaison Worker hours to support the planned extension of opening times for community mental health services.

The four paradigms can be applied to help in gaining understanding about actions and to consider limitations.

The *Functionalist* perspective is seen in Dr Maddox's identification of symptoms which need treating as opposed to trying to understand Anna's lived experience.

The *Interpretive* perspective is seen in the interventions of the psychologist who takes time to listen to Anna's lived experience and helps to find some ways to make improvements. People from BME communities (as for all marginalised groups who are not given opportunities to use their voice) value the chance to explore meaning for their experience. Talking and listening re-humanises when so much that happens to BME de-humanises them.

The Chinese women's group helped members to identify that the way that services operate systematically disadvantages them. The attempt to change the outside world as a result of identifying common experiences rather than focusing upon individual pathology is a hallmark of the *Radical Humanist* perspective.

Radical Structuralism does not rely upon collectives of individuals to identify trends. It is built upon a strategic analysis of problems (low uptake of services by Chinese) and the setting of targets and strategies to bring about change. In the case study, managers had a policy on equality and identified low uptake by Chinese people. They made an investment to reduce potentially unfair variations in uptake of mental health services.

The key learning here is that the early paradigms in this model have limitations in terms of strategic change. Clinical improvements in individuals can be made in the bottom half of the diagram. However, overall negative trends and patterns of experience of services or outcomes will continue to persist for certain groups unless the contributory factors are identified and tackled.

The four paradigms provide a framework for analysing the relative merits of different approaches to prevent suicides. Some individual work of an extremely high quality is possible even in the context of failure to address structural issues. The result, however, is likely to be that overall trend data still shows disadvantage in terms of outcomes.

Current models of service promoted by the National Service Framework: What works?

Much literature dating back to the 1970s records the poor experiences and outcomes for people from BME in mental health. Research on effective interventions with people from BME groups is much more difficult to find. This is because the types of interventions that are favoured by many people from BME groups, documented in many reports such as *Breaking the Circles of Fear* (SCMH 2002) are not of a traditional medical or psychological model. They are not easily suited to randomised controlled trials (RCT). The lack of a platform for such 'pure' scientific research has acted against the interest of BME service users. The perception of RCT as the holy grail of research has meant that the many valuable studies into the *experience* of people from BME groups have little kudos and therefore little power to affect funding or shape policy. For many people from BME groups this is interpreted as yet another attempt by funders and policy makers to silence their voices. The reality is that policy development is presented as being based upon scientific evidence when on occasions other imperatives drive this process.

The views of people from BME groups in relation to mental health services are by no means uniform. There is however a fair deal of consistency as demonstrated in studies that look at BME experience in mental health services (Parkman *et al.* 1997; Sandamas and Hogman 2000; Wilson 1997). Many of these studies focus on African Caribbean and African service users, mirroring the areas of greatest discrepancy in outcomes.

Services that achieve engagement recognise and address the perceptions and experiences of many people from BME groups. The issues may be perceived by readers as controversial but will be familiar to those who listen to people from BME groups. Put another way, services that are effective in working with BME communities *understand things differently* and *do things differently*.

Effective services understand and appreciate the following perceptions held by many BME service users:

- A White person is racist unless they prove otherwise – the experience of BME service users reinforces this.

- Black people may identify gaps in their 'Blackness': feelings of inadequacy; not belonging and internal dissonance. This may be particularly so for people of mixed race parentage or those who grew up in care, or with White families.

- Some will be anxious that they will be judged by other BME people for being too compliant.

- The experience and effects of racism are likely to be as bad as the person (and research) suggests. Socioeconomic needs must be addressed if trust is to be developed.

- The fact that there are not more BME suicides (in the light of such poor experiences) indicates that significant strengths exist within individuals and wider communities. This needs to be capitalised upon.

- People from BME groups use a different language to communicate, sometimes more obviously so than others. Sometimes it is literally a different language, sometimes a dialect, emphasis or a way of speaking imbued with cultural history.

As well as understanding the above, effective services do the following:

- adopt a whole systems approach
- reflect the service user's background in staffing, attitudes and the decor of buildings
- behave non-judgementally – not based upon assumptions and stereotypes; and
- find creative ways to 'hook into' the interests of service users from BME groups.

The final bullet point addresses head-on one of the key challenges that mental health services face in relation to engaging with people from BME groups. Certain models of service within the Mental Health NSF lend themselves more readily to creative engagement. Assertive outreach teams (AOTs) and crisis intervention teams (CRTs) are prime examples. AOTs are designed specifically to 'meet the service user where they are at' where services have a history of failing to engage in this way. CRTs often rely upon close supportive networks such as families. The need to include family and community is often referred to by service users from BME groups.

Engagement: Positive examples

The Antenna Assertive Outreach service for young African and African Caribbean people in Haringey has been successful in engaging service users by hooking into their interests. For example, programmes of activity include sport such as soccer. Support is provided to tackle any problem that contributes to social exclusion of their service users. The outreach work with families, carers and communities is key to their success.

The Mellow Campaign in East London works with young Black men. Mellow organises club nights and provides DJing and other musical opportunities and training. Again, the connection is made with the interests of those being targeted by services. Mellow provides opportunities in art for specific minority groups.

The MARES Project in Buckinghamshire provides agricultural and equestrian opportunities for people from BME groups. This service connects with what Consultant Psychologist Sue Holland refers to as the 'psychic landscape' described by BME service users. Sue Holland found in her work that, contrary to popular belief, many service users express their ideal place as not within a major city or town, among congestion and high rise flats. The image painted is of something more tranquil, rural and green. MARES provides horse riding opportunities in a rural setting for BME service users from cities such as London and Birmingham.

An assumption that often creeps into discussions about services that engage successfully is that these services must be led by people from the specific ethnic groups. This is an inaccurate and unacceptable assumption. It is important however to acknowledge the point made earlier. Unless services demonstrate emphatically that they are aiming to engage with people from BME groups the perception by service users will usually be that they have no interest in doing so. History has taught them that a service is racist unless otherwise demonstrated.

Specific groups

People with dual heritage

Much literature on working with BME groups fails to recognise that many young people are growing up with dual racial or cultural heritage. This is important in understanding internal conflict. A mixed-race young man brought up by a White mother in the absence of a Black male role model can have a host of internal conflicts. This can be particularly so if the mother is perceived as having a weak anti-racist approach. This is noted here not to be stereotypical but rather to illustrate some of the complexities of the lived experience of people with dual heritage.

Black people previously in care

The complexities of a 'Black identity' are often overlooked. Not all people from a particular minority ethnic group identify easily with that group. Some do identify with the group but do not feel confident about how to behave like a member of that group. BME young people who grew up in a care environment where they have been severed from cultural ties can feel like an impostor among members of their own ethnic group. Lack of language, cultural habits or knowledge of history may cause them to feel dissonance. Services that assume that all people of a particular ethnic group will automatically prefer to be with ethnically matched services or professionals may overlook the experience of vulnerable individuals.

Refugees and asylum seekers

Research into depression within asylum seeker and refugee groups highlights the fact that the experience that led to flight is not the sole contributor to depression. The experience in host countries and social factors such as isolation, poverty and poor housing are contributory (Silove *et al.* 1997). Mental health services cannot affect the past but can certainly influence the future. Tackling social exclusion must be a priority.

Conclusion

This chapter has demonstrated that there are no formulaic answers to working effectively with individuals and communities from BME groups. It is the case however that the *method* of finding the answer is simple. Services need to hear and act upon the needs of BME groups. The nature of these needs may be socioeconomic, linguistic or to do with the quality of relationships with BME service users. Front-line workers rely on managers in organisations to model these behaviours and attitudes. Those in leadership positions within mental health organisations must lead and must be accountable.

References

Department of Health (2001) *Safety First: Five-Year Report of the National Confidential Inquiry into Suicide and Homicide by People with Mental Illness.* London: DoH.

Department of Health (2002) *National Suicide Prevention Strategy for England.* London: DoH.

Fernando, S. (1991) *Mental Health, Race and Culture.* Basingstoke: Macmillan.

Fernando, S., Ndegwa, D. and Wilson, M. (1998) *Forensic Psychiatry, Race and Culture.* London: Routledge.

Health Education Authority (1994) *Black and Minority Ethnic Groups in England.* London: HEA.

Holland, S. (1995) 'Interaction in women's mental health and neighbourhood development.' In S. Fernando (ed) *Mental Health in a Multi-ethnic Society.* London: Routledge.

Hunt, I., Robinson, J., Bickley, H., Meehan, J., Parsons, R., McCann, K., Flynn, S., Burns, J., Shaw, J., Kapur, N. and Appleby, L. (2003) 'Suicides in ethnic minorities within 12 months of contact with Mental Health Services.' *British Journal of Psychiatry 183,* 155–160.

McKenzie, K., van Os, J., Samele, C., van Horn, T. and Murray, R. (2003) 'Suicide and attempted suicide among people of Caribbean origin with psychosis living in the UK.' *British Journal of Psychiatry 183,* 40–44.

McKenzie, K., Serfaty, M. and Crawford, M. (2003) 'Suicide in ethnic minority groups.' *British Journal of Psychiatry 183,* 100–101.

Modood, T., Berthoud, J., Lakey, J., Nazroo, J., Smith, P., Virdee, S. and Beishon, S. (1997) *Ethnic Minorities in Britain: Diversity and Disadvantage.* London: Policy Studies Institute.

National Institute for Mental Health in England (2002) *Inside Outside: Improving Mental Health Services for Black and Minority Ethnic Communities in England.* Leeds: NIMHE.

Parkman, S., Davies, S., Leese, M., Phelan, M. and Thornicroft, G. (1997) 'Ethnic differences in satisfaction with mental health services among representative people with psychosis in South London: PRiSM Study 4.' *British Journal of Psychiatry 171,* 260–264.

Raleigh, V. and Balarajan, R. (1992) 'Suicide and self-burning among Indians and West Indians in England.' *British Journal of Psychiatry 161,* 365–368.

Sainsbury Centre for Mental Health (2002) *Breaking the Circles of Fear: A Review of the Relationship Between Mental Health Services and African and African Caribbean Communities.* London: SCMH.

Sandamas, G. and Hogman, G. (2000) *No Change?* London: National Schizophrenia Fellowship.

Silove, D., Sinnerbrink, I., Field, A., Manicavasagar, V. and Steel, Z. (1997) 'Anxiety, depression and PTSD in asylum-seekers: Associations with pre-migration trauma and post-migration stressors.' *British Journal of Psychiatry 170,* 351–357.

Wilson, M. (1997) 'African Caribbean and African people's experience of the UK mental health services.' *Mental Health Care 1,* 3, 88–90.

Chapter 10

Assisting Self-harm: Some Legal Considerations

David Hewitt

Introduction

Where users of psychiatric services wish to harm themselves, those who would assist them practise in a vacuum. There is little to guide or protect them, whether in the form of primary or secondary legislation, departmental or professional policy, or case law. This chapter does not fill that vacuum; rather, it seeks simply to set out some of the legal issues to which the practice may give rise, and to suggest some ways in which the law's harsher consequences might be avoided.

Defining terms

In this chapter, the term 'self-harm' is used to describe a variety of 'insults' that one might visit upon one's own person. They include, but are not limited to, cutting; burning; and abusing drugs, alcohol or other substances.

The formulation '*assisted* self-harm' describes a spectrum of interventions, each of which differs from the others, albeit possibly only in subtle ways. Those interventions are examined in the context of the patient who seeks to harm him/herself by cutting. It is assumed that this – and not self-burning or self-strangulation (for example) – is the context in which intervention will seem most attractive from a clinical point of view.

In the context of this chapter, it is envisaged that these interventions will be made – or at least considered – by health care professionals. The person who is their imagined subject is referred to, perhaps inappropriately, as the 'patient'.

Box 10.1: Assisting self-harm
by cutting – a spectrum of interventions

- Applying the blade.

- Holding a patient's arm while s/he applies the blade.

- Supervising the patient as s/he applies the blade.

- Monitoring the patient passively, in case the worst should happen.

- Providing the blade and withdrawing from the scene.

- Agreeing to dress the wound afterwards.

- Advocating use of self-harm in a general sense.

- Discussing with a patient what self-harm might involve.

- Declining to discuss the practice at all, but providing support to the patient.

The interventions set out in Box 10.1 differ both in nature and in degree, and there are many others that might, perhaps, be found in the interstices. This chapter does not assume that all forms of assisted self-harm are equally effective or acceptable, or that a practitioner who espouses one form of intervention feels the same about them all.

The 'health care' basis for intervention

It is necessary to consider whether there is a legal box into which 'assisted self-harm' can be put. Without one, the practice should be beyond the purview of health care practitioners, and for them to indulge in it would probably be unlawful. In fact, it is likely that there *is* a legal basis for the practice, and that at least some forms of assisted self-harm will constitute 'medical treatment'.

Medical treatment

According to the definition contained in the Mental Health Act (MHA)1983, 'medical treatment' includes nursing, and also includes care, habilitation and rehabilitation under medical supervision.

Subsequently, the term has been extended still further, so that it includes the alleviation of mere symptoms, even if it is ineffective against the mental disorder that creates them. Further, the term 'care' has long been given an expansive definition: in 1954, Lord Justice Denning (as he then was) called it the art of making people comfortable and providing for their well-being.

The more intensive forms of assisted self-harm – in other words, those that appear first in Box10.1 – are least likely to be regarded as 'medical treatment' and, therefore, to have a lawful basis.

However, it is possible that some less intensive interventions will exert a disproportionate influence upon patients who propose to harm themselves. That might be so, for example, if a patient believes that his or her self-imposed wounds will be sutured. Such a belief might provide the patient with all the reassurance he or she needs, and it might be acquired from an actual promise given by health care staff or merely from the fact that such wounds have been sutured before.

If a particular form of assisted self-harm does constitute 'medical treatment', how might it lawfully be provided? In order to answer this question, it is necessary to consider the Mental Health Act 1983 and the common law.

Mental Health Act 1983

In fact, for the reasons set out below, the provisions of MHA 1983 are unlikely to be relevant to assisted self-harm.

Section 58

Most patients detained under MHA 1983 fall within the 'consent to treatment' provisions in part IV. Usually, the most relevant requirement is MHA 1983, section 58, which concerns the obtaining of patient consent or a second opinion. However, this section applies only to electroconvulsive therapy (Mental Health (Hospital, Guardianship and Consent to Treatment) Regulations 1983, Reg. 16) or 'medicine'. Because it is neither of these, assisted self-harm falls outside MHA 1983, section 58.

Section 63

MHA 1983, section 63 again relates to patients detained under that Act. It states:

> The consent of a patient shall not be required for any medical treatment given to him for the mental disorder from which he is suffering, not being treatment falling within [section 58], if the treatment is given by or under the direction of the responsible medical officer.

As has been explained, many forms of assisted self-harm will probably amount to 'medical treatment'. In order to show that it fell within MHA 1983, section 63 – and therefore, that it might be made without his or her consent – it would be necessary to show that a particular intervention was given for the mental disorder from which the patient was suffering. However, this is unlikely to be relevant, as it will prove extremely difficult – and may not be considered appropriate – to attempt to assist a patient to self-harm without his or her consent.

Therefore, and even in the case of a detained patient, MHA 1983 is unlikely to be relevant to the practice of assisted self-harm.

Self-harm outside the MHA

Capable patients

In the case of informal psychiatric patients, the question of what medical treatment they can – and in some cases *must* – be given depends on whether they are capable of giving informed consent to that treatment.

A capable patient may decide for him or herself whether to consent to medical treatment. Any attempt to impose that treatment without consent may constitute an assault, and therefore a civil wrong and/or a criminal offence. The test for capacity is a common law one. It is summarised in the MHA Code of Practice.

There is a general presumption that an adult has the capacity to consent to treatment. However, that presumption may be rebutted – and, a patient may be shown to be *in*capable – in a number of ways. The incapable patient:

- is unable to take in and retain information material to the treatment decision, especially as to the likely consequences of having or not having the treatment, or
- is unable to believe the information, or
- is unable to weigh the information in the balance as part of the process of arriving at a decision.

Therefore, in the case of a capable patient, health care professionals may make only those interventions:

- that constitute 'medical treatment'; and

- to which the patient has consented.

Even then, in order to be lawful those interventions will also have to be non-negligent *per se*, and to have been made in a non-negligent fashion.

Incapable, informal patients

In the case of incapable, informal patients, the common law doctrine of 'necessity' provides that they may be given such medical treatment as is in their 'best interests'. Treatment is in a patient's best interests if it is carried out in order to:

- save his/her life

- ensure an improvement in his/her physical or mental health, or

- prevent a deterioration in his/her physical or mental health.

Therefore, in the case of an incapable patient, health care professionals may make only those interventions:

- that constitute 'medical treatment'; and

- are in the patient's 'best interests'.

Again, in order to be lawful those interventions will also have to be non-negligent *per se*, and to have been made in a non-negligent fashion. The implications of capacity and consent for the practice of assisted self-harm are:

- In some circumstances it may be lawful to assist a capable patient to self-harm and, depending on its nature, the assistance may constitute medical treatment.

- Although an incapable patient may be compelled to accept medical treatment that is in his/her best interests, it is unlikely to prove possible to compel a patient to receive assisted self-harm.

- The robust infliction of cutting, for example, is unlikely to be 'medical treatment', and is likely to amount to an assault in both criminal and civil law.

Possible challenges

There are many ways in which the practice of assisting patients to harm themselves may be subjected to challenge or censure. For example, an individual practitioner may find him/herself involved in disciplinary proceedings before the General Medical Council or the Nursing and Midwifery Council. Alternatively, an inquest may have to be held if the self-harming patient has died. Finally, there is the prospect of criminal proceedings or civil proceedings. This chapter will consider all but the first of these undesirable possibilities.

Inquests

Professionals whose practice embraces self-harming patients are likely at one time or another to be involved in inquest proceedings before Her Majesty's Coroner.

When is an inquest necessary?

A Coroner must hold an inquest where there is reasonable cause to suspect that:

- the deceased died a violent or unnatural death
- the cause of death is unknown; or
- the deceased died in a place or in circumstances that require an inquest.

Therefore, it is likely that an inquest will be held where a patient is thought to have died while attempting self-harm, whether or not he or she was in hospital at the time.

When is a jury necessary?

Where a patient is thought to have died while attempting self-harm, an inquest must take place before a jury where the circumstances of death would be prejudicial to the public if they were to recur. It is common for a jury to be summoned where there is a question as to the involvement of hospital staff in a patient's death.

What is the purpose of an inquest?

The purpose of a Coroner's inquest is to find facts, not to apportion guilt, and it may not be used to gather evidence for criminal or civil proceedings.

At one time, a Coroner's jury that returned a 'verdict' of murder, manslaughter or infanticide was required to state the name of the person responsible, and its verdict would stand as an indictment of that person in criminal proceedings. This practice was ended in 1977, and now no verdict may determine any question of civil or criminal liability. Furthermore, no person may be obliged to answer a question that might incriminate him or herself, and anyone who has not been called to give evidence but whose conduct is likely to be called into question must be given notice of the inquest.

However, subject to these limited protections, where a patient has died following contact with health care services, questions may be asked of the staff concerned, and any necessary inferences may be drawn.

The verdict

At the conclusion of an inquest, the Coroner or jury must state, among other things, how the deceased came by his or her death. Although they are neither compulsory nor exhaustive, several possible 'verdicts' are commonly used. Where a person has died following self-harm, the most relevant are:

- dependence on drugs
- non-dependent abuse of drugs
- suicide
- accident/misadventure
- open verdict
- unlawful killing.

In fact, the most likely verdict in the case of a patient who has died following attempted self-harm is 'accident' (or 'misadventure'). For a verdict of 'unlawful killing' to be justified, the form of assisted self-harm will have to have been so coercive as to have exceeded all but the most intensive of the interventions set out in Box 10.1.

To the first two forms of verdict a Coroner or jury may add that death was 'aggravated' by a lack of care. However, it may be that such a qualification is now available in a wider range of circumstances.

'Neglect' as a verdict

The 'lack of care' qualification is now more often expressed as 'neglect'. At one time, neither a Coroner nor a jury could make such a qualification in respect of a primary verdict of 'suicide', and there was no prospect that 'neglect' could amount to a verdict in its own right. That position has changed.

The Court of Appeal has held that, in order to comply with their obligation to act compatibly with the European Convention on Human Rights, Coroners might have to return a free-standing verdict of 'neglect', especially where the circumstances of the death were suggestive of 'system neglect'.

On the basis of previous decisions, it would seem that a finding of 'neglect', whether as a primary verdict or merely a qualification, may be appropriate in a number of circumstances:

- There has been a gross failure to provide basic medical attention for someone who, because of age or illness, is unable to provide it for him/herself.

- This is so where it is the person's adverse *mental* condition that calls out for medical attention.

- There must be a clear causal connection between the neglect and the cause of death.

- The neglect must consist of a distinct act or omission.

It is possible that, where a patient has died following attempted self-harm, the failure of health care professionals to adopt a sufficiently robust response will be held to constitute 'neglect'.

Civil claims

Increasing claims; increasing damages

The cost of clinical negligence claims, in particular, is rising at a considerable rate:

- As at 31 March 2002, the aggregate value of clinical negligence claims made against or awaited by the NHS was £5311 m.

- Total world-wide clinical negligence compensation has risen by 200,000% since 1952.

- The average compensation award against a general practitioner rose from £30,000 in 1993 to £70,000 in 2002; and against a private hospital doctor, from £40,000 to £72,000.

- In 1991, the bill for claims against the NHS was £85m; by 1999/2000, it had risen to £375m.

So, if there hasn't so far been a significant legal case about assisted self-harm, that probably means nothing more than that the practice isn't yet widespread.

Any civil claim resulting from an act of self-harm may be made by:

- the patient him or herself. The largest claims often come from patients who attempted to commit suicide but survived. This is because in some cases their injuries are so great that they now require extensive care.

- if the patient has died, by his/her estate for any pain and suffering he or she endured immediately before death, and for any expenses incurred as a result.

- by relatives whom the deceased was supporting at the time.

Against what legal criteria will any claim be judged?

The test for negligence

Whether medical treatment was negligent – and whether, therefore, damages may be payable – will depend first of all upon the so-called 'Bolam test'. This states that a particular clinical intervention will be lawful where it is consistent with 'a standard of practice accepted as proper by a responsible body of medical opinion skilled in that art' (Bolam v Friern Hospital Management Committee 1957).

Assisted self-harm in theory

Because the practice of assisted self-harm is still far from established, its exponents should expect, in any legal proceedings in which they become embroiled, to have to justify its very existence. This is not usual in a clinical context: for example, a surgeon who is alleged to have performed a sterilisation procedure negligently probably won't have to defend the procedure per se.

The Bolam test

It is likely that most forms of intervention by which a patient might be assisted to self-harm are 'accepted as proper' by someone. Therefore, the most significant question will be whether those who accept them can be said to constitute 'a responsible body of medical men [sic] skilled in' the psychiatric art (Bolam v Friern Hospital Management Committee 1957).

Many forms of assisted self-harm have their devotees. However, in terms of the *Bolam* test, a small group of adherents will not constitute a 'responsible body of medical men', no matter how fervently their views are held. If it were otherwise, almost any medical practice advocated by one or two zealots would be defensible in law, even though the vast majority of doctors roundly condemned it. Therefore, the House of Lords has held that, if it is to provide the benchmark against which an allegation of negligence is to be tested, a medical intervention must be capable of withstanding logical analysis.

When deciding whether the *Bolam* test is met, any court will wish to hear the views of the proponents and opponents of assisted self-harm, and it might also wish to consider any documentary guidance that there might be.

The Code of Practice (and other guidance)

The MHA 1983 is silent on the subject of assisted self-harm. However, its Code of Practice is rather more forthcoming on the subject. The Code acknowledges that '[t]he [1983 Mental Health] Act does not impose a legal duty to comply with the Code but as it is a statutory document, failure to follow it could be referred to in evidence in legal proceedings' (Department of Health (DoH) and Welsh Office 1999, p.1). Furthermore, the Court of Appeal has recently confirmed that hospitals should observe the Code of Practice unless they have a 'good reason' for departing from it.

The Code of Practice has something very clear to say about what it calls 'patients at risk of self-injury': 'Patients *must be protected from harming themselves* when the drive to self-injury is a result of mental disorder for which they are receiving care and treatment' (DoH and Welsh Office 1999, para 18.30). This sentence could be read – and it is probably intended to be read – as requiring that patients be protected from harming themselves *at all*. If so, since, by definition, it results in harm of some description, any form of assisted self-harm probably breaches the Code of Practice. Those holding a contrary view might argue that patients who are assisted to harm themselves are actually protected from even greater harm. while that may be true, it is also incontestably the case that patients who harm themselves have not been 'protected' from doing so.

It might be argued that this passage of the Code is relatively unsophisticated by current standards, and that if it were being rewritten today it would have to acknowledge more subtle gradations of practice. However, that argument is unattractive, for, although it was first published in 1983, the Code of Practice was last revised only in 1999, and the passage in question was introduced at that time.

In fact, it is instructive to compare this passage in the current Code of Practice with what preceded it. The comparable passage in the last edition, which was published in August 1993, is entitled 'Observation and care of patients at risk of self injury', and it states: 'Patients *may reasonably expect* that they will be protected from harming themselves when the drive to self injury is a result of mental disorder for which they are receiving care and treatment' (DoH and Welsh Office 1999, para 18.30). It is clear, therefore, that patients who in 1993 'may reasonably expect that they will be protected from harm' now 'must be protected from harming themselves', and it would seem that the later passage imposes a more explicit and more onerous obligation.

It is unlikely that a court called upon to reach a view about assisted self-harm would confine itself to the Code of Practice, and it would probably wish to range as widely as possible and to consider everything that has been said about the practice. The most recent contribution to the debate came from the National Institute for Clinical Excellence (NICE). Its draft guidelines, which were published in November 2003, state:

> Where service users are likely to repeat self-injury, clinical staff, service users and carers may wish to discuss harm minimisation issues/techniques. Suitable material is available from many voluntary organisations;

> Where service users are likely to repeat self-injury, clinical staff, service users and carers may wish to discuss appropriate alternative coping strategies. Suitable material is available from many voluntary organisations.

> (NICE 2003, para 7.12.6.8–9)

Although a court might wish to consider these draft guidelines, or any substantive guidelines that follow them, it will surely notice that they:

- extend no further than the 'discussion' of the appropriate techniques and strategies

- do not impose a positive obligation to discuss those techniques and strategies

- only embrace '*appropriate* alternative coping strategies' (which rather begs the question).

It might be argued that at the very least, the NICE draft guidelines help to establish that the discussion of assisted self-harm is no longer unconscionable. However, the suggestion that 'suitable material is available from many voluntary organisations' is imprecise at best, and it may be downright dangerous. It does not distinguish between material advocating practices that would pass the *Bolam* test and material advocating practices that almost certainly would not pass that test. It is inaccurate to imply that a clinical practice may be appropriate simply because it finds favour with a particular voluntary organisation. If that practice is to be lawful, it will have to be consistent with a practice accepted as proper by a responsible body of relevant medical opinion. That is a far more rigorous test and, from the perspective of the civil court, it is likely to be the only one that matters.

Forging a consensus

On the basis of the MHA Code of Practice, it is likely that the practice of assisted self-harm would be ruled unlawful in the abstract. Furthermore, it is unlikely that the recent NICE draft guidelines will be of substantive value in this regard, either to practitioners or to a court. Therefore, if a particular intervention is to fulfil the *Bolam* test, those who advocate it should attempt to have it accepted as proper by a 'responsible body of medical men [*sic*]' skilled in psychiatry.

However, it is by no means certain that consensus must precede practice, for the President of the High Court's Family Division, Dame Elizabeth Butler-Sloss, has said that the *Bolam* test ought not to be allowed to inhibit medical progress. And it is clear that if one waited for the *Bolam* test to be complied with to its fullest extent, no innovative work such as the use of penicillin or performing heart transplant surgery would ever be attempted.

Practitioners who wish to change perceptions of assisted self-harm and who find the strictures of the Code of Practice unacceptable, may find it helpful to say so often and prominently. They might also foster discussion as to whether particular forms of assisted self-harm fulfil the *Bolam* test, or as to how they might be made to do so.

Assisted self-harm in practice – breach of duty

Even if it could be shown that a particular method of assisting patients to harm themselves fulfilled the *Bolam* test in the abstract, it would still be necessary for professionals to defend its application in particular circumstances.

It might be said, for example, that it was inappropriate to assist a patient to self-harm because he or she hadn't previously done so and was unlikely to do so in future. (It may be significant that the recent NICE draft guidelines envisage that the relevant techniques or strategies may be discussed 'where service users are likely to repeat self-injury'. This implies that at the point of discussion self-injury will already have occurred.) In considering this suggestion, the court would be operating at a less exalted level, and would probably wish to focus on such matters as the detail of the clinical history that was taken and the quality of the risk assessment that was performed. It might ask:

- How thoroughly was the patient's psychiatric background – and, in particular, any history of self-harming behaviour – researched, and how thoroughly understood?

- How carefully were the patient's needs considered and how closely did they match the form of assisted self-harm chosen?

- How adroitly was the patient assisted to self-harm?

It is possible that a form of assisted self-harm that passed the *Bolam* test and was considered lawful in the abstract would be held to have been negligent in its application to a particular patient.

Protocols

For the reasons set out above, it might assist those who wish to operate in this area – and those who might subsequently have to defend them – if there were protocols governing the appropriateness and practice of assisted self-harm. There are many questions that such protocols might address:

- Is it appropriate for a patient presenting a particular kind of risk to be encouraged to self-harm?

- Are there some kinds of risk that should never be addressed in this way?

- If patients are to be assisted to harm themselves, how extensive should such assistance be?

- Are there some forms of assistance that may be appropriate in one circumstance but not in another?

These issues are relevant to the question of civil *liability*; in other words, whether it is negligent according to *Bolam* to assist a patient to self-harm, either at all or in the light of that patient's particular presentation.

The other element in any civil claim is *causation*: in order to succeed, the patient-claimant will have to show, not only that the defendant was negligent to assist him or her to self-harm, but that that negligent assistance actually caused harm.

Assisted self-harm in practice – causation

Defendants facing a claim of clinical negligence in respect of a patient who has come to grief during an episode of self-harm will not be able to deny that harm, nor to suggest that it is not a result of their intervention. They will simply have to argue that the harm in question was less severe than the claimant would have sustained if there been no such intervention.

However, this approach requires the defendant to prove a negative: that but for the intervention, the patient would have been more seriously injured. That is likely to be an extremely difficult task, because:

- there is no guarantee that the patient would have chosen to harm her or himself at that time in any event; and

- there may be no pattern to previous self-harm attempts, and therefore no way of predicting what form the attempt that was forestalled would have taken.

This suggests that it will be safest to practise assisted self-harm with patients who have tried to harm themselves before, and who have done so in a fairly consistent way and to a fairly consistent degree.

However, on balance, it is likely that the practice of assisting psychiatric patients to self-harm would be held to be negligent *per se*; and even if it were not, its application in particular circumstances would be susceptible to challenge in the civil courts.

Of course, the *Bolam* test is not confined to the *positive* acts of health care professionals: if the practice of assisted self-harm were to become 'accepted as proper' the *failure* to indulge in it might be equally likely to result in a legal challenge.

Criminal offences

Unless it is done publicly – in a way that is likely, for example, to cause a breach of the peace – it is not a criminal matter to cut or otherwise harm oneself.

Assault and battery

However, it might be regarded as an assault or a battery for a clinician to assist a patient to self-harm. This would certainly be so if it were the clinician him or herself who wielded the knife. At least as far as the more serious charge of '*assault* occasioning actual bodily harm' is concerned, the 'consent' of a patient would be irrelevant (even if he or she were fully capable). It might also be so where, although it was the patient that applied the knife, the clinician had been particularly adamant that he or she do so. It is even possible that a particularly assertive form of assisted self-harm that had a particularly serious result would lead to prosecution for wounding or for the causing or inflicting of grievous bodily harm.

Suicide

There might also be difficulties where the patient died as a result of the self-harm with which he or she had been assisted. Although suicide is no longer a crime offence, it *is* still an offence to 'aid, abet, counsel or procure' someone else's suicide – or, indeed, their attempted suicide – and upon conviction, it is punishable by a maximum of 14 years' imprisonment.

A practitioner may believe that he or she is merely assisting a patient to harm her or himself more safely, and death may be the result the practitioner desires least. Nevertheless, the patient may be of a different mind. A majority of all suicides are by people who have a history of self-harm (see Chapter).

Although, for the Suicide Act offence to be committed, the perpetrator must intend to 'aid, abet, counsel or procure' the suicide, it is not necessary that she or he actually intends to cause – or even desires – the patient's death. It is only necessary that she or he intends to provide the relevant assistance, and is 'reckless' as to whether the patient dies.

Where a patient who has been assisted to self-harm commits suicide by cutting, the relevant practitioner may have justified his or her intervention by the fact that the patient had a long history of self-harm and of suicidal ideation. However, that long history may make it more, not less, reckless to give the patient a blade. Paradoxically, this is precisely the sort of patient upon whom it would be safest from a civil law, clinical negligence perspective to practise assisted self-harm.

Manslaughter

A final, and possibly even more frightening, possibility has been created by a recent case. In *R* v *Stephen Rogers*, the defendant had applied a tourniquet so that a friend could inject himself with heroin. The friend collapsed with a heart attack and died eight days later. The defendant was convicted of manslaughter, but he appealed, claiming that it was not an offence either to apply a tourniquet or to inject oneself with heroin, and that it was his friend's act and not his own that had led to death. The Court of Appeal did not agree. Lord Justice Rose said:

> It is artificial and unreal to separate the tourniquet from the injection. The purpose and effect of the tourniquet, plainly, was to raise a vein in which the deceased could insert the syringe. Accordingly, by applying and holding the tourniquet, the appellant was playing a part in the mechanics of the injection which caused death. It is therefore, as it seems to us, immaterial whether the deceased was committing a criminal offence.

Upon conviction for manslaughter, Mr Rogers was sentenced to three years' imprisonment, and the Court of Appeal upheld that sentence.

Some of the lessons of this case are:

- Someone who participates in the process that leads to death may be guilty of manslaughter.

- This is so, even though the act that precipitates death isn't itself a criminal offence.

- Although death has to be the result of the process, there is no requirement that it resulted directly from the defendant's own act.

Most forms of assisting self-harm will be far removed from the circumstances of this unfortunate case. However, some – the more direct forms – may be broadly analogous. Where a health care practitioner indulges in one of those forms with a patient who then dies, it is neither fanciful nor alarmist to suggest that the practitioner might be charged with manslaughter.

Comment

There seems to be uncertainty, not only as to the number of people who practise self-harm, but also as to how many people assist them and how far that assistance extends. This is a dangerous state of affairs, and one that NHS Trusts should take steps to address.

It is ironic, and one of several paradoxes bedevilling the practice of assisting self-harm, that every attempt to devise or even discuss an appropriate level of care runs the risk of elevating that level. Nevertheless, for their own protection, practitioners should not be discouraged from bringing the practice out into the light.

Box 10.2: Some conclusions on assisted self-harm

- Assisted self-harm is likely to constitute 'medical treatment'.

- However, because it will prove difficult to practise without a patient's capable consent, it is unlikely to engage MHA 1983.

- When a patient dies after self-harm, any practitioner who assisted him/her may be required to give evidence at an inquest and may even face a charge of manslaughter.

- NHS practitioners and the Trusts that employ them should ensure that a particular form of assisted self-harm satisfies the *Bolam* test, and that no form is practised that does not.

- Detailed protocols should be developed to guide staff and protect Trusts against the consequences of controversial or ill-considered interventions.

- Any such protocols should be the product of wide consultation, among those who practise similar interventions and those who do not.

- The wider the consultation and the greater the consensus it achieves, the more likely it is that the practice would be held to be accepted as proper by a responsible body of clinicians.

Given the present state of knowledge about the nature and degree of assisted self-harm, any guidance that can be offered at this stage is likely to be somewhat rudimentary and somewhat qualified. However, those involved should not be discouraged from seeking to promote acceptance of – and lawful authority *for* – the practice, for it is only by so doing that they will protect themselves, as well as their clients, from the more unfortunate consequences of assisted self-harm.

References

Appleby, L., Shaw, J., Amos, T., McDonnell, R., Bickley, H., Kiernan, K., Davies, S., Harris, C., McCann, K. and Parsons, R. (1999) *Safer Services: Report of the National Confidential Inquiry into Suicide and Homicide by People with Mental Illness.* London: Stationery Office.

Department of Health and Welsh Office (1999) *Mental Health Act 1983 Code of Practice.* London: Department of Health.

NHS Litigation Authority (2001) *Report and Accounts 2001.* www.nhsla.com

National Institute for Clinical Excellence (2003) *Self-Harm: Short-term Physical and Psychological Management and Secondary Prevention of Intentional Self-harm in Primary and Secondary Care.* London: NICE. www.nice.org.uk

Legislation – Primary

Coroners Act [1887] Chapter 71

Coroners (Amendment) Act [1926] Chapter 59

Coroners Act [1988] Chapter 13

Criminal Law Act [1977] Chapter 44

Fatal Accidents Act [1976] Chapter 30

Human Rights Act [1998] Chapter 42

Law Reform (Miscellaneous Provisions) Act [1934] Chapter 41

Mental Health Act [1983] Chapter 20

Offences Against the Person Act [1861] Chapter 100

Suicide Act [1961] Chapter 60

Legislation – Secondary

Coroners Rules [1984] SI 1984 No 552

Mental Health (Hospital, Guardianship and Consent to Treatment) Regulations [1983] SI 1983 No 893

Relevant Cases

Bolam v Friern Hospital Management Committee [1957] 1 WLR 582

Bolitho v City and Hackney Health Authority [1997] 3 WLR 1151

Dianne Pretty v United Kingdom [2002] 35 EHRR 1

Donald Simms v Jonathan Simms and A NHS Trust; PA v JA and A NHS Trust [2002] EWHC 2734 (Fam)

F v West Berkshire Health Authority and another (Mental Health Act Commission intervening) [1989] 2 All ER 545

Laskey, Jaggard and Brown v United Kingdom, European Court of Human Rights, 17 February 1997, 109/1995/615/703–705

Minister of Health v Royal Midland Counties Home for Incurables at Leamington Spa [1954] Ch 530

Reid v Secretary of State for Scotland [1999] 2 WLR 28

R v Ashworth Hospital Authority, ex parte Munjaz [2002] Administrative Court, 5 July 2002

R v Attorney General for Northern Ireland, ex parte Devine [1992] 1 WLR 262, HL

R v Birmingham Coroner, ex parte Home Secretary [1990] 155 JP 107, DC

R v Brown [1993] 2 All ER 75, CA

R v Director of Public Prosecutions, ex parte Dianne Pretty and Secretary of State for the Home Department [2001] UKHL 61, [2001] 3 WLR 1598

R v Dr M and others, ex parte N [2003] 1 WLR 562

R v Fernando Augusto Megalhaes Dias [2001] EWCA Crim 2986

R v HM Coroner for West Somersetshire, ex parte Jean Middleton; R v Secretary of State for the Home Department and HM Coroner of West London, ex parte Imtiaz Amin [2002] 3 WLR 505

R v Kennedy [1999] Crim LR 65

R v North Humberside Coroner, ex parte Jamieson [1995] 1 WLR 31

R v Poplar Coroner's Court, ex parte Thomas [1993] 2 WLR 547

R v Stephen Rogers [2003] EWCA Crim 945

R v South London Coroner, ex parte Thompson [1982] 126 SJ 625, DC

R v Southwark Coroner's Court, ex parte Kendall [1988] 1 WLR 1186, DC

Sacker v HM Coroner for the County of West Yorkshire [2003] 2 All ER 278

S v Airedale NHS Trust [2003] Lloyd's Rep Med 21

Chapter 11

'Shouting at the Spaceman' – A Conversation about Self-harm

Clare Shaw and Christine Hogg

Working therapeutically and effectively with people who engage in self-destructive behaviours is perhaps one of the most complex and challenging issues in mental health care. Maintaining a sense of hope and optimism while dealing with self-destructive injuries may leave the carer with a sense of overwhelming helplessness and despair. In this chapter we attempt to explore some of these complex and challenging issues and to provide some light into the experience of someone who has used self-harm as a way of coping with distress. The chapter is a dialogue between Clare, who has used mental health services, and Christine, who has worked as a mental health nurse.

Clare: I was 20 when I first came into contact with the psychiatric services. I was a high achieving academic star who had suddenly gone off the rails and taken an overdose. In some ways it was a big relief to be given a diagnosis and having an illness that can be cured with tablets and whatever. But it was so opposite to what I imagined! The ward was just unbelievably chaotic and terrifying.

Christine: Why did they keep you in – for taking an overdose?

Clare: Yes. Looking back I couldn't tell you what their rationale was at all – I think it was automatic, overdose therefore psychiatric ward. I don't think there was any kind of thinking through of 'What can we do for this person?' or 'What help could we get in this setting?' because there was nothing offered – it was just a case of 'You get transferred to this ward' because there was obviously a mad thing going on.

Christine: What was happening to make you take the overdose?

Clare: Well, I think it was a mounting combination of circumstances and there was an awful lot of traumatic baggage I was carrying from my childhood that had never been looked at, never been supported appropriately. I was living a life which was completely inappropriate to where I was at. I just couldn't cope any more with that, but I couldn't see anyway of changing it. I just couldn't see a way out of it. So I wasn't trying to kill myself, it wasn't an act of suicide, I knew I wasn't going to die. It was an act of 'Oh for God's sake, something has to change somehow'.

Christine: Did anyone realise how desperate you were?

Clare: I think something that is perceived as suicide does probably get that across quite effectively, doesn't it! At that point, self-injury wasn't something that anybody was aware that I had been doing before. So, it was like this and everything's taken seriously. But I kind of speculate that maybe they hoped that this was a temporary blip and with the right medication it would be sorted within months. I don't think that anybody at that point predicted how long and how severe it was going to be. I wouldn't have been thinking that five years later I would still be in psychiatric wards.

Christine: So really, the overdose you took was almost like a catalyst for change?

Clare: Yes, but the first couple of nights in there was a dramatic rewriting of all of my expectations of what I was going to get from that service. I would have liked to have been in a kind of safe and friendly space. But the psychiatric ward wasn't safe or friendly. I think to have had somebody to have said in a calm and safe way 'What is going on for you? What is this about?' and help me to look at it. Just something as basic and obvious as that, rather than to say 'You have clinical depression.' Well, it was catastrophic really, suddenly you're in this space that's just about the opposite of any space that you would expect or want to be in and it is so completely outside of everything that I had ever experienced. It was like a complete rupture.

Christine: In some ways would you say it made things worse for you, I wonder if it compounded your distress?

Clare: Completely. I think in lots of different ways. Being put into a place that's completely depressing and frightening, it's going to make you feel worse. Going into psychiatric hospital and realising 'Actually what I'm going to get here is pretty useless' is a bit like ringing the police when you've got a burglar in the house and realising they're not going to come out to you. So it was a really hopeless, despairing feeling. This help I assumed was there is actually not there, you know, or exists in a form that is just not going to be any use to me.

Christine: So what happened next?

Clare: The beginning of this cycle of 'in and out of hospital'. I started to self-injure very, very badly at that point.

Christine: Was there a difference in the self-injuring and the overdosing?

Clare: They definitely serve different functions in different ways. Most of my overdoses weren't about trying to die. I actually had a sort of a knowledge of what I could take and what wasn't going to kill me, but make me look like it was, that sort of game. Cutting is generally something I did a lot more just for me. It was generally just about getting through a crisis, and it wasn't necessarily about ending up in hospital or making any contact with the services or even telling anybody about it. Whereas overdose tended to be where self-injuring and all the other ways I had of harming myself weren't working, and it was like 'This is really, really bad. I really don't know what else to do, I don't want to die but if I take an overdose it will take me out of this situation.'

Christine: So would you say the overdose is the next step up from the injury?

Clare: It was for me though I know it isn't for other people. I know people who overdose quite regularly. I know it's not safe. I never felt quite safe in what I was doing. But for me cutting was an everyday thing. And then I'd take an overdose when that wasn't working.

Christine: So overdosing is probably taken more seriously than cutting, because cutting is something you can do on your own at home and you can look after yourself?

Clare: A lot of people cut and never come into contact with services. But I also know someone who used to take a lot of small overdoses and never had any contact with services, so there again it is possible that somebody could be overdosing in that way. Minor is not a good word but it's a form of self-injury that isn't going to land them in hospital.

Christine: What sort of things were you using to overdose?

Clare: I kind of had enough knowledge to know paracetamol was a pretty terrible thing to use and if I used paracetamol I'd get help immediately. After I gradually learned enough about the effects of paracetamol, I thought 'I really don't want to be doing that' so I would use like aspirin and ibuprofen and Prozac. Prozac makes you feel really terrible, but it's probably not going to kill you. It does make you very ill. You feel awful. So it has this massive impact and you've got to be in hospital for a few days, but you're not going to die.

Christine: And you knew you weren't going to die?

Clare: Yes, but it has this effect of, you know, halting all the other problems for a few days and getting me a lot of attention, dare I say it, and taking me out of the situation that I was in, sort of announcing 'This is how distressed I am'. It did serve those functions – this feeling of just letting out bad feelings, tension and chaos, like somehow I could leak it out.

Christine: Did it help you actually feel any different?

Clare: Oh yes, otherwise I wouldn't have done it so much. Yes, it did work, and even now it's really tempting when I feel really bad – but I know there's something there that really does work, really effectively. It's really quite difficult not to use that and to go for other ways of coping that are not quite as effective.

Christine: Was overdosing the same then, did overdosing make you feel better?

Clare: Yes, in a very different way. I think overdosing was a lot more about changing circumstances whereas self-injury was a lot more about immediate relief from overwhelming feelings. Overdosing did have that element while you were swallowing the tablets that you are not as focused on the pain but definitely was more about trying to escape from or affect circumstances, whereas self-injury was about immediate relief from how I was feeling. I had a couple of experiences of waking up the next day after overdosing and everything feeling quite new. It was almost like pronouncing this was a fresh start. I have spoken to other people who have had that and who have actually taken overdoses again as a way of seeking that experience, it's a bit like taking an overdose and 'Tomorrow's a fresh start, I'll try all over again'.

Christine: Can I ask you about cutting? Have you ever put your life in danger from cutting?

Clare: I have a couple of times. I once needed surgery through nerve and arterial damage. Generally I think that was through ignorance. I just wasn't aware of where things like nerves and arteries were, which for me brings us to this issue about informing people where it's safe to cut and where it's not safe to cut. It's very important because I didn't actually mean to cause artery damage. The time when I really, really did some terrible damage to myself, I was on the psychiatric ward of the General Hospital and I found a razor and it was just like 'Quick! While I can!' I remember being squashed in this little space in between a bed and a wall and just going for it as quickly as I could before anyone found me. But I didn't know how sharp the blade was because it wasn't mine. So this really was out of control, largely because of the circumstances. I couldn't take my time like I used to do at home when there was control about it – and that's when I did really major damage to myself. Actually, every time that I did major damage to myself was while I was in hospital because I was doing it as hurriedly as I could, before they found me. At home I had sort of a ritual, I was relatively safe around what I was doing. I didn't want to cause damage. I tended to cut very slowly and gradually. I was really in control of the amount of damage. In the psychiatric ward the main thing was about the system. I'm not allowed to do it, so how do I get round that? There was me and countless other people on the ward engaged in this game which was 'we were going to do it no matter what'.

Christine: As a nurse, I've been in that situation. It's like a cat and mouse game! But there is an expectation for nurses that they have this duty of care, almost a protection role. What's your perception on that, when they've got a duty of care?

Clare: I have quite a complicated view on that. I think there are all sorts of different ways of understanding care. When you kind of look at my experience I think actually hospital for me did me more harm than good. I self-injured much more severely and dangerously in hospital than out of hospital. So was that care? I'm crossing over here a bit to suicide rather than self-injury, but the person who was most helpful for me when I was suicidal was someone who was themselves quite depressed and sometimes suicidal. She was the person I had the greatest connection with because she was able to sort of speak my language. I was concerned about her, I didn't want her to die, that would have been awful. And she was caring for me because she didn't want me to kill myself. And it wasn't this sort of 'Oh my God' stop this at all costs, she was able to use the same points of reference as me and to understand how I was experiencing the world at that time. I also remember a nurse who was really helpful. She was like the kind of nurse who liked hanging round with the really difficult patients and I kind of fell into that category after a bit. She had a very human response that wasn't actually particularly getting into anything very deep but you were really clear she would be very upset if you died, or really didn't want you to be doing great big damage to yourself. From her I did get a sense of acceptance of 'Alright, so this is where you're at.' It was a level of trust that 'Somehow you're going to find your way and do the right thing for yourself and I'm just going to hang around and be friendly and have a laugh with you.' So it was important for me to have a sense that actually people do care that I'm so distressed that I'd cut myself or think about ending my life. That's really important I think, to be like that.

Christine: Yes, I can understand that. I've heard a lot of how people in this situation feel a great sense of isolation? I've always thought that if you feel isolated, then you might think it doesn't matter whether I live or die?

Clare: Actually, I've read accounts of suicide and people talking about this suicidal trance they go into. And it makes loads of sense to me. For short periods when I was really suicidal it did feel quite trance-like in the sense that I felt really, really disconnected from everything; from people, from life in general. So I think what was really key for me was that there was somebody who could get through that disconnection. To set up a sense of connection again, which is where I think being able to talk the same language is really, really important in giving somebody a connection with other human beings and life in general.

Christine: Is it almost like bringing somebody back into the world?

Clare: Absolutely. I have a really clear visual image of it. I was like a spaceman who was out there floating out in space, not on the earth, but looking down on everyone! That's how I felt and really it was only by somebody floating out into space that they could bring me back. You know, people would be like standing on the surface of the earth shouting 'Come back, come back!' It was no good, somebody had to come out and get into the same space. You've kind of got to get into that frame of experience to be able to talk or make a connection.

Christine: How long did it take you to recover?

Clare: I think it was forever! Everything is just a process really and I don't think there is a point at which you could go 'Oh, everything is fine I am cured.' About four or five years ago I was at the point where I was very determinedly suicidal for a few months and then I actually came out of it and began to change. Before that I just remember a great period of being in and out of hospital self-injuring and trying to get things that were not gettable and trying to change things in a way that wasn't going to change. I remember this as a painful period, and then reaching this point where it became unbearable. That's the point where it was like 'I do want to kill myself.' It was having that sense of connection during that period that allowed me to come back. I'm not that convinced I would have come back without that connection. I don't know about that, but I think that allowed me to continue living and that's the point at which I began to make some really big changes in my life and they were absolutely key to coming back from that brink.

Christine: So it's almost like you have to go to the brink?

Clare: It felt that way, and a lot of people I've talked to, other people who have self-injured, people who have been suicidal – a lot of people have said they have had to hit bottom before they can kick back up again. One friend I'm thinking of took an overdose and that was her lowest point, it was the point where everything changed for her. Whereas for other people they were taking five overdoses a week, and that wasn't their lowest point. They had to go through other experiences before they came to the point where everything is going to change.

Christine: Five overdoses a week sounds like a lot?!

Clare: Absolutely, yes, like you say that's what people look at and think this must be a suicide attempt, people can't be taking overdoses just as a way of getting through the day surely, that doesn't make sense. But people do!

Christine: Clare, what's your opinion about showing people how to self-injure safely?

Clare: I'm in favour. When I was self-injuring badly, I thought I had only four arteries. I didn't realise you had them all over! So I really didn't know what I was doing. People have this big reaction, you shouldn't tell people where the arteries are because they'll just go and cut them. The vast majority of people won't. There are people who are self-injuring and doing it in safe controlled ways. Loads never have any contact with services, you know, it would really be a tiny minority who would use that information to kill themselves or to do great damage. And to me that's better than more people killing or damaging themselves badly because they don't know how to do it safely.

Christine: What would you say then if you came across someone who had taken paracetamol, say 8 to 12, would you say that that person is suicidal or not?

Clare: I don't think you should ever make assumptions, not on the basis of what somebody has done. I mean, being part of STEPS [a self-help group for people who self-injure] where you have loads and loads of different women coming into the group who were self-injuring in different ways, you could just never make assumptions about anything. Somebody could say 'I've eaten six paracetamol' and they really intended to die, but somebody else could be dangling from a noose and it's just their way of self-injury and they don't intend to die. You can't make that assumption.

Christine: But if you're dangling from a noose though, people might pull out all the stops and say 'Oh my God, she's serious!' But what you are saying is, they might be really worried about something, but they might not really be trying to kill themselves. So although it looks serious it might not be?

Clare: Well, they are serious, aren't they? They're serious about being distressed. But the ways that people self-harm are also connected to the circumstances they are in. I've come across people using ligatures in prisons. That's where they don't have access to many other ways of self-injury, so it's maybe not that you would freely choose to hang yourself from a noose and nearly pass out as your chosen way of self-injuring, it's just it's the only one that's available at the time. No, you can't ever make assumptions. I think the only assumption you can make is someone is distressed and needs help, but you can't assume in what form or that they want *your* help, just that they might need a bit of support from somewhere.

Christine: Another issue I'd like to explore with you, one you often hear staff saying, that it's not distress at all, that's it's just learnt behaviour?

Clare: What I think it is that people come to hospital and places like that because they are distressed. So it's obviously about distress. Maybe self-injury is then presented as a coping strategy, because you see that other people use it as a coping strategy. Maybe you learn this coping strategy as a way of coping in your own internal world, and, as well as that, coping with the external world of the ward. So maybe in one sense it is a learnt behaviour, in the sense that you learn the possibility of coping with distress through self-injury. But it's not learnt behaviour in the patronising way that people often mean it, like 'You haven't got anything better to do with your time!'

Christine: What about contagion? Which is another explanation given: 'It's not serious, just contagious.'

Clare: Yes, like in institutions or whatever, one person self-injures and you see other people self-injure afterwards. So it may seem to be contagious. But really you should be asking questions about it. I think you should approach it as a coping strategy, it gives you a lot more insight into the situation. Maybe then you would start asking questions about the kind of environment that you put people in.

Christine: So it's related to the environment that people are in?

Clare: Yes. I've never understood the whole sort of psychiatric set up of putting distressed and anxious people into a ward full of distressed and anxious people. It just doesn't seem right! You know, imagine if you yourself are feeling down or anxious, saying 'Oh well, I will just put myself in a situation where I'm completely surrounded by incredibly distressed and anxious people!' Of course you wouldn't do it – it's completely counter-intuitive. It makes you feel worse. I have often thought there is no logic to it!

Clare: What are your feelings about it, Christine? How do you approach somebody who has self-injured?

Christine: It was only when I came out of nursing on wards that I got an understanding of it properly. If I were to go back in that situation now, I think I would see and do things very differently.

Clare: In what way?

Christine: Well, for example, I had been working with somebody, a young girl, I thought I got on really well with, and then she went and cut herself on the ward. I felt really despondent. I felt like the work I'd done was for nothing or that she had let me down really by doing it.

Clare: She'd let you down?

Christine: Yes, because as a nurse you want to help people and you want to help them get better and move on, and not do things like this.

Clare: So the fact she'd gone and cut herself then meant something was wrong that should have been fixed?

Christine: Or that she didn't need to cut herself, she could have come and talked to me. And I thought I got on well with her and I did actually get on well with her. Looking back I realise it's nothing about me, the act is not about me, it's about her. But trying to disconnect yourself from that is very difficult and I remember at the time thinking, 'Have I caused this? Am I not good enough? Could I have done something more, so she wouldn't have had to do this? What can I do so it won't happen again?' And there's all that anxiety that someone might point the finger of blame at you!

Clare: Really?

Christine: Oh yes, and that you have failed in your duty of care. That's how it feels, and that this has happened because you weren't doing your job properly. You know, it's your job to look after people in your care, to protect them? So really you have failed to do a good job. It can be very stressful. I was on a ward one day and I took a young woman to casualty three times in one shift. Can you imagine? Looking back it was 'Let's see how far can I push you before you'll reject me,' because that's what she'd been used to in the past.

Clare: How was she? Where would she get the stuff to cut herself?

Christine: Well, you let her go to the toilet on her own, because you would give some leeway, a bit of dignity. So she would go into the bathrooms and take bits of plastic off the door. Anything she could get her hands on! I remember she got a plastic cup and smashed it up really quickly in her room and cut herself really badly.

Clare: That's quite a key point, isn't it – no matter how much you do someone can still self-injure.

Christine: But you had this feeling really that it was escalating. And some days she used to say she could see spiders everywhere. So I always had this unease that she would go off and really damage herself so badly that she could end up in a wheelchair really or something like that. But I think looking back we helped her to get to that state. We were all part of her problem.

Clare: Again, that's really key isn't it, because sometimes we are presented with this kind of scenario and people ask 'Well, what would *you* do here?' It's really hard because you want to unpick it, to ask 'Well, how did it get to this point where you are so locked in this game that neither of you can get out of it?'

Christine: But you don't, at the time, you don't see it and think. We were so preoccupied with formulating new care plans and looking for the 'magic key' to cure her problems that we lost sight of what was therapeutic. Or even the possibility that we had somehow contributed to her distress!

Clare: When I look at the period I had when I was suicidal, I'm glad that the services were there to stop me from killing myself at that point. But when I look at the preceding six years of spending so much time in these horrible, chaotic, depressing places, being told that I was crazy, and this gradual losing of hope, people saying you're mentally ill and we can cure you with tablets and realising that actually this is not happening – there was this setting in of great despair and all the other shit that goes with being a mental patient. When you're talking about that level of confusion you can then see how appealing medication is and why it is so over-used really. You can predict that 'this type of pill, it will have this effect'. Whereas just listening to this person and giving them support and space – how can you predict what's going to happen then, how can you measure it? Yet it's so important. I'm back to beating the same drum. Listen to people. That really is the key. Forget all your fancy theories and just come back to listening. If you are allowed, or helped, to be able to articulate what's going on for you and articulate how you feel, if you can talk about what it's like, then that's half the battle to me. There is a key in there somewhere. One of the ironies of the vicious circles is the reason I wanted to self-injure was that I didn't feel I had a right to communicate my distress. So at a certain point self-injury became the way to say 'Look! This is how I'm experiencing things.' Yet it seemed like a lot of the service responses were about stopping me being able to say that and not offering me any other way of saying it.

Some months after this conversation Clare and Christine reflect on some of the issues that have been raised.

Clare: This chapter started out by acknowledging that the issue of how to work therapeutically with people who self-injure is one of the most challenging and complex in mental health care today. In some ways, our conversation confirms this. Effective care raises important questions at every level from emotional to ethical to institutional: from 'How do we deal with our own human responses of shock, anger and anxiety?' to 'How do we – and the institutions we work within – understand our duty of care with regard to self-injury?' Yet at the same time as illustrating the complexity of therapeutic work with self-injury, the chapter also gives a sense of its essential simplicity. Ultimately, we return to the profound value of communication. Beyond the shock and horror, the desire to listen and to respond. Beyond the procedural complexities, the ability to accept and to trust. Beyond the psychiatric and psychological theorizsing, to learn from the framework of understanding of the person who self-injures. And ultimately, that most basic necessity of human communication – to speak the same language. In my experience, everything follows from that.

Christine: I have been involved in researching and thinking about self-harm for about 10 years now but I think this is probably one of the most interesting discussions I have ever had. I was very interested in the issues around interchanging self-injury and overdosing and how in fact people manage to use both methods successfully without accessing services. This confirms my belief that there are large numbers of people who self-harm in society and who remain without any help or support. The conversation also reminded me of the difficulties and the futility of trying to manage and control self-injurious behaviour on in-patient settings. Like other health care professionals, I have spent many days and weeks in cat and mouse games trying to prevent people inflicting damage on their bodies through whatever means. This action only seems to compound people's distress and frustration and so ultimately we may be causing more harm than good and thus becoming part of the problem!

Chapter 12

Adolescents and Developmental Group Psychotherapy

Gemma Trainor

Introduction

This chapter will explore important aspects of both completed and attempted suicides in young people and consider a range of treatment options, focusing on development group psychotherapy. As background to a discussion of this and other innovative approaches to preventing suicide in adolescents it is useful to explore some common features and risk factors in young suicide completers and attempters. Some important features are given in Box 12.1.

Box 12.1: Features of adolescent suicide

- *Incidence:* Suicide in children and early adolescence is rare in all countries. In the UK the overall suicide rate is around 13 per 100,000 population, but 17 per 100,000 in adolescence.

- *Age:* In the mid-1980s, 20 per cent of suicides in the Western world were adolescents (Hill 1995) but very few children under 12 died by suicide.

- *Gender differences:* It has been observed that girls make suicide attempts as much as ten times as often as boys, but boys die by suicide two to three times as often as girls (Hawton, Zahl and Weatherall 2003).

- *Methods and lethality*: Gender differences may be due to the fact that young men are more likely to choose more 'active' methods such as hanging rather than 'passive' methods such as self-poisoning.

- *Secular trends*: Diekstra and Movitz (1987) observed that by the mid 1980s one fifth of suicides in the Western world were adolescents, compared with one ninth in the 1950s. In the UK, an increase in adolescent (age 15–19) female suicide rate has been noted over the period 1990–2000 (Office of National Statistics 2002) while adolescent male suicide rates did not change over this period. This is in contrast to trends in other age groups, where the suicide rate in both males and females has decreased by 15 per cent.

- *Imitation and contagion*: Many researchers have investigated the idea of suicide being contagious and there is a further suggestion that suicide clusters among 15–19-year-olds occur more frequently than would be expected by chance. The media ensures coverage of suicides and it is a popular script used by television and films. There have been many debates about the effect of such portrayals on young people.

Risk factors of completed suicide

Deliberate self-harm is recognised as the strongest risk factor for future suicide, but there is very limited data on the extent of the risk, particularly for younger people. A mortality follow-up study of over 11,000 patients who had presented to UK hospitals after an episode of deliberate self-harm between 1978 and 1997 included some information on the younger age group (10–24 years). For this group the risk of suicide ranged as follows:

- 0.3% 1 year after the DSH episode
- 0.7%, 5 years post episode
- 1.3%, 10 years post episode
- 1.8%, 15 years post episode,

the risk being between two and four times higher for males than females (Hawton *et al.* 2003).

While only a minority of teenage attempters go on to die by suicide, studies have demonstrated that the suicide rate among this group is much higher than that of adolescents in the general population (UK suicide rate is 13 per 100,000, i.e. around 0.01%), reaching over 11.3 per cent in male attempters in one study (Table 12.1). Shaffer (1974) stated that about half of all suicides have threatened or discussed suicide within 24 hours of their death and 50 per cent of female suicides and 25 per cent of males have made previous attempts.

Table 12.1: Analysis of suicide in treated suicide attempters

Study	No.	Treatment	Length of follow-up	Age range	Suicide rate
Males					
Otto 1972	321	In-patient	5	10–20	11.3%
Garfinkel, Froese and Mood 1982	124	In-patient	1–9	8–19	–
Goldacre and Hawton 1985	641	Out-patient	1–5	12–20	0.7%
Females					
Otto 1972	1226	In-patient	5	10–20	3.0%
Garfinkel, Froese and Mood 1982	381	In-patient	1–9	6–21	–
Goldacre and Hawton 1985	1851	Out-patient	1–5	12–20	0.1%

Adapted from Shaffer *et al.* 1988.

Other important risk factors are summarised in Box 12.2.

Box 12.2. Other risk factors

- *Life events*: One study suggests that many teenagers die by suicide in the context of disciplinary action, humiliation or rejection. (Shaffer and Gould 1987)

- *Birth history*: Neurological sequelae of obstetric morbidity, the effects of inadequate parenting or maternal psychopathology may be factors (Jacobson *et al.* 1987; Salk *et al.* 1985).

- *Family dysfunction*: Issues such as family conflict, history of family suicide, family violence and lack of parental skills, loss of a parent and lack of cohesion resulting in the young person feeling abandoned (Kerfoot *et al.* 1996; Shaffer and Gould 1987).

- *Psychiatric disorder*: Researchers have observed that in recent years more children, adolescents and young adults now suffer from serious mental health problems (Brent *et al.* 1997; Runeson 1989). Shaffi *et al.* (1985) noted that clinical psychiatric disorders were found in a high proportion of suicide cases.

Deliberate self-harm (DSH)

Attempted suicide among adolescents constitutes an important and increasing health problem. Deliberate self-poisoning is a frequent cause of hospital admission. Referrals to hospital because of deliberate self-poisoning are high for the adolescent age group. Indeed, rates of DSH are higher in the UK than in most parts of Europe (Hawton *et al.* 1999) and British child mental health professionals therefore spend much time in the aftercare of vulnerable adolescents (Kerfoot and Huxley 1995).

The Royal College of Psychiatrists guidelines advise that young people who deliberately harm themselves should always be taken seriously and assessed by a mental health professional afterwards (Royal College of Psychiatrists 1998).

Some features of deliberate self-harm are presented in Box 12.3.

Box 12.3: Features of deliberate self-harm

- *Prevalence*: Rates of DSH in the UK are among the highest in Europe (Schmidtke, Bille-Brahe and DeLeo 1996): there are approximately 100,000 general hospital admissions for attempted suicide each year in England and Wales; 19,000 of these involve teenagers, mostly girls (Hawton *et al.* 1996). Every hour in the UK, two young people self-harm (Samaritans 2003); according to parental information the highest rate of self-harm (3.1% of 10,000 schoolchildren studied) was found among 13–15-year-old girls (Meltzer *et al.* 2001); a survey of 6020 pupils aged 15 and 16 reported 398 acts of DSH in the previous year (6.6%), few of these 398 episodes (12.6%) resulted in a presentation to hospital.

- *Secular change:* Recent years have seen changes in the extent of estimated self-harm in the 15–19 age group, with estimated numbers falling from 24,000 in 1998 to 17,000 in 1999, but rising to 19,000 in 2000 (Samaritans 2003).

- *Age:* Most studies report that there are very few cases of DSH in children under 12 years of age, although it increases in frequency throughout the adolescent years.

- *Gender:* DSH is far more common among girls than boys, especially in younger adolescence. In a follow-up study over the period 1989–1995 of 1264 young people (aged 15–19) with episodes of DSH, the female to male gender ratio ranged between 2.0 and 3.1 (Hulten *et al.* 2001). A female:male ratio of over 3 was recorded in a questionnaire survey of 15–16 year olds (Hawton *et al.* 2002).

- *Ethnicity:* Research into the suicidal behaviour of ethnic groups is sparse and conflicting (see Chapter 9).

- *Methods and lethality:* In the EURO Multicentre Study of Suicide Behaviour (Hulten *et al.* 2001), repetition of DSH was more frequent in those who used 'hard' methods compared with those who used 'soft' methods (Odd Ratio = 1.51).

Outcomes in adolescents who self-harm

Three main outcomes of DSH in adolescents are:

- *Repetition of DSH:* Follow-up studies of adolescent suicide attempters have suggested that approximately 1 in 10 will make a further suicide attempt during the year after an attempt. Goldacre and Hawton (1985) studied repetition by 2492 self-poisoners aged 12–20 years in the Oxford area. Out of the number investigated 6.3 per cent repeated within one year of their first admission. Data from 149 UK children looking at which variables may predict repetition of self-harm, found that a history of previous attempts as well as parental mental ill health were the strongest predictors (Chitsabesan *et al.* 2003).

- *Adverse psychiatric and psychosocial outcomes*: In addition to repetition, suicide attempts have been associated with other outcomes, such as difficulties with social and psychological adjustment. The strongest risk factor for a repeat suicide attempt was the presence of a mood disorder. Pfeffer *et al.* (1993) found that repetition is often linked to episodes of depression and that suicidal ideators and attempters were more likely to have a variety of psychiatric disorders and poorer social adjustment. Kerfoot *et al.* (1996), on the other hand, observed that major depressive disorder often remits following acts of DSH.

- *Completed suicides*: It is notoriously difficult to predict effectively those young people who will go on to die by suicide. Follow-up studies in the past few decades have usually been between only 5 and 10 years in duration. Granboulan, Rabain and Basquin (1995) found that out of a sample of 265 hospitalised adolescents 15 had died within a follow-up period of 9 years.

Promising treatments of deliberate self-harm

This chapter has reviewed the epidemiology and risk factors of completed suicide and DSH among young people. There are important differences between the two phenomena, as well as some common features. Both problems are strongly associated with family dysfunction and with mental disorder.

What, then, are the implications of research findings on epidemiology and risk factors for prevention and treatment of attempted suicide and suicide among the young? The first implication is that DSH needs to be taken seriously. Young people who deliberately harm themselves are at increased risk of completed suicide, and conversely people who have completed suicide have often deliberately harmed themselves in the past. Second, it is possible to identify some groups who are at particularly high risk of suicide. These include male gender, increasing age, substance abuse and psychiatric disorder. Additionally, the sections above have highlighted some of the potential psychological mechanisms that could be targeted by treatment programmes. These include family problems, impulsivity, poor problem solving and depression.

These young people present greater concern because of the psychological co-morbidity and the increased risk of suicide. Knowledge regarding prevention is limited. There has been relatively little empirical work on the treatment of adolescent suicides. There remains considerable uncertainty about which forms of psychosocial and physical treatment are the most effective. Some of these difficulties and promising treatments will be explored below.

Individual treatment options

Treatment options include psychological interventions, behavioural techniques, medications targeted at co-existing mental health problems, family therapy and group psychotherapy. The mental state of the presenting young person can be complex and involve a host of environmental, interpersonal and internal difficulties. Although many different treatment strategies are used, less evidence is available on whether these are effective or not.

- *Individual therapy* with suicidal children and adolescents is often based on the principles of crisis intervention. Crisis or problem-solving therapy is likely to be brief, intensive and focus on current difficulties.

- *Cognitive behavioural interventions and problem-solving treatments* are increasingly becoming used with suicidal adolescents. However, most of the studies investigating effectiveness are of older adolescents and adults. There has been some evidence to suggest that cognitive behavioural therapies are effective in reducing suicidal behaviours (Salkovskis, Atha and Storer 1990).

- *Psychotherapeutic intervention* aims to explore feelings, thoughts and experiences. Role-play, play therapy and other creative therapies may be employed in order that the young person can use different mediums of communication. Linehan (1993) has written extensively on a treatment strategy referred to as dialectical behaviour therapy. Hawton *et al.* (1998) felt the randomised controlled trial of this treatment was promising but an evaluation of a shorter form of this treatment is needed.

- *Family therapy:* most of the literature on the treatment of suicidal young people suggests that family therapy or family involvement is an important component in treatment. Harrington *et al.* (1998) used a brief home-based family intervention which targeted difficulties such as poor communication and difficulties with problem solving. Although much has been said about strong associations with family dysfunction, a family approach is rarely presented as the sole treatment, nor is it recommended for all suicidal youngsters, particularly older adolescents.

- *Psychopharmacological interventions:* psychotropic drugs can be used in the treatment of DSH, particularly when there is evidence of co-morbidity such as anxiety states, psychosis and depressive symptomatology. Pharmacotherapy of suicidal youngsters with, for example, anti-depressants, needs to be a cautious undertaking, given the high level of toxicity of some of these drugs.

Group treatments

A review of the literature revealed only one randomised controlled trial (Wood *et al.* 2001) and one uncontrolled study of group intervention with suicidal adolescents (Scheidlinger and Aronson 1991). Most of the treatment activities developed in suicide prevention to date have focused on individual therapy, and have mainly concerned adults.

There is a paucity of group therapies available for the treatment of suicidal adolescents. This is probably partly because of anxiety about grouping suicidal people together. Another problem is the lack of training for therapists wishing to work with adolescents in groups. Moreover, some psychotherapists recommend exclusion of suicidal persons from groups. One literature review on grouping delinquent boys together reported that it caused them to increase their anti-social behaviour (Julian and Kilman 1979). There has, however, been no evidence to suggest that this is true of grouping suicidal youngsters together in a therapeutic setting. The experience of development group psychotherapy did not see an adverse influence on treatment (Clark 1996; Trainor 2001).

Developmental group psychotherapy

Group intervention has seldom been used with suicidal adolescents, even though it has been recognised widely as the treatment of choice when dealing with this age group. Adolescents are known to form groups more easily than adults. Crisis intervention, hospitalisation and individual long-term therapies tend to be the most used treatments in the UK and the USA.

Developmental group therapy was specifically devised to meet the complex needs of this client group. Before its implementation the intervention was piloted over a three-month period at an outpatient department of a hospital in the north of England (Clark 1996). This short pilot study suggested that groups were a good setting for dealing with some of the problems that are especially prevalent among suicidal adolescents, such as peer relationships and impaired problem solving. It appeared to reduce the need for other forms of therapy and it was accessible to the young person at a critical time (Trainor 2001). Subsequently, a randomised controlled trial has confirmed the promising findings of this intervention (Wood *et al.* 2001).

Developmental group therapy is 'developmental' in the sense that it seeks to support the adolescent to grow, or develop, through their difficulties using the group as a responsive, corrective experience. The group intervention is an integrative eclectic model of treatment embracing cognitive behavioural techniques, dialectical behaviour therapy and person-centred approach. As with all group therapies there is a heavy reliance on the knowledge and insights of Yalom (1975). Determining any therapeutic change is complex and occurs through the therapist guiding the group experience. Yalom's key principles, his 'curative factors', have been adapted to the treatment of suicidal youngsters: for example, the instillation of hope for young people who have long abandoned any idea of another way out. The therapist's main aim is to facilitate the young person negotiating the developmental task of adolescence in a nurturing and safe environment. Unlike other group approaches, the therapist adopts a para-analytical stance, and at times will be directive and provide education. It is thought that young people are more likely to absorb such observations when they can explore them in a setting with other members who have followed a similar path.

The programme

The group intervention is currently based at the an outpatient service attached to an adolescent in-patient service. The programme of treatment comprises:

- an initial assessment and engagement phase
- attendance at six acute group sessions; and
- on-going participation in weekly group therapy sessions until the young person feels ready to leave.

Young people may also be receiving medication and individual family treatment programmes and may have support from social services and education. However, present experience is that few of the young people attending the long-term group have been receiving any other treatments.

The young people are referred mainly by a mental health care professional from the Child and Adolescent Mental Health Services when they present with repeated self-harming behaviours. Many present in crisis and have complex and psychosocial co-morbid mental health problems. The assessment will always involve the young person's parents/carers and any professional from social services who has been involved with them. The assessment of suitability for inclusion in the developmental group therapy programme may be conducted over a series of sessions. Key criteria for inclusion in the programme are the presence of repeated self-harm, absence of severe eating disorder or severe learning difficulty, and that the young person is motivated to 'try' the therapy.

The young person is first invited to attend six initial weekly sessions known as the acute group. This group operates an open, rolling programme and sessions are orientated around themes these young people often struggle with:

- relationships
- school problems and peer relationships
- family problems
- anger management
- depression and self-harm
- the future.

Each session lasts one hour and is conducted by two therapists (a consultant in child and adolescent psychiatry and a nurse practitioner). Usually between five and eight young people attend. The group aims to support the young people in crisis by adopting an 'active' problem-solving approach. Each session begins with a review of the previous week, after which the young people are encouraged to explore each other's problems. Role-play and other experiential techniques may be used. After six weeks' attendance, a review of progress is held with the young person and their carers. They are invited to give feedback on attending the group and invited to attend on a longer-term basis. In this instance, the long-term group takes place weekly and is facilitated by the same therapists.

The longer-term group members are more attuned to the process and are often more responsive to each other as they are likely to have come through the acute phase of their illness. In this setting the therapists take on a less directive stance and the young people do not require the same encouragement to participate. Group members tend to discuss their current dilemmas. The therapist's role is to link the themes the young people present, for example, difficulties with peers, risk-taking behaviour or family problems. The members are more familiar with each other and have a better understanding of each other's situations. The structure is more informal, for example, the review of the preceding week will be much more spontaneous as the young people will often ask about how a group member tackled a particular problem they presented at the previous session. Frustration and enthusiasm are more easily absorbed. There is an expectation that new members are supported by older members. This is helpful for both, and can be seen as a form of progression.

Once the young person has become engaged in the process they usually determine their own disengagement. On the whole this has been a voluntary announcement by the group member and can be precipitated by more positive life events such as sitting examinations or getting involved in college life.

Case studies

The following three case studies provide examples of young people who could be involved in the developmental group psychotherapy programme. The characters depicted are fictional. However hypothetical, presenting problems and experiences will help illustrate the therapeutic process that may typically take place.

Case study 12.1: Tracy (aged 15)

Tracy was a slim attractive girl with multiple body piercings who frequently changed her appearance. She was referred to the service following an overdose and received some individual therapy. She took a further overdose and expressed on-going suicidal intent and multiple somatic complaints. She remained on the paediatric ward for a few days before she was discharged. Tracy attended her first group session from the paediatric ward. Tracy lived with her natural parents and was the younger of two children. She has a close relationship with her mother and they described this as 'like best friends'. Tracy's father suffered from depression and anxiety. The trigger to Tracy's difficulties was an alleged rape by a boyfriend. She did not confide in her parents immediately and felt betrayed by the legal system. Although capable academically, Tracy had missed a lot of school and described difficulties with peer relationships. In the group she was initially silent and complained of somatic symptoms. She listened to others but was aloof and distant. In the session focusing on relationships, Tracy spoke about the relationship which had led to her attack. This was difficult for Tracy and the other group members but enabled issues of trust, guilt and anger to be explored by the group. Tracy seemed to establish a level of trust, acceptance and regard from the group that allowed her to work through her distress. The group also allowed her to separate and individuate from her mother and feel accepted by her peers. She subsequently returned to school and attended the group intermittently.

Case study 12.2: Angela (aged 14)

Angela was a small slightly built gregarious teenager who lived with her mother, stepfather and half brother. Her stepfather was blind and had mental health problems. Angela had a 12-month history of oppositional defiant behaviours at home and in school. She described low moods and had taken three overdoses, all in the context of severe conflict with her stepfather. She was bullied in primary school and has had some difficulties in peer relationships in secondary school. The most recent overdose, which led to her starting to attend the group, involved Angela taking paracetamol tablets and hiding from her parents. She was found the following day by a friend. Angela quickly engaged with the group and attended regularly for more than 12 months. She talked about her overdose and her out of control behaviour. She was very supportive of other young people in crisis and took the role of 'leader' in the group. She used the group to explore her conflicted relationship with her stepfather and her feelings of anger towards her mother. Angela was able to return to school and find a way of living with her stepfather for her mother's sake.

Case study 12.3: Barry (aged 14)

Barry was referred for a child and adolescent psychiatric assessment at the age of 13 due to self-laceration and out of control behaviours both at home and at school. Barry lived with his mother and two younger sisters. His mother had suffered from difficulties as a teenager and had taken overdoses. She had separated from Barry's father when Barry was five and subsequently had a series of difficult and often violent relationships. For the past three years she had been with a partner who had more or less lived with the family and with whom Barry was developing a good relationship. Barry engaged very readily with the group and attended regularly. He was of medium build but rather immature for his years. He was often distractible in sessions and tended to be disruptive. He was encouraged by the group to talk about his worries about his mother and to work through his problems rather than act out. At times he missed school and talked with bravado about his drug use and delinquent behaviour. The group attempted to set limits on his behaviour and encouraged him to take responsibility. Alongside the group sessions, Barry attended occasional meetings with his mother to facilitate communication between them. For Barry, the group was 'parental' and nurturing. He was an emotionally needy boy who used self-harming behaviours as a communication within a reversed care relationship with his mother.

The group psychotherapy experience is a result of a complex inter-relationship of group interactions guided by the therapist. The course is unpredictable and the therapist's task is to create and convene the group and act as gatekeeper, recognising deterring issues which may threaten the group process (Yalom 1975). The treatment has been manualised and describes the various structural techniques which are used to enhance discussion and communication (Wood and Trainor 2001). The group is beneficial in validating the young persons' experiences and helps facilitate the use of alternative coping strategies. These young people are often excluded by peers, school and home and describe feeling that they do not 'fit'. For adolescents it is important to feel included and being part of the group can be the first step in learning new ways of thinking and behaving.

Conclusions

This chapter has explored suicidal behaviour in adolescents and some of the more promising treatment options available. A specific focus has been upon young people who repeatedly self-harm and who are likely to be at higher risk of adverse psychiatric and psychosocial difficulties and completing suicide. Given the complexity of their problems and needs, a comprehensive service for such young people needs to call on a variety of therapies. In many cases self-harming behaviour is a symptom of significant unmet need. Because of this, longer-term, multi-modal forms of intervention are needed. These young people are difficult to engage in conventional treatment programmes, therefore new and more creative ways of working are needed. Developmental group psychotherapy has been proven to be successful in reducing self-harming behaviour (Wood *et al.* 2001) and it is currently the subject of a large randomised multi-centre trial. It is hoped that the results of this research will see this approach becoming more widely used and contribute to the range of suicide prevention approaches being developed to support younger people.

References

Brent, D., Holder, D., Kolko, D., Birmaher, B., Braugher, M. and Roth, C. (1997) 'A clinical psychotherapy trial for adolescent depression comparing cognitive, family and supportive treatments.' *Archives of General Psychiatry 54*, 877–885.

Chitsabesan, P., Harrington, R., Harrington, V. and Tomenson, B. (2003) 'Predicting self-harm in children. How accurate can we expect it to be?' *European Journal of Child and Adolescent Psychiatry 12*, 23–29.

Clark, G. (1996) 'Children Have a Right to be Fully Grown.' Unpublished MA thesis, University of Manchester.

Diekstra, R.F.W. and Movitz, B.J.M. (1987) 'Suicidal behaviour among adolescents: An overview.' In R.F.W. Diekstra and K. Hawkes (eds) *Suicide in Adolescence*. Dordrecht: Martinus Nijhoff.

Garfinkel, B.P., Froese, A. and Mood, J. (1982) 'Suicide attempts in children and adolescents.' *American Journal of Psychiatry 139*, 1257–1261.

Goldacre, M. and Hawton, K. (1985) 'Repetition of self-poisoning and subsequent death in adolescents who take overdoses.' *British Journal of Psychiatry 146*, 395–398.

Granboulan, V., Rabain, D. and Basquin, M. (1995) 'The outcome of adolescent suicide attempts.' *Acta Psychiatrica Scandinavica 91*, 265–270.

Harrington, R.C., Kerfoot, M., Dyer, E., McNiven, F., Gill, J., Harrington, V., Woodham, A. and Byford, S. (1998). 'Randomised trial of a home based family intervention for children who have deliberately poisoned themselves.' *Journal of the American Academy of Child and Adolescent Psychiatry 37*, 512–518.

Hawton, K., Arensman, E., Townsend, E., Bremner, S., Feldman, E., Goldney, R., Gunnell, D., Hazell, P., van Heeringen, K., Owens, D., Sakinofsky, I. and Traskman-Bendz, L. (1998) 'Deliberate self-harm: Systematic review of psychosocial and pharmacological treatments in preventing repetition.' *British Medical Journal 317*, 441–447.

Hawton, K., Fagg, J., Simkins, S., Harris, L., Bale, E. and Bond, A. (1996) 'Deliberate self poisoning and self injury in children and adolescents under 16 years of age in Oxford 1976–1993.' *British Journal of Psychiatry 169*, 202–208.

Hawton, K., Kingsbury, S., Steinhardt, K., James, A. and Fagg, J. (1999) 'Repetition of deliberate self-harm by adolescents: The role of pyschological features.' *Journal of Adolescence 22*, 369–378.

Hawton, K., Rodham, K., Evans, E. and Weatherall, R. (2002) 'Deliberate self-harm in adolescents: Self report survey in schools in England.' *British Medical Journal 325*, 1207–1211.

Hawton, K., Zahl, D. and Weatherall, R. (2003) 'Suicide following deliberate self-harm: Long term follow-up of patients who presented to a general hospital.' *British Journal of Psychiatry 182*, 537–542.

Hill, K. (1995) *The Long Sleep: Young People and Suicide.* London: Virago Press.

Hulten, A., Jiang, G.-X., Wasserman, D., Hawton, K., Hjelmeland, H., De Leo, D., Ostamo, A., Salander-Renberg, E. and Schmidtke, A. (2001) 'Repetition of attempted suicide among teenagers in Europe: Frequency, timing and risk factors.' *European Journal of Child and Adolescent Psychiatry 10*, 161–169.

Jacobson, B., Ekland, G., Hamberger, L., Emersson, D., Sedvall, G. and Valverius, M. (1987) 'Perinatal origin of adult self destructive behaviour.' *Acta Psychiatrica Scandinavica 76*, 364–371.

Julian, J. and Kilman, P. (1979) 'Group treatment of juvenile delinquents: A review of the literature.' *International Journal of Group Psychotherapy 29*, 3–38.

Kerfoot, M., Dyer, E., Harrington, V., Woodham, A. and Harrington, R. (1996) 'Correlates and short term course of self poisoning in adolescents.' *British Journal of Psychiatry 68*, 38–42.

Kerfoot, M. and Huxley, P. (1995) 'Suicide and deliberate self harm in young people.' *Current Opinion in Psychiatry 8*, 214–217.

Linehan, M.M. (1993) *Cognitive Behavioural Treatment of Borderline Personality Disorder.* New York: Guildford.

Meltzer, H., Harrington, R., Goodman, R. and Jenkins, R. (2001) *Children and Adolescents who Try to Harm, Hurt or Kill Themselves.* London: Office of National Statistics.

Office of National Statistics (2002) *Estimated Numbers of Deaths Assigned to Suicide, 1997–2000: Annual Reference.* London: HMSO.

Otto, U. (1972) 'Suicidal acts by children and adolescents: A follow up study.' *Acta Psychiatrica Scandinavica 233*, 5–123 (Supplement).

Pfeffer, C.R., Klerman, G.L., Hurt, S.W., Kakurma, T., Peskin, J.R. and Siefker, C.A. (1993) 'Suicidal children grow up: Rates and psychological risk factors for attempts during follow-up.' *Journal of the American Academy of Child and Adolescent Psychiatry 32*, 106–113.

Royal College of Psychiatrists (1998) *Managing Deliberate Self-Harm in Young People.* (Document CR64) London: Royal College of Physicians.

Runeson, B. (1989) 'Mental disorder in youth suicide: DSM-111-R axis 1 and 11.' *Acta Psychiatrica Scandinavica 79*, 490–497.

Salk, I., Stumer, W., Pipsett, I., Reilly, B. and Bevar, R. (1985) 'Relationship of maternal and perinatal conditions to eventual adolescent suicide.' *Lancet i* 624–627.

Salkovskis, P.M., Atha, C. and Storer, D. (1990) 'Cognitive behaviour problem solving in the treatment of patients who repeatedly attempt suicide: a controlled trial.' *British Journal of Psychiatry 157*, 871–876.

Samaritans (2003) *Suicide Statistics.* Available at www.samaritans.org.uk

Schleidlinger, S. and Aronson, S. (1991) 'Group psychotherapy of adolescents.' In M. Slomowitz (ed) *Adolescent Psychotherapy: Clinical Practice.* Washington DC: American Psychiatric Press.

Schmidtke, A., Bille-Brahe, U. and DeLeo, D. (1996) 'Attempted suicide in Europe: rates, trends and sociodemographic characteristics of suicide attempts during the period 1989–1992. Results of the WHO/Euro multicentre study on parasuicide.' *Acta Psychiatrica Scandinavica 93*, 327–338.

Shaffer, D. (1974) 'Suicide in childhood and early adolescence.' *Journal of the American Academy of Child Psychology 15*, 275–291.

Shaffer, D., Garland, A., Gould, M., Fisher, P. and Trautman, P. (1988). 'Preventing teenage suicide: A critical review.' *Journal of the American Academy of Child and Adolescent Psychiatry 27*, 675–687.

Shaffer, D. and Gould, M. (1987) *Study of Completed and Attempted Suicides in Adolescents. Progress Report.* Bethesda, MD: National Institute of Mental Health.

Shaffi, M., Corrigan, S., Whittinghill, J.R. and Derrick, A. (1985) 'Autopsy of completed suicide in children and adolescents.' *American Journal of Psychiatry 142*, 1061–1064.

Trainor, G. (2001) 'Learning to live with life.' *Mental Health Care 4*, 273–275.

Wood, A. and Trainor, G. (2001) *Developmental Group Psychotherapy. A Manual for Mental Health Professionals.* Manchester: Withington Hospital.

Wood, A., Trainor, G., Rothwell, J., Moore, A. and Harrington, R. (2001) 'Randomised trial of group therapy for repeated deliberate self harm in adolescents.' *Journal of the American Academy of Child and Adolescent Psychiatry 40*, 1246–1253.

Yalom, I. (1975) *The Theory and Practice of Group Psychotherapy.* New York: Basic Books.

Chapter 13

The Role of the National Confidential Inquiry in Relation to Suicide Prevention

Jo Robinson and Harriet Bickley

This chapter describes the contribution of the National Confidential Inquiry into Suicide and Homicide by People with Mental Illness in preventing suicide. The first part of the chapter will describe the background and aims of the Inquiry, its methodology, and what the Inquiry data can tell us about suicide in England and Wales. It will then discuss how Inquiry data are used at a national level, some of its key findings and recommendations and its role in the development of national policy. The chapter will then consider how the Inquiry data can be used locally for audit purposes and service development before finally discussing some new developments for the Inquiry.

Background to the Inquiry
Background and aims
The National Confidential Inquiry into Suicide and Homicide by People with Mental Illness was established at the University of Manchester in 1996, having previously been based in London. It is one of three confidential inquiries in England and Wales that were set up with funding from the Department of Health in order to investigate adverse outcomes under health services. In 1997, the Inquiry also obtained funding from the Scottish Office and the Health and Social Services Executive in Northern Ireland and data collection began in these countries, making the Inquiry a UK-wide audit.

The Inquiry was initially established following public and governmental concern about homicides by patients in contact with mental health services, specifically the case of Christopher Clunis (Ritchie, Dick and Lingham 1994). Further, following government targets for the reduction in suicide rates (Department of Health (DoH) 1992), suicide as an adverse outcome was also to be investigated. Thus, the Inquiry was set up aiming to:

- collect detailed clinical data on people who die by suicide or commit homicide and who have been in contact with mental health services

- make recommendations on clinical practice and policy that will reduce the risk of future suicides and homicides occurring under services.

How the Inquiry is conducted

There are three stages to the data collection process for suicide.

1. The first stage is the collection of a comprehensive national sample of all suicides, irrespective of mental health history. Information about people who die by suicide or who receive an open verdict at coroner's inquest is obtained from the Office for National Statistics. The majority of open verdicts are suicides and it is conventional for these to be included in studies of suicide (Neeleman and Wessley 1997). In the Inquiry, all open verdicts are included unless it is clear that suicide was not considered at inquest.

2. The second stage is the identification of those people who had been in contact with psychiatric services in the year before death. This is achieved with the help of a named contact at each NHS Trust via a comprehensive system of record searches in the deceased person's district of residence, and district of death if different. Individuals identified through this system become 'Inquiry cases'.

3. The third stage of data collection involves obtaining detailed clinical information about each case, provided by the responsible consultant psychiatrist in consultation with the clinical team. The consultant psychiatrist is asked to complete a questionnaire which covers the following areas:

    - demographic details
    - clinical history

- details of the suicide
- details of contact with services
- events preceding the suicide
- the respondent's views on prevention.

Questionnaires are returned to the Inquiry in 95 per cent of cases.

What the Inquiry can tell us

The Inquiry uses this information to describe the antecedents of suicide for all patients under psychiatric care during the 12 months before their death.

For example, the Inquiry can describe the number of suicides that occur among psychiatric inpatients. It can say how many of these patients died on the ward itself, at what stage in their admission their suicide occurred, whether or not they were under high levels of observation and how many were on agreed leave.

Similarly, the Inquiry can tell us how many people who commit suicide do so within three months of discharge from an inpatient unit; the nature of their last admission to, and discharge from hospital; and whether or not they live alone, thus enabling services to build up a picture of the circumstances under which suicides most frequently occur.

while the Inquiry collects information on *all* suicides under mental health services, it is particularly interested in certain groups of patients (*priority groups*) for whom recommendations are most needed. These are:

- psychiatric inpatients
- recently discharged patients
- patients under the Care Programme Approach (CPA)
- patients who are non-compliant with medication
- patients who miss their final appointment with services
- patients from an ethnic minority group
- patients who were homeless at the time of their death.

People within these groups are known to be at high risk, to have greater treatment needs and to experience difficulty in maintaining contact with services. They are also patients who are often in close proximity to services and are already identified as being at high risk. By examining common events preceding a suicide the Inquiry can make recommendations that aim to strengthen services as a whole and provide better care for all patients.

Further, by targeting the priority groups services can focus interventions where they are most likely to have an impact.

The Inquiry therefore holds a national database of the clinical characteristics of all people who die by suicide while under the care of psychiatric services in the UK. These data are analysed regularly and the findings disseminated in a range of ways, e.g. reports, academic publications, presentations etc. The next part of this chapter summarises the Inquiry's most recent findings, published in the report *Safety First* (Appleby *et al.* 2001).

How the Inquiry data are used

The national picture: Key suicide findings for England and Wales

The findings presented here are for England and Wales and relate to deaths registered between April 1996 and March 2000; thus the sample is a four-year consecutive case series. Key findings are provided for:

- the general population
- the overall Inquiry sample
- the 'priority groups'.

Recommendations arising directly from these key findings are highlighted by vertical bars, and where available specific actions arising from the recommendations are detailed.

Suicides in the general population

In England and Wales, the Inquiry was notified of 20,927 suicides and probable suicides during the four years from April 1996, an annual rate of 10.0 per 100,000 population. Of these, the proportion in contact with psychiatric services was 24 per cent. while this is a significant figure, it is only a quarter of all suicides and it is clear that mental health services alone cannot meet the present national targets for suicide reduction (DoH 1999). Therefore, the first recommendation included in the report was that:

Each country [i.e. England, Wales, Scotland and Northern Ireland] develops a broad-based suicide prevention strategy, which sets out the actions required of mental health services, as well as other health and social care organisations.

Progress: A suicide prevention strategy for England was launched (Department of Health 2002).

Among the general population 75 per cent of suicides were men, although this varied with age – among the 25–34-year-olds 82 per cent of suicides were men compared to 62 per cent of over 75s.

Cause of death: Three methods of suicide accounted for the majority of deaths: hanging (the most common method overall); self-poisoning and carbon monoxide poisoning using car exhaust fumes. Among women, however, overdose was the most common method, followed by hanging. Violent or 'active' methods such as jumping from a height or in front of a moving vehicle were more common among men than women.

Inquiry suicides

Of the total sample, 5099 (24%), were known to be in contact with mental health services in the year before death. The Inquiry received completed questionnaires on 4859 cases – a response rate of 95 per cent. These 'Inquiry' cases form the basis for the rest of the findings presented here.

As in the general population, Inquiry suicides were more often by men and the preponderance of men was again higher in the younger age groups (see Figure 13.1). Again the most common methods of suicide were hanging and self-poisoning.

Tables 13.1 and 13.2 present the key social, behavioural and clinical characteristics of the Inquiry cases.

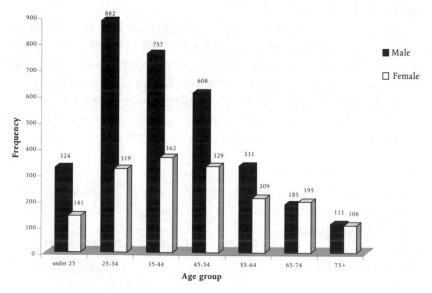

Figure 13.1 Age and sex profile of suicides

Table 13.1: Suicides in contact with services in the 12 months before death – demographic and behavioural characteristics

	Number	%
Demographic features		
Age: median (range)	41 (13–95)	
Not currently married	3405	70
Male	3198	66
Unemployed/long-term sick	2765	57
Living alone	2006	41
Ethnic minority	282	6
Lone carers of children	192	4
Homeless	131	3
Behavioural features		
History of self-harm	3077	63
History of alcohol misuse	1899	39
History of drug misuse	1348	28
History of violence	920	19

Note: Total sample n=4859

Table 13.2: Suicides in contact with services in the 12 months before death – clinical characteristics

	Number	%
Priority groups		
Under the CPA	2243	46
Missed final contact	1131	23
Recently discharged patients	1100	23
Non-compliance	929	19
Inpatients	754	16

Continued on next page...

Table 3.2 continued...

	Number	%
Clinical features		
Primary diagnosis		
Affective disorder	2036	42
Schizophrenia	960	20
Personality disorder	505	10
Alcohol dependence	439	9
Drug dependence	216	4
Any secondary diagnosis	2460	51
Duration of history under 12 months	1000	21
Over 5 previous inpatient admissions	712	15
Contact with services		
Estimate of immediate risk: low or none	3950	81
Symptoms at last contact	2990	62
Estimate of long-term risk: low or none	763	16
Last contact within 7 days of death	2308	48
Out of contact with services	1153	24
Suicide thought to be preventable	876	18
Requested contact but not taken place	161	3

Note: total sample (n=4859)

Other differences were evident among the sample. The Inquiry is able to highlight the different features of suicide between patients of different age groups; for example:

Rates of schizophrenia were highest among the under 25s and decreased steadily with age. In contrast, rates of affective disorder were lowest among the under 25s and increased with age – reaching a peak among the over 65s. Further differences were evident between older and younger cases particularly with regard to behavioural characteristics and engagement with services. Looking at the data in this way allows the Inquiry to build up a picture of the antecedents to suicide among these different groups of patients and enables specific recommendations to be made to services for different patient groups.

The Inquiry also collects information about patients' final contact with clinicians.

Last contact with services

Almost half of Inquiry cases had been in contact with services within the week prior to their deaths and in the majority of cases this contact was routine and not urgent. During this last contact immediate risk of suicide was estimated to be low or non-existent in 85 per cent of cases and high in only 2 per cent of patients. It was most frequently reported that current mental state and suicidal ideas were the most important factors when assessing risk. Those thought to be at high risk were more likely to have a history of self-harm, non-compliance with treatment and a primary diagnosis of personality disorder.

Priority groups
INPATIENTS

During the four years of data collection there were 754 suicides that occurred while the patient was an inpatient on a psychiatric unit – this represents 16 per cent of Inquiry cases and 4 per cent of *all* suicides that occurred during this period.

As expected the inpatient sample had greater morbidity than the overall sample, with 34 per cent having a primary diagnosis of schizophrenia and around a quarter of these suicides clustered around admission.

The methods of suicide used by inpatients differed from those used by the overall sample. The majority of inpatients died by hanging and jumping was the second most common cause of death. Around a third of inpatient suicides occurred on the ward itself and of these three quarters died by hanging, with the most commonly used ligature being a belt and the most common ligature point being a curtain rail. These findings generated two important recommendations to services:

Inpatient units should remove, or make inaccessible, all likely ligature points.
Progress: This became a Department of Health policy directive and by March 2002 all non-collapsible curtain rails were reported to have been removed from inpatient psychiatric units in England.

Inpatient teams, in consultation with user representatives, should develop protocols that allow the removal of potential ligatures from patients at high risk, in particular from those detained under the Mental Health Act (1983) and those placed under non-routine observation because of suicide risk.

Among the inpatient sample, 25 per cent were under non-routine observations and 3 per cent were under one-to-one observations at the time of death. These findings generated the following recommendations:

Patients under non-routine observations should not normally be allowed time off the ward or home leave.

Inpatient services should ensure that there are no gaps, however brief, in one-to-one observation.

Thirty-one per cent of inpatients died while on home leave agreed by the clinical team. Inpatient services should therefore make provision for:

Close community follow-up of patients during periods of leave, particularly for those who live alone.

Mental health teams considered inpatient suicides to be the most preventable with closer supervision of patients being one route to reducing suicide risk.

POST-DISCHARGE PATIENTS

Around a quarter of the suicide sample were patients who had left hospital in the previous three months. Post-discharge suicides were linked to short admissions (i.e. less than seven days), readmission within three months of a previous discharge and self-discharge. These suicides were at a peak during the first two weeks following discharge and 40 per cent took place before the first follow-up appointment. After the first two weeks the number of suicides declined steadily, see Figures 13.2 and 13.3.

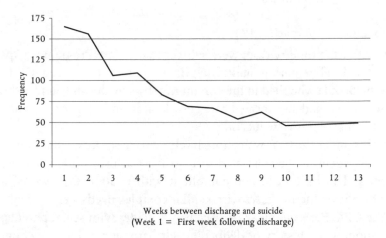

Figure 13.2 Number or suicides per week following discharge

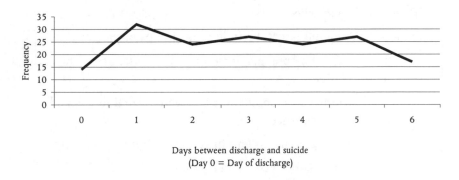

Figure 13.3 Number of suicides per day following discharge

These findings generated a further recommendation to services:

All discharged inpatients with a severe mental illness or a recent history of deliberate self-harm should be followed up within one week.

Approximately one third of the recently discharged group were patients who had initiated their own discharge. Compared to the rest of this group these patients had higher rates of personality disorder, previous violence and alcohol and drug misuse. .

Care Programme Approach (CPA)

Almost half of the Inquiry cases were subject to the Care Programme Approach at a level requiring multidisciplinary review (enhanced CPA). Among the people who died in the community by suicide while under the CPA, 94 per cent had an allocated care coordinator, and 76 per cent had a date set for the next review meeting.

Suicides under the CPA were more likely to have severe mental illness, to be an inpatient at the time of death, to have a history of deliberate self-harm and to have been non-compliant with treatment. However, a number of suicide Inquiry cases with similar complex needs were not subject to the CPA. For example, 25 per cent of suicides with schizophrenia, half of whom had a history of deliberate self-harm and a third of whom were non-compliant with treatment, were not under the CPA.

The following actions are therefore needed:

The establishment of national criteria for enhanced CPA, which emphasise the importance of risk

Enhanced CPA should target the following groups of patients:

- those with schizophrenia, including those who are in the early stages of illness
- those who have a combination of severe mental illness and self-harm or violence
- those who are homeless and have been admitted to hospital
- lone parents with severe mental illness.

Monitoring of this should be a priority for local clinical governance bodies.

NON-COMPLIANCE AND LOSS OF CONTACT

Almost a quarter of suicide Inquiry cases were non-compliant with medication in the month before death and one third of suicides in the community missed their final appointment with a member of the mental health team. In the non-compliant group, mental health teams made a face-to-face attempt to encourage compliance with treatment in 62 per cent of cases. For the group who missed their final appointment in the community, mental health teams made an assertive attempt to re-establish contact in just over half of cases.

It would be unrealistic to expect services to respond assertively to every person under their care who refused treatment or did not attend an appointment. However, for patients with severe mental illness and/or indicators of risk, services need to be prepared to make a direct response to disengagement. An obvious group might be those patients already under enhanced CPA. Therefore, the Inquiry recommends that:

All care plans for enhanced CPA should include explicit plans for responding to non-compliance and missed contact.

Ethnic minority groups

The Inquiry sample included 282 people from an ethnic minority group. This is 6 per cent of the overall sample. Patients in this group were more likely to have been unemployed but less likely to have lived alone at the time of their death. There was a higher proportion of people with a primary diagnosis of schizophrenia, especially among Black Caribbeans.

Suicides among ethnic minorities were more likely to follow non-compliance with medication. Although negative side-effects of medication were common, the reason most frequently given by staff for non-compliance was lack of insight into the illness.

These findings add to the evidence that services need to find successful ways of working with patients from ethnic minorities, especially those with severe mental illness and social difficulties. Therefore the Inquiry recommends that:

All local services should develop a strategy for the care of people from ethnic minority groups and that this should include staff training, recruitment and links with the voluntary sector.

Homeless patients

There were 131 suicides by homeless people, which is 3 per cent of the sample. These suicides appeared to cluster around acute inpatient admission; almost half were inpatients at the time of death, and a further 22 per cent died within three months of hospital discharge. Around half of this group were under the higher levels of the CPA.

Homeless suicides in the community were more likely to have missed their final appointment with services and two thirds were considered to be out of contact with services altogether, largely due to self-discharge. These findings led the Inquiry to emphasise the need for patients who are homeless to be given priority under the CPA and for the work of assertive outreach teams.

The findings discussed here are necessarily brief and are designed to demonstrate what the Inquiry can tell us about suicides that occur under psychiatric services. A fuller account of the findings can be found in the *Safety First* report (Appleby *et al.* 2001). Many of the findings discussed here have led to clear recommendations as highlighted above. However the Inquiry has also produced a summary of its key clinical recommendations from both its reports, *Safety First* and *Safer Services* (Appleby *et al.* 1999) and this is referred to as the *Twelve Points to a Safer Service*.

The twelve points to a safer service

The twelve points to a safer service are intended as a practical checklist for local services. They comprise the key clinical recommendations made by the Inquiry and their implementation should lead to the improvement of services generally and thereby to a reduced number of suicides occurring under similar circumstances in the future.

1. Staff training in the management of risk – both suicide and violence – every three years.

2. All patients with severe mental illness and a history of self-harm or violence to receive the most intensive level of care.

3. Individual care plans to specify action to be taken if a patient is non-compliant or fails to attend.

4. Prompt access to services for people in crisis and for their families.

5. Assertive outreach teams to prevent loss of contact with vulnerable and high-risk patients.

6. Atypical anti-psychotic medication to be available for all patients with severe mental illness who are non-compliant with 'typical' drugs because of side-effects.

7. Strategy for dual diagnosis covering training on the management of substance misuse, joint working with substance

misuse services, and staff with specific responsibility to develop the local service.

8. Inpatient wards to remove or cover all likely ligature points, including all non-collapsible curtain rails.

9. Follow-up within seven days of discharge from hospital for everyone with severe mental illness or a history of self-harm in the previous three months.

10. Patients with a history of self-harm in the last three months to receive supplies of medication covering no more than two weeks.

11. Local arrangements for information-sharing with criminal justice agencies.

12. Policy ensuring post-incident multidisciplinary case review and information to be given to families of involved patients.

The twelve points to a safer service form the mental health objective of the Suicide Prevention Strategy for England, thereby demonstrating one of the ways that Inquiry findings have informed national policy and subsequently service change. Services are expected to implement these recommendations as part of their wider suicide prevention agenda and it is the responsibility of the National Institute for Mental Health in England (NIMHE) to support them in doing so. Early monitoring by NIMHE suggests that one local implementation team (LIT) is now able to indicate full compliance with the twelve points and the remainder are making good progress towards this.

The local picture: How Inquiry data can be used locally

The findings described above apply to the whole of England and Wales, and while they can tell us about the pattern of suicide among certain groups they do not tell us what is happening within a particular area or service. Nor do they tell us whether suicides under one service differ from the national average, both of which are important for identifying local development priorities. However, under the right circumstances the Inquiry does provide local services with this sort of information (anonymised and aggregated). Local Trusts regularly contact the Inquiry and request key findings for their service along with national figures for comparison. Table 13.3 gives an example of the sort of local information that can be extracted from the Inquiry data; the local data would be provided in the blank column 'Local Service'.

Table 13.3: Data available to local services

Date of notification of death April 1996 – March 2001	Local service Number (%)	England and Wales Number (%)
Number of suicides and probable suicides		25,924
Number in contact with mental health services within one year prior to death		6294 (24)
Data are available on 6275 of those in contact with services in England and Wales.		
TOTAL		6275
Age (years) min–max		13–95
Sex		
Male		4151 (66)
Female		2124 (34)
Inpatient at time of death		973 (16)
Died within 3 months of discharge from inpatient care		1414 (23)
Non-compliant with drug treatment during the month before death		1233 (20)
Regular multidisciplinary review occurred under Care Programme Approach		2902 (46)
Primary psychiatric diagnosis:		
Affective disorders		2696 (46)
Schizophrenia and other delusional disorders		1250 (20)
Personality disorder		606 (10)
Alcohol dependence		568 (9)
Drug dependence		276 (4)
Other		648 (10)
History of deliberate self-harm		3987 (64)
History of alcohol misuse		2497 (40)
History of drug misuse		1791 (29)
History of violence		1189 (19)
Last contact with services:		
Between 1 and 7 days before death		1805 (29)
Within 24 hours prior to death		1181 (19)
Period between onset of primary diagnostic disorder and death less than 12 months duration		1290 (21)
Suicide thought to be preventable by patient's mental health team		1110 (18)
Over 5 previous psychiatric inpatient admissions		910 (15)
Patient requested contact but contact did not take place		218 (3)

The Inquiry also regularly presents findings at conferences and NHS Trust training. This enables Trusts to understand the pattern of suicide both nationally and locally and to consider potential areas for development within their service. Further, the Inquiry regularly provides copies of its questionnaire for Trusts to use in local audit and when conducting post incident case reviews.

Thus the Inquiry can describe the antecedents of suicide for all those under mental health care, and can help Trusts identify local priorities for suicide prevention activity. However there are limitations with the Inquiry data and there are some things that the Inquiry cannot yet tell us. The next part of this chapter describes the new work programme highlighting the studies the Inquiry will be conducting over the next three years and how they can improve our knowledge and understanding of suicide and suicide prevention.

New directions

The Inquiry has recently agreed an expanded three-year programme of work with its funders. This guarantees continued funding for the core work programme as described above and allows the Inquiry to introduce several new studies.

A study of the relationship between suicide and service configuration

The Inquiry has developed a study into the relationship of suicide to service configuration. In this study questionnaires about service configuration are sent to Clinical Directors and the information gained will be correlated with rates of suicide under that particular service. This study therefore should be able to tell us, for example, how many suicides occur under services with assertive outreach teams compared to those without. More specifically, we should also be able to see how many suicides occur in people who are homeless, what services have done to keep these patients engaged and whether or not they have specialist outreach teams in an attempt to prevent such outcomes.

The questionnaire for this study also includes questions about the implementation of some of the Inquiry recommendations, including the twelve points to a safer service, and is a way of auditing the implementation of the recommendations and any potential effect they may have upon the rate of suicide.

Case control studies

while the Inquiry data can tell us a great deal about the pattern of suicides under psychiatric services, it is an audit. This means that because data are uncontrolled it can only describe patterns of behaviour and cannot attribute suicide to independent risk factors. However, the Inquiry has now established two case control studies, one for inpatient suicides and one for recently discharged suicides, i.e. the Inquiry now collects information about 'live controls' for both of these groups.

The aims of these studies are to:

- compare suicides by inpatients and recently discharged patients with living controls on a range of possible risk factors

- identify differences in the care of suicides and controls

- develop models of suicide that could be the basis of further recommendations on prevention and the development of risk assessment tools.

Data are being collected on 200 inpatient controls and 200 recently discharged controls from the Nationwide Clearing Service and the methodology follows that already established by the Inquiry. These studies are both underway and it is anticipated that the findings will be published in 2004 and 2005 respectively.

Suicide psychological autopsy study

This is an extension of the current Inquiry methodology to include data collection from General Practitioners, A&E departments and the families of people who have died by suicide, using the psychological autopsy methodology. The psychological autopsy has been an accepted method for characterising the mental and psychosocial features of suicide victims for several years (Arato *et al.* 1988; Barraclough *et al.* 1974). Its main advantages are that the interviews provide detailed information about the circumstances leading up to death (Curphey 1967), which supplements information gathered quantitatively from other sources. Furthermore, it has been described as 'probably the most direct technique currently available for determining the relationship between particular risk factors and suicide' (Cavanagh *et al.* 2003).

This study will include current Inquiry cases, that is, people who were under psychiatric care, but will mean that data will be obtained from a broader source enabling a much more detailed picture of the antecedents of suicide to be developed.

It is noted that three quarters of those people who die by suicide in England are not under the care of psychiatric services (Appleby *et al.* 1999; 2001). It is also noted that many of these people will have recently seen their GP (Andersen *et al.* 2000; Luoma, Martin and Pearson 2002) and the Inquiry acknowledges that research is needed into the antecedents of suicide for this group. The psychological autopsy study currently being developed is a step towards this. For the first time data will be collected from GPs, A&E departments and bereaved families by the Inquiry, albeit only for those under secondary care. This study will also assess the feasibility of broadening the remit of the Inquiry to include those who were only under primary care and not specialist mental health services.

The aim of these additional studies is to increase the Inquiry's ability to describe the clinical circumstance of those patients who die by suicide while under psychiatric care. They will also enable the Inquiry to relate patterns of suicide to service configuration and to make comparisons between inpatients and recently discharged patients who do and do not die by suicide. Finally, the Inquiry will be able to supplement its current data from specialist mental health services with data gathered from primary care as well as A&E departments and the families of patients. These studies will enable the Inquiry to enhance its understanding of suicide by psychiatric patients and to consider expanding its investigation into primary care.

In summary

The Inquiry has an important and continually developing role in contributing to the prevention of suicide in the UK. As far as we are aware the Inquiry is unique. There is no other research project in this field that has a virtually complete national sample upon which to base its recommendations. Therefore not only can the Inquiry contribute to the reduction of suicide through its recommendations but also through the successful dissemination of its findings and methodology within the academic community.

A close relationship with the Department of Health and its sponsor the National Institute for Clinical Excellence (NICE) has meant that Inquiry work remains policy directed and feeds into the clinical governance agenda. It also means that Inquiry recommendations can inform and be informed by NICE guidance and national policy. On a local level Inquiry recommendations have led to service change and in time it is hoped that the Inquiry will be in a position to demonstrate how these combined approaches have led to a clear reduction in the rate of suicide under psychiatric services.

References

Andersen, U.A., Andersen, M., Rosholm, J.U. and Gram, L.F. (2000) 'Contacts to the health care system prior to suicide: a comprehensive analysis using registers for general and psychiatric hospital admissions, contacts to general practitioners and practicing specialists and drug prescriptions.' *Acta Psychiatrica Scandinavica 102,* 126–134.

Appleby, L., Shaw, J., Amos, T., McDonnell, R., Bickley, H., Kiernan, K., Davies, S., Harris, C., McCann, K. and Parsons, R. (1999) *Safer Services: Report of the National Confidential Inquiry into Suicide and Homicide by People with Mental Illness.* London: Stationery Office.

Appleby, L., Shaw, J., Sherratt, J., Robinson, J., Amos, T., McDonnell, R., Bickley, H., Hunt, I.M., Kiernan, K., Wren, J., McCann, K., Parsons, R., Burns, J., Davies, S. and Harris, C. (2001) *Safety First, Report of the National Confidential Inquiry into Suicide and Homicide by People with Mental Illness.* London: Stationery Office.

Arato, M., Demeter, E., Rihmer, Z. and Somogyi, E. (1988) 'Retrospective psychiatric assessment of 200 suicides in Budapest.' *Acta Psychiatrica Scandinavica 77,* 454–456.

Barraclough, B.M., Bunch, J., Nelson, B. and Sainsbury, A. (1974) 'A hundred cases of suicide: Clinical aspects.' *British Journal of Psychiatry 125,* 355–373.

Cavanagh, J.T.O., Carson, A.J., Sharpe, M. and Lawrie, S.M. (2003) 'Psychological autopsy studies of suicide: A systematic review.' *Psychological Medicine 33,* 3, 395–405.

Curphey, T.J. (1967) 'The forensic pathologist and the multi-disciplinary approach to death.' In E.S. Shneidman (ed) *Essays in Self Destruction.* New York: Science House.

Department of Health (1992) *The Health of the Nation: Strategy for Health in England.* London: HMSO.

Department of Health (1999) *Saving Lives: Our Healthier Nation: A Contract for Health.* Cm4386. London: Stationery Office.

Department of Health (2002) *National Suicide Prevention Strategy for England.* London: DoH Publications.

Luoma, J.B., Martin, C.E. and Pearson, J.L. (2002) 'Contact with mental health and primary care providers before suicide: A review of the evidence.' *American Journal of Psychiatry 159,* 6, 120–127.

Neeleman, J. and Wessley, S. (1997) 'Changes in classification of suicide in England and Wales; time trends and associations with coroners' professional background.' *Psychological Medicine 27,* 467–472.

Ritchie, J., Dick, D. and Lingham, R. (1994) *The Report of the Inquiry into the Care and Treatment of Christopher Clunis.* London: HMSO.

Chapter 14

Using Audit

Lester Sireling

Why do suicide audit?

Introduction

To audit suicide means different things to different people. In this chapter it
will be taken as the retrospective examination of individual cases of suicide,
either by the practitioners who had been caring for that person, or by others not directly involved but feeding back their findings to those practitioners. This examination usually involves looking at the casenotes to learn
about how the case had been managed, sometimes also talking to the professionals concerned and to the bereaved relatives and friends. The primary
purpose of such an audit is to learn how to do things better in future. Audit
is not a witch-hunt or a blame-finding exercise and, except in the case of serious negligence, should not lead to disciplinary action. (If people knew
that revealing their actions to colleagues would put them at serious risk of
being disciplined or reported to their professional regulatory body, few
would be willing to engage in suicide audit, and even fewer would be prepared to be honest about their actions.)

Because of the stigma surrounding death and particularly suicide, carrying out audit of this mode of death is challenging. And for those left behind, whether family or staff, a suicide almost always brings with it feelings
of regret and guilt. Usually these feelings are not justified, but they can act
as a potent fuel to ignite inappropriate emotions and behaviour which can
make suicide audit even more challenging. Where they feel particularly
guilty, staff will sometimes refuse to participate in suicide audit. Alternatively they may attend a meeting to discuss the case but 'have to' leave on
urgent business within a few minutes. (The same phenomenon can be seen

in committees, where items for the agenda regarding suicide audit tend to get relegated to the very end of the meeting or postponed.)

So why audit suicide? Surely there are easier and less emotive subjects to examine in day-to-day practice? One reason is that suicide is one of the few clearcut outcome measures in psychiatry. It can act as a proxy for the quality of a service. However the suicide rate in a particular service is governed probably as much by the demographics of that area as by the quality of the service. It is the change and direction of change in the suicide rate over time which is important for a local service. Suicide rates can also be compared between services, but this has to be done with caution because subtle differences between services (such as the proportion of the population with a serious mental illness in the catchment area, or specialist expertise within one team) can make a big difference to suicide rates.

Suicide audit builds on the soul-searching which starts when we hear the news that a patient/client has committed suicide. We ask ourselves 'What did I do wrong?': the answers to this can form the basis for an audit of the suicide.

Importantly, suicide audit can also identify service gaps, and particular populations at high risk within a service.

National policy

The first move to set targets for a national reduction in suicide rates came in 1992 with the publication of the Government White Paper *The Health of the Nation* (Department of Health (DoH) 1992). The rate was targeted to be reduced by 15 per cent over the following few years, coupled with a 33 per cent reduction in the suicide rate of severely mentally ill people. In 1999 a further White Paper *Saving Lives: Our Healthier Nation* (DoH 1999a) set an even more challenging target of reducing suicide rates by 20 per cent by 2010. In the same year the National Confidential Inquiry into Suicide and Homicide by People with Mental Illness (see below) published their first report *Safer Services* (DoH 1999b), which reported on their first few years of collecting data about suicide by patients in contact with mental health services. This and their subsequent report *Safety First* (DoH 2001) make a number of detailed recommendations about actions which should reduce the suicide rate in future. Also in 1999 the National Service Framework for Mental Health set out seven standards for mental health services, one of which was concerned with the prevention of suicide (DoH 1999c).

The *National Suicide Prevention Strategy for England* (Department of Health 2002) examined the evidence based interventions for reducing suicide, and set out a strategy for doing so, incorporating the 12 most important clinical recommendations of *Safety First*. Recently the National Institute for Mental Health in England (NIMHE) has published *Preventing Suicide: a Toolkit for Mental Health Services* (NIMHE 2003) which takes the recommendations of *Safety First* and the *National Strategy for Suicide Prevention*, and suggests ways of auditing these, following the patient's pathway of care. This is an excellent place to begin suicide audit, for the reader who has had no previous experience in this area. It requires the examination of clinical records, and the inspection of current policy statements, testing them against the standards set out in the Toolkit. The standards are summarised in Box 14.1.

Box 14.1: Preventing suicide: A toolkit for Mental Health Services

Summary of standards to be tested:

1. Patients in certain high-risk groups (at known risk of suicide or violence; with schizophrenia; with a combination of severe mental illness and harm to self or others; homeless people; lone parents with severe mental illness) are allocated to the enhanced level of the Care Programme Approach.

2. Inpatient units are audited to minimise opportunities for hanging, likely ligature points are removed, observation policy and practice reflect current evidence about risk factors, and patients under increased observation are not allowed leave or time off the ward.

3. Inpatients have a case review and risk assessment before discharge: discharge care plans specify arrangements for promoting compliance/engagement with treatment. Inpatients are followed up within 48 hours of discharge if they had been at high-risk of suicide during the admission. Assertive outreach teams prevent loss of contact with vulnerable and high risk patients.

4. Families/carers know how to make contact with a member of the clinical team and are given appropriate prompt information following a suicide.

5.   Patients at risk of suicide taking antipsychotic or antidepressant medication receive the right medication in the right amounts. Discharge prescription is for no more than 14 days, and GPs are advised explicitly about appropriate prescribing quantities.

6.   A strategy exists for the comprehensive care of people with comorbidity/dual diagnosis, e.g. people with mental health problems who also engage in alcohol and/or substance misuse. Staff who provide care to people at risk of suicide are trained in the management of cases of comorbidity/dual diagnosis.

7.   Suicides are reviewed in a multidisciplinary forum: all staff, patients and families/carers affected by a suicide are given prompt and open information and the opportunity to receive support.

8.   All direct care staff in contact with patients at risk of self-harm or suicide receive training in the recognition, assessment and management of risk at intervals of no more than three years.

Following these recommendations would provide a sound basis for developing more sophisticated suicide audit at a later date, once the principle of systematic suicide audit has been accepted within the service.

Literature review

With several publications at national level aiming to reduce suicide rates and promote suicide audit, it is surprising how little exists on suicide audit in the British literature. A paper by Redpath *et al.* (1997) reports on the use of case discussions of suicide in primary care, concluding rather pessimistically that the wider social and economic context was thought to be more important than any preventative measures identified. Most publications on suicide in the British literature report on short-term or retrospective studies rather than ongoing audits. Long-term audits in Bristol and Oxford remain the exception.

The NHS Management Executive has published a practical guide to suicide audit: *Clinical Audit of Suicide and Other Unexpected Deaths* (Morgan 1994).

National Confidential Inquiry

The Inquiry was set up in 1992 in London and moved to the University of Manchester in 1996. Public Health Departments forward information to the Inquiry about people who die by suicide or who receive an open verdict at coroner's inquest. The Inquiry then ascertains from local mental health services which of these people had been in contact with the service, and issues a detailed questionnaire to the team which had been caring for that patient. Returned questionnaires are collated, and every few years a report is published summarising the findings and making recommendations for practice to reduce the suicide rate. The reports tend to focus on populations at high risk of suicide, such as patients recently discharged from psychiatric inpatient care.

Local statistics

Although the targets for reductions in suicide rates are set at national level, clearly they cannot be achieved without reductions at local level. However, the more local the level examined, the smaller the figures become and the more prone to year-on-year fluctuations which make it difficult to establish trends. Nevertheless it is interesting to examine data on suicide rates for populations of local areas such as Mental Health Trusts or Boroughs, because staff relate to the areas they serve and have more of a sense of ownership of local figures. Wide variations between individual years can be smoothed out by using three-year rolling averages. Such data is available through the publications of the Office for National Statistics. Local Health Improvement or Public Health Departments usually have these publications.

What settings to audit?

Primary care

The large majority of mental health problems are dealt with by primary health care teams, 10 per cent or less being referred to secondary mental health services. Only about one in four people who commit suicide had been in contact with the mental health services in the previous year. The majority of people who commit suicide had seen their general practitioner (GP) within the previous three months (58% in a local audit in Barnet). So it seems logical to audit cases of suicide in primary care. There are, however, several drawbacks. For example, a GP will only have one case of suicide on average every four or five years so GPs tend to view suicide audit as not among their highest priorities, unless they have recently had a case of suicide. Similarly, GPs are accustomed to auditing their work either individually or within their group practices, but have less experience of their clinical work being audited by others, such as the secondary mental health services. In Barnet, to reduce the suspicion that suicide audit in primary care could be punitive, it has been designated as a voluntary activity. Once the audit project has been notified of the death of a patient which may have been by suicide, the GP is contacted and invited to participate in the audit. Only a small proportion of GPs decline.

Secondary care

It tends to be less difficult to audit suicide in secondary care, i.e. in the hospital and community mental health services. Audit has been well established in hospitals, there are mechanisms for obtaining agreement from the professional bodies involved such as medical staff committees, and all hospitals collect activity data, with a greater or lesser degree of accuracy.

Although the mental health services only see a minority of people who subsequently commit suicide, psychiatric populations are at relatively high risk, which is additional justification for commencing suicide audit in secondary care. (In Barnet, secondary care suicide audit began in 1991. In 1993 it was proposed to extend the audit into primary care, but negotiations took a further five years and seven drafts of the protocol!)

What practice to audit?

When starting an audit of suicide it is easiest to commence with the casenotes. They are usually accessible, often legible and provide enough material to get a 'feel' for the case and the way it was managed. The drawback of casenote audit is that it only provides part of the picture. Often one can learn much more about the case and the way it was managed by interviewing the professionals concerned. For a complete picture (insofar as that can ever be obtained) the family, other carers and friends need to be heard as well. They must be approached with sensitivity, bearing in mind that they are very likely to feel traumatised, may have negative feelings towards health professionals and may have bad memories triggered off by receiving official letters. Most, however, are willing to talk about their experiences.

One challenge of suicide audit is knowing what to make of the themes identified. For example, an audit might discover that 30 per cent of cases of suicide in the previous year were aged under 30. Without knowing the age distribution of the general population in that area, this finding does not mean much. If 15 per cent of the catchment area population were aged under 30, the audit finding is indicating a high-risk population, but if 30 per cent of the catchment area population were aged under 30, the audit has not found a high-risk group. Discovering that 20 per cent of the patients who committed suicide had taken an overdose in the previous six months might invite the issuing of a warning to staff doing assessments that a history of taking an overdose leads to a particularly high risk of suicide in the following six months. But if 20 per cent of *all* patients referred to the mental health service had taken an overdose in the previous six months, a history of recent overdose would not be a predictive factor at all. One solution to this is also to audit a sample of cases who did not proceed to suicide, seen by the same service in the same time period.

Who should do audit and who should lead it?

Suicide audit is not the prerogative of one profession: it is most useful as a multidisciplinary effort. Many services have access to local Clinical Effectiveness (or Audit) Departments, which can be helpful sources of advice. Clinical Effectiveness staff can also sometimes carry out casenotes audit, and would need little training in auditing basic information such as whether the date and manner of death were recorded, or whether offers of help to the survivors had been documented.

For a more in-depth look at management of the case a system of 'peer review' is required. In Barnet we started by having a professional from the same discipline and at the same level of seniority examine the casenotes, for example a consultant psychiatrist would review the casenotes of the consultant of the patient who had committed suicide, a basic grade Occupational Therapist (OT) would look at the notes written by the basic grade OT who had been in contact with the patient, and so on. This had the advantage of being straightforward, but could lead to a plethora of overlapping findings and recommendations being made on the same case by different professionals. We now ask a multidisciplinary team to sit down with the casenotes of all the professionals who had been involved with the case, and one joint report is produced, based around a semi-structured questionnaire.

Similarly, in primary care the GP's notes will be audited by a GP from another part of the borough. To remove any risk of personal bias, and to reduce fears of audit findings being used in any future litigation, the casenotes are photocopied and anonymised before being passed to the peer reviewer.

When should audit be carried out?

There is a case for starting the audit as soon as possible after learning of the death. Memories are still fresh, casenotes are more likely to be available and staff are engaged in self-questioning. But at this stage there may be uncertainty about the cause of death, with staff often hoping against hope that the death will turn out to have been an accident or due to natural causes. (One audit officer was told by a consultant that his patient's death by electrocution 'might have been accidental, because Mr X had a medical condition which could have led him to accidentally touch a live appliance'. The reviewer later discovered that the patient had three times in the previous two weeks attempted to kill himself by electrocution.)

Once the inquest is over there is usually less doubt about the cause of death, as most suicide audit and research include open or 'undetermined' verdicts with suicide verdicts. But the inquest can be several weeks or even months after the death; memories have become more selective, the casenotes may be missing or with the coroner, and generally there may be a reluctance to 'rake over old ground'. If the service is conducting an internal inquiry there may be objections to holding an audit at the same time.

Each service will have to decide whether and to what extent to keep the audit and any internal inquiry separate. It seems very inefficient for two sets of people to be questioning staff about the same events, and poring over the same casenotes. Yet rightly or wrongly, most staff worry that an inquiry by managers or senior clinicians could lead to disciplinary action. Inquiry reports are usually phrased in circumspect language and are circulated to other agencies, which makes it less likely that they will be overtly critical of the service. A suicide audit report, by contrast, tends to be more frank and open about identified deficiencies. (But not always. At one time in Barnet we carried out a comparison. We selected several cases which had been peer reviewed by local consultant psychiatrists. The casenotes were sent to another consultant psychiatrist working in a different Trust. He did not see the peer reviews carried out by the local consultants, but when his peer reviews came back it was apparent that he had seen deficiencies in the service which had not been picked up by local consultants. We had clearly got used to local services as they were, warts and all. An outsider was able to see things more clearly, and to notice where the deficiencies lay.)

Completing the audit cycle

To find out the demographic details of people who had committed suicide and to document what proportion of survivors had been offered care is an important exercise which may identify local risk factors or areas. But to learn clinical lessons two things need to happen. First, the management of the case needs to be examined critically, looking for issues of service provision and areas of case management which could be improved in future. Second, the findings need to be fed back to the relevant people. Problems with case management, and recommended ways of improving them, need to be brought to the attention of the clinicians involved, and also, in a form which does not disclose the identity of the clinician, to other clinicians in the service. Gaps in or problems with service provision need to be brought to the attention of relevant managers and other stakeholders.

How can this be done without breaching confidentiality? It is possible to phrase the clinical recommendations in a general way which does not allow identification of individual cases. However if only one case of suicide had arisen in the six months before the recommendations were issued, it would not take a genius to realise which case was being discussed. It may therefore be better to wait until three or four cases have accumulated, before making recommendations trawled from those cases. When making recommendations, it is important to distinguish between problems unique to a particular case and problems which underlie several cases. For example, in a service with very busy outpatient clinics, it may be standard practice for patients discharged from hospital to be offered 'the next available outpatient appointment', only to find that that is two months hence. The period soon after discharge is a particularly high-risk time, so several cases of suicide may have been detected as having occurred after discharge and before being seen in clinic. This would be an underlying issue, common to several cases. It should be drawn to the attention of all those concerned, with a strong recommendation that patients are seen within a short time of discharge from psychiatric wards (one of the recommendations of *Safety First*). But in an isolated case where, for example, the suicide occurred after a patient had managed to smuggle pills onto the wards in their socks, it would be foolish to make a recommendation that no psychiatric inpatients should be allowed to wear socks! A balance needs to be struck between the zealous protection of the few and the human rights and dignity of the many.

To complete the audit cycle, the audit must check whether the recommendations have been met and implemented, and if so, whether this has had an impact on practice. It would be wonderful if this were reflected in a drop in suicide rates, but suicide rates fluctuate considerably year to year in a local service. It is therefore usually impossible to demonstrate that introduction of a particular recommendation has led to a fall in suicide rates. Individual clinicians may be able to name particular patients whom they believe have not committed suicide because of a certain intervention or change of practice, but it is never possible to 'prove' such an assertion. (The situation is analogous to the control of high blood pressure. If 10 people need to take medication to control blood pressure in order to prevent one case of stroke, it is not possible to point to a particular one of these 10 people and say that this person would have had a stroke had they not taken the treatment.)

Converting recommendations into practice needs a combination of enthusiasm, tact and patience, the last in considerable degree. Recommendations in secondary mental health services seem to get swallowed up in a 'black hole', perhaps after having been considered by one committee and referred to another. With perseverance all things are possible: our first attempt at sifting through the recommendations from individual cases came up with more than 10 common themes, which were converted into recommendations. After none of these had been implemented within a couple of years, we identified three as 'priority recommendations' and made them more operationalised. We then focused on having these three implemented, and within a further two years all three recommendations had become practice.

A practical guide to comprehensive suicide audit

To audit suicide comprehensively requires the inclusion of all cases in a particular area. Depending on the resources available this could be a Borough or Primary Care Trust (a third to half a million population), a population served by a Mental Health Trust (about one million population) or by a Strategic Health Authority (more than one million population). All residents of the defined area who may have committed suicide should be included in the audit, whether or not they had contact with the primary health care team or with the mental health service. One of the first challenges therefore is case ascertainment. Trying to obtain cases by word of mouth or by looking at hospital records will yield only a small proportion of the potential cases. It is helpful at the onset to agree on a definition of the phrase 'who may have committed suicide'. The simplest definition would be 'anyone who receives a verdict of suicide or undetermined death from the coroner', although this will include a few cases where an undetermined verdict has been brought for reasons which are not related to suicide, for example cases of asbestosis or where a body has decomposed before being found and the cause of death cannot be determined.

In the early stages of suicide audit in Barnet an attempt was made to collect information from all possible sources including local GPs and consultant psychiatrists, post-mortem rooms, health authorities, coroners and the Office of National Statistics (then called the Office of Populations and Censuses). No one source provided precisely the same list as any other source. The coroner's list was the most comprehensive but only included people who had died within that coroner's jurisdiction. A Barnet resident who had travelled to the coast to jump off a cliff would therefore not be dealt with by the Barnet coroner. Departments of Public Health, now sometimes called Health Improvement Departments, do receive notification of all deceased residents of that area, including the cause of death on the death certificate or ascertained at inquest. However, this information can take months to arrive at the Public Health Department, and to filter out the suicide and undetermined death verdicts requires someone to screen through many names and causes of death. Surprisingly the Office of National Statistics is not always accurate in allocating a resident to the correct Trust or Local Authority by address and their statistical reports have at times listed deaths by the date of the coroner's verdict rather than the date of the actual death.

We have found a 'belt and braces' approach to be best, obtaining most of the data from the coroners covering the areas in which we are interested, and supplementing this with data from the Public Health Department when it arrives, as this will include local residents who have committed suicide elsewhere. This approach is only possible if the people doing the audit are able to establish and maintain a good relationship with the local coroner(s). The coroners and their officers will not have time to search through databases for audit information, and – as they have the duty of keeping the data confidential except where there is a 'need to know' – they may question the auditor's justification in seeking this information. It would be wise to clarify with the coroner from the onset that the audit will require minimal time from the coroner's staff.

Having set up a system for case ascertainment which should be updated for new cases every month or two, a database must be created, either paper or electronic, to store the data in a manageable and digestible form. At this stage it is useful to decide precisely what information is to be kept on each case. This will of course include the date of birth and date of death, together with the manner of death and the person's status at the time of death (whether an inpatient on the ward, an inpatient absent without leave or on planned leave, someone who had previously been in contact with the mental health service within the previous 12 months, or someone with no contact with the mental health service, etc.). Some of this information may be available from the coroner's records and some from health records. There is a wealth of potentially useful information in these records: over the years we have steadily increased the number of fields in the database to take account of new questions raised.

Now that a list of names and some information is available, the next step would be to audit the casenotes, preferably by peer review. This would include any mental health service casenotes and ideally also those of the primary health care team. It is suggested that a semi-structured questionnaire be developed for the person or team carrying out the casenote audit, including not only easily obtainable data such as the date of the last contact with the deceased but also open-ended questions such as 'Could the case have been managed any better? If so, how?'

As the audit proceeds the amount of data will soon become too much to assimilate by just looking at the database. Someone with the relevant skills will need to put the data together as tables, graphs and charts. Eventually it should be possible to look at trends over time, but initially the most interesting data will come from the demographic information, the proportion of patients seen by the mental health service and the causes of death. It is very important to proceed beyond these 'interesting' findings to the next step, which is identifying areas for heightened attention (for example certain patient groups, times of year or geographical 'hotspots' at high risk) and making recommendations for improvements in practice. The recommendations could range from changes in policy, for example in observation levels on wards, to finding a different way of assessing former patients who arrive at a mental health service setting asking to be seen. Once these recommendations have been discussed, modified, accepted and implemented, the effects can be monitored through the continuing audit.

Confidentiality and trust

One question sometimes asked of people working in suicide audit concerns the law. Health and social services staff may be fearful of litigation by aggrieved relatives. They may also be worried about criticism by the coroner and by senior managers or clinicians. We are told that we should be working towards a 'no blame culture', but the reality is that we are in a 'blame

culture' which can be exacerbated by hasty actions after a high-profile suicide.

If suicide audit is to obtain honest answers to its questions, the ques-
tioner needs to have the trust of the person being interviewed. So can suicide audit staff honestly say to the clinician 'Your answers will not lead to
any possibility of disciplinary action'? This would not be true. If suicide audit were to uncover evidence of gross negligence, there would be an obligation to report this to somebody more senior in the organisation. Reminding
the clinician of this fact immediately before interviewing them for suicide
audit may not be the best way of helping them relax: it is more sensible to
ensure that all employees in the service are aware of this when they join the
service, or when suicide audit is introduced into the service.

All documents in the health service, including audit documents, are liable to subpoena by the courts. The most conscientious and exemplary clinician may be reticent in answering questions if he or she is aware that the
answers could be read out in court in front of hostile litigants. One way to
avoid this possibility is to ensure that documents retained for suicide audit
are rendered anonymous as soon as possible.

Final thoughts

There are mandatory requirements from the Department of Health for
health staff to carry out suicide audit. These requirements are monitored,
for example Primary Care Trusts are asked annually about their progress
with suicide audit. Despite this, auditing suicide is not easy. Suicide is an
emotive issue. Professionals who have been involved with somebody who
has committed suicide usually feel a greater or lesser degree of guilt and responsibility for the suicide. They may also fear that they are going to be
scapegoated, either by managers or by the family.

Establishing suicide audit has to be done with sensitivity to these issues
or it will be met with hostility and rejection. But if it is done well, the components of a comprehensive audit – the non-judgmental questioning, the
opportunity for reflection and disclosure, and the honest feedback – are
helpful both to the bereaved family and to the bereaved staff, and raise
standards of practice throughout the service.

References

Department of Health (1992) *The Health of the Nation: A Strategy for Health in England.* London:
    HMSO.
Department of Health (1999a) *Saving Lives: Our Healthier Nation.* London: HMSO.

Department of Health (1999b) *Safer Services: National Confidential Inquiry into Suicide and Homicide by People with Mental Illness.* London: Department of Health.

Department of Health (1999c) *National Service Framework for Mental Health.* London: Department of Health.

Department of Health (2001) *Safety First: Five Year Report of the National Confidential Inquiry into Suicide and Homicide by People with Mental Illness.* London: Department of Health Publications.

Department of Health (2002) *National Suicide Prevention Strategy for England.* London: Department of Health Publications.

Morgan, H.G. (1994) *Clinical Audit of Suicide and Other Unexpected Deaths.* London: NHS Management Executive.

National Institute for Mental Health in England (NIMHE) (2003) *Preventing Suicide: a Toolkit for Mental Health Services.* Leeds: NIMHE.

Redpath, L., Stacey, A., Pugh, E. and Holmes, E. (1997) 'Use of the critical incident technique in primary care in the audit of deaths by suicide.' *Quality and Health Care 6*, 25–28.

Chapter 15

Carrying Out Internal Reviews of Serious Incidents

Suzette Woodward, Kathryn Hill, and Sally Adams

Introduction and background

In healthcare there are two main myths:

- the perfection myth: if we try hard enough we will not make any errors
- the punishment myth: if we punish people when they make errors they will make fewer of them. (Leape 2002)

The truths are:

- Everyone makes errors both at home and work.

- Incidents are caused by complex systems and human factors such as interruptions, short term memory, attention span, pressure to hurry, fatigue, anxiety, fear, boredom, complacency and habit.

- Despite some high profile cases, the overwhelming majority of incidents that affect patient safety are not caused by care workers' malicious intent or even lack of competence.

- An error is not misconduct unless there was some intent behind the error.

An Organisation with a Memory (Department of Health (DoH) 2000) and *Building a Safer NHS for Patients* (DoH 2001) set out the development of a new national system for learning from incidents that affect patient safety and this led to the creation of the National Patient Safety Agency (NPSA). They also describe how an improved system for handling investigations and inquiries across the NHS will be developed, and recognise the complex interplay of issues that leads to errors occurring in healthcare settings.

In the future the most serious incidents, including individual cases of death by suicide by those in touch with specialist mental health services, could be investigated by the NHS Trust concerned using a Root Cause Analysis (RCA). There are situations which warrant the RCA being carried out by an investigator external to the Trust involved. These include all homicides perpetrated by someone currently or recently in receipt of specialist secondary mental health services and suicides that are of a particular concern, such as a number of suicides committed in the same area over a short period of time.

RCA should support the *Saving Lives: Our Healthier Nation* (DoH 1999) target of reducing the death rate from suicide by at least 20 per cent by 2010. The government-published *National Suicide Prevention Strategy for England* (DoH 2002) strategy identifies high risk groups for suicide of which one is mental health service users. To reduce the number of mental health service users who attempt or commit suicide, local services must take a multi-disciplinary approach to reviewing and learning lessons and create constructive environments that allow for changes in practice to be identified and implemented.

The purpose of this chapter is to outline what constitutes a patient safety incident; a prevented patient safety incident; and how an emerging open and fair approach to investigations increases the opportunity for lessons to be learnt and solutions implemented. There is also a detailed look at the RCA process. The term 'patient safety incident' is used throughout to describe any unintended or unexpected incident(s) which could have or did lead to harm for one or more persons receiving healthcare.

Patient safety

Patient safety encompasses assessing risk, identifying and managing patient-related risks, analysis, generating solutions and ultimately improving patient care. The term patient safety replaces the traditional terms of clinical risk, non-clinical risk and the health and safety of patients.

Patient safety is defined as: the processes by which an organisation reduces the risk and occurrence of harm to patients as a result of their healthcare.

Patient safety incidents

A patient safety incident could be a single incident or a series of incidents over time. It includes incidents relating directly to patient care, and indirect patient care incidents such as equipment issues, staff shortages and confusing labels. A patient safety incident is any event which impacts negatively on patients or their care. This could be a direct care event such as an overdose of medication or an indirect system event such as missing test results, lack of training for a new piece of equipment or lack of induction for temporary staff. These can be defined specifically as care delivery problems.

Grading of incidents

A patient safety incident which impacts on patients is graded according to the severity of impact: no harm, low, moderate, severe or death (see Figure 15.1). The key factor for the severity category is the patient's condition. This is the injury or harm, and the level of care required following the incident.

Figure 15.1: Levels of severity of harm

Models of investigation

For some time, chronological chain of event models have been used (Lagerlof and Andersson 1979) to identify a sequence of events. These work back from the accident in the hope of identifying the cause.

When a patient safety incident occurs, the important question is not 'Who is to blame?' but 'How and why did it occur?' The answer to the latter tells us more about the system in which we work (Vincent 2002). This is a move away from passive learning, where lessons are identified but not put into practice, to active learning, where lessons are embedded into an organisation's culture and practices (DoH 2000). In healthcare the main approaches to investigations have been local inquiries, major public inquiries (for example the Bristol Royal Infirmary Inquiry), significant event audits (mainly in primary care) and most recently root cause analysis.

Significant Event Audit (SEA)

SEA is a form of RCA used in primary care and, in particular, general practice. Individual episodes with significant consequences, either beneficial or harmful, are analysed in a systematic and detailed way to ascertain what can be learnt about the overall quality of care. Changes that might lead to future improvements are identified (Pringle *et al.* 1995).

SEA is a work-based local forum for identifying and analysing incidents as well as celebrating success. It is seen as a positive and proactive approach to incident management (Berlin *et al.* 1992; Buckley 1990; Firth-Cozens 1992; Pringle and Bradley 1994; Robinson *et al.* 1995).

Root Cause Analysis (RCA)

The NPSA has developed an RCA model which is largely based on the work of Rasmussen (1983), Reason (1990), Vincent *et al.* (2000) and Taylor-Adams and Vincent (2004).

The NPSA has identified the following factors as the reasons why patient safety incidents happen:

1.   Active failures.

2.   Latent conditions.

3.   Contributory factors.

4.   Influencing factors.

5.   Causal factors.

RCA is a retrospective review of a patient safety incident which identifies the above factors, and finds out how the incident happened. The analysis identifies areas for change, recommendations and sustainable solutions that minimise the chances of the incident happening in the future. It is equally applicable to complaints and claims.

Getting started: classifying incidents

Latent conditions

Decisions taken at the higher levels of an organisation, while well thought out and considered, can introduce unrecognised (latent) problems into the system. Organisational processes can have a direct bearing on how accidents develop.

Active failures

Active failures are unsafe acts or omissions by those at the 'sharp end' of the system that have immediate adverse consequences. These unsafe acts are influenced by error-producing conditions (contributory or influencing factors) such as stress, inadequate training and assessment, poor supervision and high workload. They arise in the process of care, usually actions or omissions by members of staff. Examples include failure to monitor, observe or act, decisions that are incorrect with hindsight, not seeking help when necessary and failure to establish a training system for a new procedure or piece of equipment.

Contributory factors

The significance of a contributory factor varies. These factors tend to be specific to the incident and are often present in the working ethos of the system.

Not all contributory factors are negative. They can mitigate or minimise a more serious outcome. It is important that positive factors are drawn out during the investigation and are used to support and promote good safety practice. The opportunity to provide positive feedback to those involved in an incident influences safety culture in the long run.

Contributory factors are classified as follows:

1. *Patient factors.* These tend to be unique to the patient involved and could be the complexity of their condition. They can be grouped into social and cultural factors.

2. *Individual factors.* These are unique to the healthcare worker(s) involved in the incident such as their psychological state, home life and relationships with colleagues.

3. *Task factors.* These could be guidelines, procedures and policies that are unavailable, unclear, incorrect or too complicated.

4. *Communication factors.* These are all types of communication, whether verbal or written, that have affected the task or performance.

5. *Team and social factors.* These are predominantly communication issues. However, they also include management style, hierarchical structures, lack of respect for junior team members and individuals' perception of their role.

6. *Education and training factors.* The lack of availability and quality of training programmes affects the ability to perform to job specifications and respond appropriately under difficult or emergency circumstances. The effectiveness of training, as a way of improving safety, is dependent on content, delivery style, assessment of skill acquisition, monitoring and updates.

7. *Equipment and resource factors.* This refers to faulty or missing equipment. Resource factors could be a lack of skilled staff or the funds to train staff and buy new equipment.

8. *Working conditions,* These are any factors that affect the ability to function at optimum levels in the work place. They could be uncomfortable heat, poor lighting, overcrowding, noise from equipment and building works.

9. *Organisation and strategic factors,* These are factors that are either inherent in or imbedded in the organisation. They can lie dormant and unrecognised or they could be recognised but not viewed as a priority.

Influencing and causal factors

An influencing factor plays a key part either in an incident happening or in the outcome of such an incident. Causal factors are those that play a significant part in the incident happening. Removal of these factors will either prevent, or reduce, the chances of a similar type of incident happening in similar circumstances in the future. There may be more than one causal factor. Identifying and removing these factors is the prime aim when undertaking an RCA.

Stages of a Root Cause Analysis

The first thing local organisations need to do is establish the basic facts and assess the incident to determine whether a low or high level investigation is appropriate. This is dependent on the level of harm to the patient(s).

Low level investigation

This is for incidents where no permanent injury or significantly increased level of care was required. The healthcare worker completes an incident report form which includes any identified contributing factors. The information is put into a local database and subjected to aggregate review which highlights any trends or themes. These should be reported across the organisation to raise awareness. If a trend appears, the organisation can combine a cluster of incidents and conduct an RCA. As part of the investigation, the patient(s) harmed should be given an explanation by a nurse or doctor.

High level investigation

This is appropriate for all unexpected or unintended deaths which were directly related to an incident; those incidents which resulted in permanent injury, loss of function or body part; or those incidents which become either a complaint or civil claim. A high level investigation may also be conducted for an incident where the patient needed further surgical intervention, transfer to intensive care or the incident was prevented but is considered worthy of an in-depth review.

Potential bias

The person doing the investigation should not be biased by the outcomes or hindsight. They must take into account the situation and circumstances that the healthcare workers faced at the time.

Stage one: Being Open

Being Open is the principle of discussing the incident with healthcare workers, patients and their carers. It can include a factual explanation of what happened and what steps are being taken to manage and review the incident. It can also mean the patient or carer are involved in the investigation. It is essential that this is done before starting the RCA. The organisation should acknowledge and apologise when things go wrong and reassure patients and carers that lessons learnt will help to prevent a recurrence (Osborn and Carthey 2003).

The key principles of Being Open are:
- All patient safety incidents are acknowledged as soon as they are identified.
- Information about an incident is given to patients and their carers in a truthful, timely and open manner by an appropriate person.
- Patients and carers receive a sincere expression of sorrow or regret for the harm that has resulted from a patient safety

incident in the form of an appropriately worded and agreed form of apology, as early as possible.

- Patients and carers are treated sympathetically, with respect and consideration and given support appropriate to their needs.

- Healthcare workers are encouraged to report patient safety incidents and supported throughout the incident investigation. Counselling services should be available.

- RCA, SEA or similar techniques are used to discover the underlying causes of patient safety incidents.

- Being Open should include healthcare workers who have key roles in the patient's care. Most healthcare provision involves multi-disciplinary teams so Being Open should therefore have multi-disciplinary representation.

- Being Open requires the support of clinical risk and quality improvement processes through governance frameworks. It also involves a system of accountability through the Chief Executive to Trust Board to ensure these changes are implemented and their effectiveness reviewed.

- Policies and procedures for Being Open should be developed by NHS organisations and their independent contractors, with full consideration of and respect for patient, carer and staff privacy and confidentiality, and in line with the national guidance, i.e. *National Suicide Prevention Strategy for England* (DoH 2002).

Stage two: Gathering and mapping information

This stage of the analysis is critical and can result in a vast array of documents from many sources in the organisation. The following points should be considered when collecting data:

- The protocols and guidelines in place during the planning and delivery of care should be reviewed.

- Copies of all clinical guidance documents are preserved in the investigation file.

- Information should be tracked at all times including when it was requested, if it was received, and where it is being kept.

- Give all documentary evidence, including photographs, a reference number and use this as an integral part of keeping track of them.

- Keep information in a ring binder with a numbered or lettered index system. This makes information easier to find and less likely to be accidentally destroyed.

- It is important to distinguish between original documents and copies. Originals should be kept centrally. All information must be kept securely in line with the Data Protection Act 1998.

If many staff have been asked to provide a written account of events it is worth considering making copies of the relevant part of the patient's health records to enable easy access in a timely manner.

Stage three: Interview process

In stage three, the healthcare workers involved are asked for their witness statements. This can be followed by interviews. Each person should be interviewed alone. The interview should be in a private room without interruptions. At the end of the interview, they should be asked if they would have done anything differently or what changes they think are required to prevent the incident from happening again.

Stage four: Mapping the information

Multi-disciplinary group meetings

In some instances it may be necessary to arrange for a group discussion with the healthcare workers involved in the incident. Investigators will need to be flexible and may need to arrange meetings outside normal office hours. The discussion requires planning, expert facilitation, setting of rules and should be seen as a positive process, providing a chance to review all the events leading up to the incident. The purpose is to clarify events and make sure nothing has been forgotten.

The meeting should be minuted and everyone should be made aware that this is happening. Any recordings must be agreed with everyone. It is advisable to get legal advice on disclosure issues.

There are a number of ways to collect the information and three techniques are outlined below.

BRAINSTORMING

The aim is to identify what happened; ways in which the incident could have been prevented; and recommendations for change in the future. The group needs a facilitator and a scribe. The scribe uses either a plain pad or flip-chart to record what is being said. The process can be either structured or unstructured. In a structured process, otherwise known as 'round-robin', each person states their involvement and what they would have done differently; this can be quite daunting for those who do not feel able to speak freely. In an unstructured process, otherwise known as 'freewheeling', people speak up spontaneously. This can sometimes mean some individuals dominate the discussion or inhibit others from speaking. The facilitator should ensure the process is open and fair and that it does not degenerate into individual criticism or arguments.

BRAINWRITING

This is similar to brainstorming but allows the group to generate information and ideas anonymously. Rather than speak out, each participant is asked to write down key points on cards or post-it notes. The scribe collects these and writes the points on a flip-chart, so that individuals' handwriting is not identified. Brainwriting is very useful if there are potential conflicts in the group, where some individuals may dominate the process or there is a mix of senior and junior staff.

NOMINAL GROUP TECHNIQUE

This is a form of 'silent voting' used to prioritise the issues that have been discussed in a group session. It can help identify the key, causal or contributory factors, and prioritise recommendations for change. Once the factors have been agreed, through brainstorming or brainwriting, each participant is asked to rank them in order of priority on cards or post-it notes. The scribe takes these cards and allocates scores to the factors or recommendations. The investigator then has a prioritised list to work with.

Stage five: Analysis

Five 'whys'

This is an extremely effective and simple process for identifying all the questions that need to be asked. 'Why?' is asked at least five times in a row to detect the root cause or meaning of a particular incident (Ross 1994).

> Because of no nail, the horseshoe got lost,
> Because of no horseshoe, the horse got lost,
> Because of no horse, the rider got lost,

Because of no rider, the battle got lost,
Because of no battle, the kingdom got lost.

(Traditional, cited by Lynch and Kordis 1988)

It can take more or less than five 'whys' to identify the latent failure, contributory factor or root cause. This process generally ends when the investigator finds it hard to identify any new questions. The question 'why' can be applied to either written documents or asked to people in a group process or one-to-one interview. The investigator starts by identifying the active failures and asks 'Why did this happen?' Each question can generate more than one answer, which can take the investigator down various avenues.

For example:

Q1. *The patient died by suicide through taking an overdose. Why did this happen?*

A1. Because the patient had accumulated a number of doses of their medication.

Q2. *The patient had accumulated a number of doses of their medication. How did this happen?*

A2. Following administration the patient was not observed or checks made to see if they had taken their medication.

Q3. *The patient was not observed or checked to see if they had taken their medication. Why was this not done?*

A3. *This could generate a number of responses, such as the nurses were:*

- short-staffed and busy
- not aware of the policy to stay and observe
- inexperienced and new to the area.

These are then listed as contributory factors and further questions could elicit latent system failure which led to each factor.

The Fishbone diagram or Ishikawa diagram

Kaoru Ishikawa, a Japanese quality control statistician, invented the fishbone diagram. The fishbone diagram is an analysis tool that provides a systematic way of looking at effects and the causes that create or contribute to those effects. The design of the diagram looks much like the skeleton of a fish. The multiple branches represent direct, contributory and root causes. An example is found in Figure 15.2.

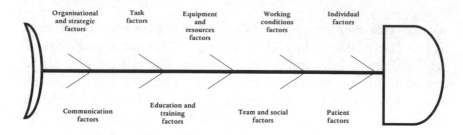

Figure 15.2: Fishbone diagram

Gantt charts

Gantt charts are bar graphs that help identify time lines. They can also be used to indicate the relationship between factors. Gantt charts can also be used in the report stage to plan implementing recommendations, and assign those responsible for each task.

TASKS	Month 1	Month 2	Month 3	Month 4
Task A	▨			
Task B		▨	▨	
Task C			▨	▨
Task D				

Figure 15.3: Gantt chart

Time lines

Time lines are useful tools for mapping out the chronology of the event using dates and times. There are a number of different versions.

Patient found hung in bathroom ⟶ Cardiac arrest team called
07.45   07.46

Figure 15.4: Time line

Staff involved/Time	07.45	07.46
Ward domestic	Found patient in bathroom; called for nursing assistance	Asked other patients to stay out of the way
Nurse in charge	In shift handover	Called cardiac arrest team
Nurse caring for the patient	In shift handover	Rang to collect equipment

Figure 15.5: Tabular time line

Event date and time	16 June 2003 07.45	16 June 2003 07.46
Event	Patient found hung in the ward bathroom	Cardiac arrest team called
Supplementary information	Patient had been on 15-minute observations	
Good practice		Team called promptly
Active failure	Patient not being observed for more than 15 minutes	
Contributory factor	Shift handover taking place	
Latent failure	Policy decision that all staff leave patients to take part in shift handover	

Figure 15.6: Time person table

Stage six: Barrier analysis

Controls and defences exist in all healthcare process to act as barriers to incidents. A barrier analysis identifies whether or not controls and defences have worked. It can be useful to brainstorm controls and defences and recommend those for the future.

Physical barriers

- Insulation on hot pipes
- Bar coding
- Lead aprons for radiographers
- Keypad controlled doors
- Computer programmes which prevent further progression if a field is not completed

- Double-locked cabinets for controlled drugs which require two keys to open and these are kept separately
- Filing cabinets constructed so that opening one drawer locks all the rest, reducing the chance of tipping
- Bathroom sinks with an overflow hole helping to prevent flooding

Natural barriers (distance, time or place)

- Procedure for level one observation every 15 minutes
- System for checking prescriptions in community pharmacy, for example, supervised consumption of methadone
- Checking informed consent at different stages
- Sending debit and credit cards separately from their pin numbers

Human action barriers

- Checking the temperature of a bath before getting in
- Control and restraint of violent patients
- Patients asking the healthcare staff if they have washed their hands
- Checking patient's identification with the patient, carer or relative

Administrative barriers

- Protocols and procedures
- Supervision and training
- Two people signing for controlled drugs
- Checklists
- Notices
- Professional registers
- Computer passwords
- Expiry dates

Of these four types of barrier, physical barriers are the most reliable in terms of providing failsafe solutions to safety problems. Natural barriers, while less effective, generally provide a more robust solution than human action and administrative barriers which rely on human action and behaviour.

Stage seven: Report and recommendations

The final stage is to put together a report with sustainable recommendations. This report may need to be in different formats for different audiences. The report may be required by some or all of the following:

- the patient and relatives
- organisational management committees, for example, clinical governance committee
- Trust Board
- Coroner's office
- local and national media
- strategic health authority
- Department of Health.

The report should be easy to read and staff should not be identifiable. Do not use first names or surnames of staff involved. They can be referred to as Dr A or Nurse Y and a central master copy of who A and Y are should be kept securely.

- Start with a summary section.
- All evidence must be referenced.
- Use a content list and clear headings.
- Number every page.
- Use the header for the title of the document and label it as a draft, including which version, or final.
- Use the footer for the version date, reference initials, document name and location on computer and page number.
- Headings should include: summary, introduction, incident details, active and latent failures, contributory factors, conclusions and recommendations.
- Appendices should include: recommendations table with the name of those responsible for implementation; list of documentary evidence; fishbone diagrams; flow charts; control charts and time lines.

Questions to ask when considering recommendations:

- Consider the 'side effects' of improvements – is more risk being introduced?
- Can they be shared?
- Are they cost-effective?
- Are they realistic and sustainable?

The organisation should monitor all RCA reports and recommendations at least quarterly. This can be done by the clinical governance or risk management committee. The Board should also be informed and assured that actions are being taken and monitored.

Conclusion

Healthcare is a complex system of processes and procedures which are carried out by a vast number of hugely committed staff. These staff endeavour to create a safe environment despite working in a complex system, preventing things from going wrong by resolving issues, detecting incidents and anticipating hazards on a daily basis (Reason 2000).

The NHS is constantly striving to learn from patient safety incidents that occur in mental health settings. Improving the safety of NHS patients is a key component of quality improvement and clinical governance. Extensive research in industry has shown that most failures do not have a single explanatory cause for the event and are usually a result of a series of problems in the system (Bogner 1994; Reason 2000; Vincent 2001). However, when things fail, human actions and human error are often the easiest things to identify as the cause of the incident. The usual response is to find 'the culprit' and blame that individual (DoH 2000; Reason 2000).

The new approach outlined in this chapter should help staff and services move away from this and begin to develop a culture that allows lessons to be learnt and systems to be changed following a suicide.

References

Berlin, A., Spencer, J.A., Bhopal, R.S. and van Zwanenberg, T.D. (1992) 'Audit of deaths in general practice: A pilot study of the critical incident technique.' *Quality in Health Care 1*, 231–235.

Bogner, M.S. (ed) (1994) *Human Error in Medicine.* Hove: Lawrence Erlbaum Associates Publishers.

Buckley, G. (1990) 'Clinically significant events.' In M. Marinker (ed) *Medical Audit and General Practice.* London: BMJ Publishing.

Data Protection Act (1998) London: The Stationery Office. www.hmso.gov.uk/acts/acts1998/19980029.htm

Department of Health (1999) *Saving Lives: Our Healthier Nation.* London: HMSO.

Department of Health (2000) *An Organisation with a Memory.* London: The Stationery Office.

Department of Health (2001) *Building a Safer NHS for Patients.* London: DoH.

Department of Health (2002) *National Suicide Prevention Strategy for England.* London: Department of Health Publications.

Firth-Cozens, J. (1992) 'Building teams for effective audit.' *Quality in Healthcare 1,* 252–255.

Lagerlof, E. and Andersson, R. (1979) *The Swedish Information System on Occupational Injuries.* Stockholm: The Swedish National Board of Occupational Safety and Health.

Leape, L.L. (2002) 'Reporting of adverse events.' *New England Journal of Medicine 347,* 20, 1633–1638.

Lynch, D. and Kordis, P. (1988) *Dolphin Strategies.* Brain Technologies Corp. German Edition: *Delphin Strategien,* PAIDA Verlag.

Osborn, S. and Carthey, J. (2003) *Being Open: Open Disclosure of Adverse Incidents.* National Patient Safety Agency unpublished policy.

Pringle, M. and Bradley, C. (1994) 'Significant event auditing: A user's guide.' *Audit Trends 2,* 1, 20–23.

Pringle, M., Bradley, C.P., Carmichael, C.M., Wallis, H. and Moore, A. (1995) *Significant Event Auditing.* RCGP Occasional Paper 70. Exeter: Royal College of General Practioners.

Raef, S. (2002) 'Exploring 7 levels of safety.' Annenberg IV Conference April 22–24. Paper presented by C. Vincent. *Editor Focus on Patient Safety.* www.npsf.org

Rasmussen, J. (1983) 'Skills, rules, knowledge: Signals, signs and symbols and other distinctions in human performance models.' *IEEE Transactions: Systems, Man & Cybernetics 13,* 3, 257–267.

Reason, J.T. (1990) *Human Error.* New York: Cambridge University Press.

Reason, J. (2000) 'Human error: models and management.' *British Medical Journal 320,* 768–770.

Robinson, L.A., Stacy, R., Spencer, J.A. and Bhopal, R.S. (1995) 'How to do it: Use facilitated case discussions for significant event auditing.' *British Medical Journal 311,* 315–318.

Ross, R. (1994) 'The five whys perspective.' In P. Senge, A. Kleiner and C. Roberts (eds) *The Fifth Discipline Fieldbook: Strategies and Tools for Building a Learning Organization.* New York: Doubleday.

Taylor-Adams, S.E. and Vincent, C. (2004) *A Protocol to Investigate and Analyse Adverse Incidents.* London: BMJ Publishing. (Available on RCA e-learning site).

Vincent, C. (ed) (2001) *Clinical Risk Management. Enhancing patient safety.* 2nd edn. London: British Medical Journal Publishing.

Vincent, C., Taylor-Adams, S., Chapman, E.J., Hewett, D., Prior, S., Strange, P. and Tizzard, A. (2000) 'How to investigate and analyse clinical incidents: Clinical risk unit and association of litigation and risk management protocol.' *British Medical Journal 320,* 737–745.

Chapter 16

Developing Training Packages

Jenny Droughton, Linda Gask,
Gill Green and Clare Dixon

This chapter identifies the main principles which statutory and voluntary services, teams, and staff trainers/educators should consider when developing training programmes in suicide risk assessment and management. The authors present background information underpinning the need for effective training in suicide prevention among staff in a wide range of settings and agencies and identify some key components required to develop effective training. The Skills Training on Risk Management (STORM) project is then reviewed as an exemplar of an effective, evidence-based training programme. Finally, a checklist of good practice recommendations in suicide prevention training is provided and the reader is encouraged to reflect on specific questions and challenges within this crucial area.

Background: The policy imperative, the evidence base and the challenges ahead

Earlier chapters in this manual describe the growing clinical and empirical evidence underpinning strategies and interventions likely to prevent or reduce suicide and related behaviour. The key challenge is then to disseminate and target this knowledge to where it will have the maximum impact and applicability. This can be achieved through training staff who manage suicide risk in various locations or who work with groups and populations at high risk of suicide. As the *National Suicide Prevention Strategy for England* (Department of Health (DoH) 2002) recommends, providing and regularly repeating such training for staff and personnel across a wide range of settings is a vital ingredient in the campaign to prevent and reduce suicides and deliberate self-harm.

Initially, a logical starting point in relation to suicide prevention training might be to use staff who work in mental health services to train personnel in other locations in the practical skills and theoretical knowledge of risk assessment and management. This would involve specialist mental health staff routinely cascading their skills and knowledge to colleagues in other locations, who work with diverse client groups. It is based on the robust premise that workers and agencies (not just mental health services) in contact with key high risk groups such as prisoners, unemployed people and young males all require some level of training in suicide prevention if a reduction is to be achieved, given the fact that the majority of suicides occur among individuals *not* known to specialist mental health services.

There are, however, clear difficulties with such a proposal to the training question: first, there is the assumption that at least *qualified* mental health practitioners such as psychiatrists, mental health nurses, clinical psychologists and social workers have all received a minimum amount and quality of suicide prevention training in their respective professional training. This is clearly not the case and the training that is provided is often on an ad hoc basis with no standards of quality, content or tutors' qualification. This leaves a mental health workforce with a surprisingly poor general standard of competence and a limited knowledge base in effective suicide prevention strategies, though some small pockets of excellence exist. A second difficulty is that of the limited capacity of those mental health staff who are well trained and skilled in suicide prevention to provide sustained, rolling programmes of training to staff in other settings, given the national shortage of all disciplines within the entire mental health workforce.

A final challenge is that while mental health experts can act in a consultative role, helping other agencies to develop training which incorporates the core principles of effective suicide risk assessment and risk management (which are generalisable across most settings), such experts may not have a full appreciation of the specific issues unique to any particular setting. There is no single approach to suicide risk training, no off-the-shelf, empirically validated training package suitable for all the diverse areas / workers who have a legitimate role to play in suicide prevention. However, a range of training courses and providers both within and outside the mental health arena exists among both statutory and commercial agencies, though actual details are sparse and there is no national database/directory nor any agreed standards/codes of practice.

One obstacle in progressing the training agenda for suicide prevention is that there is a lack of intervention studies, at both epidemiological and micro levels. This means that there is very little robust evidence identifying the core principles underpinning effective training available to guide those planning training packages. A notable exception to this is the STORM research study, which is described in detail later in this chapter, and the earlier work undertaken by Tierney (1994) which will now be considered briefly.

This series of Canadian research studies evaluated the impact of the 'Suicide Intervention Workshop' (SIW) – a standardised training programme based on adult learning principles. The SIW contained modules on attitudes, knowledge and intervention skills and was aimed at both mental health personnel and other public sector and community staff, e.g. teachers, police, youth workers. The goal of the two-day programme was:

> to provide caregivers with intervention strategies and competencies to prevent the immediate risk of suicidal behaviour. It was designed to assist caregivers in the development of attitudes, knowledge, and skills to recognise persons at risk of suicide, to assess the level of immediate risk, and to undertake appropriate management or referral of a person at risk (Tierney 1994, p.70).

Using various methodologies, including a pre–post comparison study design, random samples of people undergoing the SIW completed various structured measures which evaluated aspects of their knowledge, attitudes and intervention skills (Tierney 1994). Results demonstrated significant increases in participants' self-reported and observed skills in suicidal intervention. Some preliminary trends towards improvements in attitudes towards the feasibility and effectiveness of suicide intervention and in knowledge of suicide and of intervention strategies were also identified.

The general dearth of robust research into effective suicide prevention training programmes in mental health is mirrored in the lack of published evidence reporting training initiatives and packages delivered in non-health settings, e.g. prisons or non-statutory agencies working with adolescents. Some agencies have published descriptive data regarding numbers of personnel trained but fail to supply details of any other outcome measures or to share the content or curriculum of their particular training programme.

There is a clear need to improve access to, and the quality of, suicide prevention training programmes within and across many sectors. However, in the push to increase the throughput in terms of numbers of staff trained it is important not to lose sight of a key principle of adult learning, namely that training which only addresses knowledge is insufficient to achieve sustained changes in behaviour. Undoubtedly, training which relays information about the demographic risk of certain groups of individuals and the

standards and goals of the National Suicide Prevention Strategy is important. However, without combining this factual knowledge with basic skills
training in how to assess if someone is at risk of suicide, staff will remain ill
equipped to prevent and manage suicidal behaviour. Clearly, the relative
proportion of skills-based training within a programme compared to the
knowledge and awareness component will depend on the target audience,
including their roles and responsibilities in suicide prevention. For instance, some staff, e.g. college counsellors or General Practitioners, may
have a role in identification and referral of suicidal individuals while other
staff, e.g. community mental health nurses, will be directly involved in delivering treatment. There is therefore a need for a hierarchy of training to be
available to match the needs of different staff groups in specific roles and
settings. This hierarchy of suicide prevention training should start with basic awareness courses for all staff, with a next stage of general assessment
and management skills and knowledge and extending, where necessary, to
a higher level of advanced and specialist training.

    As with all effective education and training, optimum outcomes will
not be achieved by just addressing knowledge and skills deficits. For any
type of training programme to achieve sustained learning and changes in
behaviours, a third strand is required: the attitudinal dimension. In suicide
prevention training, this final part of the learning triangle of Knowledge –
Skills – Attitudes is particularly important as negative attitudes towards
suicidal individuals and misinformation regarding suicide and deliberate
self-harm abound in our society. As a result, unhelpful attitudes or inaccurate myths, such as 'people who say they are going to kill themselves don't
tend to do it', are still commonplace even among practitioners and staff in
frequent contact with people or groups at high risk of suicide (Williams
1997).

    If suicides are to be prevented it is crucial that such negative beliefs and
myths are tackled as a fundamental part of training programmes as otherwise any improvements in skills or knowledge achieved through training
will be compromised. An additional attitudinal aspect of suicide prevention, which may impact on the effectiveness of training programmes, is the
negative beliefs that some staff may hold about those in their care. For instance, if staff express, or even privately hold, beliefs that the future is hopeless for their client group or that they are incapable of positive change (e.g.
mental health staff believing there is no future for people with schizophrenia or prison officers of the opinion that all prisoners are necessarily
recidivists) this may well be inadvertently transmitted to those in their care
and so increase the risk of suicide. Clearly it would be unrealistic to expect a

brief training course to totally eliminate such polarised and fatalistic attitudes. However, trainers need to be aware that the pre-training attitudinal climate of their audience and organisational culture will be very influential in determining how receptive trainees are to gaining new knowledge and learning and trying out new skills.

Key components in the development of training programmes in suicide prevention

Mapping existing training activity and programme quality

The lack of any coherent data to clarify the level and quality of training activity within even the areas which serve 'high risk groups' such as mental health services or the prison service is a major challenge nationally, regionally, and often even locally. Anecdotal evidence suggests an unacceptably wide variability in the availability, content, format and quality of training programmes. A common theme emerges of poor co-ordination and limited sharing of good practice and resources despite the existence of a few small pockets of excellence. There is a clear need for national mapping exercises to identify all training courses and packages in suicide prevention currently available in the key risk areas and to review their evidence base as well as the credentials of their tutors and trainers.

Delivery and content of training

Even within settings where staff have access to some sort of mandatory training in suicide prevention, there may be an over-emphasis on didactic teaching methods and a content focused on statistics and epidemiological data. This may be coupled, particularly in mental health settings, with an over-reliance on paper measures and rating scales as the main 'intervention'. As Holloway (2002) highlights, within suicide prevention training targeted at mental health services, a shift is needed from an emphasis on bureaucratic activities and service structures to the provision of effective treatment and care for underlying problems and disorders, and increased sensitivity to the ever-changing risks presented by each service user.

An interpersonal focus

In all settings, trainers need to market the message that an essential ingredient of suicide prevention is high quality suicide risk assessment and management and that this in turn is in fact predominantly an interpersonal process. As such, it is somewhat immaterial whether staff undertake brief screening interviews or instead are involved in more in-depth suicide assessment, management and preventative work. Instead, they need to be enabled to develop a helpful, collaborative and honest interpersonal style and an ability to discuss sensitive areas in a supportive but open manner rather than just focusing on completing tick-box questionnaires or reading through checklists. This shift in paradigm and practice will take time and sustained effort together with frequent repetition of the message as it challenges the beliefs held by many services, managers and workers about how best to reduce, assess and manage suicidal risk.

Measuring gains in skills, attitudes and knowledge

Trainees who demonstrate high levels of confidence and competence in using any new approach are more likely to use new skills after any training course. Therefore, training programmes in suicide prevention need to identify and include methods of evaluating skills and measuring knowledge acquisition and positive attitude change.

Implementation into routine practice after training and the lasting effects of training need to be researched as does the frequency of refresher courses.

Trainer qualities and background

Findings from other successful training initiatives indicate that an additional factor in providing effective suicide prevention training programmes is the qualities and skills of the trainers. In a discussion of the optimal qualities of tutors delivering psychosocial training for staff working with people with severe mental illness, Bradshaw (2002) identified several key attributes. His work suggests that tutors need to be sufficiently skilled themselves in the practical application of suicide prevention intervention and techniques; preferably to be drawn from a workforce similar to that they are training and, ideally, to still actively be involved in working with clients who may present a risk of suicide. Other attributes, such as a facilitative and collaborative rather than a directive and confrontational style of teaching, and competence and confidence in training groups and the use of different training methods, are also essential ingredients.

Good practice guidelines

- Consider the involvement of bereaved relatives and people who self-harm or have survived a suicide attempt as trainers in training programmes, i.e. 'experts by experience'.

- Recognise the impact of media reporting and stereotypes regarding suicide and self-harm on the attitudes and practice of even highly qualified and experienced health and social care staff as well as workers in other settings.

- Address commonly held 'myths' and anxieties about working with suicidal and self-harming individuals early on in any training programme.

- Recognise that several occupational groups of public sector workers are themselves at increased risk of suicide: how will this impact on their response to any training?

- Encourage organisations hosting training programmes to undertake a review of how they promote the mental health and well-being of their own staff.

- Ensure training courses offer instruction in the core practical skills as well as referring to the background theory and facts.

- In addition to the core skills which are generalisable across diverse settings, each course should include issues specific to that setting, e.g. cultural issues pertinent to a training programme for staff working with South Asian women/security issues pertinent to prison officers.

- Training courses must be linked to 1) an audit cycle 2) an implementation plan.

- Any training and implementation plan or initiative must be owned, led, valued and frequently reinforced by the entire organisation from chief executive level down to front-line staff.

- Training needs to be supported by access to high quality clinical or case supervision.

The Skills Training on Risk Management (STORM) project

STORM is an innovative training package that offers a useful framework and addresses the key components highlighted above as prerequisites for effective suicide prevention and management training programmes. It has been developed over the last five years, initially in Preston in collaboration with the University of Manchester and more recently also with the University of Liverpool. A large number of people have been involved in its development and evaluation.

How does STORM differ from other risk management training packages which are currently available?

STORM can be adapted to professionals working in a range of different settings. It is not a prescriptive approach. But the key difference is that STORM training is concerned with *acquisition of skills*, not with learning how to apply a checklist or other paper exercises. Although it utilises evidence-based methods and its effectiveness has been evaluated, further research is required to inform its wider implementation.

The training package

There are four training modules each lasting approximately two hours. These are: assessment, crisis management, problem solving and crisis prevention. Some groups of workers will only want to take part in the first two of these. Different groups of workers have different needs, so the training videotape also contains a variety of different material to enable the trainers to match with the group they are working with. For example, initial assessment is demonstrated being carried out by a General Practitioner, a community psychiatric nurse and a police surgeon. A single group would not need to see all of these examples.

A great deal of training on suicide focuses on making professionals aware of the identification of risk factors which have been determined by careful epidemiological research. While this is undoubtedly important, it does not help the individual professional to assess individual degree of risk and manage the person sitting in front of them. For this it is essential not only for them to be aware of the interview tasks that must be carried out to make such an assessment, but also for them to have some *model* in their mind of levels of risk; good communication skills and the ability to ask difficult questions about such issues as the nature of any specific plans for suicide.

The training method that we use incorporates brief didactic presentation and modelling from the teaching videotape alongside much more active approaches such as role-play and video feedback. These are not popular methods and require some considerable skill on the part of our facilitators to engage groups positively. Many people would like to think that they can develop skills simply from watching a videotape alone. We are quite certain that this is not the case.

Researching STORM

We have now carried out three evaluation projects. In the first project the staff whom we recruited had no formal training or qualifications in mental health, nor had they any previous interview skills training specific to suicide assessment or management. Four two-hour weekly sessions of interview skills training, using role-play with modelling and video feedback, were held with 33 health and voluntary workers from a geographical area bordered by three towns (population 540,000). We successfully demonstrated improvement in confidence and attitudes towards suicide and that it was possible for these workers to acquire new skills (Morriss *et al.* 1999).

In the second, much larger study (Appleby *et al.* 2000), staff in three health care settings, primary care, A&E departments and mental health services, were offered STORM training. This was provided by trained facilitators, two of whom were nurses and one a psychologist by training, in a district-wide programme across South Lancashire. It was possible to deliver training to 167 health professionals – 47 per cent of those eligible during a six-month period – and of these 103 (62%) attended all training sessions. The courses were very well received, with changes in attitudes, confidence and skills all most marked in those who attended from A&E departments.

Example 16.1: General Practices in South Lancashire

Overall, GPs found STORM training useful. Flexibility in the delivery of training was crucial if GP's were to find time to take up training. Adaptations included:

- delivering each module separately over lunch, or after evening surgery
- delivering the package as part of a practice development day
- excluding modules not seen as essential at this point (e.g. problem-solving) although some practices worked through all four modules
- including all practice staff in training, including reception staff.

Issues of responsibility were discussed in relation to appropriate referral to mental health services. Clear discussion of assessment of levels of risk and crisis management which forms part of the STORM training on assessment helped to clarify the decision making process.

A practice strategy for future management of people at risk of self-harm was drawn up.

Example 16.2: A&E in South Lancashire Hospitals

Out of all professionals trained Accident and Emergency staff found STORM training the most useful.

Staff trained included doctors and nurses of all grades with an emphasis on assessment and crisis management.

Staff found it useful to train together as a team with modules spread over a period of a few weeks.

Contingency plans were drawn up as a consequence of team discussions around the management of a person who is suicidal.

In the third study, we focused on delivery of STORM via locally seconded mental health nurse trainers to four mental health trusts in the northwest of England. Four hundred and fifty-eight front-line mental health professionals in four clinical services in the northwest have been recruited to the study. Results have shown:

- significant improvements in confidence and attitudes both immediately and four months after training

- the importance of the culture of learning within an organisation and training group for successful training

- targeting training appropriately achieves maximum effect

- the significance of increased confidence as an outcome of attending STORM training

- positive feedback in terms of satisfaction about the course, in particular on the relevance of the skills and techniques taught to clinical practice.

Additions to the videotape and materials have subsequently improved the suitability of the package for a broader audience. HM Prison Service has commissioned a version of STORM applicable to the needs of prisoners and this is being piloted in a number of key local prisons.

Example 16.3: Mental Health Trusts in the northwest of England

Staff from a variety of specialist mental health settings, including acute in-patient wards; low secure units; community mental health teams including crisis, assertive outreach and homelessness, were trained.

The majority of Trust staff trained were either qualified mental health nurses, including ward managers, or unqualified nursing assistants and Health Care Assistants, though some occupational therapists, social workers, junior doctors and psychologists also attended.

Adaptations included:

- delivering three modules in a full one-day session to minimise the impact of the training on already stretched ward staffing levels in one of the Trusts

- ensuring flexibility in the venues provided when training a workforce spread across several geographical bases

- aiming to train groups of staff who work together in the same team on the same day

- modifying role-play scenarios to reflect the setting in which the participants usually work.

Implementation of STORM

The next stage is to facilitate the implementation of STORM training into service areas. This means moving from the pure research phase to disseminating the training package for wider general application. This next phase began in the northwest and Ireland during 2003 and will move further outwards during 2004–5. Staff will be trained as STORM trainers who will themselves set up and run 6–8 hour training courses within the Trusts. Training will initially be aimed at front-line mental health staff. In some Trusts this training has begun and requires consolidation with more trainers. We envisage the STORM training and assessment method becoming embedded in the culture of training assessment and supervision within Trusts.

In the past we have demonstrated the acceptability of STORM to a wide range of professionals including primary care, A&E, voluntary agency and social care staff as shown in the examples. Supervision and support will continue to be offered to Primary Care Trusts and other agencies in the health and social care community. We see trust trainers, with their mental health expertise, as best placed to contract to provide training within their local communities.

The course aims to train staff (Student Trainers) to become trainers of STORM. A 'Training the Trainers' model incorporates familiarisation of the package and teaching in the delivery of the package. As trainers, they will deliver training to staff within their organisation. Professional development accreditation is being sought for both trainers and trainees. In addition, we envisage the trainers receiving Higher Education credits.

Stage 1 – Familiarisation with the STORM package

Student Trainers will be taught in *all* modules of the package, engaging in role-play activity and videotaped feedback as would be expected of all trainees. This section will be revised as more STORM 'trained' staff wish to become trainers.

Stage 2 – Training to be Trainers

Student Trainers will learn the skills needed to facilitate STORM training. They will be asked to return approximately one week after stage one having learned the package content. Each Student Trainer will practice facilitating teaching, role-play and videotaped feedback. Feedback and guidance will be provided. Time will also be given for discussion of practical issues related to delivery of the training.

Continued support

Supervision will be offered to each trainer for one year following the course. This comprises one hour every three months and telephone support if necessary and when needed. We aim to provide video-conferencing facilities in the future.

Quality assurance

We wish to ensure that STORM continues to be effective and are constantly evaluating its impact within and across organisations. It is hoped that Trusts and organisations wishing to take up STORM training will help by allowing us to collect certain qualitative and quantitative data relating to course outcomes and the progress of the training.

Conclusion

Recent research has led to some degree of pessimism about the effectiveness of training interventions. Our response to this would be that a great deal of money is still being invested in training and education. We have to ensure that it is being used wisely. Research suggests that educational interventions are most effective when they are 'multi-faceted', meaning that they utilise a range of different training approaches and offer options for people with different training needs. Educationalists need to draw on the expertise and success demonstrated by the pharmaceutical industry in effectively selling to doctors the idea that their product is essential. Training will not work unless it is accompanied by structural change in many organisations in order to allow it to be properly effective. Front-line workers will not risk using new skills unless they have back-up supervision and support to help them when they feel out of their depth. All these elements must be built in to the provision of training interventions.

Questions for consideration

1. What is the minimum level of suicide prevention skills you are hoping to develop in your own service/team/practice? And why?

2. What different levels of training will different staff or teams or sectors within your area of work or profession require, in addition to the basic, core skills and awareness?

3. What specific issues relevant to the population/individuals you work with need to be included in any training course developed in your area?

4. How will the content of the course integrate with and be supported by (or conflict with) existing organisational policies, practices and philosophies?

5. How can courses which support a shift towards a more longitudinal and individualised emphasis in 'suicide prevention' be developed in your area?

6. What will encourage staff to continue to implement and refine their skills in suicide prevention in their everyday work, after they have participated in training programmes?

7. What will prevent or hinder staff from implementing and refining their skills?

8. How can good practice in suicide prevention training be shared beyond your organisation?

9. How can you and your service work across traditional boundaries to improve and develop training?

10. What flexible training and learning methods of assessing and updating your workforce's suicide prevention skills, e.g. CD-ROMs or web-based interactive learning programmes, can be developed?

References

Appleby, L., Morriss, R., Gask, L., Roland, M., Pery, B., Lewis, A., Battersby, L., Colbert, N., Green, G., Amos, T., Davies, L. and Faragher, B. (2000) 'An educational intervention for front-line health professionals in the assessment and management of suicidal patients (the STORM project).' *Psychological Medicine 30*, 4, 805–812.

Bradshaw, T. (2002) 'Training and clinical supervision.' In N. Harris, S. Williams and T. Bradshaw (eds) *Psychosocial Interventions for People with Schizophrenia.* Basingstoke: Palgrave Macmillan.

Department of Health (2002) *National Suicide Prevention Strategy for England.* London: Department of Health Publications.

Holloway, F. (2000) 'The 5-year report of the National Confidential Inquiry into Suicide and Homicide by People with Mental Illness. I. Clinical Practice.' *Journal of Forensic Psychiatry 13*, 1, 131–137.

Morriss, R., Gask, L., Battersby. L., Francheschini, A. and Robson, M. (1999) 'Teaching front-line health and voluntary workers to assess and manage suicidal patients.' *Journal of Affective Disorders 52*, 1–3, 77–83.

Tierney, R.J. (1994) 'Suicide intervention training evaluation: A preliminary report.' *Crisis15*, 2, 69–76.

Williams, M. (1997) *Cry of Pain: Understanding Suicide and Self-Harm.* Harmondsworth: Penguin.

Chapter 17

International Perspectives in Suicide Prevention, Education and Training

Richard Ramsay

Introduction

This chapter addresses suicide prevention training from two perspectives. One looks at the relevance of an international guideline for nations to use in formulating and implementing national suicide prevention strategies (United Nations 1996). The other looks at the use of social R&D (research and development) methods (Rothman 1980) to develop suicide intervention training for community and potentially international dissemination. The Applied Suicide Intervention Skills Training (ASIST) program developed by LivingWorks Education in Canada is presented as an international dissemination example (Appendix 1).

National strategies

Although suicide dates to ancient times (van Hooff 2000), it attracted little international interest until late in the twentieth century when the World Health Organization (WHO) identified it as a priority public health issue (WHO 1985). The importance of this priority is underlined in WHO's recent global violence survey, which reports that the annual loss of life to suicide is now close to a million, more than all deaths from wars, other civil strife and homicide (WHO 2002). Several nations have acknowledged the magnitude of the issue in their own country, but few have developed policy-guided strategies to assist human service practitioners. Finland, in the early 1990s, was one of the first to launch a government-initiated strategy (Uppanne 1999) that coincided with a serendipitous interest by the social development sector of the United Nations (UN) to participate in developing national strategy guidelines for international distribution. What prompted the UN to get involved is significant because it points to the danger of isolating priority health concerns as single sector issues when, to be truly effective, suicide prevention requires a multi-sector approach. Practitioners should know what happened as a reminder that suicide prevention should not be treated as a one-sector issue in mental health, public health, social development, injury control or other health related domains, locally or internationally.

Development of the UN national strategy guidelines

The stage was set for the UN to become involved at the 1987 meeting of Ministers Responsible for Social Welfare and with General Assembly approval of the *Guiding Principles for Developmental Social Welfare Policies and Programmes in the Near Future* (United Nations 1987). Four years later, the Secretary General asked government and non-government organisations, and universities (for the first time), to help with a global review of national and local progress toward achievement of the social welfare recommendations in the 1987 document. The request to the University of Calgary was passed to the dean of social work and I was assigned the task of preparing the university response. The scope of the response was narrowed to mostly review progress related to the Alberta Model of suicide prevention (Boldt 1985) and the work of four human service practitioners (the author included) who had been working with the Canadian Mental Health Association and various governmental groups in Canada and the United States to develop an innovative suicide intervention program (Ramsay, Cooke and Lang 1990).

The Secretary General's report to the General Assembly highlighted suicide prevention and the UN's reply to the University of Calgary acknowledged that suicide was 'a problem we have neglected hitherto, and we are grateful to you for having stimulated the idea that this neglect should not continue' (personal communication, Michael Stubbs, Developmental Social Welfare Unit, 9 August 1991). This was the beginning of a developmental process that led to an interregional 'experts' meeting, hosted in Canada in 1993, to develop UN supported prevention of suicide guidelines for the formulation and implementation of national strategies (UN 1996). LivingWorks Education and Alberta's Suicide Information and Education Centre, now the Centre for Suicide Prevention, organised the meeting held in Calgary with funding support from several federal and provincial government departments. Fifteen representatives from twelve countries (Australia, Canada, China, Estonia, Finland, Hungary, India, Japan, Netherlands, Nigeria, United Arab Emirates and the United States) attended, along with WHO and UN representatives and observers from Sweden and Australia.

The UN guideline

The UN guideline, designed to facilitate strategy development within different socio-economic and cultural contexts, is linked to three principles that practitioners can use to evaluate the status of national strategy development in their respective countries. These principles underline the sovereign right of national governments to set policy priorities, implement their priorities in relation to institutions responsible for individual, family and community well-being and, perhaps most important, to appoint and adequately fund a coordinating body responsible for suicide prevention. The first test is to find out if suicide is treated as a policy priority by their national government. The real litmus test is to find out if a coordinating body has been appointed and actual funds have been committed to the formulation and/or implementation of a national strategy.

Organising principles

If a national strategy is being formulated or implemented, practitioners can determine if it addresses the eight organising principles in the guideline (UN 1996, p.14). Several are of particular interest to practitioners because their endorsement (or lack of) will affect how suicide prevention approaches are organised at the community level; these are:

- no single discipline or level of social organisation is solely responsible for suicide or suicide prevention
- individuals in many roles and at all levels of community/society can contribute to the prevention of suicidal behaviour
- the mosaic of community resources for suicide prevention operates most effectively when its activities are coordinated and integrated.

The UN guide is clear that no single discipline or organisation should be solely responsible for suicide prevention. The corollary to this is that individuals in many roles and at all levels in a community/society can contribute to suicide prevention, and that the network of community resources available (or in need of developing) will work best when they are coordinated and integrated as part of a common strategy.

Objectives

Practitioners are encouraged to be familiar with the 13 suggested objectives in the UN guideline (UN 1996, pp.14–15) and use them to evaluate an existing strategy or to recommend their inclusion in proposed or revised strategies. Questions should be asked to determine if the strategy:

1. Has a conceptual framework that is specific to suicide for implementing, monitoring and evaluating programs.

2. Supports a standardised taxonomy (classification) system for suicidal behaviours.

3. Includes early identification, assessment, treatment and referral for professional care.

4. Supports public and professional access to all information about suicide prevention.

5. Includes the need for an integrated data collection system to identify at-risk individuals, groups and settings.

6. Supports public awareness of mental health, suicide risks, consequences of stress and effective crisis management.

7. Includes the importance of training programs for gatekeepers.

8. Supports the adoption of media protocols for reporting suicidal events.

9. Includes access to services for both those at risk and those affected by suicidal behaviours.

10. Recognises the importance of having both supportive and rehabilitative services to persons who are at risk or who have been directly affected by suicidal behaviours.

11. Supports the reduction in availability, accessibility and attractiveness of the means for suicidal behaviours.

12. Includes the establishment of organisations to promote and coordinate research, training and services related to suicide prevention.

13. Supports the development or modifications in relevant legislation and regulations to facilitate the implementation of national strategy objectives.

Strategy approaches

Practitioners should be aware that the guideline endorses two strategy development approaches that support either a government or citizen/community-initiated process to formulate a strategy. Each approach has detailed steps that can be followed. The goal of both approaches is to end up with a strategy that is guided by a national policy on suicide prevention and recognises that neither government nor community interests should dominate implementation.

Impact

Prior to the UN guideline, countries interested in national suicide prevention strategies had little guidance from the international community. Since their publication in 1996, they have had an advocacy and a template impact on national strategy developments.

Advocacy impact

The basic elements of a national strategy should include a 'government policy; supporting conceptual framework; general aims and goals; measurable objectives; identification of agencies/community organisations to implement the objectives; monitoring and evaluation' (UN 1996, p.15). British researchers used these elements to survey national strategy progress in several countries (Taylor, Kingdom and Jenkins 1997). From nine responding countries (60% response rate), they identified three groups: nations with comprehensive strategies (or setting them up), nations with national preventative programs and nations without national action. Finland, Norway, Australia, New Zealand and Sweden were in the first group. The United States, Netherlands, England, France and Estonia were in the second group. Canada, Japan, Denmark, Austria and Germany were in the third group. In a follow-up article Jenkins and Singh (2000) concluded '[t]he endorsement by both the World Health Organization and the United Nations of the framing of national strategies has put particular onus on governments to respond in an area of health in which they traditionally have had little interest' (p.613). Although the sovereign right principle must be respected, practitioners can use the advocacy potential of the UN guideline to encourage the formulation and implementation of a national strategy.

Template impact

The rapid transition of the United States from the second group to the first group is a great example of the template impact. In 1994, Jerry Weyrauch, whose physician daughter died by suicide some years before, obtained a copy of the guideline drafted at the Calgary meeting. He concluded that a community-initiated approach was needed, as previous government-initiated efforts had never resulted in the formulation of a national strategy. Since survivors, from his perspective, were the obvious group to mobilise public opinion, he and his family established SPAN (Suicide Prevention Advocacy Network), a survivor-led organisation, to initiate the approach. His dedication to this process was motivated in part by a remembered Abraham Lincoln quote:

> Public opinion is everything. With public sentiment, nothing can fail. Without it, nothing can succeed. Therefore, he who moulds public opinion goes deeper than he who enacts statutes or pronounces decisions.

SPAN's grassroots success in mobilising survivors, politicians, government experts, academics, state organisations, health professionals and the private sector was remarkable. By 1998, a national summit was held in Reno, Nevada with 450 delegates representing a diverse group of national strategy advocates. Their task (i.e. to develop a draft national strategy) was to accomplish in four days what fifteen international representatives had six days to accomplish in Calgary, along with the added pressure of knowing that the Surgeon General of the United States would be attending the closing session to receive the completed draft. What seemed like an impossible expectation was completed and delivered on schedule. In the *Call to Action* report that followed, the Surgeon General acknowledged that the UN template clearly 'motivated the creation of an innovative public/private partnership to seek a national strategy for the United States' (Satcher 1999, p.1). The final strategy, released in 2001, restated the positive impact of the UN guideline on the development of their strategy (US Department of Health and Human Services 2001, p.1).

Education and training

Although suicidology is still a young science, scholars in the field had concluded by the 1970s that a core knowledge base existed, which was not being adequately disseminated (Maris 1973). Practitioners were reporting the lack of adequate preparation about suicide and the absence of continuing education opportunities (Boldt 1976; Royal 1979). Those most in need of training were 'gatekeeper' professionals and other community caregivers who were in a position to give 'first-aid' assistance and link people to other sources of help (Snyder 1971).

The Alberta Model

When the Canadian government named a suicide prevention provincial advisory committee in 1981 to develop the Alberta Model, they had a mandate to establish an information centre, training program, research centre and networks of coordinated community services. As a member of this committee, and assigned to provide leadership to the training program component, I worked with three partners from psychiatry and psychology and many others between 1982 and 1985 to develop a two-day Foundation Workshop to teach basic (first-aid) suicide intervention. The work of the partners continued and was the basis for establishing LivingWorks Education in 1991 to disseminate the training program beyond Alberta, with assistance and encouragement from the University of Calgary's technology transfer company, University Technologies International. Rothman's social R&D guided the on-going development of the workshop and its subsequent evolution to ASIST.

Rothman, a social work academic, was interested in whether 'it was possible to develop R&D procedures for social intervention and thus to solve both the problem of ineffective methods and the problem of dissemination and utilization...' (Kirk and Reid 2002, p.23). Adequate preparation and training in effective methods is still an important challenge. The United States strategy is very clear about this:

> key gatekeepers, those people who regularly come into contact with
> individuals or families in distress, must be trained to recognize
> behavioral patterns and other factors that place individuals at risk for
> suicide, and be equipped with effective strategies to intervene before
> the behaviors and early signs of risk evolve further. (US Department
> of Health and Human Services 2001, p.78)

Social R&D and the development of ASIST

Social R&D has four easy-to-follow phases that developers can use to convert existing knowledge into practical and user-friendly intervention programs. Although the developmental process is straightforward, sustaining the process to the final phase can be challenging, frustrating and time consuming, but ultimately highly rewarding.

Research/retrieval

Practitioners will recognise the literature review nature of this phase that includes gathering knowledge from both academic and other sources. In developing ASIST, this phase revealed the core knowledge pool (Maris 1973) and supporting evidence that caregivers were inadequately prepared (Boldt 1976). Out of this review, three design questions were identified:

1. Could a standardised curriculum be designed for a diverse group of gatekeepers?

2. Could the curriculum be delivered on a large-scale basis?

3. Could quality control standards be developed and enforced?

The challenge was to develop an early identification program and prepare caregivers with first-aid intervention skills.

Conversion and design

Converting the knowledge pool to a core curriculum, developing a province-wide delivery strategy and conducting pilot tests were the focus of this phase in 1982 and 1983. Two curriculum pilots were conducted: one with community caregivers in a rural setting and the other in an urban setting with counsellors and support staff from a community college. Eighty candidates were selected from a pool of three hundred applicants to pilot and field test a three-day Training for Trainers (T4T) course.

Development

This phase is often underdeveloped because of insufficient funds or inadequate time provided to properly field trial the program. Not doing this phase well can easily lead to premature implementation and disappointing evaluation results. With adequate support from the Alberta government, the developers were able to conduct eight curriculum field trials over an entire year in diverse settings and locations. Correctional Services of Canada supported a ninth, out-of-province, trial in federal prison settings. Curriculum revisions, manual preparations, audiovisual productions and workshop handouts were developed. Policies were made to embed the principle of having a core curriculum with adaptable flexibility to meet the needs of practitioners working with varied population groups in different cultural contexts. Finished materials and trainer's manuals were finalised in 1985. A procedural policy to periodically return to this phase for review and updating was approved.

Several reviews and adjustments were made in the first 15 years of ASIST that culminated in the production of Edition 6 in 1997, followed by an extensive two-year review beginning in 2001. The changes from the latter review advanced the program several editions beyond Edition 6, leading the developers to release Edition X in 2003. LivingWorks will continue dissemination support for Edition 6 until 2005, the target date for its vast trainer network to be converted to Edition X. The commitment to continuously revisit the development phase has resulted in award winning audiovisuals, state of the art workshop materials and three editions of a take-home *Suicide Intervention Handbook* (Ramsay *et al.* 1999). More recently the commitment has led to a leading edge partnership with the Johns Hopkins University Applied Physics Laboratory to provide the United States Department of Defence with ASISTR, a take-home computer-assisted program to reinforce ASIST training (Curwen 2003).

Diffusion

Canada-wide diffusion of ASIST was launched in 1985. International diffusion began in 1986 with the California Department of Mental Health to provide state-wide youth suicide intervention training. After California, state-wide implementation expanded to Washington (1996), Virginia (2000), Colorado (2001), Tennessee (2001) and Oregon (2002), with regional implementation in Oklahoma (2000) and Texas (2000) and large system implementation with the United States Army (1989 and 2000) and Air Force (1999).

International diffusion extended to Australia in 1995 as part of a three-year Suicide Intervention Field Trial (SIFTA) in partnership with Lifeline Australia and funding support from the Commonwealth Government. The success of these trials led to the establishment of LivingWorks Australia and national dissemination as part of Lifeline Australia and its network of national services.

Expansion to Norway occurred in 1998 through the Department of Psychiatry, University Hospital of North Norway. VIVAT (Latin for 'let him/her live'), located at the Centre for Suicide Prevention of northern Norway, delivers ASIST as part of the national training strategy of the Norwegian Plan for Suicide Prevention (Mehlum and Reinholdt 2000).

After more than 20 years of developmental research and implementation experience, the two-day ASIST workshop and expanded five-day T4T course is supported by an effective quality control system, an international network of close to 2000 trainers and over 400,000 ASIST trained gatekeepers, mostly in Australia, Canada, Norway and the United States, but also in Guam, Northern Ireland, Russia, Scotland and Singapore.

Evaluation

Best practice guidelines suggest that gatekeeper training programs should be evaluated against three indicator levels: short-term, mid-term and long-term (White and Jodoin 1998). Short-term indicators include satisfaction feedback, increased confidence in intervention abilities and demonstration of suicide intervention skills that are measured immediately after and up to two months post-training. Mid-term indicators include measures of skill retention and referral patterns, usually evaluated between three and six months post-training. Long-term indicators measure changes in suicidal behaviour rates between two and five years post-training. ASIST has been subjected to more than 15 independent evaluations since 1982, including two University of Calgary doctoral dissertations (McDonald 1999; Tierney 1988). These and other evaluations in Australia, Washington and Norway show that ASIST effectively produces positive short-term and mid-term indicators of effectiveness (Eggert, Karovsky and Pike 1999; Soras 2000; Turley and Tanney 1998). Although sufficient long-term evaluations have not been conducted, the benefits of working in coordinated and collaborative partnerships have shown some promising reductions in suicides between pre- and post-intervention measures. For example, a small rural-urban area of western Canada, after establishing a base of over 300 ASIST trained caregivers in a coordinated network of youth service programs, went from a rate of 1–2 youth suicides over several years to a five-year post-intervention rate of no youth suicides (Walsh and Perry 2000).

Why ASIST is a good way to learn suicide first-aid

A common approach to suicide prevention is targeting at-risk groups and directing population-specific prevention and/or treatment approaches to selected members of these groups (Guo, Scott and Bowker 2003). In contrast, ASIST is directed to caregiver groups who are most likely to encounter individuals in any at-risk category. The advantage of this approach is that first-aid practitioners are prepared to use their skills with anyone, any place, any time. The target groups for workshop participation include both professional and other caregivers based on evidence that almost half of those who die by suicide have had some contact with mental health or medical professionals within the year of their death, leaving an equal number or more who have not had such contacts (Pirkis and Burgess 1998).

The United States Institute of Medicine (IOM) in *Preventing Suicide: A National Imperative* concluded that 'changes in helping behavior will not occur by simply fostering helping attitudes and increasing intentions to help' and 'brief, didactic suicide prevention programs with no connection to services should be avoided' (IOM 2002, pp.294 and 297). Overall, IOM concluded that 'evidence-based programs, especially longer-term approaches couched in a broader context of teaching skills and establishing appropriate follow-through and services appear to be the most effective against suicide' (p.317). ASIST is a frequently recommended and widely implemented program for gatekeeper training that meets these expectations (Centres for Disease Control and Prevention 1992; Eggert, Pike and Karovsky 1999; IOM 2002; White and Jodoin 2003).

Summary

The international perspectives discussed in this chapter have significance for human service practitioners interested in advancing suicide prevention at the community level. The UN Prevention of Suicide guideline provides a template to evaluate the elements in an existing or proposed national strategy and also provides international support for the importance of community gatekeeper training programs. The social R&D process is a credible way to evaluate the developmental research quality of existing gatekeeper training programs or to guide the formulation and implementation of new programs.

Appendix: Applied suicide intervention skills training (ASIST)

ASIST is a LivingWorks Education program, designed for caregivers to provide suicide first-aid to prevent the immediate risk of suicidal behaviour. It is comparable to the CPR (cardiopulmonary resuscitation) program of the American Heart Association. Workshop instructors take a five-day T4T course and agree to be part of a quality control program that supports them in their trainer roles and encourages them to provide ongoing development feedback to LivingWorks. ASIST provides a common language link within and between groups of caregivers that strengthens their ability to provide immediate and follow-up assistance, and encourages them to participate in coordinated and collaborative strategies at a broader community level. Workshops with a mix of caregiver backgrounds are preferred to begin their exposure to the benefits of a common language and to seed the advantages of working collaboratively in their communities.

Goal and objectives

Edition X of ASIST has several objectives that participants are able to achieve:

1. Recognise the effect of personal and societal attitudes on a person at risk.

2. Talk directly about suicide with a person at risk.

3. Identify risk alerts and develop safeplans.

4. Demonstrate basic suicide intervention skills.

5. Know the resources available to a person at risk of suicide, including themselves.

6. Commit to improving community resources.

7. Recognise that suicide prevention is broader than suicide first-aid.

Organisation

ASIST has five sections to help caregivers learn suicide first-aid. Preparing sensitises participants to evidence that suicide is a serious community problem. The Connecting, Understanding and Assisting sections helps them integrate life-assistance attitudes and first-aid knowledge with a unique skill-facilitating Suicide Intervention Model (SIM). The networking section sensitises them to the importance of self-care and the value of coordination and collaboration at the community level. All workshops require at least two trainers and the minimum number of participants is recommended to be 14, 7 in 2 workgroups. The norm is 20–24 participants. The maximum number recommended is 45, using 3 trainers, 15 in each workgroup.

The knowledge transfer process of ASIST

Preparing

Suicidology evidence is clear that several contributory sources (e.g. biological, psychological, social and attitudinal) are involved in suicide risk that can be close (proximal) and/or somewhat removed (distal or predisposing) to a specific suicidal act (Moscicki 2001). These sources converge in different ways to push adaptive thresholds to their breaking points. A good indicator that someone's threshold has been breached may be thoughts of suicide, although they may not be immediately known to or suspected by others.

Connecting

Once a threshold is breached, early detection approaches are needed that practitioners and others can use quickly and effectively. Risk factor approaches are objective attempts to find demographic and psychosocial indicators of risk, but once identified their predictive powers are generally limited (Plutchik 2000). Measurement instruments have predictive value in some populations; however, current evidence suggests that a single 'best' instrument is unlikely to be developed (IOM 2002, p.231). Risk factors have become so numerous that each one has little predictive power unless there is also evidence of co-occurring suicidal thoughts. To date, the only reasonably reliable way to detect someone at risk is to start by asking if they have thoughts of suicide. However, the sensitivity needed to detect these 'invitational' messages and ask about suicide thoughts is not naturally obvious to many untrained in suicide first-aid.

Understanding

The admission of suicidal thoughts poses another challenge. The listening skills of empathy, genuineness and positive regard for others are important in suicide first-aid. These skills, however, are often associated with assessing, estimating or diagnosing levels of risk (high, medium, low) and less with using them to genuinely hear the meanings associated with these thoughts, and inviting them to openly share the reasons they have for wanting to die and to live, and the ambivalence that is often present in these back and forth feelings.

Current and background risk factor information presented in ASIST is regularly updated. All factors can be detected using direct questions (i.e. Are you having thoughts of suicide? Have you attempted suicide before? Do you have a plan? and so on). Replies do not require secondary analysis or further consideration. The concept of 'risk alerts' has been added to extend the process of risk review beyond a risk estimation objective. Alerts suggest danger (i.e. prepared to do it; unbearable pain; aloneness) as well as targets for safeplan actions (i.e. personal supports; treatment referrals; disable the plan; help with pain relief) to counter the circumstances that led to the risk alert alarm.

Assisting

With the introduction of risk alerts, the first-aid focus is more on safeplan and follow-up actions to counter individualised risk alerts. Participants learn how to use the structure and interactive process of the Suicide Intervention Model and are given ample time to try the model in practice simulations.

Networking

This is not a big section but it is an important part of linking first-aid training to the networking challenges of creating suicide safe communities. Following training, 'networking is the second most important strategy identified by projects for enhancing the capacity of communities or service systems to refer young people [and adults] to appropriate support once they have been identified as being at risk' (Mitchell 2000, p.125). The importance of self-care for caregivers is also stressed in this section to sensitise caregivers to the risk of 'compassion fatigue' that is increasingly recognised as a significant side effect of crisis work (Figley 1995).

References

Boldt, M. (chair) (1976) *Report of the Task Force on Suicides to the Minister of Social Services and Community Health.* Edmonton: Government of Alberta.

Boldt, M. (1985) 'Toward the development of a systematic approach to suicide prevention: The Alberta Model.' *Canada's Mental Health 30,* 2, 12–15.

Centres for Disease Control and Prevention (1992) *Youth Suicide Prevention Programs: A Resource Guide.* Atlanta: US Department of Health and Human Services.

Curwen, T. (2003) 'Learning to detect the enemy within: The army turns to a computer program emulating the pain of a suicidal GI. Will this avert real-life tragedies?' *Los Angeles Times,* 17 September, 1.

Eggert, L., Karovsky, P. and Pike, K. (1999) *Section III: Selective Prevention – Gatekeeper, Training and Crisis Services. The Washington State Youth Suicide Prevention Program: Final Report.* Seattle: University of Washington School of Nursing.

Figley, C. (1995) *Compassion Fatigue: Coping with Secondary Traumatic Stress Disorder in Those who Treat the Traumatized.* New York: Brunner/Mazel.

Guo, B., Scott, A. and Bowker, S. (2003) *Suicide Prevention Strategies: Evidence from Systematic Reviews.* Edmonton: Alberta Heritage Foundation for Medical Research.

Institute of Medicine (IOM) Goldsmith, S., Pellmar, T., Kleinmann, A. and Bunney, W. (eds) (2002) *Reducing Suicide: A National Imperative.* Washington: The National Academies Press.

Jenkins, R. and Singh, B. (2000) 'General population strategies for suicide prevention.' In K. Hawton and K. van Heeringen (eds) *The International Handbook of Suicide and Attempted Suicide*. London: John Wiley and Sons, Ltd.

Kirk, S. and Reid, W. (2002) *Science and Social Work: A Critical Appraisal*. New York: Columbia University Press.

Maris, R. (chair) (1973) 'Education and training in suicidology for the seventies.' In H. Resnick and B. Hathorne (eds) *Suicide Prevention in the Seventies*. Washington: US Government Printing Office.

McDonald, M. (1999) *Suicide Intervention Training Evaluation: A Study of Immediate and Long Term Effects*. Unpublished doctoral dissertation, University of Calgary.

Mehlum, L. and Reinholdt, N. (2000) 'The Norwegian plan for suicide prevention: Follow-up project 2000–2002: building on positive experiences.' *Norwegian Journal of Suicidologi 1*. http://www.med.uio.no/ipsy/ssff/engelsk/menuprevention/Mehlum.htm

Mitchell, P. (2000) 'Building capacity for life promotion: Technical report volume 1.' *Evaluation of the National Youth Suicide Prevention Strategy*. Melbourne: Australian Institute of Family Studies.

Moscicki, E. (2001) 'Epidemiology of completed and attempted suicide: toward a framework for prevention.' *Clinical Neuroscience Research 1*, 310–323.

Pirkis, J. and Burgess, P. (1998) 'Suicide and recency of health care contacts: A systematic review.' *British Journal of Psychiatry 173*, 462–474.

Plutchik, R. (2000) 'Aggression, violence, and suicide.' In R. Maris, L. Berman and M. Silverman (eds) *Comprehensive Textbook of Suicidology*. New York: Guilford Press.

Ramsay, R., Cooke, M. and Lang, W. (1990) 'Alberta's suicide prevention training programs: A retrospective comparison with Rothman's developmental research model.' *Suicide and Life-Threatening Behavior 20*, 4, 335–351.

Ramsay, R. and Tanney, B. (1996) *Global Trends in Suicide Prevention: Toward the Development of National Strategies for Suicide Prevention*. Mumbai: Tata Institute of Social Sciences.

Ramsay, R., Tanney, B., Lang, W., Tierney, R. (in memoriam), Kinzel, T. and Turley, B. (1999) *Suicide Intervention Handbook*. Calgary: LivingWorks Education.

Rothman, J. (1980) *Social R&D: Research and Development in the Human Services*. Englewood Cliffs: Prentice-Hall.

Royal, P. (1979) *Report of the Committee on the Nature of, and Response to Personal and Family Crisis in the Province of Alberta*. Edmonton: Government of Alberta.

Satcher, D. (2001) 'Preface from the Surgeon General.' In *National Strategy for Suicide Prevention: Goals and Objectives for Action*. Rockville: US Department of Health and Human Services, Public Health Service.

Soras, I. (2000) 'The Norwegian Plan for Suicide Prevention 1994–1999: Evaluation findings.' *Norwegian Journal of Suicidologi 3*. http://www.med.uio.no/ipsy/ssff/engelsk/Soeraas.htm

Snyder, J.A. (1971) 'The use of gatekeepers in crisis management.' *Bulletin of Suicidology 8*, 39–44.

Taylor, S., Kingdom, D. and Jenkins, R. (1997) 'How are nations trying to prevent suicide? An analysis of national suicide prevention strategies.' *Acta Psychiatrica Scandinavica 95*, 457–463.

Tierney, R. (1988) *Comprehensive Evaluation for Suicide Intervention Training.* Unpublished doctoral dissertation, University of Calgary.

Turley, B. and Tanney, B. (1998) *SIFTA Evaluation Report.* Melbourne: Lifeline Australia.

United Nations (1987) *Guiding Principles for Developmental Social Welfare Policies and Programmes in the Near Future.* Vienna: Centre for Social Development and Humanitarian Affairs.

United Nations (1996) *Prevention of Suicide: Guidelines for the Formulation and Implementation of National Strategies.* New York: UN Department of Policy Coordination and Sustainable Development, ST/ESA/245.

Uppanne, M. (1999) 'A model for the description and interpretation of suicide prevention.' *Suicide and Life-Threatening Behavior 29,* 242–255.

US Department of Health and Human Services (2001) *National Strategy for Suicide Prevention: Goals and Objectives for Action.* Rockville: US Department of Health and Human Services.

van Hooff, A. (2000) 'A historical perspective on suicide.' In R. Maris, L. Berman and M. Silverman (eds) *Comprehensive Textbook of Suicidology.* New York: Guilford Press.

Walsh, M. and Perry, C.M. (2000) 'Youth based prevention strategies in a rural community, Quesnel, BC: A community suicide prevention study.' Paper presented to Canadian Association of Suicide Prevention 11th Annual Conference, October 11–14, Vancouver, BC.

White, J. and Jodoin, N. (1998) *Before the Fact Interventions A Manual of Best Practices.* Vancouver: Suicide Prevention Information and Resource Centre of British Columbia, CUPPL, University of British Columbia.

White, J. and Jodoin, N. (2003) *Aboriginal Youth: A Manual of Promising Suicide Prevention Strategies.* Calgary: Centre for Suicide Prevention.

World Health Organization (1985) *Healthy Living for All.* Geneva: WHO.

World Health Organization (2002) *The World Report on Violence and Health.* Geneva: WHO.

Chapter 18

Supporting Staff
and Patients after a Suicide

Victoria Pallin

Approximately one quarter of suicides in Britain have been in contact with mental health services in the year before their death. Sixteen per cent of suicides in England and Wales were psychiatric in-patients at the time of their death and 23 per cent died within three months of discharge from in-patient care (Department of Health 2001). It is not surprising, therefore, that so many health care professionals working on psychiatric wards and in Community Mental Health Teams (CMHT) have direct experience of a patient suicide during their career. Seventy-five per cent of nursing staff (Midence, Gregory and Stanley 1996), 51 per cent of psychiatrists and one third of psychiatrists in training report at least one suicide, often more (Valente and Saunders 2002).

As hospitals admit patients with higher acuity, more hospitalisations are involuntary, and as high demand for beds tends to lead to early discharge, the likelihood of staff experiencing a suicide increases (Bultema 1994).

The impact on the psychological well-being of staff can be profound. A national survey of 259 psychiatrists reported 57 per cent experienced post-trauma symptoms following a patient suicide (Chemtob *et al.* 1988). Cooper describes it as a 'significant occupational hazard' for psychiatric nurses and ancillary staff, resulting in psychological distress which can 'seriously compromise the quality of patient care' (1995, p.26).

while there is a wealth of information on suicide, there is virtually no research into its impact on staff or what staff need to cope with the experience. It is as if hospital management, trainers and researchers, and even staff themselves, collude to avoid thinking about it for fear of 'making it happen'.

Models of support that are described tend to have evolved in response to the experiences of a particular ward's trauma. As such, they lack an evidence base. However, given the need to provide staff with appropriate support following an incident as traumatic as a patient suicide and the lack of a rigorous research base, these sometimes very personal accounts are invaluable in providing a framework with which to begin. It is a synthesis of this literature which forms the basis of this chapter.

The impact of suicide on staff

Patient suicide has a profound effect on staff as individuals and the team as a whole. Staff experience a wide range of emotional, cognitive and behavioural responses. Cooper's (1995) extensive literature review identified 40 reported reactions, of which many were associated with post-traumatic stress and grief reactions. The severity and extent of these effects can cause significant disruption to the individual's functioning, both on and off the job, and it is not surprising that patient suicide has been linked to burnout, absenteeism and staff turnover.

Bereavement theory is helpful in understanding the responses of staff to a suicide because loss is at the heart of the experience. Grief encompasses a range of emotional responses – shock, disorganisation, denial, desolate pining, despair, guilt, anger, anxiety, resolution and reintegration (Parkes 1972). In his account of an in-patient suicide Hodgkinson (1987) identified that shock and disorganisation were universally experienced by the staff team. All the other components, with the exception of pining, were experienced but were distributed among individuals or subgroups of staff. He suggests that the success, or otherwise, of resolution and reintegration was dependent upon a sharing of the emotional components among the whole staff group.

Cotton et al. (1983), interviewing staff one year after four suicides, highlighted three phases of staff reaction. The initial shock reaction was followed by a period in which staff, exhausted and demoralised, were overwhelmed by a 'flood of rage, guilt, anxiety and depression' (p.389) and the fear of blame.

Garland (1998) notes that the group in distress functions much like the individuals of which it is comprised. It, too, is flooded with unmanageable, often incomprehensible feelings, communication breaks down and the integrated functioning of the whole is thrown into disarray. Like the individual it is at risk of 'losing its head' and, as such, risks losing sight of its primary task – the provision of a safe, contained, therapeutic environment – at a time when the patients, particularly those who are suicidal, are most in need of it.

Unless staff feel contained, by being supported in processing and making sense of their feelings, these feelings will tend either to be avoided or to emerge to interfere with clinical work. For example, according to Cotton *et al.* (1983), anger towards the deceased was displaced onto colleagues, guilt was expressed through blaming, and self-doubt through inefficient, unproductive overwork. Others withdrew from work, either literally through absenteeism and sickness, or psychologically. Bartels (1987) cautions that self-doubt may characterise the team for many months, manifesting subtly but significantly, in impaired clinical judgement and an avoidance of decision-making.

Hodgkinson (1987) noted that staff became very preoccupied, sometimes with good reason, but largely out of guilt, with potentially suicidal clients in an attempt to make reparation. Angry feelings towards the deceased were projected onto other patients resulting in some staff being overly restrictive or even punitive, and lack of trust and fear of future incidents disrupted existing therapeutic relationships and hindered the formation of new ones. A number of authors, including Hodgkinson, report staff turning to self-destructive defences against anxiety such as excessive drinking (see Bartels 1987; Cooper 1995).

The final phase of staff reaction identified by Cotton *et al.* (1983) is one of 'new growth' in which feelings of sadness and demoralisation diminish as commitment to the work is renewed. Central to this is the renegotiation of relationships undermined by the experience and re-engaging in work with suicidal patients. This can only be achieved once feelings have been processed and the individual is, once again, able to tolerate the possibility of future losses to suicide (Bartels 1987). Cotton *et al.* (1983) noted that those staff who had been less able to express their feelings took longer to renew their commitment and, for some, a new job was needed to facilitate recovery. while not common, pathological grief reactions, disability and suicide have been reported among clinicians who have not been able to arrive at some resolution of the loss.

Why is suicide so difficult for staff to bear?

Whatever the circumstances, the death of a patient is traumatic for mental health staff and represents a significant loss. This is partly because, in contrast to medical or surgical staff for whom treatment of the dying patient is an essential part of care, the death of a patient on an in-patient psychiatric unit or within a CMHT is relatively rare. Familiarity with procedures or 'mastery by repetition' is never achieved (Bartels 1987). Instead, staff are constantly faced with the *prospect* of death in their suicidal patients which evokes a state of underlying tension and anxiety.

Being so hard to tolerate, staff may unconsciously defend against this anxiety by invoking the omnipotent belief that suicide is within their control; that is, preventable. This is a belief which is paradoxically reinforced by the absence of patient deaths.

In addition, death by suicide evokes a range of different and often more powerfully felt emotions than those associated with another form of death. These feelings, of themselves, contribute to the experience of trauma. Of these, the feeling of failure, fear of blame, and feelings of guilt and shame are most commonly reported.

Feeling of failure

The staff member's perception of self as a competent mental health care provider may be severely challenged by a patient in their care committing suicide. This is likely to be accentuated the closer the therapeutic relationship and the greater their investment in the patient's recovery. For many people personal identity is inextricably linked to what they do. The more omnipotent their beliefs in their professional role – what they believe they can and should do for their patients – the more intense the feelings of failure following a suicide.

Feelings of failure in staff are also generated by the nature of the act of suicide itself and the hostility that is being unconsciously communicated to the survivors by the deceased, if only in terms of making apparent their failure to help.

Fear of blame

The feeling of failure and fear of blame go hand in hand. A key role of mental health nursing is to provide a safe, secure environment in which vulnerable individuals can recover. Central to this ideal for many is the belief that suicide can and should be prevented (Bultema 1994). This omnipotent belief is reinforced by the assumption in society at large that if an individual commits suicide, someone must be to blame (Henley 1983) and by an organisation which denies its possibility by failing to train or prepare staff for it. In failing to do this they 'appear to be maintaining a hopeful denial that such a situation will never occur' (Gibson and Gornell 2001, p.11) and by implication are suggesting that, in the event, someone is to blame.

In addition, Cooper's (1995) study revealed that institutional reactions to patient suicide commonly included panic, denial, attempts to minimise the incident, and active scapegoating. All these reactions are presumably driven by the institution's wish to distance itself from the suicide and locate responsibility for it elsewhere. The effect on staff already traumatised is that they feel unsupported at best and, at worst, blamed.

The fear of blame is often exacerbated by the formal review process. The Suicide Review or 'psychological autopsy' is an attempt to understand the suicide and objectively review treatment. As such it is a laudable enter-prise but, in the absence of other forms of staff support and often occurring before staff have been able to fully process the experience, the questioning tends to be experienced as punitive and blaming. Its potential to be experi-enced as traumatic in its own right is exemplified by a study in which 95 per cent of nursing staff likened the in-house investigation to 'being on trial' (Midence *et al.* 1996, p.118).

Feelings of guilt and shame

A consistent finding in the psychotherapy research literature is that the quality of the therapeutic alliance is the best predictor of good outcome in therapy. However, suicidal patients frequently suffer from a high degree of aggression and/or hopelessness, helplessness and despair. Aggression and dependency are particularly likely to arouse negative feelings in staff.

In the absence of understanding staff will protect themselves from the impact of these feelings and behaviours in a number of ways, of which one is to minimise or negate the suicidal potential of the patient (Modestin 1987); that is, to emotionally disengage from the patient's distress. This failure to empathise will be experienced by the patient as a form of aban-donment – often the very state from which the patient is endeavouring to protect him/herself through the behaviour.

In suicidal patients this disengagement by staff is 'potentially lethal' (Modestin 1987, p.383). In his study of therapist/patient relationships where institutional suicides had taken place, Modestin found that failure to recognise or manage negative feelings evoked by the relationship (particu-larly patient hostility and dependency) was responsible for 6 per cent of the suicides. In Morgan's (1979) study of 12 suicides during treatment he found that staff had felt 'critical and indeed hostile' to two thirds of these patients, seeing the expressed suicidal intent as untrue or the client as over-dependent.

Watts and Morgan (1994) have conceptualised the process by which potentially therapeutic relationships become dangerously undermined as 'malignant alienation'. Malignant alienation is 'characterised by a progressive deterioration in [the patient's] relationships with others, including loss of sympathy and support from members of staff, who tend to construe these patients' behaviours as provocative, unreasonable, or overdependent' (p.11). Patients for whom this is likely to happen typically have a lifelong difficulty with intimacy and find it hard to express their needs directly or receive help when it is offered. Thus, for example, the patient who cannot tolerate feelings of vulnerability may express their dependency in angry, attacking behaviour. This alienates staff who avoid the patient. Feeling more needy and hurt than ever the patient becomes more angry and, inevitably, more alienating. In this way, a dynamic becomes established in which the most vulnerable not only elicit the least help but drive people away. If they are suicidal, the outcome may be fatal. Using a case study approach, Duffy (2003) provides a graphic description of this dynamic from the perspective of a patient as well as a nurse for whom the process is very much alive in the relationship, but understood.

It is important to note, however, that while staff attitudes may contribute to the occurrence of patient suicide it is not sufficient cause. Fragmented leadership, disagreement over treatment, staff demoralisation and faulty supervision have also been found to contribute to poor patient care resulting in fatal outcomes.

What do staff need?

The package of support proposed in this chapter is a synthesis of recommendations made by nurses, psychologists and psychiatrists directly involved in an in-patient suicide. A broadly similar protocol is applicable to a CMHT following an out-patient suicide. Needs particular to CMHT staff will be addressed at the end of sections.

The in-patient unit or CMHT passes through a predictable series of stages following a suicide. These are characterised by the feelings and psychological tasks outlined in Table 18.1.

Table 18.1: Feelings and psychological tasks
in the aftermath of a patient suicide

Stage	Time-frame	Feelings	Psychological task
Phase 1	Immediate aftermath	Shock	Containment
Phase 2	Middle phase	Overwhelming feelings	Finding meaning and managing affect
Phase 3	Post-traumatic phase	Self-doubt and questioning	Restoring integrity and relationships
Phase 4	Recovery	Renewed confidence	Coping and anticipation

As loss is at the heart of the experience it is no coincidence that the feelings and psychological tasks parallel the tasks of grieving which all, at some level, focus on the capacity to reflect on and make sense of feelings (Worden 1982):

1. Accept the reality of the loss.

2. Experience the pain of grief.

3. Adjust to the environment in which the deceased is missing.

4. Withdraw emotional energy and reinvest in another relationship.

The practical tasks and support systems which enable staff to cope with the experience are shown in Table 18.2, beginning with the immediate aftermath of the suicide and ending at its anniversary.

Table 18.2: Team activities following a patient suicide

	Activity	Timing	Participants	Main tasks
Phase 1	Staff meeting	Immediate	Duty Team Lead: ward manager or in-patient service manager	• Review event, plan rest of shift • Acknowledge common responses
	Patient community meeting	Same day	All patients – mandatory	• Inform patients, respond to feelings • Risk assessment
	Process meeting	2–3 days	All nursing and ancillary staff involved, CMHT, psychiatrist, hospital administrator Lead: in-patient service manager	• Share responses/mutual support • Information – what happens next
Phase 2	Memorial service	1 week	Staff and patients (optional)	• Facilitate grieving
	Suicide Review (psychological autopsy)	3–4 weeks	All main caregivers Lead: in-patient medical director and service manager	• Understand suicide • Review treatment • Identify problems and plan corrective action
	Staff meeting	Post-Suicide Review	All main caregivers plus additional team members wishing to attend Lead: ward manager	• Address issues/feelings arising out of Suicide Review
Phase 3	Continuous process opportunities	Ongoing: team meetings, case reviews, supervision, new staff induction	As appropriate	• Work collectively through continual feelings • Review treatment regimes, policy, training
Phase 4	Anniversary meeting	1 year	All staff (optional)	• Complete grieving work

Phase 1: The immediate aftermath

Shock and confusion may be accompanied by emotional flooding and panic. The first few hours after the suicide represent a critical period for staff and patients and it is vital that the unit leadership provides clear information, direction and support. The psychological task at this time is containment and it is the function of the staff meeting and the patient community meeting to facilitate this.

The staff meeting

A staff meeting should be called immediately. Ideally the whole team should be present including unqualified and auxiliary staff. The purpose of the meeting is to:

- inform the entire staff
- plan the rest of the shift
- assign tasks
- identify patients and staff most at risk
- acknowledge shared responses
- provide team with demonstrable support by senior management.

Organising the shift

while there is no reliable data in the nursing literature, crisis intervention studies have shown that staff are significantly less traumatised by a critical incident if they have undergone pre-incident training (Richards 2001).

The first task is to assign tasks and implement procedures regarding the:

- deceased – who needs to be notified and by whom?
- ward – planning the rest of the shift, closure of the ward to new admissions, cancellation/review of leave passes, organisation of extra cover/staff relief
- patients – community meeting, risk assessments, follow-up support.

Taking care of staff

The staff meeting is the first opportunity to identify staff who may be at risk. Those who had developed a good rapport with the patient may be left with unresolved and difficult feelings, as will those whose feelings were most negative. The person who found the body may be left with lasting images, especially where the death was violent or if resuscitation was attempted.

Often qualified staff lose sight of the needs of the unqualified staff who may have been closely involved with the patient. Cotton *et al.* (1983) reports that some of the most severe staff reactions occur among unqualified staff and young staff for whom the suicide may be their first experience of death.

The role of the organisation

Feeling supported by the organisation is of singular importance in determining whether staff experience an intervention as helpful or not (Rick and Briner 2000). The in-patient service manager should be present to 'represent' the organisation and demonstrate its support.

The process meeting

A process meeting should take place within three days involving all those most closely involved. A hospital administrator should be present who, ideally, is also a clinician. The in-patient service manager is best placed to lead this large and potentially difficult group meeting as the affected ward managers need to be able to participate without the burden of this responsibility.

The purpose of this meeting is to:

- discuss shared responses
- provide mutual support
- educate – what to expect, normalise feelings, provide coping strategies
- identify staff who are struggling
- disseminate information – what happens next, etc.
- alleviate fears of blame
- plan memorial service.

There is a growing consensus in the trauma literature that 'psychological first aid' is the most appropriate initial intervention (Litz *et al.* 2002); that is, the provision of support, practical assistance and education. The emphasis of this meeting, therefore, is not to provide psychological interventions to facilitate remembering and mourning but to ensure that these 'safety needs' are met.

Shared responses

while reflecting on feelings about the suicide will be a focus this should be nothing like the intense re-exposure to the experience that forms the basis of psychological debriefing. This carries the risk of increasing trauma and heightening arousal and distress (Ormerod 2002). Instead, thinking about clinical work with the patient in the context of 'unpressurised sharing of concerns, fears and feelings' is advocated (Hodgkinson 1987, p.390).

Mutual support

while not sufficient alone, social support has been identified as a major protective factor post-trauma, enhancing the opportunity for recovery and ameliorating the need for more formal psychological interventions. The focus on supporting and listening to one another in the process meeting models and makes explicit the expectation for this to continue.

Monitoring staff

The process meeting provides continued opportunities to monitor individual staff. It is too early to determine whether a member of staff may require subsequent psychological support but indicators of risk may be already apparent. Where further intervention is needed, early detection is critical in preventing the development of psychopathology following trauma (Rose, Bisson and Wessely 2001).

Organisational support

The presence of a hospital administrator communicates to staff that the organisation values them and is aware of the distress they are experiencing. Bultema (1994) stresses that the role of the administrator at this time is facilitative rather than managerial; that is, *the process meeting is not the forum for reviewing the circumstances of the suicide.*

Thoughts for the CMHT following an out-patient suicide

- Greater risk of isolation, guilt, fear of blame if only one or two workers were involved in the patient's care. Same day meeting with team leader is essential.

- Process meeting led by community service manager should involve the full multi-disciplinary team in order to prevent splits occurring between professions and to provide tangible support to those directly involved.

- Regularly updated pre-incident procedural training essential for all staff.

- Roles/responsibilities of senior staff (from different disciplines) clearly delineated in protocols.

Phase 2: The middle phase

As time passes the spontaneous energy and comradeship within the team decreases, leaving staff exhausted, demoralised and overwhelmed by feelings (Cotton *et al.* 1983). The psychological tasks are to make sense of the experience and cope with the feelings. As in the immediate aftermath, the act of processing must be counterbalanced by containment. Opportunities should be taken during supervision, staff meetings, case reviews and informal contact to provide this support and direction (see Phase 3).

More formally in this phase, the rituals of death provide a focus for the expression of feelings and the psychological autopsy a forum for questioning and finding meaning.

The memorial service

The memorial service facilitates the grieving process and provides an opportunity for patients and staff to come together in a shared expression of grief.

The Suicide Review

The function of the Suicide Review or 'psychological autopsy' is to reconstruct the suicide and its antecedents. The purpose is to develop understanding by answering two questions:

1. What happened to this patient that resulted in suicide?

2. What can be learned about patient treatment from this death?

This is achieved by reviewing the details of the death and the medical and psychiatric history. Individual caregivers should then be given the opportunity to summarise their assessment of and interactions with the suicide victim.

This meeting should be smaller than the process meeting, involving only the multi-disciplinary team directly involved in the patient's care and for whom it is mandatory.

The purpose is not to assign blame because scapegoating is likely to ensue. On the other hand, reviews that fail to address actual errors in judgement or contain key oversights may be experienced as 'whitewashing', and will leave staff feeling isolated and unsupported in their feelings of responsibility and guilt (Bartels 1987). In this context it is useful to clarify that a clinician's mismanagement can only increase the probability of suicide, never cause it.

If sensitively handled the Suicide Review can facilitate grief work and expression of feelings. Staff typically agonise over questions and doubts and the review can help to dispel myths about suicide prevention.

The timing of the Suicide Review requires sensitive management and the urge by hospital administration to convene it hastily should be resisted. It has been found to be especially unhelpful, and even harmful, if performed immediately following the suicide (Bartels 1987).

Staff meeting

The memorial service and the suicide review are both difficult events in the life of the team. An additional full staff meeting may be needed, particularly if the team is left feeling vulnerable after the review or where it is having to undergo an external enquiry.

External enquiries

The coroner's inquest, which all too often takes place many months after the suicide, places an additional strain on staff. Anticipated as threatening in itself, the wait can be equally burdensome, disrupting the return to ordinary working and delaying the grieving process. More difficult still is litigation which may hang over staff for years. Managers are at risk of forgetting the strain that this causes staff and need to ensure that regular support is available during the waiting period and adequate preparation is provided when the inquest/court hearing takes place.

Phase 3: The post-traumatic phase

Once the internal enquiries have taken place, managers may be tempted to think that the worst is over and, therefore, the work is done. However, the survival of the team is dependent on the way in which the ensuing months are managed because the focus of this time is the psychological adjustment to the fact of a suicide having occurred.

This will involve enabling staff to regain belief in themselves and trust in their colleagues. Conflicts, blame and disappointments strain staff relationships in the wake of a suicide and if not addressed have the potential to poison the team's capacity to return to a competent, functioning whole. The challenge with patients is to feel able to work, once again, with those who are suicidal.

Restoring integrity and relationships is thus the key task during this time and is achieved through what Bultema (1994) calls the 'continuous process opportunities' already available to the team.

Continuous process opportunities

Opportunities for this work occur through the course of supervision, regular team meetings, shift hand-overs, case reviews and training. The team's success is dependent, though, on senior staff nurturing a culture in which reflection and open discussion are acceptable and safe.

Ongoing opportunities for informal support, such as breaks, continue to be important. If possible, staff movement to cover other wards, etc. should be kept to a minimum in order to promote team cohesiveness, communication and a sense of belonging.

Thought for the CMHT

Whole team processing opportunities are needed to foster multi-disciplinary collaboration, shared learning and support for the individual(s), particularly when only one or two CMHT workers were directly involved. To take place alongside intra-disciplinary processing opportunities.

Review of procedures

During this time the team also needs to review treatment regimes, procedures and policies in light of the suicide. This will occur in the context of team meetings but a formal review in which these issues are a focus is also recommended.

Phase 4: Recovery

Recovery is underway when staff as individuals and the team as a whole have regained confidence in their professional integrity and worth and, once again, feel invested in the work of patient care. This includes the capacity to tolerate the likelihood of future suicide.

Anniversary meeting

Some staff may have a significant grieving response on the anniversary date. Recognition of the death at this time is thought to help staff complete their grief work.

Training needs

Contemplating the suicide of a patient is anxiety provoking. It is perhaps for this reason that so many organisations fail to prepare front-line staff for its occurrence or train senior staff to support them. The staff support outlined in this chapter requires careful preparation and training at all levels. This includes:

- pre-incident training as part of standard training and induction for all staff, including instruction on procedural policy, how it may feel, coping strategies, available support systems
- training for senior staff in managing all serious incidents and, in particular, suicide
- training for senior staff in providing support to staff following a suicide and, in particular, facilitating process meetings and Suicide Reviews
- training for senior staff in providing support to patients and, in particular, facilitating patient community meetings
- training for all qualified staff in supporting patients affected by any serious incident.

What do patients need?

A suicide on the ward will have a profound effect on the patient group. A mandatory community meeting should be called within hours of the suicide. The tasks of the meeting are to share information, assess responses and indicate a willingness to listen to patients' feelings. Above all, the emphasis of the meeting is to contain.

Patients most at risk are those who are currently suicidal, those who have made a prior suicide attempt, and those who are depressed. Patients who had been especially close to the patient during the hospitalisation or who have shared similar psychiatric histories are also particularly vulnerable.

The community meeting needs to be followed by individual risk assessments, alongside small and large group opportunities in which patients can continue to deal with their feelings. Caution is needed here, however, because the aim is not to challenge patients' defences. Denial, for example, may be very protective at this time. The primary task is to help patients feel contained and supported, not 'opened up'.

The ward routine should continue but it is advisable that it is closed to new admissions. Cancelling all leave is advised until staff have instituted individual risk assessments. This also helps to maintain the integrity of the patient group.

Conclusion

It is essential that hospitals and CMHTs provide staff and patients with appropriate support following the suicide of a patient. The model outlined in this chapter is derived from experiential accounts supported by research published in the trauma literature. However, systematic research is still needed to investigate the particular needs of those involved in a suicide and to evaluate the practice that has evolved in the absence of an evidence base. In particular, the needs of staff in different settings require careful examination; the group dynamics on a ward comprised principally of nursing and medical staff are very different, for example, to those of a CMHT where individual staff may represent different disciplines working autonomously and often alone.

References

Bartels, S.J. (1987) 'The aftermath of suicide on the psychiatric inpatient unit.' *General Hospital Psychiatry 9*, 3, 189–197.

Bultema, J.K. (1994) 'The healing process for the multidisciplinary team: recovering post-inpatient suicide.' *Journal of Psychosocial Nursing 32*, 2, 9–24.

Chemtob, C.M., Hamada, R.S., Bauer, G., Kinney, B. and Torigoe, R.Y. (1988) 'Patients' suicides: frequency and impact on psychiatrists.' *American Journal of Psychiatry 145*, 2, 224–228.

Cooper, C. (1995) 'Patient suicide and assault: their impact on psychiatric hospital staff.' *Journal of Psychosocial Nursing 33*, 6, 26–29.

Cotton, P.G., Drake, R.E., Whitaker, A. and Potter, J. (1983) 'Dealing with suicide on a psychiatric inpatient unit.' *Hospital and Community Psychiatry 34*, 55–59.

Department of Health (2001) *Safety First: National Confidential Inquiry into Suicide and Homicide by People with Mental Illness.* London: DoH.

Duffy, D. (2003) 'Exploring suicide risk and the therapeutic relationship: a case study approach.' *Nursing Times Research 8*, 3, 185–199.

Garland, C. (1998) 'The traumatised group.' In C. Garland (ed) *Understanding Trauma – A Psychoanalytical Approach.* London: Duckworth.

Gibson, L.M. and Gornell, N. (2001) 'Client suicide and the effects on the therapist: how we prepare ourselves could make the difference.' *Clinical Psychologist 8*, 11–14.

Henley, S. (1983) 'Bereavement by suicide.' *Bereavement Care 2*, 5–6.

Hodgkinson, P.E. (1987) 'Responding to in-patient suicide.' *British Journal of Medical Psychology 60*, 387–392.

Litz, B., Gray, M., Bryant, R. and Adler, A. (2002) 'Early intervention for trauma: current status and future directions.' *Clinical Psychology Science and Practice 9*, 112–134; also at www.ncptsd.org/facts/disasters/fs_earlyint_disaster.html

Midence, K., Gregory, S. and Stanley, R. (1996) 'The effects of patient suicide on nursing staff.' *Journal of Clinical Nursing 5*, 115–120.

Modestin, J. (1987) 'Counter-transference reactions contributing to completed suicide.' *British Journal of Medical Psychology 60*, 379–385.

Morgan, H.G. (1979) *Death Wishes: The Understanding and Management of Deliberate Self-Harm.* Chichester: Wiley.

Ormerod, J. (2002) 'Current research into the effectiveness of debriefing.' In N. Tehrani (ed) *Psychological Debriefing: Professional Practice Board Working Party.* Leicester: British Psychological Society.

Parkes, C.M. (1972) *Bereavement: Studies in Grief in Adult Life.* London: Routledge and Kegan Paul.

Richards, D. (2001) 'A field study of critical incident stress debriefing versus critical incident stress management.' *Journal of Mental Health 10*, 3, 351–362.

Rick, J. and Briner, R. (2000) *Trauma Management vs Stress Debriefing: What Should Responsible Organisations Do?* London: Institute of Employment Studies.

Rose, S., Bisson, J. and Wessely, S. (2001) 'Psychological debriefing for preventing post traumatic stress disorder (PTSD) (Cochrane Review).' In *Cochrane Library 3*, 2002. Oxford: Update Software.

Valente, S.M. and Saunders, J.M. (2002) 'Nurses' grief reactions to a patient's suicide.' *Perspectives in Psychiatric Care 38*, 1, 5–14.

Watts, D. and Morgan, G. (1994) 'Malignant alienation.' *British Journal of Psychiatry 164*, 11–15.

Worden, J.W. (1982) *Grief Counselling and Grief Therapy.* New York: Springer.

Chapter 19

Samaritans

Working with Everyone, Everywhere

Sarah Nelson and Simon Armson

Context: The founding of Samaritans and development of its approach to suicide reduction

Samaritans was founded 50 years ago, in 1953, by Chad Varah, a young vicar in the London parish of St Stephen's, Walbrook. His initiative was prompted by the death of a 15-year-old girl, whose funeral he had conducted. She had taken her life when she started menstruating. Lacking anyone to turn to for help or advice and believing herself to have contracted a venereal disease, she killed herself. Chad was horrified that a lack of knowledge could cause someone to end their life prematurely, and thought that if he made himself available to answer questions, particularly for young people or young couples, that he might be able to prevent others from ending their lives in the same way.

Initially Chad advertised the service, wrote articles in newspapers about it, and held face-to-face consultations in one of the rooms in St Stephen's Church. As demand grew, members of the parish volunteered to man the waiting room, to act as receptionists to people waiting to speak to Chad or answering the phone to people calling to make an appointment. Often, the callers would pour out their problems to these 'receptionists' and many felt no need to speak to Chad afterwards, or intimated that it had been helpful to talk about how they were feeling. It was at that point that Samaritans as people know it today was born.

Chad and the volunteers began to understand that the action of speaking to someone they did not know, who would simply listen to what they had to say, could be beneficial for suicidal people, and could help alleviate suicidal feelings. Because the volunteers were not known to the callers, they were able to be more honest and open about their feelings and they did not feel judged as they might have by a professional or someone they knew, while the volunteers, who were not trained at this time, would not interrupt and felt unable to offer advice. Inadvertently, some years before the benefits of counselling as we now know it were widely recognised, Samaritans was able to give people a space where they could potentially find objectivity and perhaps a way forward, through being listened to. The emotional support service offered by Samaritans today is based on these same principles. Although it is impossible, because of the confidential nature of the service, to understand how effective it is, personal testimony and anecdotal reports suggest that Samaritans could have saved thousands of lives over the past 50 years.

Today, Samaritans is – wrongly in some ways – synonymous with suicide prevention in the UK and Republic of Ireland. In the last 50 years the organisation has grown considerably and now has 203 branches across the UK and Republic of Ireland, while 18,300 volunteers give up over 2.7 million hours each year to provide a service to people in distress and despair. The vast majority of people in the UK, 97 per cent (NOP Solutions 2001) are aware of the organisation, testament to the role of Samaritans within society and its ability to connect with everyone, everywhere. It is the original telephone helpline, offering support in each of the 4.5 million contacts it receives each year. Each of our volunteers receives thorough training, which is so respected that it is now used by other not-for-profit and commercial organisations. And yet Samaritans is still a charity that is volunteer-led, and it receives 97 per cent of its income from general donations.

Samaritans was involved in the development of the government's 2002 Suicide Prevention Strategy document and continues to work closely with statutory and respected academic bodies to develop new methods to address the issue of suicide and emotional distress. Over 100 other organisations in more than 50 different countries have set up similar services – some called Samaritans and which are affiliated to our organisation – such is the belief in the original premise of 'listening' as a way to help people with feelings which may lead to suicide or despair.

Although many people assume that Samaritans is a suicide prevention organisation, this is not strictly the case. It was originally envisaged as a sort of emergency service for the suicidal, akin to calling 999 for help with more obvious emergencies such as a fire or burglary. An aim as lofty as suicide prevention was never considered by this amateur group of volunteers – there were doctors out there to help prevent suicide, whereas Samaritans were just ordinary people who wanted to help people who had nowhere else to turn. Samaritans' focus in the early years was far more centred on the individual in need of help and how they, as ordinary people without specialist training, could do something for those in distress.

Given the above, it is unsurprising that the rights of individuals still remain paramount within Samaritans. Central to Samaritans service is the belief in 'self-determination', that is, a person's right to make decisions about their life, including the decision to die by suicide. This belief is reinforced by the non-judgemental approach of the service. After all, to say that someone should not kill himself or herself would be making a judgement about someone else's life, without fully understanding how they have come to that decision.

while Samaritans may not refer to itself as a suicide prevention charity, reducing the number of people who take their own lives is very much at the heart of Samaritans' ethos. Three years ago, in the run up to our 50th birthday, a review was carried out of the entire organisation called 'Facing the Future'. We examined the services we offer, our beliefs and where we wanted to go in the next 50 years. This was with a view to shaping an organisation that would be able to continue to offer support to those in need, reaching out more clearly to people in distress, strengthened by a shared understanding of what Samaritans means.

One of the most important results of the review was the formalisation of Samaritans' beliefs and vision. Samaritans work towards a vision of society where fewer people die by suicide, where people are able to respect the feelings of others and recognise the benefits of being able to speak openly about difficult feelings and where people are able to express their feelings without fear of judgement. Our mission is to be available to offer confidential emotional support to people in distress, 24 hours a day, 365 days a year.

Samaritans in the 21st century – what has changed?

In many ways this is a broader, bolder vision than that of the 1950s but it is, we believe, more appropriate and also more fundamentally important if we are to play our full role in society. It provides a platform for us to extend our work from the reactive role of supporting people who are both literally and metaphorically at the end of the line, to reach out to society as a whole. So how is this reflected in the work now being carried out by Samaritans? The answer is, unsurprisingly, in the services we offer, how we present ourselves to people in need, the partnerships we are developing and the work we do with the media.

In terms of the 'traditional' Samaritans service, we are looking at ways to expand our services, exploiting new technology and ways to reach people who – for whatever reason – cannot, or do not make contact through our more traditional existing services which comprise telephone, face to face in branches and correspondence. For example, there is a large body of evidence to suggest that young men find it hard to articulate difficult feelings, so we decided to look at ways of working which did not involve this high-risk group needing to speak to a volunteer to receive support. From 1994, Samaritans piloted an email support service, which was formally launched in November last year – the first tangible results of this strategy. We now receive around 300 emails a day from people in distress and initial anecdotal reports suggest that many of the users of this service are young people.

We are also looking at whether text messaging might be an appropriate way of helping people to seek emotional support from us. Obviously there are many issues around whether this would be possible, and the various options are currently being investigated. For example, it might make most sense for the service to allow people to give Samaritans their number so they can be called back, rather than making the call themselves. Since over 55 million texts are sent in the UK each day (Mobile Data Association 2003), many by young people, a text-based service would, we believe, allow us to increase our reach to this at-risk group.

As well as age, environment can play a role in determining not only suicide risk but also propensity to access help services such as Samaritans. Samaritans has worked hard to identify risk groups and develop services to meet these specific needs or to work in partnership with others better placed to provide services directly to these communities. Over the last 10 years, Samaritans has worked in partnership with HM Prison Service in England and Wales and equivalent bodies in Scotland, Northern Ireland and the Republic of Ireland, to develop services for those in custody, who are seven times more likely to take their own life than people in the general population. Samaritans branches offer support directly to prisoners, but have also been instrumental in setting up 133 'Listener' schemes whereby approximately 1500 prisoners have received Samaritans training to offer face-to-face emotional support to other prisoners in need. Thousands of hours of listening are provided each year, and it is hoped to extend the number of prisons running the scheme as awareness grows of imprisonment as a risk factor in suicidal behaviour.

As well as extending our range of services, we have also taken a long, hard look at how Samaritans is perceived by the world around us as part of the Facing the Future review. The conclusion was reached that it would be impossible for us to work towards our vision if we were not seen as a contemporary and relevant organisation. In today's society, how we 'sell' our services has a huge effect on whether people feel able to seek help from us and is, therefore, in some ways, almost as important as the services themselves. Research into the attitude of the general public towards Samaritans showed that work needed to be done to build a reputation that was different to how we were perceived then. Nearly everyone in the UK had heard of 'Samaritans' – we found that we had 97 per cent awareness among all areas of society – but hardly anyone knew what exactly that meant or what would happen if they used our services (NOP Solutions 2001). In a recent survey carried out on behalf of Samaritans by Keith Hawton, Karen Rodham and Emma Evans of The Centre for Suicide Research, Oxford, among 15 and 16 year olds, the idea that we need to take our image more seriously was reinforced by the finding from this group, that Samaritans should advertise the organisation more so people in need would know it is available to them (Hawton, Rodham and Evans 2003).

Although we continue to receive high levels of contacts each year, it was clear that with suicide rates remaining high, we needed to be able to extend our reach, and to be able to communicate with high-risk groups among the population, particularly young people and men in general, to encourage them to use our service. If people did not know about our service, or did not understand what it did, there was little chance of us being successful in supporting them. Some of the comments made about us prior to setting up the scheme with Portsmouth are: 'You only do suicide', 'Email would be great for young people' and 'Didn't know callers could visit? Do you need an appointment?'

Samaritans secured the services of the respected brand consultancy, Wolff Olins, on a pro bono basis. Wolff Olins, who have developed brand ideas with Orange, UNICEF, BT, Odeon and Honda, worked with Samaritans to research and develop a new look and feel for the charity to communicate effectively with everyone we needed to reach about who we are and what we do. After 18 months of hard work, in October 2002, the new brand identity was launched. Since then, a number of high-profile campaigns have been developed, attracting millions of pounds of media space to raise awareness of our service, thanks to the generosity of media owners across the UK, while coverage of the rebranding and what it means has appeared in 65 national and regional publications. More use has been made of digital communications in our marketing campaigns, which has more appeal for younger, PC-literate audiences and is more cost effective than traditional marketing. The reception has been positive from the media and the general public alike. Director of English Heritage, Jamie Lister, commented in *Marketing* magazine:

> At some point, over a lifetime of being aware of The Samaritans, I had consigned it to the 'not for me' pile. There were other charities with which I felt much more comfortable… I now consider Samaritans to be contemporary, valuable and acutely relevant in the 21st century. I'm impressed by the level to which a simple piece of marketing has changed my mind. (Lister 2003)

Large-scale research is yet to be carried out to determine how the public's perception of what Samaritans means has changed quantitatively, but we are confident from initial feedback that we are moving towards where we need and want to be.

From reactive to proactive – education and partnerships

As an organisation that has traditionally been seen as very reactive, after 50 years, Samaritans is now undertaking a range of initiatives that are broadly aimed at reaching out to people more proactively. Service provision and development continues to be central to what Samaritans is, plus we are building on these in several ways. We want to connect with potential users more effectively and also to change the attitudes and behaviour of society as a whole towards suicide and emotional health. Our new vision, of a society where feelings are respected and can be expressed without fear of judgement, is at the heart of these new developments. For Samaritans this is a central part of 'suicide reduction'.

We see society as a whole – everyone, everywhere – as having a shared responsibility for reducing suicide. By allowing and encouraging people to share difficult feelings, our belief is that ultimately fewer people will decide to take their own lives. It is only through a fundamental change in how society views talking about feelings that people will be able to understand each other better and support others directly, or indirectly by encouraging them to get external help, as well as having appropriate skills to deal with difficult emotions in themselves and in others. Our Emotional Health Promotion Strategy, which will be launched in 2004 to coincide with our 50th birthday, sets out how we intend to undertake this challenge. Samaritans believe that by giving people information, changing attitudes and enabling the development of healthy coping skills we can promote people's emotional health and bring society closer to our vision. The Emotional Health

Promotion Strategy sets out our framework, rationale and priorities in a range of settings including the media, rural communities, schools, prisons, statutory health services and the workplace.

It is important to emphasise that we recognise that this is not an all-encompassing model that will prevent everyone from taking his or her life. It is clear that there are limitations in Samaritans' approaches to suicide reduction. For example, although our services are aimed at everyone everywhere, clearly, even thoroughly trained volunteers' emotional support is not a substitute for suitable counselling or suicide prevention service for people with severe mental health issues. Some people need professional medical help and care on an ongoing basis to minimise the risk of suicide.

Moreover, as a charity, we do not have the resources to change society's attitudes towards suicide and talking about feelings overnight and we are aware of how ambitious a task we have set for ourselves. But by doing what we can, we believe we can create an improved awareness of behaviour that indicates emotional or mental health problems so that people are able to access the services they need sooner, without fear of stigma from the people around them. It is akin to changing attitudes about race, sexuality and gender. These changes happen generationally over tens of years, not over the course of one conventional marketing campaign. But we believe it is a change worth working towards, and like race, gender and sexuality, that it is possible to achieve real change on a societal level.

Much of the activity being undertaken as part of a more proactive approach to connecting with high-risk groups and also promoting emotional health is simply an extension and formalisation of activities that have been carried out for many years by our 203 branches across the UK and Republic of Ireland. Throughout its history, Samaritans has undertaken 'promotional', or proactive work at a local level in community groups of all types such as clubs, associations and businesses. By discussing Samaritans in a fundraising or volunteer recruitment context, suicide itself is a key element of any discussion, even if it is not the primary reason for meeting. Contextualising the issue of suicide in the UK and making the scale of the problem clear is vital in order to make people aware of the extent of Samaritans' need, for people to give either time or money to maintain our service. In turn, this helps people to understand and be more aware of the issue, which is, we believe, the first step in moving towards reducing suicide within society. In addition, Samaritans has always visited schools and colleges in an educational capacity, explaining to both teachers and pupils how to spot the signs of suicidal thoughts or behaviour as well as encouraging any who need the service to use it. Anecdotally, many people have

said that this is the basis for anything they know or understand about suicide and the signs of suicidal behaviour over and above what is learnt from
the mass media.

At a local level, many longer-term relationships with gatekeeper groups
have developed from these initial contacts, leading to ongoing work with,
to name just a few, young people, the homeless, older people and those in
care. This enables Samaritans to raise awareness of and offer its services
among high-risk groups who might not otherwise be reached by our attempts to encourage them to use the service, through contact with people
that they already trust and respect. The groups with whom we work get access to a service that they cannot offer themselves, that they know they can
trust and that their users can gain something from. In response to an increasing understanding that both Samaritans and communities can benefit
from these partnerships, Samaritans is piloting a Local Needs project across
the UK. This helps branches to identify groups within their community
that are at particularly high risk, establish whether there are existing support networks and where appropriate, begin to develop relationships with
support from the charity's central office.

Samaritans believe projects that initiate direct contact with high-risk
groups are vital in encouraging potential users towards the service. Marketing alone cannot reach high-risk groups. Many Samaritans callers say that
the first call is the most difficult. Despite the enormity of their suffering,
they struggle to find reasons to call us or to speak when they get through.
At the same time, mental health legislative framework, primarily set out in
Our Healthier Nation (Department of Health 1999) and more recently in the
government's National Suicide Prevention Strategy for England (DoH 2002) requires that primary care providers play a role in suicide reduction but many
do not have appropriate resources in place, while Samaritans has 18,300
such resources in the form of trained volunteers.

Recognising this, two years ago, when Samaritans Portsmouth branch
was approached by its local A&E department with a view to getting involved in any relevant projects, a scheme was developed that was so successful that it is now being extensively tested by nine other branches across
the UK with a view to replicating the benefits (Edinburgh, Bridgend,
Derry, Brent, Ryegate, Taunton, Yeovil, Nottingham and Shrewsbury). Any
patient who is admitted to A&E having been identified as having self-
harmed is assessed prior to discharge. They are then asked whether they
would like Samaritans to contact them if an official psychiatric follow-up is
not required. The response to date has been extremely positive: 37.5 per
cent of patients wanted a follow-up call or visit from a volunteer, and 92 per

cent said it was beneficial to them. Samaritans has worked closely with the Trust to monitor the scheme and evaluate the benefits and any issues that may arise. Someone involved in the scheme, who wishes to remain anonymous, said, 'I couldn't bring myself to make that first call. Now I can.'

It is becoming increasingly apparent that joint-working projects can help to fill any resource gaps at a local level, and the scheme has been welcomed by all the NHS Trusts which Samaritans has approached. Long-term success is too early to judge, but we are confident that if replicated faithfully and with commitment on both sides, the scheme could help many vulnerable people. NHS Direct in both England and Wales has expressed an interest in developing similar referral schemes, and Samaritans is currently exploring how schemes might work with social work groups, GP surgeries and midwifery organisations.

Many of the gatekeeper groups mentioned above work on an almost daily basis with people who experience suicidal behaviour. Through developing strong, formalised relationships with them, locally and nationally, we believe we can extend our reach to help the people who cannot or do not ask for help themselves.

Communicating with everyone, everywhere

Gatekeeper groups exist outside the medical and statutory framework. The media, in particular, has the ability to influence people's attitudes towards emotional health, suicide and suicidal behaviour. A large body of research exists to demonstrate how graphic images of suicide in the media can provoke copycat behaviour (see 'The media and suicide' below), not just in the UK but globally. This research not only demonstrates a direct link between how suicidal behaviour is portrayed and the consequences for society, but also that there are ways in which the media can have a protective effect. The media's portrayal of suicide can often seem to be based on a combination of desperation for a good story, and ignorance about the effect of writing about suicide in explicit detail. Suicide is difficult to represent because it is the polar opposite of the format in which news is packaged. Suicide is the result of a complex series of events and perhaps predicating factors, whereas news is more often than not a 50-word soundbite. Suicide is shades of grey, whereas news is black and white.

In a society where people spend more time watching TV than they do talking to their friends or parents as a form of stress relief (MORI 2003), the media is therefore incredibly important in terms of suicide prevention as the first point of contact for many people considering suicide, as well as a primary educative voice.

About 10 years ago, Samaritans compiled its first set of guidelines for the media. This document is available to anyone from our website and is updated and distributed to journalists regularly. It is a short 15-page booklet aimed at helping those working in the media, whether in development of factual or fictional stories, to develop stories that include suicide with an understanding of how their choices will affect people watching, reading or listening. In practical terms it simply lays out the facts about how the media can influence suicidal behaviour, backed up with salient examples such as the one below, and it offers ways in which stories can be approached in a positive way. We also offer a free consultancy service for anyone wishing to develop stories around suicide. In the past six months, we have worked with BBC1 to develop appropriate EastEnders and Holby City scripts, with Granada on Coronation Street episodes, and we are approached to provide input into many other fictional and factual media productions on a regular basis. In the future, we also hope to work with education bodies to try to ensure that sensitive reporting of suicide is an issue that will be part of any journalism training. Not only is this vital in terms of limiting copycat behaviour, but also in shaping people's attitudes towards and understanding of the wider issue of emotional health. If more people working in the media were aware that one in four people in the UK has been affected directly by suicide, we believe the media would influence society in a different way.

The media and suicide

The media is well known for its flightiness. Most people remember how the tabloid press in particular cast David Beckham as Britain's biggest villain when he got sent off for fouling an Argentine player in the 1998 World Cup. He was roundly pilloried, and it would be fair to say that public attitudes reflected what was in the media. Today, he and his wife Victoria have been recreated by the media as Britain's second royal family – living in 'Beckingham Palace' and enjoying all the media attention that was once reserved for Britain's aristocracy. Research shows that the media, both fictional and factual, has a similar power when it comes to forming attitudes about suicide.

Professor Keith Hawton, of the Centre for Suicide Research in Oxford, has undertaken a wide-ranging body of research to show how the media can directly influence people's behaviour. One of the studies that has been most influential in shaping Samaritans' beliefs about the media and suicide is discussed below.

A Casualty episode was screened in the mid 1990s which depicted a suicide attempt through paracetamol overdose. The method was not only graphically portrayed, showing images of the attempt itself, but it was also discussed in detail, including how many paracetamol tablets were taken. In the week following the screening of the episode, which was seen by mil-lions across the UK, admissions to hospital for paracetamol overdose in-creased by 17 per cent, and for the subsequent week it was 9 per cent greater than the previous year. Twenty per cent of patients who were ques-tioned about whether the episode had affected them said it had influenced their decision to attempt suicide (Hawton *et al*. 1999). Interestingly, the media was also shown to have had a protective effect in the long term on this occasion. There was a great deal of coverage in the media about the epi-sode in question, and one of the longer-term results was that more people became aware of the fact that large but non-fatal doses of paracetamol re-sult in permanent liver damage.

Many other examples have been found world-wide that demonstrate the power of the media in relation to suicide. Most recognise the damage that media can do rather than recognising its protective effects, reflecting the reality of how suicide is reported today.

Different types of media wield varying power. Research undertaken into how the death of celebrities by suicide (Wasserman 1984) provoked imitative behaviour found that stories which appeared in printed media were more likely to have an effect, probably because details of the story can be kept, studied repeatedly and retained in the memory more than broad-cast reports.

Samaritans is not aware of any research that has been carried out to date to establish where new media and the Internet in particular sits in compari-son to forms of traditional media in terms of influencing. However, with newsgroups and chatrooms freely accessible to billions of people globally where explicit information on suicide methods is readily available, where people joining in are actively encouraged to take their lives, where people offer assisted suicide services online, it is only a matter of time before the effect of this relatively recent type of communication becomes a subject for scrutiny, not only from the academics but potentially from lawyers or statu-tory bodies. while they may perhaps offer a seemingly secure environment for people to share their feelings, it is crucial that more is understood about the risk factors as well as the benefits of these online resources.

Education and training

Although suicide is unlikely ever to be on the national curriculum, Samaritans is working hard to ensure that its wider message of emotional health, and the importance of learning coping strategies for difficult times as well as recognising and accepting emotional issues in others, is part of everyone's mainstream education. As with our initiatives in other areas, our work primarily takes the form of working with existing groups to provide them with resources that can supplement what they do already. Education initiatives are also designed to dovetail with existing branch outreach into schools, and because we already have a known and trusted presence in many schools, we are hopeful that our messages will be disseminated widely.

Several years ago, Samaritans developed a Youth Pack, which is designed to help teachers to understand suicide. As most teachers are not experts in the area, it has been well received, since it offers facts, statistics, and ideas for group exercises that make the subject accessible and easy to contextualise in classroom situations. As described above, Samaritans has also supplied materials and speakers to schools on request for decades. The advent of the national curriculum and subjects that focus on personal development, such as Personal, Health and Social Education (PHSE), has provided Samaritans with a new opportunity to work within the existing education system to help people to understand more about suicide. In 2002, Samaritans received funding that enabled us to work with a well-known forum theatre company, ARC, to develop an emotional health promotion resource that can be used as part of the PHSE modules taught to 15 and 16-year-olds. It comprises a 40-minute play on video, complemented by a set of exercises on which group exercises can be based. All elements have been specifically designed to be user friendly, requiring no extra work by the teacher, and each branch has a copy that they can loan out to schools at no charge.

Another setting in which Samaritans is working to develop relationships is that of the workplace. Increasingly, there is an acceptance in the world of employment that issues such as stress can lead to depression and suicide – issues that directly affect organisations' abilities to attract good employees and manage successful business relationships. By placing ourselves in the context of emotional health rather than simply suicide, it is clearer to businesses why we are relevant to them and they are more interested in what we have to say. Not only does this give us access to new sources of funding, but it also opens the door to developing programmes to assess stress or emotional health levels at work and to working together with these organisations to provide their employees with skills to protect and promote their emotional health.

Samaritans has already begun to offer a training course in listening skills that is increasingly popular. A half-day and one-day course have been developed to teach people what are essentially communications skills based on the thorough training for Samaritans volunteers. An ability to listen actively, to ask appropriate questions, to understand what the person is really trying to say are all vital communications skills that are of benefit to everyone – both socially and in business – and can be delivered by Samaritans. More than 20 organisations have had the training and all the feedback so far has been extremely positive.

Conclusion

Much of the success of Samaritans' new initiatives in reaching out to society as a whole depends on factors integral to a charity and which are largely outside our control, such as the legislative environment, which dictates the extent to which statutory bodies want to work with the voluntary sector, or the economic climate, which determines our financial status.

However, in comparison with many other organisations, we have a huge advantage, in that our 18,300 volunteers are untouched by these factors. They have remained hugely committed to our cause over 50 years, helping countless people, whether at the end of the line, or through educating them about emotional health in general. We are confident that the next 50 years will offer new challenges that they can meet with the same passionate diligence and dedication as they have done over the last 50. Through them, we hope not only to help the people at the end of their tether, but society as a whole – by being a first stop rather than a last call on the issue of suicide and emotional health in general, exploiting our 50 years of experience to the benefit of everyone, everywhere.

For further information about Samaritans, visit our web site: www.samaritans.org.

References

Department of Health (2002) *National Suicide Prevention Strategy for England.* London: DoH.

Department of Health (1999) *Saving Lives: Our Healthier Nation.* London: The Stationery Office.

Hawton, K., Rodham, K. and Evans, E. (2003) *Youth and Self-harm: Perspectives – A Report.* London: Samaritans.

Hawton, K., Simkin, S., Deeks, J.J., O'Connor, S., Keen, A., Altman, D.G., Philo, G. and Bulstrode, C. (1999) 'Effects of a drug overdose in a television drama on presentations to hospital for self-poisoning: Time series and questionnaire study.' *British Medical Journal 318*, 972–977.

Lister, J. (2003) 'Direct Choice: Samaritans.' *Marketing*, 30 January.

Mobile Data Association (2003) *Mobile Data Association Announces 55 Million Texts Per Day*. Essington: Mobile Data Association.

MORI (2003) *Stressed Out Survey*. London: Samaritans.

NOP Solutions (2001) *Brand Usage: Samaritans*. London: NOP Solutions.

Wasserman, I. (1984) 'Imitation and suicide: a re-examination of the Werther effect.' *American Sociological Review 49*, 427–436.

Chapter 20

PAPYRUS

An Example of Voluntary Sector Work

Tony Cox, Anne Parry and Anna Brown

Introduction

Sadly many of those who belong to PAPYRUS have lost young people to suicide. This horrifying and tragic personal experience gives them a unique insight into prevention and the powerful motivation to work with other organisations to help those at risk of taking their own lives. Information from *Making Use Of Hindsight* (Stanley and Manthorpe 2001), a study of 46 parents who had lost young people through suicide, and 'When our children kill themselves' (Harvey 2002), provides some of the evidence from the parents' perspective.

An attempted suicide is a real opportunity to examine an individual's values, lifestyle and coping skills. Often the episode is treated as 'a mistake', 'attention seeking', and not a 'life threatening' attempt. PAPYRUS members know that a range of interventions, particularly those which focus on empowering individuals to take charge of their own lives and build on their strengths, have an important role to play in preventing a further attempt.

The power of peer support is a very strong and valuable resource. Engaging this support and providing training are challenging issues. Nevertheless, it is a challenge which may prove to be a powerful and positive tool for preventing suicide in young people (Cowie and Wallace 2000). Parents and peers are in an ideal situation to support and act as mentors. There are times when the relationship between young people and parents is described as 'toxic' (Cowie and Wallace 2000) – but this aspect alone can be a driver for change. Parents need information and guidance in order to be effective. If they do not know or recognise that there is a problem, or are not engaged in managing the issues, they may be a negative influence. Where relationships or individuals are antagonistic to one another an alternative 'prop' or person (e.g. friend, sibling) can be employed to handle the situation.

Box 20.1: Aims of PAPYRUS

1. To promote an understanding of the unique contribution that parents, families and carers can make to suicide prevention by:

    (a) providing assistance to parents and others, in a caring or professional role, in supporting vulnerable young people

    (b) being represented in policy making decisions at all levels and monitoring their implementation

    (c) encouraging, initiating and taking part in the development of learning opportunities for all

    (d) encouraging, taking part in and/or initiating research into suicide prevention

    (e) campaigning for adequate mental health services for young people, and an easily accessible route to such help on an informal basis.

2. To promote public awareness of the importance of emotional well-being and good mental health by:

    (a) promoting awareness of the risk of mental or emotional distress during adolescence and throughout life, and helping to remove the stigma of such occurrences

    (b) encouraging the promotion of emotional well-being and good mental health at all levels of education

    (c) co-operating with professional and voluntary bodies working in the suicide prevention field

    (d) encouraging and disseminating examples of good practice in suicide prevention

    (e) encouraging the provision of appropriate support, either voluntary or professional, for those bereaved by suicide.

PAPYRUS

PAPYRUS is a national charity founded by parents who have been bereaved by suicide. Members include parents, professionals from many different fields, and others who are interested in the prevention of suicide. Since it was formed in 1997, PAPYRUS has been involved in policy discussions around the country at both local and national level. Although it is still a relatively small organisation, PAPYRUS is working across boundaries to support and disseminate initiatives which may contribute to a reduction in the number of people, especially young people, who ultimately die by suicide.

Making use of hindsight

The findings of a UK survey of parents whose children took their own lives provides a unique insight into suicide prevention and the impact of suicide on families. The research was a collaboration between PAPYRUS and the University of Hull.

A confidential questionnaire was sent by PAPYRUS to its members and of these, 46 were returned (62% of those distributed, n=74). The responses were analysed by independent researchers from the Department of Social Work at the University of Hull who had prior experience of research into student mental health issues (Stanley, Manthorpe and Bradley 1999). Only one parent reported for each family so there was no overlap between the cases reported.

The questionnaire explored a range of issues but was deliberately kept as brief as possible. Most questions were open-ended to allow parents to write about their own feelings and experiences. The survey provided a range of information which parents thought other parents should know. With the benefit of hindsight, they were able to identify and reflect on issues arising from their own experience. Their most consistent message was that they advised other parents to take depression and any expression of ideas about suicide seriously. Many now thought they had not realised the full extent or depth of the problems experienced by their son or daughter. One parent reflected:

> I didn't realise that [his] seeming lack of interest in the future was due to depression and that even small decisions caused him distress.

> I wish I had picked up on some of the things he said and tried to discuss further.

The issue of waiting lists was raised by those parents who felt that young people's problems should be responded to more urgently. They considered that help for young people within the NHS should be 'fast track' and some suggested that young people should have a dedicated service.

Parents identified a need to seek support for themselves when struggling to care for a son or daughter who was distressed or experiencing problems. They provided a variety of suggestions about what worked for them. Eight commented on the value of accessing help from someone outside the immediate family and eleven noted the importance of seeking support or advice for parents when a son or daughter was actively suicidal:

> Parents themselves need guidance from psychologists/psychiatrists/counsellors on how to best deal with the situation.

In summary, the survey suggested that parents whose child is actively expressing a wish to die by suicide need particular support. Professionals working in this area, including the police, coroners, health services, education and religious organisations, may benefit from training on the most effective means of support both before and after a death by suicide. The impact of the death of a child in such circumstances may endure over many years, so support should not be seen as a one-off or single event.

University Suicide Intervention Initiative (USIi)

The evidence from parents identified the mental health of students as an area of concern. Subsequently the University Suicide Intervention Initiative was set up. Ten voluntary sector organisations – each concerned about suicide in higher education establishments (Samaritans, National Schizophrenia Fellowship, MIND, Manic Depression Fellowship, Depression Alliance, National Student Bureau, National Union of Students (NUS), NUS Scotland Disabilities, University of Oxford Nightline, University of London Nightline) collaborated with PAPYRUS to produce a set of guidelines. These were presented to the Committee of Vice Chancellors and Principals (CVCP), now Universities UK, and the Association of Managers of Student Support in Higher Education (AMOSSHE) and have been circulated to higher education institutions around the country.

Many of the recommendations are appropriate for health service personnel who have contact with students and other young people. They cover areas such as stigma and culture, effectiveness of support, education and staff development, and resources. As a result of this report Universities UK and SCOP (Standing Conference of Principals) commissioned specific research into student suicide and self harm. Their management guidance, published in December 2002 (Universities UK 2002), highlights the need for closer working between higher education establishments, health agencies and the voluntary sector to disseminate examples of good practice and to provide mechanisms for better staff training opportunities.

The contentious issue of confidentiality was discussed and the guidance recommends that higher education institutions:

> should give particular consideration to establishing protocols that define the boundaries of confidentiality both within their institution and in any communications to those outside the institution, including community health practitioners and relatives.

Case study 20.1: Amanda's story

Amanda's story highlights some of these points: problems with confidentiality, problems with the legal status of some young people and the need for a networked service. Her mother writes:

> Amanda finally succeeded in taking her own life in May 1998. She was just six days short of her eighteenth birthday. She drove her car to a motorway services and put a hosepipe in the exhaust. She survived on a life support machine for a day and was then declared brain dead.

> Amanda had tried over a period of eighteen months to commit suicide so many times that I have actually lost count of the number of times that I was called from one intensive care unit to another throughout the country.

> Amanda was highly intelligent and, as I have a legal background, was possibly more aware than most young adolescents of her rights under the Children Act. Following one suicide attempt, again using a hosepipe in her car, she was sectioned under the Mental Health Act. She appealed using her basic legal knowledge and convinced the Mental Health Tribunal that she should be let off the section. At that time she was just 17.

> Amanda spent about six weeks in a top hospital. However, she kept running away and trying to take her own life. In January 1998 they refused to offer her any further treatment as an inpatient and would only treat her on a voluntary outpatient basis. They said that if she was sectioned she would always be able to appeal successfully.

I think that Amanda's story highlights the very grey area that exists in the law to protect such vulnerable people. I found that whenever she was admitted to hospital there was a lack of information passed to me because Amanda could control what was said to me.

The weekend Amanda died she was found driving erratically by the police. They arrested her and tried to have her sectioned. By this stage her car had what is known as a suicide marker so they were aware that she was vulnerable. She was then seen by the hospital doctors and social workers who attempted to obtain her records from other hospitals where she had previously been admitted. They decided, despite objection by the police, not to section her. They released her and by Monday morning she was dead.

Much of the information I found out about my daughter was at the inquest. For some time after the inquest I felt that the last hospital who saw her were negligent in not sectioning her. I am sure that she had tried on at least 10 occasions to end her life and that the last hospital had that information. When I did obtain information about Amanda it was always along the lines of an inevitability that she would end her life. I wish that she had been able to receive better support and that as a parent that I had known how to get help for her.

To the outside world Amanda was a gifted child who had every advantage in life but hated herself and did not want to grow up.

Questions for consideration:

1. What would have happened to Amanda if she had presented in your department with this history?

2. How would you have involved the parents in this scenario?

3. What is the procedure you follow for releasing information to other hospitals?

4. What determines the legal status of people under 18 years of age?

5. List the agencies which may have been able to offer help to Amanda following discharge from A&E.

Case study 20.2: John's story

John's father feels that his son gave him every chance to help him. Unfortunately, lack of resources and an inflexible system of mental health care compounded John's sense of hopelessness:

> My son completed a successful Business Studies course – gaining a BA first class honours degree – in June. I was not aware of any mental problem until a visit home in August of that year. I soon began to realise that all was not well, but it was very difficult for him to talk to me about his depression.
>
> I accompanied him on a visit to a local GP who told us that we would have to wait 11 months for a referral to a Clinical Psychologist. During the next few weeks I spent some time contacting drop-in centres and the local psychiatric hospital – all to no avail. I was so desperate for help that I took him to our General Hospital. The doctor in A&E told John that he had a psychological problem and should see his GP.
>
> Eventually I paid privately for a consultation with a doctor in London. After an hour and a half, I was invited in with them both to be told that John was very ill and that he could be admitted to the clinic immediately, at a cost of £300 per day. I could not afford to do this and had to refuse the offer, but the doctor told me that there would be help at hand when we arrived home. At 8 pm that night the local GP phoned to confirm that she would be coming around within the hour.
>
> The following day the local psychiatric hospital agreed to accept John as a voluntary patient. While he was in there, much to my surprise, one of the nurses said to me 'You know he's suicidal, don't you?' This was the first intimation I had had that he was suicidal. I was very shocked but felt a sense of relief that he was in a safe place. He spent just short of a week in hospital before walking out. He just could not cope with being in an alien situation alongside acutely mentally ill patients. There was no follow-up appointment at outpatients and I don't know whether he was given any medication to take home.
>
> During October, John visited family abroad. One day in November he again phoned to say that he wanted to come to stay with me. On the following evening, thinking that I had got home before he had arrived, I discovered him in my garage. He was in his car with the motor running. I was too late to save him and he was pronounced dead on arrival at the General Hospital.

Some of the signs that may have been picked up on seem very apparent now. While he was in college he had locked himself in his room for three days – and no one had asked him why! while at home with me, he sat on his own one night and drank a considerable amount of whiskey, making himself sick and, I found out later, he had taken some tablets. I'm sure this was a suicide attempt. His final note to me said 'Had you really known how I felt about myself, and the emotional suffering I had been going through over many years, you might accept my decision.'

It is some consolation to know that at least I had the opportunity to help him and I respect him for this. Even so – in the end it didn't stop him doing what he did.

Questions for consideration:

1. Is it really easier for privately referred patients to be treated?

2. What protocols are there for informing someone of the possibilities resulting from their self-discharge when they are voluntary/informal patients?

3. John's father had been involved in his decision to enter hospital. Should he have been involved in follow-up suggestions?

4. John discharged himself but his GP – who was outside the hospital's area – was not informed. What information should be released on discharge and to whom?

5. If patients discharge themselves, what contact numbers would be given to them by your service?

Case study 20.3: Barbara's story

Making contact with a therapist is often very difficult for someone who is depressed. Barbara managed to put into words how depression feels from the point of view of the person who lives it. Depression may have been there for a long time before it comes to the attention of a clinician. A suicide attempt may be the first indication of the need for intervention, but there are often early signs of a developing problem.

I think depression has always been a part of me. I remember as a very young child having a sense of life being sad and difficult. It always seemed hard for me to be happy. Other people managed it – but I had a sense of foreboding, of isolation and despair. I tried not to think about it most of the time. But when I did I thought that maybe other people had got the knack of life and I just didn't know the rules. I felt cut off – separate and different. I never really knew how to put it into words. And I didn't know how to try and explain it to anyone. You feel that no one else can understand, no one else has ever felt like this. They can't have because it's so hard and so painful.

The suicidal thoughts began to be a part of these feelings when I was about 15. They were fleeting at first, but gradually over the years they began to creep forward in my thinking. So by the time I was in my early twenties I had almost got used to the idea of killing myself as being one way of ending the pain I felt inside. If a sure way to stop the pain was to end my life – then sometimes that seemed to be the only option available to me.

When I was 28, despite the fact that I had reached a senior position in my career, had a wide circle of friends and was deeply in love with my boyfriend and saving to buy my first home, these thoughts had been a part of me for so long and were so overwhelming that I felt the only option I had left was to take an overdose.

I'm 30 now – and only really beginning to get used to approaching life with an acceptance of my illness. I've only recently been able to try and put these feelings into words. It's perhaps the hardest thing I've ever attempted in my life. Trying to explain to anyone how I felt and feel when I am depressed goes against everything my depression is about. Words don't seem to work properly with the kind of emotions you have inside you when you are depressed. At my worst times there is still no one I want to tell the feelings I have, no one I want to see or hear me. Depression can make me retreat so far into myself at times that it is totally impossible to come out until the worst is past. I implode.

When I am in the middle of a severe depressive episode it seems absolutely impossible that I will ever be able to be 'normal'. To interact with anyone else. To do the things that people take for granted – like going to the shops, eating a meal with friends, even having a relationship. Depression makes me feel completely and utterly isolated. Despite having friends who love and care about me and who I could call at anytime and tell anything.

For me living with clinical depression is characterised by a battle, an argument with my innermost thoughts. I have had to learn to accept the feelings, to sometimes let them wash over me and tell myself that they will pass eventually. It's made easier when other people accept it too. As I have had to learn, so have those who care about me and who share my life. Some people in my life have found it impossible to accept and understand my situation. Some tried and tried but found it too difficult. I understand that. I have found myself exasperated by depressed people. Even when I loved them and cared for them. I found myself thinking – oh for God's sake pull yourself together – get a grip – can't you see it's not that bad? So I know how hard it can be for those around me.

No matter how much support is around me though – the most important thing I have had to do is learn to accept what is inside me and be willing to try and open up about it. That has taken years and has been a frightening and slow process.

Questions for consideration:

1. Barbara describes a sense of feeling 'separate and different' from early on in her life. What can be done to help children who feel this difference?

2. Would a wider acceptance of suicide as a possible consequence of stress and depression help people to recognise when their options are running out?

3. Barbara has been helped by an informed and supportive network of friends. Do you suggest to clients that they can benefit from letting friends help?

4. Cognitive behaviour therapy gave Barbara her start on a road to recovery. Other techniques work better for some people. How flexible is your service in offering alternative treatments for depression?

5. Involving family in assessment can often indicate how long a problem has existed, how serious it is, and what might help. Are clients asked if family can be approached?

Resources

From parents' testimonies, PAPYRUS has identified three groups where a major input of information and guidance is required:

- staff and students in schools and colleges
- young people who are suicidal
- those who are caring for them.

With this in mind, two booklets, *Not Just a Cry for Help* and *Thinking of Ending it All?*, have been published. The feedback from professionals, parents and the young people who have used them to date has been positive.

Not Just a Cry for Help

Often family members and/or friends are left to pick up the pieces after a suicide attempt. An inappropriate reaction can compound feelings of low self-esteem, helplessness and lack of hope in the suicidal. *Not Just a Cry for Help* addresses the needs of these people and is suitable for all who come into contact with attempted suicide – family, police, social workers, teachers, accident and emergency staff, ambulance personnel and so on.

Box 20.2 (from *Not Just a Cry for Help*)

DO keep 'ALERT'…

Ask them how they were feeling before it happened and how they are feeling now. Talking about suicide does not make it more likely to happen. Try to be patient if they are angry or refuse to talk. It may be that writing things down is an easier way for them to communicate with you.

Listen – this is the most important thing you can do. Treat them with respect, and try not to be judgmental or critical.

Empathise by showing that *you really are trying to understand* things from their point of view. Words don't always matter. The touch of a hand or a hug can go a long way to show that you care.

Reassure them that desperate feelings are very common and can be overcome. Things can and do change, help can be found and there is hope for the future. People *do* get better!

Try to give practical support, and help them to cope with any extra pressures. It may not be possible to deal with all the things that are troubling them, but between you agree on what you will do if a suicidal crisis happens again.

...and DON'T 'PANIC'...

*P*ut *them down* or do things that might make them feel worse. A suicide attempt suggests that self-esteem is already very low.

*A*bandon *or reject* them in any way. Your help, support and attention are vital if they are to begin to feel that life is worth living again. Don't relax your attentions just because they seem to be better. It doesn't mean that life is back to normal for them yet. They may be at risk for quite a while.

*N*ag – although it may be well meant. Nobody wants to be pestered all the time. Don't intrude – try to balance being watchful with a respect for privacy.

*I*gnore what has happened.

*C*riticise their actions – however you may be feeling about their suicide attempt, try to remember the pain and turmoil that they were, and may still be, going through. Don't take their behaviour personally – it was not necessarily directed at you.

Box 20.3 (from *Thinking of Ending it All?*)

So what can you do about it?

Tell someone you trust how you are feeling. This could be someone in your family, your doctor, a teacher, the school nurse, college counsellor... If the person you are telling doesn't seem to understand, don't be put off – tell someone else. If you reach a suicidal crisis where the desire to kill yourself is overwhelming, you *must* tell someone. Ask them to keep you company until the feelings pass.

Thinking bad thoughts about yourself all the time (especially about killing yourself) makes you feel worse. You might be thinking that you're a failure or nobody likes you or that nothing will get better. There might be some thoughts that are very private to you.

Tell yourself about the good things you've done today instead of the bad things.

Just thinking about your bad thoughts a bit less often can be a great achievement. It can help you realise that you are starting to win the battle.

If you find it difficult to talk, write it down and send a letter, an e-mail, or text someone.

Don't be afraid of going to see a specialist like a counsellor or psychiatrist. There are some very good 'talking treatments' which work really well, especially if you go in the early days of feeling unwell. If you are not able to relate to the person you are seeing – *ask to see someone else.*

Try to get help with the problems which may be causing your depression.

If you have been given medication (tablets) to help with your suicidal feelings, make sure you understand how long it takes before they start having an effect. If they don't seem to be working, tell your doctor so that he/she can try something else. Don't stop taking them because you feel better or because you are having side effects. Get advice from your doctor first. You can also talk to your pharmacist about your medication.

Avoid alcohol and drugs. Although at first they give you a lift, they are known to make depressed people feel even worse in the long run. Under their influence you may do things or make decisions you would not normally make. Using alcohol and other drugs can actually make some people suicidal. Even cannabis can have this effect too.

Stop any risk taking behaviour – where you want the decision as to whether you live or die to be left to chance. Like driving the car in a way that could kill you (or someone else). Don't be pressured into doing risky things by other people.

Be very careful of making an impulsive decision to kill yourself.

Don't listen to sad music when you're really down.

Start looking after yourself with regular meals and plenty of exercise. Get out into the daylight and try to stay out of bed until night time. Find something to do which gives some structure to your day.

Don't expect to feel OK all at once. Just knowing that life is slowly getting better means that there is light at the end of the tunnel.

Thinking of Ending it All?

Thinking of Ending It All? can be used as a starting point for opening up a dialogue – something which men in particular seem to find difficult. From PAPYRUS' experience, the opportunity for suicidal people to see the emotions/feelings they are experiencing written in a booklet can give immense relief. Reassurance that other people have felt the same, that they are not 'going mad', that there is 'light at the end of the tunnel' can be helpful in the healing process.

The text of both booklets can be downloaded from www.papyrus-uk.org

Don't Die of Embarrassment

PAPYRUS has produced a video and teachers' resource pack for use in schools, colleges, youth work and group therapy. Based around a piece of drama by boys from West Derby Comprehensive School, Merseyside, it deals with issues that young men in particular find difficult to acknowledge. The drama follows the events in one young man's life – the contacts he has with peers, parents and professionals, and how circumstances lead him to suicide. This powerful expression of the struggle with stereotypes and stigmas that teenagers face in growing up needs to be introduced sensitively as part of an ongoing programme of mental health education.

In conclusion

Parents and other carers often feel excluded from the helping circle by their ignorance of what is going on. They want to know which treatments are available and how they may be accessed. Worries about medication, misinformation from the Internet and scaremongering by the media can add to their concern. Some services do not involve parents as a matter of policy, particularly if the client is over 16 years of age. Parents are a valuable and underused resource for many young people. Where they have not requested confidentiality, young people may be introduced to the concept of involving their parents/carers in their treatment, especially when medication is prescribed. Medication can cause a change in behaviour which may not be apparent to the young people themselves.

In his 1999 Thematic Review, the Chief Inspector of Prisons for England and Wales entitled his report *Suicide is Everyone's Concern*. PAPYRUS endorses this view and will continue to work with and support all who are concerned with the prevention of suicide.

References

Cowie, H. and Wallace, P. (2000) *Peer Support in Action: From Bystanding to Standing By.* London: Sage. http://www.childsafe.net.au/SCOUTS/scysp1.html (accessed 8 July 2003)

Harvey, M. (2002) 'When our children kill themselves: Parental perspectives following suicide.' In N. Stanley and J. Manthorpe (eds) *Students' Mental Health Needs.* London: Jessica Kingsley Publishers.

HM Chief Inspector of Prisions for England and Wales (1999) *Suicide is Everyone's Concern: A Thematic Review.* London: HMSO.

Stanley, N. and Manthorpe, J. (2001) *Making Use of Hindsight: Report.* Hull: University of Hull and PAPYRUS.

Stanley, N., Manthorpe, J. and Bradley, G. (1999) *Responding Effectively to Students' Mental Health Needs: Project Report.* Hull: University of Hull.

Universities UK (2002) *Reducing the Risk of Student Suicide: Issues and Responses for Higher Education Institutions.* London: Universities UK.

Chapter 21

Community Whole-System Approaches

Jude Stansfield and Pippa Sargent

Introduction

Two thirds of suicides are by people who do not have contact with mental health services. We know that certain groups are more at risk than others and that they often have contact with many other agencies within the community, e.g. housing, job centre, police, GP and employer. Equally, individuals will be marginalised or excluded within a community e.g. lacking social networks and participation. A whole community approach requires developing partnerships and capacity that build protective factors and reduce risk factors to create healthy and inclusive communities.

This chapter focuses on improving mental health in order to prevent suicide. It discusses prevention and promotion, and then explains how the whole-system approach is put into practice through health promoting settings and mental health promotion strategies. Case studies of specific community interventions to promote mental health are then detailed.

Prevention and promotion

This section explores suicide prevention and links it to mental health promotion. It focuses on a holistic understanding of health, drawing on the broad influences on our mental health.

Although suicide mortality rates within a community may seem low, suicide is preventable and is a significant public health issue. Considering or attempting suicide reflects a person's state of mental health and, as the *National Suicide Prevention Strategy for England* (Department of Health (DoH) 2002) recognises, suicide rates reflect the mental health of the community as a whole. Goal two of the strategy is 'to promote mental well-being in the wider population'. This supports Standard One of the *National Service Framework for Mental Health* (DoH 1999), which focuses on mental health promotion, social inclusion and discrimination.

Box 21.1 National Suicide Prevention Strategy

Goal 2: To promote mental well-being in the wider population

Suicide rates reflect the mental health of the community as a whole. Standard one of the National Service Framework for adult mental health adopts a similarly broad approach by stating that health and social services should:

- Promote mental health for all, working with individuals and communities

- Combat discrimination against individuals and groups with mental health problems, and promote their social inclusion

We value the importance of general measures to improve mental health and to address aspects of people's life experiences that may damage their self-esteem and their social relationships.

(DoH 2002, p.13)

Equally, the US National Strategy for Suicide Prevention (United States Department of Health and Human Services 2003) calls for a whole-population, public health approach. It specifies increased awareness that suicide is a public health problem that is preventable, acknowledging a lack of understanding among individuals and organisations and emphasising that each can play an important role in tackling this issue.

Box 21.2 National Strategy for Suicide Prevention

Goal 1: Promote Awareness that Suicide is a Public Health Problem that is Preventable

By increasing public understanding that suicide and suicidal behaviors can be prevented, and that individuals and groups can play a role in prevention, beliefs and behaviours can be changed and many lines saved.

(US Department of Health and Human Services 2003)

Just as many factors influence whether someone will attempt suicide, there are many influences on a person's health. A whole-community or public health approach recognises the influences at different levels. Dahlgren and Whitehead (1991) identify five layers of influence on health. These are: age, gender and constitutional factors; individual lifestyle factors; social and community networks; living and working conditions (e.g. housing, unemployment, work environment, education, health care services); general socio-economic, cultural and environmental conditions.

Improving health is most effective, therefore, when attention is paid to all the influences and action is delivered at individual, community, organisational and structural levels. Health service interventions often focus on the first two influences – biological factors and lifestyle. Yet the last three layers are particularly important to mental health. Discrimination, income, good quality housing, employment, education and physical environment have a significant impact on mental health (DoH 2001) and access to social support and social participation are increasingly being recognised as influential (Pevalin and Rose 2003).

In promoting mental health, therefore, one first recognises that mental health is a positive state of well-being that affects all of us. Prevention, however, relates not holistically to health, but to ill health – an illness or health problem, i.e. preventing mental illness or suicide.

Defining prevention and promotion (adapted from DoH 2001)

Mental health promotion involves any action to enhance the mental well-being of individuals, families, organisations or communities.

- *Primary prevention* refers to interventions designed to prevent a disorder or problem occurring. Prevention may be:

- ° universal – interventions across the whole population, e.g. in schools
- ° selective – targeted to individuals or groups at increased risk, e.g. young women of Asian heritage
- ° indicated – individuals with early signs, e.g. contemplation of suicide, self-harm.

- *Secondary prevention* is concerned with reducing prevalence through early interventions, e.g. interventions with those who have attempted suicide.

- *Tertiary prevention* is defined as reducing disability as a result of a disorder, e.g. interventions targeting those while attempting suicide, such as providing collapsible rails.

- *Early interventions* target individuals developing or experiencing a first episode of a mental health problem.

A whole-system approach may consider interventions at each stage of prevention, as the *National Suicide Prevention Strategy for England* (DoH 2002) reflects in its goals and objectives.

Key learning points

- Mental health is a positive state of well-being that affects all of us.

- Mental health promotion can make a valuable contribution to suicide prevention.

- A broad range of factors including individual, community and socio-economic, cultural and environmental conditions influence our mental health.

Health Promoting Settings

This section describes the Health Promoting Settings approach to health improvement, giving background information on what a setting is and how this initiative seeks to improve health.

Health Promoting Settings or Healthy Settings is a health promotion approach to improving population health. As an individual's health is significantly affected by the environment in which they live and work it is those environments that we need to make healthy, i.e. moving away from a focus on individual factors and lifestyles to the broader influences on health.

A setting is any place where people live, learn, work or play, e.g. school, neighbourhood, workplace, hospital or prison. The healthy settings approach seeks to integrate health and the improvement of health within the whole system of that setting. Health is not the responsibility of health (illness) professionals but the responsibility of many within a community. The settings approach connects the different dimensions of health across the different systems within a community or organisation. The roles of each department within a hospital, school or each agency within a community all impact on health yet often function in isolation. What is required is a commitment to health throughout the cultures, structures and processes of the community or organisation, involving all key players.

The settings-based approach has been developing, internationally, over the last 10–15 years. It is rooted in the World Health Organization (WHO) strategies *Health for All* and the *1986 Ottawa Charter for Health Promotion*. Examples within the UK include healthy cities, hospitals, universities, colleges, schools, workplaces and prisons.

The settings-based approach moves services away from an illness and problem focus to one of health and the determinants of health..

A Health Promoting Setting should create a healthy working and living environment, integrate health promotion into daily activities. and outreach into the community in the form of health promoting alliances (Baric 1994).

A *health promoting mental health service* would adopt principles, policy and practice that integrate health by: improving the health and well-being of patients; creating a healthy workplace; promoting the health and well-being of carers and family members; developing a healthy role and relationship with the wider community; providing and promoting a healthy physical environment; and increasing the social inclusion of patients in the community (Stansfield 2002).

While interventions relating to the above may already exist they are often marginalised or uncoordinated. The development of a healthy settings approach would provide a framework for a co-ordinated approach throughout the whole organisation. It requires commitment from the top of the organisation and involvement of all stakeholders.

> **Key learning points**
>
> - Best practice in promoting mental health is achieved through focusing on the broad influences on health – including individual, community and socio-economic, cultural and environmental conditions.
>
> - A whole organisation approach can help to embed health improvement into the culture, structure and systems of the organisation.
>
> - A healthy setting focuses on improving the health of customers, staff and the extended community.

Strategies for whole populations

This section explores how strategies can create a whole-system response to suicide prevention. The example used is Mental Health Promotion (MHP) strategies, as the Department of Health requires each locality to produce such a strategy.

In order to achieve long-term change, a strategic focus is useful. Integrating the improvement of mental health into local strategy and policy is more sustainable than developing isolated one-off projects. Many localities have developed MHP strategies that attempt to create a sustained impact on the mental health of the local population.

Mental Health Promotion strategy

The *National Service Framework for Mental Health* (NSF) (DoH 1999) prioritises Mental Health Promotion as Standard One. The performance targets call for the production and implementation of local strategies to provide a focus and direction for promoting mental health, increasing social inclusion and combating discrimination associated with mental illness. Despite no central funding and limited incentive for local decision-makers, many localities have produced and are implementing multi-agency strategies. Some of these are also combined with Suicide Prevention strategies – Standard Seven of the NSF.

While many agencies are involved in promoting mental health and well-being, or in increasing social inclusion, this work has often been ad hoc, reactive, uncoordinated or marginalised. The DoH (2001) states that strategies should to be based on local need, use evidence-based practice and co-ordinate mental health promotion at different levels.

Why produce a strategy?

It may be thought that a strategy is just another document that nobody reads and collects dust on the shelf.

However, a strategy can:

- create ownership of the issue among stakeholders
- build partnership working
- provide a proactive, planned approach and direction
- raise the profile of the issue – make it explicit
- build a vision for achieving the long-term goals
- motivate stakeholders who each play a small part in achieving the whole
- use resources more effectively.

Ashton, Wigan and Leigh Primary Care Trust's strategy is underpinned by two key approaches to mental health promotion:

a *whole population approach* which is aimed at everyone who lives in the borough and a *targeted approach* which addresses the specific needs of those most at risk of experiencing mental health problems. These complementary approaches will focus upon the following settings:

- neighbourhoods and communities
- schools and colleges
- workplaces
- prisons
- health and social care services.

Focusing mental health promotion within key settings enables us to develop activities in the context of people's lives, i.e. where they live and work.

(Ashton, Wigan and Leigh Primary Care Trust 2003)

The DoH issued guidance on producing a locality MHP strategy (DoH 2001). It included agreeing a vision, mapping initiatives, identifying key settings, policy links and stakeholders, selecting interventions, assessing evidence, establishing indicators, evaluation and resource implications. A similar framework could be used for developing an organisational mental health promotion or suicide prevention strategy.

Many different strategies exist in one locality and the Government has attempted to co-ordinate these through the introduction of Local Strategic Partnerships (LSP). Each LSP has to produce a community strategy or plan to improve the social, economic and environmental well-being of communities. In order for MHP strategies and Suicide Prevention strategies to be effective within a locality it is important that they are integrated into the work of the Local Strategic Partnership and Community strategy.

> The Local Government Act 2000 gives local authorities a statutory responsibility and powers to address the needs of their population by improving the economic, social and environmental circumstances of their area. Plans should include mental well being in relation to social well being alongside the mental health impact of economic and environmental factors. [For example:]
>
> • *Community strategies* to improve individual well being and regenerate communities.
>
> • *LSPs* offering an umbrella under which mental health promotion can be threaded into policies.
>
> (St Helens Primary Care Trust 2002)

An example of an effective LSP is the Salford Partnership Plan, published in 2001. It is based on priorities identified by nine community committees representing communities across Salford to improve lives. Local community action plans have been produced but seven crosscutting themes were identified and incorporated into a citywide plan. The seven themes addressed as priorities for action are:

- a healthy city
- a safe city
- a learning and creative city
- a city where children and young people are valued
- an inclusive city with a strong community
- an economically prosperous city
- a city that's good to live in.

Promoting mental health across the settings

In developing a whole-system approach it is important to know what drives the systems and what the opportunities are to promote mental health within a system. Many systems are influenced by national and local policy. Figure 21.1 shows some of the policies and programmes relevant to improving mental health. Each of these have supporting goals or targets which, joined together, can create a whole-system approach not just within the setting, but also between settings, to produce a whole-community approach.

In Figure 21.2 four key objectives have been identified as pertinent to each setting, as informed by the supporting policy. Again, the objectives work together to create a whole-system approach across the settings. At an individual level, people move between the settings and can experience complementary environments, rather than conflicting and uncoordinated systems.

Key learning points

- A strategy can help to create ownership and build partnership between key organisations.

- Planned and co-ordinated activity is more cost-effective than developing one-off projects.

- Promoting mental health is linked to many different strategies, policies and organisations within one locality.

Mental Health Promotion and supporting policy across settings

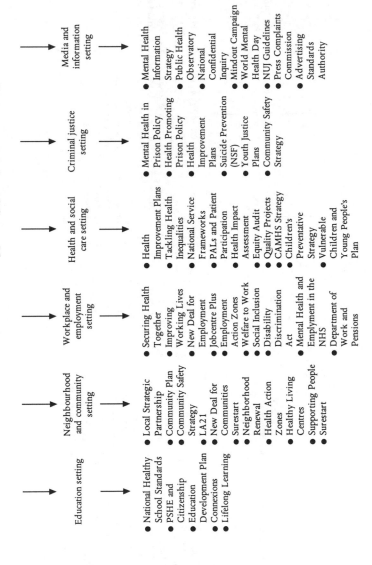

Education setting
- National Healthy School Standards
- PSHE and Citizenship Education
- Development Plan
- Connexions
- Lifelong Learning

Neighbourhood and community setting
- Local Strategic Partnership
- Community Plan
- Community Safety Strategy
- LA21
- New Deal for Communities
- Surestart
- Neighborhood Renewal
- Health Action Zones
- Healthy Living Centres
- Supporting People
- Surestart

Workplace and employment setting
- Securing Health Together
- Improving Working Lives
- New Deal for Employment
- Jobcentre Plus
- Employment Action Zones
- Welfare to Work
- Social Inclusion
- Disability Discrimination Act
- Mental Health and Emplyment in the NHS
- Department of Work and Pensions

Health and social care setting
- Health Improvement Plans
- Tackling Health Inequalities
- National Service Frameworks
- PALs and Patient Participation
- Health Impact Assessment
- Equity Audit
- Quality Projects
- CAMHS Strategy
- Children's Preventative Strategy
- Vulnerable Children and Young People's Plan

Criminal justice setting
- Mental Health in Prison Policy
- Health Promoting Prison Policy
- Health Improvement Plans
- Suicide Prevention (NSF)
- Youth Justice Plans
- Community Safety Strategy

Media and information setting
- Mental Health Information Strategy
- Public Health Observatory
- National Confidential Inquiry
- Mindout Campaign
- World Mental Health Day
- NUJ Guidelines
- Press Complaints Commission
- Advertising Standards Authority

Figure 21.1: Mental Health Promotion and supporting policy across settings

Mental Health Promotion and key objectives for settings

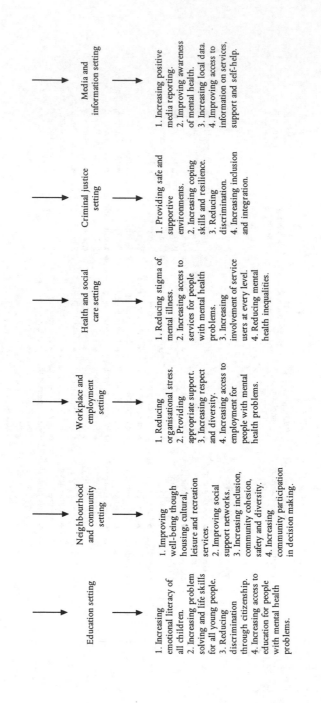

Education setting	Neighbourhood and community setting	Workplace and employment setting	Health and social care setting	Criminal justice setting	Media and information setting
1. Increasing emotional literacy of all children. 2. Increasing problem solving and life skills for all young people. 3. Reducing discrimination through citizenship. 4. Increasing access to education for people with mental health problems.	1. Improving well-being though housing, cultural, leisure and recreation services. 2. Improving social support networks. 3. Increasing inclusion, community cohesion, safety and diversity. 4. Increasing community participation in decision making.	1. Reducing organisational stress. 2. Providing appropriate support. 3. Increasing respect and diversity. 4. Increasing access to employment for people with mental health problems.	1. Reducing stigma of mental illness. 2. Increasing access to services for people with mental health problems. 3. Increasing involvement of service users at every level. 4. Reducing mental health inequalities.	1. Providing safe and supportive environments. 2. Increasing coping skills and resilience. 3. Reducing discrimination. 4. Increasing inclusion and integration.	1. Increasing positive media reporting. 2. Improving awareness of mental health. 3. Increasing local data. 4. Improving access to information on services, support and self-help.

Figure 21.2: Mental Health Promotion and key objectives for settings

Good practice guidelines

1. Identify the needs of your community and any current action or plans – find out if the following local documents exist and get hold of them from the Public Health or Health Promotion department:

    ° Mental Health Promotion strategy

    ° Suicide Prevention strategy

    ° Mental Health Needs Assessment – identifying suicide rates and mental illness prevalence

    ° Public Health report – broader health priorities, deprivation figures, mortality and morbidity rates

    ° Community strategy or plan.

2. Recognise the broad layers of influence on health when working with individuals, communities or at a policy level.

3. When planning preventative activities identify the different stages of prevention and whether interventions are needed at each stage. Some activities may work to promote mental health as well as to prevent mental ill health or suicide.

4. Identify local healthy settings work and explore how mental health can be integrated within it. Consider the healthy settings approach to improve health within your organisation or community.

5. Plan any local mental health promotion initiatives in conjunction with local plans and policies, such as the Local Implementation Team (LIT) for Mental Health who co-ordinate the Mental Health Promotion strategy.

6. Promotion or prevention activity should be planned to meet local need, work in partnership with key stakeholders, use the evidence base on what is effective practice and include evaluation of it's success.

Examples of community interventions

There are many and varied examples of community approaches to suicide prevention across the UK and internationally, encompassing a broad range of approaches and initiatives developed specifically to contribute to suicide reduction through the promotion of positive mental health. In addition, given that beyond biological and lifestyle factors a holistic approach to positive mental health promotion – and therefore suicide prevention – incorporates many facets of communities, both can be outcomes as a by-product of other community interventions.

Examples of initiatives have been chosen that target a specific sector of the community – young men – to illustrate the types of primary prevention that can contribute to suicide reduction in a high-risk group. Three examples are given that could be classed as universal, selective and indicated prevention (as detailed above).

1. Healthy schools programme
Profile

- *Environment/target*: School-aged children (5–16), 4 key stages
- *Approach*: Universal, settings-based primary prevention (all young men)
- *Range*: National intervention, via Local Education Authorities
- *Funding source*: Department of Health, Department for Education and Skills
- *Main themes/aims*: Local healthy schools programmes, managed by local education and health partnerships, provide support to schools to help them become healthy and effective via the National Healthy Schools Scheme (NHSS) quality standards guidance and accreditation.
- *Key words*: Educating in health, early intervention

Synopsis

Every Local Education Authority in England is working in partnership to manage a local healthy schools programme. Each programme has a local co-ordinator and a team from Education and Health supporting its management and delivery. The NHSS Team – based at the Health Development Agency – together with the support of nine regional co-ordinators help to build the capacity and capability of the local partnerships to implement the NHSS, and manage a system of accreditation to ensure that local healthy schools programmes are working to the NHSS.

Guiding principles

The National Healthy School Standard (NHSS) has a key contribution to make in raising pupil achievement and promoting social inclusion. It provides a framework within which local healthy schools programmes can tackle inequalities and aim to improve the health and emotional well-being of young people.

Key features

The Healthy Schools Programme is aligned to key stages (1–4) in school life and includes the themes listed below. The NHSS Guidance, launched in 1999, outlines criteria for assessing school achievements in relation to (the emotional health and well-being section has been expanded):

- local priorities
- school priorities
- PSHE
- citizenship
- drug education (including alcohol and tobacco)
- emotional health and well-being (including bullying)
    - opportunities are provided for pupils' views to inform policy and practice
    - the school has a policy and code of practice in place that is owned, understood and implemented by all members of the schools community and includes contact with external support agencies
    - the school openly addresses issues of emotional health and well-being by enabling pupils to understand what they are feeling and by building their confidence to learn
    - the school identifies and supports the emotional health needs of all staff
- healthy eating
- physical activity
- safety
- sex and relationship education.

The NHSS promotes a whole-school approach to health improvement and education that includes:

- policy development
- assessing, recording and reporting pupils' achievements
- partnerships with parents/carers and local communities
- giving pupils a voice
- curriculum planning and work with outside agencies
- school culture and environment
- staff professional development needs, health and welfare
- leadership, management and managing change
- teaching and learning
- provision of pupil support services.

Examples of the initiative in practice

Translating the principles into practice is the challenge that LEAs, and the schools involved, are addressing. Examples below are taken from the Manchester Healthy Schools Partnership (MHSP):

1. Minimum criteria which schools are encouraged to reach to meet the guidance on emotional health and well-being and a joint project 'Mindful Schools' is being piloted with four high schools involved in the Healthy School Award Scheme. The project aims to strengthen a whole-school ethos, promoting the emotional health and well-being of pupils and staff, and supporting young people with mental health problems.

2. A drama workshop called 'Happy, Safe and Confident' is used as a method to promote emotional health and well-being in Manchester primary schools, focusing on bullying and anger management. A progression of the drama workshops has been extended to include work with parents and staff to support anti-bullying policy and practice development.

Successes, lessons learnt and future developments

Local education and health partnerships are making an explicit contribution towards tackling health inequalities at both programme and school level (see website listed below for further information). An independent review of Ofsted school inspection found that the NHSS is having a greater impact in schools serving areas of socio-economic disadvantage (Wired for Health 2003): among schools involved in the NHSS:

- overall effectiveness of over four out of five primary schools and 50 per cent of secondary schools is 'good' or 'better' than the national average

- almost two thirds of primary schools and 37 per cent of secondary schools have made 'good' or 'better' progress since their last inspection

- primary and secondary schools are making improvements at a rate faster than schools nationally, in a number of key areas, including behaviour, standards of work, quality of the Personal, Social and Health Education (PSHE) programme and management and support of pupils.

e-contacts

- www.wiredforhealth.gov.uk – NHSS general information and guidance for teachers

- www.mhsa.org.uk – Manchester Healthy Schools Awards

2. Let's get serious (LGS)

Profile

- *Environment/target*: Men, long-term unemployed

- *Approach*: Targeted 'selective' primary prevention (excluded young men)

- *Range:* Local initiative in Manchester, Salford and Trafford (inner city communities)

- *Funding source*: Department of Health, Health Action Zone Innovations Fund

- *Main aim*: Set up to address health inequalities and social exclusion faced by men in socially deprived areas through the employment of Mentors providing support to Mentees locally, and contributing to a local agenda to improve life expectancy.

- *Key words*: Addressing inequalities and social exclusion

Synopsis

Socially excluded men in deprived areas experience significant health inequalities. Suicide and mental health problems are significantly associated with unemployment. LGS is a social enterprise, which employs long-term unemployed men and provides them with intensive professional training as mentors. The skilled mentors then deliver gender-specific mentoring to 'at-risk' boys and young men who may be having difficulties at school or in the wider community. This is primarily mentor rather than mentee focused work, concentrated on provision of jobs for mentors, the majority of whom are from minority ethnic communities.

Guiding principles

Addressing crosscutting themes of employment, education, and social exclusion is key to improving health inequalities in deprived areas, and impacts on improving mental health and reducing suicide. Other factors such as crime and disorder, supporting enterprise and engaging with young people are addressed as part of this approach.

Key features

MENTORS

- There are currently 26 employed mentors.
- Mentors complete 13 weeks of training in:
    ◦ the Pacific institute's 'STEPS' training
    ◦ the LGS-developed 'Men's health workout' training, covering areas such as counselling, drugs awareness, anger management, sexual health, equal opportunities and youth work, which is accredited by Greater Manchester Open College Network and provides a GNVQ2 equivalent
    ◦ A GNVQ3 level certificate in mentoring.
- Placements, initially two days per week, building up to four days per week, focus on work in schools, but also extend to other organisations such as Youth Offending Teams (YOTs), school inclusion projects, community centres, special schools, young offenders' institutions, behaviour improvement schemes and, somewhat unexpectedly, Greater Manchester Police.

MENTEES

- To date, 250 young people have become mentees.
- Mentees are referred to LGS via schools; often because of concerns regarding attendance, behaviour or attainment. The mentors themselves identify other mentees within the schools,

and there is also a degree of self-referral. Non-school
organisations may also request mentoring for an individual or
project/group.

- Mentor and mentee work together, mainly one-to-one, but also
  occasionally in groups, to establish a joint action plan
  specifically designed to deal with the individuals' concerns, i.e.
  the mentors work directly with the young people, focusing on
  their issues and concerns.

- The advantages of mentoring are many and well documented.

Examples of the initiative in practice

1. *Mentee*: Year 7 pupil, started to become disruptive at school.

2. *Mentor intervention*: Established rapport, facilitating discovery of
    reasons for mentee's disruptive behaviour. The mentee's home
    situation had changed; his parents were working shifts, and
    discipline around homework and bedtime was lacking because
    of this: he would stay up watching TV or playing video games.
    Consequently the mentee was turning up for school tired and
    unprepared for lessons, which was causing him stress, leading
    to his disruption. The mentee agreed that he wasn't enjoying
    getting into trouble at school

3. *Action*: The mentor–mentee relationship supported the mentee
    to get organised to get his homework done; he would take
    responsibility and go to bed at an appropriate time on a school
    night.

4. *Evaluation*: The mentee's behaviour generally improved, but the
    relationship continues to support the mentee. Benefits were felt
    by the school, the mentee and mentor.

Successes, lessons learnt and future developments

Let's Get Serious provides a positive example of a 'joined-up' community-
based project addressing suicide prevention. The University of Manchester
Community Justice Research Centre has monitored the work, with an in-
terim report produced in January 2003. LGS's success covers several areas,
particularly focused on mentors rather than mentees:

- 26 employed mentors, holding accredited qualifications
- all mentors were previously unemployed and although 65 per cent of mentors have had previous convictions (58% serving prison sentences), 80 per cent have retained their jobs with LGS
- 62 per cent of mentors using illegal drugs on starting with LGS have now stopped
- 50 per cent of mentors have significantly changed their attitude to sexual health
- challenges 'macho' approaches by demonstrating that nurturing and support skills are viable career options.

Future aspirations include sustainability; both continuing to develop the mentoring program and to offer the model to other areas.

e-contacts

www.letsgetserious.com

3. CALM (Campaign Against Living Miserably)

Profile

- *Environment/target*: Young men, aged 15–35
- *Approach*: Targeted, 'Indicated' primary prevention (YOUNG MEN AS A HIGH RISK GROUP)
- *Range*: Four local 'zones' in England; Manchester, Merseyside, Cumbria and Bedfordshire
- *Funding source*: Department of Health, local health/social care commissioners
- *Main aim*: To raise awareness of depression and suicide among young men, and encourage them to seek help at the onset of depression.
- *Key words*: Challenging stigma, increasing access to services

Synopsis

The CALM initiative was launched in 1997 in Manchester by the DoH in response to the high suicide rate among young men. It has since been extended to Merseyside, Cumbria and Bedfordshire. CALM consists of a

communications strategy that engages directly with young men and a dedicated freephone helpline.

Guiding principles

Suicide rates among young men have been increasing since the 1970s, with
young men three times more likely to take their life than young women.
However, young men are poor users of GP services, tend to present to primary care only at crisis point and generally focus on more problem-solving
methods to deal with problems than emotive approaches. Traditional
health services are heavily stigmatised among young men. The CALM initiative seeks to overcome this stigma and break down the barriers to recognising depression and encourage help-seeking behaviours in this group.

Key features
1. COMMUNICATIONS STRATEGY

- Locally focused communications strategy to resonate with
  young men through the language, tone and style of materials
  holding positive mental health promotion messages.

- Publicly autonomous of traditional health services (i.e. no NHS
  branding visible).

- Credible messages and music/sport events co-sponsorship
  propagate the notion of positive mental health choices and
  encourage a culture of acceptance.

- Communication themes:

  'There's no shame in feeling down or unable to cope; it happens to
  us all.'

  'Any problem, however small, is worth sharing.'

  'Taking positive action can help alleviate stress and depression.'

- Non-traditional advertising using bus tickets, urinal posters,
  beermats, CD-inners.

- Public support from local and national 'role models'
  highlighting the messages and personal reflections on them,
  usually from music, sport or media.

2. DEDICATED HELPLINE

- Open night-time hours, when few other services are available, freephone, 365 days a year.

- Support through telephone counselling, information and information about other services offering more long-term or specific services.

- Confidential, anonymous and unidentifiable on landline phone bills.

3. LOCALISED VALUE-ADDED PROJECT WORK

- Settings-based initiatives in partnership with other local organisations to target young men, e.g. in schools, the unemployed, cultural minorities.

Examples of the initiative in practice

1. Co-branding on *Cream* nightclub's flyers, posters and press adverts during 2001/2 facilitated reach to thousands of club-goers in Liverpool. In addition to promoting the helpline number, the association with an internationally known nightclub, and the visibility of CALM's materials in the venue at the promoted events, strengthened the mental health messages, reinforced autonomy from traditional 'health' services, and reached otherwise difficult to reach young men in their preferred social environment.

2. Working with The Princes Trust in Merseyside, CALM facilitated a project where young people designed and implemented a communications strategy for disseminating materials to a range of social venues in the semi-rural and difficult to access newtown of St Helens. In addition to providing a tangible proactive problem-solving challenge, a by-product of the project was increased awareness of CALM in the area.

Successes, lessons learnt and future developments

1. CALLS TO THE DEDICATED HELPLINE

- 8000 'interactive' calls annually, often long and in-depth – many more thousands of silent calls where the caller was not yet willing to talk

- 67 per cent of callers are men; most helplines are called predominantly by women
- a quarter of all callers find out about CALM by word of mouth, suggesting that young men are talking about the helpline
- targets young men at the onset of depression, and 94 per cent of callers do not have suicidal feelings
- most callers are calling for the first time and two thirds of young male callers are not in touch with any other service.

2. OTHER INDICATORS OF SUCCESS

- Promotional materials resonate with young men and command respect in their eyes, providing a powerful vehicle for otherwise unsexy messages about depression and mental health.
- High-profile role models, locally and nationally, give credibility in the eyes of the young men who consider them highly – difficult to achieve by 'health professionals' alone.
- It is a tool to access several sectors of the community not normally utilised to contribute to suicide prevention – those working in music, sport and media – often young men themselves.
- Local project work includes partnerships with others such as The Princes Trust, Healthy Schools/PSHE, CAMHS and Lifelong Learning.

Future work intends to build on the positive elements of the CALM initiative by inclusion in young men's mental health promotion pilots supported by NIMHE.

e-contacts

www.thecalmzone.net

References

Ashton, Wigan and Leigh Primary Care Trust (2003) *Mental Health Promotion Strategy.* Wigan: Ashton, Wigan and Leigh PCT.

Baric, L. (1994) *Health Promotion and Health Education in Practice: The Organisational Model.* London: Barns Publications.

Dahlgren, G. and Whitehead, M. (1991) *Policies and Strategies to Promote Social Equity.* Stockholm: Health Institute of Future Studies.

Department of Health (1999) *National Service Framework for Mental Health.* London: DoH.

Department of Health (2001) *Making it Happen: A Guide to Delivering Mental Health Promotion.* London: DoH.

Department of Health (2002) *National Suicide Prevention Strategy for England.* London: DoH.

Dooris, M., Dowding, G., Thompson, J. and Wynne, C. (1998) 'The settings-based approach to health promotion.' In A. Tsouros, G. Dowding, J. Thompson and M. Dooris (eds) *Health Promoting Universities.* Copenhagen: World Health Organization.

Pevalin, D. and Rose, D. (2003) *Social Capital For Health.* London: Health Development Agency.

Salford Primary Care Trust (2002) *Draft Mental Health Promotion Strategy.* Salford: Salford PCT.

Stansfield, J. (2002) 'Health Promoting Mental Health Services.' *Journal of Mental Health Promotion 4,* 1, 25–31.

St Helens Primary Care Trust (2002) *Mental Health Promotion Strategy.* St Helens: St Helens PCT.

United States Department of Health and Human Services (2003) *National Strategy for Suicide Prevention.* SAMHSA National Mental Health Information Center, www.mentalhealth.org

Wired for Health (2003) 'Whole school approach, National Healthy Schools Scheme.' www.wiredforhealth.gov.uk

Websites

www.thecalmzone.net Department of Health CALM campaign

www.hda-online.org.uk Health Development Agency

www.nimhe.org National NIMHE

www.nimhenorthwest.org.uk National Institute for Mental Health in England (NIMHE) Northwest Centre

www.mentality.org.uk UK Mental Health Promotion charity

www.mindout.net UK campaign to combat stigma

www.who.org.uk World Health Organization

Chapter 22

Useful Resources

Rowan Purdy

Introduction

This chapter contains a selected list of references to policy, guidelines, reports and resources of relevance to the subject of suicide prevention from a variety of information sources. The resource list is intended to promote knowledge and improve the capacity of policy, services and professionals to prevent suicide and be of help to people at risk and to their families.

No attempt has been made to be exhaustive. A selective 'snapshot' of resources was identified using a variety of different methods between August and September 2003. Over the course of time many of the websites and individuals referred to here may change although the resources should remain available. At the time of writing all of these addresses permitted access without financial subscription. Some websites may have access restrictions; some, for example, are limited to a professional group and can only be accessed by members of the profession.

Many of the resources initially identified appear in other chapters and are therefore not repeated here. This is especially true in relation to the resources from central government such as the Department of Health, which would otherwise have appeared in the books and reports section of this list. The reader should therefore consider these lists of resources as an adjunct to those covered in the rest of the book rather than a summary of all the work gathered in this volume.

Search strategy used to create this resources list

1. The following bibliographic databases were searched using the keywords *suicide* and *suicide prevention*:

- Medline
- PsycINFO
- Embase
- CINAHL
- Kings Fund Database.

2. Meta-searches of numerous websites were searched and are referenced in the organisations and websites section below.

3. The reference sections of various resource materials relevant to the subject area were also consulted.

4. Experts in the field of suicide prevention, both individuals and organisations, were contacted directly for recommended resources in this subject area.

Organisations and websites

Action for Prisoners Families
London Head Office
Riverbank House, 1 Putney Bridge Approach
London SW6 3JD
Tel: 020 7384 1987   Fax: 020 7384 1855
Email: info@actionpf.org.uk   www.prisonersfamilies.org.uk/

Agency for Healthcare Quality and Research (AHQR)
www.ahcpr.gov/

Alcohol Concern
Waterbridge House, 32–36 Loman Street
London SE1 0EE
Tel: 020 7928 7377   Fax: 020 7928 4644
Email: contact@alcoholconcern.org.uk   www.alcoholconcern.org.uk/

American Foundation for Suicide Prevention
www.afsp.org/index-1.htm

Anti-Bullying Network
Moray House School of Education
University of Edinburgh
Holyrood Road
Edinburgh EH8 8AQ
Tel: 0131 651 6100   Fax: 0131 651 6100
Email: abn@education.ed.ac.uk   www.antibullying.net

At Ease
c/o Rethink
30 Tabernacle Street
London EC2A 4DD
Tel: 020 7330 9100   Fax: 020 7330 9102
Email: at-ease@rethink.org   www.rethink.org/at-ease/

Audit Commission
www.audit-commission.gov.uk

Australian Commonwealth Department of Health and Aged Care: Suicide Prevention Strategy
www.mentalhealth.gov.au/sp/

The Australian Patient Safety Foundation (APSF)
www.apsf.net.au

Bandolier
Evidence Based Mental Health Care
www.jr2.ox.ac.uk/bandolier/booth/booths/mental.html

British Medical Association Library Catalogue
www.bma.org.uk/ap.nsf/content_hub+library

British Official Publications Current Awareness Service
www.soton.ac.uk/~bopcas/

Campaign Against Living Miserably (CALM)
Tel: 0800 58 58 58 (5 pm–3 am)
www.thecalmzone.net/

Caring for Carers
The Department of Health
Public Enquiry Office
Richmond House, 79 Whitehall
London SW1A 2NL
Tel: 020 7210 4850 (line open from 9.00 am to 5.00 pm Monday to Friday)
Minicom: 020 7210 5025
dhmail@doh.gsi.gov.uk   www.carers.gov.uk/

Centre for Drug Misuse Research, at the University of Glasgow
www.gla.ac.uk/centres/drugmisuse/

Centre for Evidence Based Mental Health (CEBMH)
http://cebmh.warne.ox.ac.uk/cebmh/

Centre for Evidence Based Social Services
www.ex.ac.uk/cebss/

Centre for Research on Drugs and Health Behaviour, at University College, London
www.med.ic.ac.uk/divisions/template_divisions_departments.asp?id=65

Centre for Suicide Prevention
School of Psychiatry and Behavioural Sciences
7th Floor Williamson Building
University of Manchester
Oxford Road
Manchester M13 9PL
Tel: 0161 275 0700/1
Email: nci@man.ac.uk   www.national-confidential-inquiry.ac.uk/

Centre for Suicide Research, Oxford
http://cebmh.warne.ox.ac.uk/csr/mainscreen.html

Changing Our Minds
Tel: 08457 90 90 90
Admin office: Samaritans HQ
The Upper Mill, Kingston Road
Ewell
Surrey KT17 2AF
Tel: 020 8394 8300   Fax: 020 8394 8301
Email: admin@samaritans.org   www.changeourminds.com

Chief Medical Officer
www.doh.gov.uk/cmo

Childline
24-hour helpline on 0800 111111 for children and teenagers
Textphone service on 0800 400 222
ChildLine HQ
45 Folgate Street
London E1 6GL
Tel: 020 7650 3200   Fax: 020 7650 3201
www.childline.org.uk/

CJS online
www.cjsonline.org/

Cochrane Collaboration
www.cochrane.org

The College of Pharmacy Practice
www.collpharm.org/

COPAC
www.copac.ac.uk/

Counselling in Primary Care
www.cpct.co.uk

Cruse Bereavement Care
Cruse House, 126 Sheen Road
Richmond
Surrey TW9 1UR
Tel: 020 8939 9530   Fax: 020 8940 7638
Email: info@crusebereavementcare.org.uk   www.crusebereavementcare.org.uk/
Day by Day Helpline: 0870 167 1677   Email: helpline@crusebereavementcare.org.uk
Young people between the age of 12 and 18 should call Freephone 0808 808 1677

Database of Abstracts of Reviews of Effectiveness (DARE)
http://nhscrd.york.ac.uk/welcome.html

**Department of Addictive Behaviour at St George's Hospital Medical School,
London**
www.sghms.ac.uk/depts/addictive-behaviour/welcome1.html

Department of Health: Mental Health section
www.dh.gov.uk/policyandguidance/healthandsocialcaretopics/mentalhealth/fs/en

Department of Health: Prison Health website
www.dh.gov.uk/policyandguidance/healthandsocialcaretopics/prisonhealth/fs/en

Drug Education Forum
www.drugeducation.org.uk/

Drug Misuse Information: Drug misuse statistics
www.publications.dh.gov.uk/public/ionh

drugs.gov.uk
www.drugs.gov.uk/Home

DrugScope
32–36 Loman Street
London SE1 0EE
Tel: 020 7928 1211   Fax: 020 7928 1771
General enquiries email info@drugscope.org.uk
Membership enquiries email membership@drugscope.org.uk
www.drugscope.org.uk/

Drugs-Info.co.uk
www.drugs-info.co.uk/

**ECRI (Health Services Research Agency, formerly the Emergency Care
Research Institute)**
UK HQ Weltech Centre, Ridgeway
Welwyn Garden City
Herts AL7 2AA
Tel: +44 (1707) 871 511   Fax: +44 (1707) 393 138
Email: info@ecri.org.uk
www.ecri.org

electronic Library for Social Care (eLSC)
www.elsc.org.uk/

European Association for the Treatment of Addiction (UK)
www.eata.org.uk/

Federation of Drug and Alcohol Professionals (FDAP)
www.fdap.org.uk/

Health and Safety Executive
www.hse.gov.uk/

Health Development Agency (HDA)
Holborn Gate
330 High Holborn
London WC1V 7BA
Tel: 020 7413 1899   Fax: 020 7413 8913
Email: communications@hda-online.org.uk   www.hda-online.org.uk

Healthcare Workforce Development Portal
www.healthcareworkforce.org.uk/

HM Prison Service
www.hmprisonservice.gov.uk/

Home Office
www.homeoffice.gov.uk

Home Office Research Development and Statistics Directorate (RDS)
www.homeoffice.gov.uk/rds/index.htm

Hospital In-Patient Data (based on Hospital Episode Statistics)
www.dh.gov.uk/publicationsandstatistics/hospitalepisodestatistics/fs/en

Howard League for Penal Reform
1 Ardleigh Road
London N1 4HS
Tel: 020 7249 7373   Fax: 020 7249 7788
Email: howardleague@ukonline.co.uk   www.howardleague.org

The Institute for Safe Medication Practices (ISMP)
www.ismp.org

The Institute of Mental Health Act Practitioners (IMHAP)
www.markwalton.net/index.asp

The Institute of Prison Law
www.prisonshandbook.co.uk/ipl/home.html

The Joint Commission on Accreditation of Healthcare (JCAHO)
www.jcaho.org

Joseph Rowntree Foundation
The Homestead, 40 Water End
York
North Yorkshire YO30 6WP
Tel: +44 (0)1904 629241   Fax: +44 (0)1904 620072
Email: info@jrf.org.uk   www.jrf.org.uk/

Lifeline
Head Office, 101–103 Oldham St
Manchester M4 1LW
Tel: 0161 834 7160   Fax: 0161 835 2160
www.lifeline.org.uk/

The London Development Centre for Mental Health
11–13 Cavendish Square
London W1G 0AN

Mental Health Act Commission
Maid Marian House, 56, Hounds Gate
Nottingham NG1 6BG
Tel: 0115 943 7100   Fax: 0115 943 7101
Email: ChiefExec@mhac.trent.nhs.uk   www.mhac.trent.nhs.uk

Mentalhealthdata.org.uk
www.mentalhealthdata.org

Mentality
134–138 Borough High Street
London SE1 1LB
Tel: 020 7716 6777   Fax: 020 7716 6774
Email: enquiries@mentality.org.uk   www.mentality.org.uk/

National Addiction Centre, Institute of Psychiatry, King's College London
www.iop.kcl.ac.uk/IoP/Departments/PsychMed/NAC/index.shtml

National Association for the Care and Resettlement of Offenders (NACRO)
www.nacro.org.uk/

National Audit Office
www.nao.gov.uk

National Confidential Inquiry into Suicide and Homicide by People with Mental Illness
Non-confidential correspondence only:
The National Confidential Inquiry
Centre for Suicide Prevention
7th Floor Williamson Building
University of Manchester
Oxford Road
Manchester M13 9PL
Tel: 0161 275 0700/1

Email: nci@man.ac.uk
Confidential correspondence: please send to our PO Box address – for details please
contact the Inquiry office www.national-confidential-inquiry.ac.uk

National Drugs Helpline
Formerly www.ndh.org.uk/ now replaced by Talk to Frank (www.talktofrank.com/),
see below

National electronic Library for Mental Health (NeLMH)
www.nelmh.org

National Institute for Clinical Excellence (NICE)
11 Strand
London WC2N 5HR
Tel: 020 7766 9191   Fax: 020 7766 9123
Email: nice@nice.nhs.uk   www.nice.org.uk/

National Institute for Mental Health for England (NIMHE)
Blenheim House
West One, Duncombe Street
Leeds LS1 4PL
Tel: 0113 254 3811   Fax: 0113 254 3828
Email: ask@nimhe.org.uk   www.nimhe.org.uk/development/index.asp

NIMHE East Midlands Development Centre
Pleasley Vale Business Park
Outgang Lane
Pleasley
Mansfield
Notts NG19 8RL
Tel: 01623 819350   Fax: 01623 819351
www.nimhe.org.uk/development/eastmidlands/index.asp

NIMHE Eastern Development Centre
Eastern Mental Health Development Partnership
654 The Crescent
Colchester Business Park
Colchester
Essex CO4 9YQ
Tel: 01206 287 593   Fax: 01206 287 597
www.nimheeastern.org.uk/

NIMHE North East, Yorkshire and Humberside Development Centre
2nd Floor, Blenheim House
West One
Duncombe Street
Leeds LS1 4PL
Tel: 0113 254 3821   Fax: 0113 254 3828

Northern Centre for Mental Health, Durham
Suites 4 and 5, William Robson House
Claypath
Durham DH1 1SA
Tel: 0191 370 7760   Fax: 019 383 0109
Email: office@ncmh.co.uk

Northern Centre for Mental Health, York
2nd Floor, Yorkshire House
6 Innovation Close
Heslington
York YO10 5ZF
Tel: 01904 717260   Fax: 01904 717269
Email: yorkoffice@ncmh.co.uk

NIMHE North West Development Centre
Hyde Hospital
2nd Floor, Grange Road South
Hyde
Cheshire SK14 5NY
Tel: 0161 351 4920   Fax: 0161 351 4936
Email: ask@nimhenorthwest.org.uk   www.nimhenorthwest.org.uk

NIMHE South East Development Centre
Parklands Hospital
Aldermaston Road
Basingstoke
Hampshire RG24 9RH
Tel: 01256 376 394   Fax: 01256 376309
www.sedc.org.uk

NIMHE South West Development Centre
2 Tower Lane
Tower Street
Taunton
Somerset TA1 4AR
Tel: 01823 337879   Fax: 01823 272897
www.nimhe.mhsw.org.uk

NIMHE West Midlands Development Centre
Osprey House
Albert Street
Redditch
Worcestershire B97 4DE
Tel: 01527 587626   Fax: 01527 587504
www.nimhe.org.uk/development/westmidlands/index.asp

National Patient Safety Agency (NPSA)
www.npsa.nhs.uk/

National Patient Safety Foundation
www.npsf.org

National Phobics Society
www.phobics-society.org.uk

National Probation Service
www.probation.homeoffice.gov.uk

National Research Register
www.nrr.nhs.uk

National Treatment Agency for Substance Misuse (NTA)
www.nta.nhs.uk/

NHS Direct
24-hour nurse advice and health information service
Tel: 0845 46 47. Operational issues including complaints: Mr Bob Gann (Director)

NHS Direct Online
Strawberry Fields
Berrywood Business Village
Tollbar Way
Hedge End
Hants SO30 2UN
Email: complaints@online.nhsdirect.nhs.uk   www.nhsdirect.nhs.uk/

NHS Economic Evaluations Database
http://nhscrd.york.ac.uk/welcome.html

NHS Health Scotland: Suicide prevention toolkit pages
www.hebs.com/suicideprevention

NHS Modernisation Agency
www.modern.nhs.uk

NHS Modernisation Agency Improvement Leaders' Guides Website
www.modern.nhs.uk/improvementguides/

Office of the Deputy Prime Minister
www.odpm.gov.uk

Office of National Statistics
www.statistics.gov.uk/

Office of National Statistics: Suicide datasets
www.statistics.gov.uk/CCI/SearchRes.asp?term=suicide

OMNI (Organising Medical Networked Information)
www.omni.ac.uk

PAPYRUS
Rossendale GH
Union Road
Rawtenstall
Lancashire BB4 6NE
Tel/Fax: 01706 214449
Email: admin@papyrus-uk.org.   www.papyrus-uk.org

The Patient Safety Research Programme (PSRP)
www.publichealth.bham.ac.uk/psrp/

Pharmacy in the future
www.rpsgb.org.uk/nhsplan/index.html

Pharmacy Medicine Information Website
www.nmhct.nhs.uk/pharmacy/

POINT – Department of Health Publications on the Internet
www.info.doh.gov.uk/doh/point.nsf/NewSearch?openform

Primary and Community Care Pharmacy Network
www.pccpnetwork.org/

Primary Care Mental Health Education (PriMHE)
The Old Stables
2a Laurel Avenue
Twickenham
Middx TW1 4JA
Tel: 020 8891 6593   Fax: 020 8891 6729
Email: admin@primhe.org   www.primhe.org/

Prison Reform Trust
www.prisonreformtrust.org.uk/

Prison Service Statistics
www.homeoffice.gov.uk/rds/prisons1.html

Public Health electronic Library (PHeL)
www.phel.gov.uk/

PubMed
www4.ncbi.nlm.nih.gov/PubMed/

QOLID – Quality of Life Instruments Database
www.qolid.org/

QualityHealthcare.org
www.qualityhealthcare.org

Release
388 Old Street
London EC1V 9LT
Tel: 020 7729 5255   Fax: 020 7729 2599
Email: info@release.org.uk   www.release.org.uk/

'Rizer' Young Offenders Initiative
www.rizer.co.uk

Royal College of General Practitioners
14 Princes Gate
Hyde Park
London SW7 1PU
Tel: +44 (0) 20 7581 3232   Fax +44 (0) 20 7225 3047
Email: info@rcgp.org.uk.   www.rcgp.org.uk/

Royal College of Nursing Library Catalogue
http://rcn-library.rcn.org.uk/uhtbin/webcat

Royal College of Psychiatrists
17 Belgrave Square
London SW1X 8PG
Tel: 020 7235 2351   Fax: 020 7245 1231
Email: rcpsych@rcpsych.ac.uk   www.rcpsych.ac.uk/

Royal Pharmaceutical Society of Great Britain
1 Lambeth High Street
London SE1 7JN
Tel: 020 7735 9141   Fax: 020 7735 7629
Email: enquiries@rpsgb.org.uk   www.rpsgb.org.uk/

Royal Society of Medicine Library Catalogue
www.roysocmed.ac.uk/librar/libcat.htm

Sainsbury Centre for Mental Health
134–138 Borough High Street
London SE1 1LB
Tel: 020 7827 8300   Fax: 020 7403 9482
Email: info@scmh.org.uk   www.scmh.org.uk/

Samaritans
24-hour helpline and email contact: 08457 909090   jo@samaritans.org
Head Office:
The Upper Mill
Kingston Road
Ewell
Surrey KT17 2AF
Tel: 020 8394 8300   Fax: 020 8394 8301
Email: admin@samaritans.org   www.samaritans.org.uk/

Samaritans: suicide statistics
www.samaritans.org.uk/know/statistics.shtm

Scottish suicide prevention strategy
www.scotland.gov.uk/library5/health/clss-00.asp

Social Care Institute for Excellence (SCIE)
www.scie.org.uk/

Social Exclusion Unit (SEU)
www.socialexclusionunit.gov.uk

Substance Misuse Information
www.dh.gov.uk/policyandguidance/healthandsocialcaretopics/substancemisuse/fs/en

Substance Misuse Management in General Practice (SMMGP)
www.smmgp.demon.co.uk/

SubstanceMisuse.net
www.substancemisuse.net/

Suicide Information and Education Centre (Canada)
www.suicideinfo.ca

Survivors of Bereavement by Suicide (SOBS)
www.uk-sobs.org.uk/

Talk to Frank (National Drugs Helpline)
For free confidential drugs information and advice 24 hours a day talk to FRANK
0800 77 66 00
If you are deaf you can Textphone FRANK on 0800 917 8765
Email: frank@talktofrank.com   www.talktofrank.com/

Turning Point
New Loom House, 101 Backchurch Lane
London E1 1LU
Tel/Fax: 020 7702 1458
Email: se-region@turning-point.co.uk   www.turning-point.co.uk/

Turning Research Into Practice (TRIP) Database
www.tripdatabase.com

UK Psychiatric Pharmacists Group
www.ukppg.org.uk

**US Center for Mental Health Services: National Strategy for Suicide Prevention
– Goals and Objectives for Action**
www.mentalhealth.org/publications/allpubs/SMA01-3518/default.asp

WeBNF
http://bnf.org/

Women and Equality Unit (WEU)
www.womenandequalityunit.gov.uk

Women in Prison
www.womeninprison.org.uk/

World Health Organization (WHO)
Guide to Good Prescribing:
www.med.rug.nl/pharma/who-cc/ggp/homepage.htm
Suicide Prevention Section:
www.who.int/mental_health/prevention/suicide/suicideprevent/en/

Service user and carers organisations and websites

Age Concern
Astral House, 1268 London Road
London SW16 4ER
Information Line on 0800 009966, seven days a week from 7am to 7pm
Head Office: Tel: 020 8765 7200   Fax: 020 8765 7211
www.ace.org.uk/

Al-Anon Family Groups
61 Great Dover Street
London SE1 4YF
Tel: 020 7403 0888   Fax: 020 7378 9910
www.al-anonuk.org.uk/

Alzheimer's Society
Gordon House, 10 Greencoat Place
London SW1P 1PH
Tel: 020 7306 0606   Fax: 020 7306 0808
Email: enquiries@alzheimers.org.uk   www.alzheimers.org.uk/

Carers' National Association
Ruth Pitter House, 20–25 Glasshouse Yard
London EC1A 4JT
Tel: 020 7490 8818   Fax: 020 7490 8824
CarersLine: 0808 808 7777
Email: info@ukcarers.org   www.carersonline.org.uk

Chinese Mental Health Association
2nd Floor, Zenith House
155 Curtain Road
London EC2A 3QY
Tel: 020 7613 1008   Fax: 020 7739 6577
Email: info@cmha.org.uk   www.cmha.org.uk/

Depression Alliance
35 Westminster Bridge Road
London SE1 7JB
Tel: 0207 633 0557   Fax: 0207 633 0559
Email: information@depressionalliance.org   www.depressionalliance.org/
List of self-help groups: www.depressionalliance.org/Contents/groups.htm
DAtalk: Members only email group datalk-admin@depressionalliance.org

Distress Awareness Training Agency
5 Wellbank Close
Oldham OL8 1NX
Tel: 0161 627 1391
Email: info@distress.org.uk.   www.distress.org.uk/

First Steps to Freedom
1 Taylor Close
Kenilworth
Warwickshire CV8 2LW
Tel: 1926 864473   Fax: 0870 164 0567
Email: info@first-steps.org   www.first-steps.org/

Foundation for People with Learning Disabilities
83 Victoria Street
London SW1H 0HW
Tel: 020 7802 0300   Fax: 020 7802 0301
Email: fpld@fpld.org.uk   www.learningdisabilities.org.uk

Hearing Voices Network
91 Oldham Street
Manchester M4
Tel: 0161 834 5768
www.hearing-voices.org

Manic Depression Fellowship
Castle Works, 21 St George's Road
London SE1 6ES
Tel: 020 7793 2600   Fax 020 7793 2639
Information: mdf@mdf.org.uk
Self management: smt@mdf.org.uk
Groups: groups@mdf.org.uk
www.mdf.org.uk/

Mental Health Forum for England
www.nuts.cc/index.html

Mental Health Foundation
83 Victoria Street
London SW1H 0HW
Tel: 020 7802 0300   Fax: 020 7802 0301
Email: mhf@mhf.org.uk.   www.mhf.org.uk/

Mental Health Media
356 Holloway Road
London N7 6PA
Tel: 020 7700 8171   Fax: 020 7686 0959
Email: info@mhmedia.com.   www.mhmedia.com/

Mental Health Resource Centre for England
www.mhrc.cc/

The Mental Health Trainers Network
www.mhtn.org

MIND
MIND England
15–19 Broadway
London E15 4BQ
Tel: 020 8519 2122   Fax: 020 8522 1725
Email: contact@mind.org.uk   www.mind.org.uk
MINDinfoLine 0845 766 0163 open Mondays to Fridays 9:15 am to 5:15 pm

MIND Cymru
3rd Floor, Quebec House
Castlebridge, 5–19 Cowbridge Road East
Cardiff CF11 9AB
Tel: 029 20395123   Fax: 029 20402041

Rural Minds
c/o National Agricultural Centre
Stoneleigh Park
Warwickshire CV8 7LZ
Tel: 024 7641 4366   Fax: 024 7641 4369
Email: ruralminds@ruralnet.org.uk

Mood Swings Network
23 New Mount Street
Manchester M4 4DE
Tel: 0161 953 4105
www.moodswings.org.uk

National Phobics Society
Zion Centre
Stretford Road
Hulme
Manchester M15
Tel: 0870 7700 456
www.phobics-society.org.uk

Rethink
Head Office
30 Tabernacle Street
London EC2A 4DD
Tel: 020 7330 9100/01   Fax: 020 7330 9102
Email: info@rethink.   www.rethink.org/

SANE
1st Floor, Cityside House
40 Adler Street
London E1 1EE
SANELINE open from 12 noon until 2 am every day of the year 0845 767 8000 (calls charged at local rates)
Tel: 020 7375 1002   Fax: 020 7375 2162
Email: london@sane.org.uk   www.sane.org.uk

Schizophrenia Association of Great Britain
Bryn Hyfryd
The Crescent
Bangor
Gwynedd. LL57 2AG
Tel: 01248 354048
Fax: 01248 353659
Email: info@sagb.co.uk.
www.sagb.co.uk

Seasonal Affective Disorder (SAD) Association
PO Box 989
Steyning BN44 3HG
www.sada.org.uk/

UK Advocacy Network
Riverbank House
1 Putney Bridge Approach
London SW6 3JD
Tel: 020 7736 7903   Fax: 020 7736 7932
Email: info@thepatientsforum.org.uk   www.thepatientsforum.org.uk/

Young Minds
102–108 Clerkenwell Road
London EC1M 5SA
Tel: 020 7336 8445   Fax: 020 7336 8446
Parents' Information Service: 0800 018 2138
Email: enquiries@youngminds.org.uk   www.youngminds.org.uk/

Books and reports

American Association of Suicidology and CatchWord Ltd (2001) *Suicide and life-threatening behavior.* New York: Guilford Publications.

Appleby, L., Shaw, J., Amos, T., McDonnell, R., Bickley, H., Kiernan, K., Davies, S., Harris, C., McCann, K. and Parsons, R. (1999) *Safer Services: Report of the National Confidential Inquiry into Suicide and Homicide by People with Mental Illness.* London: Stationery Office.

Appleby, L., Shaw, J., Sherratt, J., Robinson, J., Amos, T., McDonnell, R., Bickley, H., Hunt, I.M., Kiernan, K., Wren, J., McCann, K., Parsons, R., Burns, J., Davies, S. and Harris, C. (2001) *Safety First: Report of the National Confidential Inquiry into Suicide and Homicide by People with Mental Illness.* London: Stationery Office.

Bird, L. and Faulkner, A. (2000) *Suicide and Self-Harm.* London: The Mental Health Foundation.

Department of Health (1999) *National Service Framework for Mental Health. Modern Standards and Service Models.* London: Department of Health.

Department of Health (1999) *Saving Lives: Our Healthier Nation.* London: HMSO.

Department of Health (2002) *Guidance on Developing Prison Health Needs Assessments and Health Improvement Plans.* London: Department of Health.

Department of Health (2002) *Health Promoting Prisons: A Shared Approach.* London: Department of Health.

Department of Health (2002) *Learning From Past Experiences: A Review of Serious Case Reviews.* London: Department of Health.

Department of Health (2002) *Mental Health Policy Implementation Guide – Dual Diagnosis Good Practice Guide.* London: Department of Health.

Department of Health (2002) *National Suicide Prevention Strategy for England.* London: Department of Health.

Department of Health (2002) *Women's Mental Health: Into the Mainstream Strategic Development of Mental Health Care for Women.* London: Department of Health.

Duffy, D., Ryan, T. and Purdy, R. (2003) *Preventing Suicide: A Toolkit for Mental Health Services.* London: Department of Health.

Ellison James, M. (2001) *Treatment of Suicidal Patients in Managed Care.* Washington, DC: American Psychiatric Press.

Goldsmith, S. K. (2002) *Reducing Suicide: A National Imperative.* Washington, DC: National Academies Press.

Hawton, K. and van Heeringen, K. (eds) (2002) *The International Handbook of Suicide and Attempted Suicide.* London: John Wiley and Sons.

HM Prison Service (2001) *Prevention of Suicide and Self-Harm in the Prison Service: An Internal Review.* London: HM Prison Service.

Howard League for Penal Reform (2001) *Desperate Measures: Prison Suicides and their Prevention.* London: Howard League for Penal Reform.

Howard League for Penal Reform (2001) *Suicide and Self-Harm Prevention: Court Cells and Prison Vans.* London: Howard League for Penal Reform.

Howard League for Penal Reform (2001) *Suicide and Self-Harm Prevention: Repetitive Self-harm among Women and Girls in Prison.* London: Howard League for Penal Reform.

Howard League for Penal Reform (2001) *Suicide and Self-Harm Prevention: The Management of Self-injury in Prison*. London: Howard League for Penal Reform.

Howard League for Penal Reform (2002) *Suicide and Self-Harm Prevention Following Release from Prison*. London: Howard League for Penal Reform.

Kenny, C. (2001) *Suicidal Children and Adolescents*. Lancaster: Quay Books.

Lester, D. (ed) (2001) *Suicide Prevention: Resources for the Millennium*. Philadelphia, PA: Brunner-Routledge.

Mann, J.J. and Hendin, H. (eds) (2001) *The Clinical Science of Suicide Prevention*. New York: New York Academy of Sciences.

Maris, R.W., Berman, A.L. and Silverman, M.M. (2000) *Comprehensive Textbook of Suicidology*. New York: Guilford Press.

Marshall, T., Simpson, S. and Stevens, A. (2000) *Toolkit for Health Care Needs Assessment in Prisons*. Birmingham: University of Birmingham.

Meltzer, H.Y. (2003) *Intervention Strategies for Suicidality*. Memphis, TN: Physicians Postgraduate Press.

Mental Health Foundation and Sainsbury Centre for Mental Health (2002) *Being There in a Crisis*. London: Mental Health Foundation.

Morgan, S. (2000) *Clinical Risk Management: A Clinical Tool and Practitioner Manual*. London: Sainsbury Centre for Mental Health.

Morgan, S. (2001) *Assessing and Managing Risk: A Training Pack for Practitioners and Managers of Comprehensive Mental Health Services*. Brighton: Pavilion.

National Collaborating Centre for Mental Health (2003) *Self Harm – NICE Guideline, First Consultation*. London: National Institute for Clinical Excellence.

National Institute for Mental Health in England (2003) *Personality Disorder: No Longer a Diagnosis of Exclusion*. Leeds: NIMHE.

O'Connor, R. and Sheehy, N. (2000) *Understanding Suicidal Behaviour*. Leicester: BPS Books.

Office of Population Census and Statistics (1999) *Non-fatal Suicidal Behaviour among Prisoners*. London: The Stationery Office.

Pavilion Publishers (2001) *Suicide in Prisons: Research, Policy and Practice*. Brighton: Pavilion.

Power, K.G. (2002) *Evaluation of the Revised SPS Suicide Risk Management Strategy*. Stirling: University of Stirling.

Ridley, J. and Scotland Central Research Unit (2002) *National Framework for the Prevention of Suicide and Deliberate Self-Harm in Scotland: Analysis of Written Submissions to Consultation*. Edinburgh: Stationery Office.

Rorstad, P. and Chesinski, K. (1996) *Dual Diagnosis: Facing the Challenge*. Kenley: Wynne Howard Publishing.

Royal College of Psychiatrists' Research Unit (2002) *Suicide in Prisons*. London: Royal College of Psychiatrists.

Rudd, M.D., Joiner Thomas, E. and Rajab, M.H. (2001) *Treating Suicidal Behaviour: An Effective, Time-limited Approach*. New York: Guilford Press.

Scotland Scottish Executive (2002) *Choose Life: A National Strategy and Action Plan to Prevent Suicide in Scotland*. Edinburgh: Scottish Executive.

Scottish Development Centre for Mental Health and Scotland Scottish Executive, Health Department, Public Health Division (2002) *Reducing Suicide and Deliberate Self Harm: Exploring Experience: A Discussion Process: Final Report.* Edinburgh: Scottish Executive.

Scottish Development Centre for Mental Health and Scotland Scottish Executive, Health Department, Public Health Division (2002) *Preventing Suicide and Deliberate Self Harm: Laying The Foundations: Identifying Practice Examples: Project Report.* Edinburgh: Scottish Executive. www.scotland.gov.uk/library5/health/lfpr.pdf www.scotland.gov.uk/library5/health/lfpr-00.asp

Scottish Development Centre for Mental Health and Scotland Scottish Executive Health Department Planning Group on the National Framework for the Prevention of Suicide and Deliberate Self-Harm in Scotland (2001) *National Framework for the Prevention of Suicide and Deliberate Self-Harm in Scotland: Consultation Document.* Edinburgh: Stationery Office.

Shaw, J., Appleby, L. and Baker, D. (2003) *Safer Prisons Report 1999–2000: A National Study of Prison Suicides.* Manchester: National Confidential Inquiry into Suicide and Homicide by People with Mental Illness.

Journal articles

Appleby, L., Dennehy, J.A., Thomas, C.S., Faragher, E.B. and Lewis, G. (1999) 'Aftercare and clinical characteristics of people with mental illness who commit suicide: A case-control study.' *Lancet 353,* 9162, 1397–1400.

Appleby, L., Morris, R., Gask, L., Roland, M., Lewis, B., Perry, A., Battersby, L., Colbert, N., Green, G., Amos, T., Davies, L. and Faragher, B. (2000) 'An educational intervention for front-line health professionals in the assessment and management of suicidal patients (The STORM Project).' *Psychological Medicine 30,* 4, 805–812.

Appleby, L., Shaw, J., Amos, T., McDonnell, R., Harris, C., McCann, K., Kiernan, K., Davies, S., Bickley, H. and Parsons, R. (1999) 'Suicide within 12 months of contact with mental health services: national clinical survey.' *British Medical Journal 318,* 7193, 1235–1239.

Appleby, L., Thomas, S., Ferrier, N., Lewis, G., Shaw, J. and Amos, T. (2000) 'Sudden unexplained death in psychiatric in-patients.' *British Journal of Psychiatry 176,* 405–406.

Batt, A., Eudier, F., Le Vaou, P., Breurec, J.Y., Baert, A., Curtes, J.P., Badiche, A. and Chaperon, J. (1998) 'Repetition of parasuicide: Risk factors in general hospital referred patients.' *Journal of Mental Health 7,* 3, 285–297.

Beck, A.T. and Steer, R.A. (1989) 'Clinical predictors of eventual suicide: A 5- to 10-year prospective study of suicide attempters.' *Journal of Affective Disorders 17,* 3, 203–209.

Bhugra, D., Desai, M. and Baldwin, D. (1999) 'Attempted suicide in West London: Rates across ethnic communities.' *Psychological Medicine 29,* 1125–1130.

Dennis, M., Read, S., Andrews, H., Wakefield, P., Zafar, R. and Kavi, S. (2001) 'Suicide in a single health district: Epidemiology, and involvement of psychiatric services.' *Journal of Mental Health 10,* 6, 673–682.

Gibbins, J. (1998) 'Towards Integrated Care for Patients With Dual Diagnosis. The Dorset Healthcare NHS Trust Experience.' *The Mental Health Review.* December, 20–24.

Gore, S.M. (1999) 'Suicide in prisons. Reflection of the communities served, or exacerbated risk?' *British Journal of Psychiatry 174,* 50–55.

Gournay, K., Sandford, T., Johnson, S. and Thornicroft, G. (1997) 'Dual diagnosis of severe mental health problems and substance abuse/dependence: a major priority for mental health nursing.' *Journal of Psychiatric and Mental Health Nursing 4*, 2, 89–95.

Grandin, L.D., Yan, L.J., Gray, S.M., Jamison, K.R. and Sachs, G.S. (2001) 'Suicide prevention: Increasing education and awareness.' *Journal of Clinical Psychiatry 62*, 25, 12–23.

Gray, S.M. and Otto, M.W. (2001) 'Psychosocial approaches to suicide prevention: Applications to patients with bipoar disorder.' *Journal of Clinical Psychiatry 62*, 25, 56–64.

Gunnell, D. and Frankel, S. (1994) 'Prevention of suicide: Aspirations and evidence.' *British Journal of Medicine 308*, 1227–1233.

Gunnell, D., Lopatatzidis, A., Dorling, D., Wehner, H., Southall, H. and Frankel, S. (1999) 'Suicide and unemployment in young people. Analysis of trends in England and Wales, 1921–1995.' *British Journal of Psychiatry 175*, 263–270.

Hawton, K., Townsend, E., Deeks, J., Appleby, L., Gunnell, D., Bennewith, O. and Cooper, J. (2001) 'Effects of pack legislation restricting pack sizes of paracetamol and salicylates on self-poisoning in the United Kingdom: before and after study.' *British Medical Journal 332*, 7296, 1203–1207.

Hawton, K., Zahl, D. and Weatherall, R. (2003) 'Suicide following deliberate self-harm: long-term follow-up of patients who present to a general hospital.' *British Journal of Psychiatry 182*, 537–542.

Higgitt, A. (2000) 'Suicide reduction: Policy context.' *International Review of Psychiatry 12*, 1, 15–20.

Kavanagh, D.J., Young, R., Boyce, L., Clair, A., Sitharthan, T., Clark, D. and Thompson, K. (1998) 'Substance treatment options in psychosis (STOP): A new intervention for dual diagnosis.' *Journal of Mental Health 7*, 2, 135–143.

King, E.A. (2001) 'The Wessex Suicide Audit 1988–1993: A study of 1457 suicides with and without a recent psychiatric contact.' *International Journal of Psychiatry in Clinical Practice 5*, 2, 111–118.

King, E.A., Baldwin, D.S., Sinclair, J.M.A., Baker, N.G., Campbell, M.J. and Thompson, C. (2001) 'The Wessex Recent In-Patient Suicide Study, 1: Case-control study of 234 recently discharged psychiatric patient suicides.' *British Journal of Psychiatry 178*, 6, 531–536.

King, E.A., Baldwin, D.S., Sinclair, J.M.A. and Campbell, M.J. (2001) 'The Wessex Recent In-Patient Suicide Study, 2: Case-control study of 59 in-patient suicides.' *British Journal of Psychiatry 178*, 6, 537–542.

O'Connor, R.C., Sheehy, N.P. and O'Connor, D.B. (1999) 'The classification of completed suicide into subtypes.' *Journal of Mental Health 8*, 6, 629–637.

Pirkis, J.B. and Jolley, D. (1999) 'Suicide attempts by psychiatric patients in acute inpatient, long-stay inpatient and community care.' *Social Psychiatry and Psychiatric Epidemiology 34*, 12, 634–644.

Powell, J., Geddes, J., Deeks, J., Goldacre, M. and Hawton, K. (2000) 'Suicide in psychiatric hospital in-patients: Risk factors and their predictive power.' *British Journal of Psychiatry 176*, 266–272.

Reid, S. (1998) 'Suicide in schizophrenia. A review of the literature.' *Journal of Mental Health* 7, 4, 345–353.

Sachs, G.S., Yan, L.J., Swann, A.C. and Allen, M.H. (2001) 'Integration of suicide prevention into outpatient management of bipolar disorder.' *Journal of Clinical Psychiatry 62*, 25, 3–11.

Shergill, S.S. and Szmukler, G. (1998) 'How predictable is violence and suicide in community psychiatric practice?' *Journal of Mental Health 7*, 4, 393–401.

Taylor, C., Cooper, J. and Appleby, L. (1999) 'Is suicide risk taken seriously in heavy drinkers who harm themselves?' *Acta Psychiatrica Scandinavica 100*, 309–311

The Contributors

Sally Adams completed a BSc (Hons) in Applied Human Psychology at Aston University in 1992 and was awarded her PhD in 1996 from Birmingham University. Sally joined the Clinical Risk Unit (CRU) at University College London, in September 1995 where she has specialised in applying human factors approaches to patient safety. Sally's main area of expertise and passion is incident investigation and analysis. In October 2000 Sally joined Greenstreet Berman as a Senior Risk Management Consultant, where she provided consultancy services on all matters pertaining to risk and safety in complex industrial environments. In April 2001 Sally returned to the CRU as a Senior Researcher to undertake a variety of patient safety research projects. In January 2003 Sally took up post at the National Patient Safety Agency as an Assistant Director of Patient Safety (Midlands and East).

Simon Armson has been Chief Executive of Samaritans since July 1989 and has been a volunteer with the organisation since 1974. Before joining Samaritans in a paid capacity, he spent 14 years employed in various management posts in the NHS. Simon was, until recently, Chairman of the National Representatives of the International Association for Suicide Prevention. He is a member of the Advisory Group for the National Suicide Prevention Strategy for England and is a member of the Development Group currently working towards a clinical guideline on intentional self-harm for use in the NHS in England and Wales. He was appointed a Mental Health Act Commissioner in 2002. In 1996 he completed an MSc postgraduate degree in mental health studies at Guy's Hospital Medical School and in 2002 completed his training as a Cognitive Analytical Therapist.

Harriet Bickley is a researcher who has worked on the National Confidential Inquiry into Suicide and Homicide by People with Mental Illness for six years. She has a background in human geography, epidemiology and statistics, and an interest in mental health research. She is co-author on Inquiry publications including papers for the British Medical Journal and the British Journal of Psychiatry and has presented Inquiry findings in Melbourne, Stockholm and Edinburgh.

Jo Borrill is Research Programme Manager at the Safer Custody Group, HM Prison Service. Jo Borrill worked as a Prison Psychologist before taking up an academic post at Thames Valley University where she lectured in Psychology with particular reference to Crime and Mental Health. This was followed by three years managing research for the Mental Health Foundation. She became interested in self-harm and suicide while working on a research project for Imperial College on prisoners with drug misuse problems. Her work for Safer Custody Group has included a study of self-inflicted deaths of Life prisoners, consultation with prison staff about their support needs following a death in custody, and interviews with prisoners who survived a suicide attempt.

Nick Bowles is a mental health nurse. He works as a senior lecturer at the University of Bradford. He also works in an independent capacity as the Director of Preferred Futures working with a number of Trusts in England and Wales, including the winners of the 2003–2004 NIMHE Positive Practice award winners, Bolton Mental Health Services, who were commended for their 'refocusing' of the acute services in Bolton. He is actively engaged in research in acute psychiatry, travels widely and has published on refocusing, solution focused therapy, supervision and leadership, all themes that appear in his chapter.

Anna Brown is a PAPYRUS Trustee. Trained as an occupational therapist, and tutor in mental health services, she has worked in England and abroad. She is a non-executive director of an NHS hospital Trust and a member of an independent monitoring board at a prison. She has been involved with the University Suicide Intervention initiative and the National Suicide Prevention Strategy for England reference group. Anna has lost a child to suicide.

Jayne Cooper qualified as a Registered Mental Nurse in 1981 and worked as a psychiatric nurse in acute psychiatric hospital settings and within the community. She obtained a distinction in a Diploma in Management Studies in 1992. In 1995 Jayne embarked on a psychological autopsy study on suicide in young people from which she gained a PhD in 2001. As project manager, Jayne set up from its inauguration in 1997 the Manchester and Salford Self-Harm (MASSH) Project, which is a deliberate self-harm monitoring scheme, under the directorship of Professor Louis Appleby. Jayne was awarded the title of Research Fellow in 2002 and currently works at the Centre for Suicide Prevention, University of Manchester, UK.

Tony Cox is PAPYRUS' Administrator. He was a registered mental health nurse, here and abroad, and was co-ordinator for a unit for people with challenging behaviours. He developed a training programme for community staff working with people who have a learning disability and was a member of a critical incident stress management team.

Nigel Crompton qualified as a mental health nurse in Liverpool and worked in a newly developing crisis service before briefly working in homelessness outreach. Nigel subsequently moved to the Royal Liverpool University Hospital offering a liaison/consultation mental health service for patients in the general hospital. He went on to establish an A&E based crisis intervention team and is involved in the development of home treatment/crisis resolution services for Liverpool. He is undertaking a PhD in Reattribution Therapy for Unexplained Medical Symptoms with other interests in suicide prevention and CBT in crisis intervention.

Clare Dixon attained a BSc (Hons) in Behavioural Science at The University of Huddersfield in 1994. Her research career has included work for The Hester Adrian Research Centre, CommuniCare NHS Trust, Blackburn and the University of Manchester in both the Department of Psychiatry and Centre for Suicide Prevention. Her PhD in 2000 involved a multi-method evaluation of a training intervention for GPs in the assessment and management of depression. Clare is currently working on the National Evaluation of Sure Start.

Jenny Droughton is Consultant Nurse, Suicide Prevention and Risk Management, for Cheshire and Wirral Partnership NHS Trust. Prior to this, Jenny was Assistant Programme Director of the Foundation Programme in Psychosocial Management of Psychoses, part of the COPE (Collaboration On Psychosocial Education) Initiative based at the University of Manchester. She has also been involved in the delivery of multi-disciplinary, evidence-based training in suicide prevention. As well as combining her training commitments with continued clinical practice with people with severe and enduring mental health problems, Jenny has undertaken research into the protective impact of employment on mental health.

David Duffy is a Nurse Consultant specialising in suicide and self-harm, employed by Bolton Salford and Trafford Mental Health NHS Trust. He has over twenty years' experience of mental health care. From 2001 to 2002 he co-ordinated the Department of Health's National Suicide Prevention Strategy for England, and is a member of the steering committee of the National Confidential Inquiry into Suicide and Homicide by People with Mental Illness. David has served as a panel member for a number of external inquiries into homicides and suicides. He was awarded an MSc and a PhD for research into suicide, and has published extensively. He is the lead author of the *NIMHE Suicide Prevention Toolkit*.

Linda Gask is Reader in Community Psychiatry at the University of Manchester and Honorary Consultant Psychiatrist at Lancashire Care NHS Trust based at the Royal Preston Hospital in Lancashire. She has a long-standing interest in research and training in the acquisition of mental health skills and mental health problems in primary care settings.

Gill Green is the STORM (Skills-based Training On Risk Management) co-ordinator responsible for developing and delivering the 'Trainers' course nationally and internationally. Her background is in mental health nursing although she began her career in the learning disabilities field. For the last seven years Gill has worked in mental health research on various projects for the Department of Psychiatry, University of Manchester. Interests have included training staff for the first feasibility study of STORM and developing a Prison STORM package. Gill has also worked for the Northwest Forensic Academic Network on various prison-based studies.

David Hewitt is a solicitor and a partner with Hempsons, one of the UK's pre-eminent health care law firms. He has been a member of the Mental Health Act Commission since 1995, and was at one time part of the Commission team that reviewed the deaths of detained patients. David is a member of the editorial board of the *Journal of Mental Health Law*, a frequent contributor to the *New Law Journal*, and writes regularly for *Health Care Risk Report*. He has lectured widely, to professional and academic audiences throughout England and overseas.

Kathryn Hill is an experienced NHS manager, particularly in the field of mental health. Kathryn has spent 14 years managing mental health services in central London. Most recently Kathryn worked as a Research Fellow at the Institute for Applied Health and Social Policy based at King's College, University of London, supporting local services in the implementation of the National Service Framework, service configuration and service re-engineering. Kathryn has a Masters in Social Policy and Sociology. Kathryn joined the National Patient Safety Agency in January 2003 as the lead for mental health.

Christine Hogg is a Senior Lecturer in the School of Nursing at the University of Salford, Manchester. Christine has held various posts in mental health nursing, including working in Regional Secure Services where she completed research examining mental health nurses' attitudes and experiences of working with people who self-harm. Since joining the School of Nursing in 1994 she has been actively involved in designing and developing education programmes to enable health staff to work more effectively and therapeutically with people who self-harm. Christine is co-author of the book *Cultural Awareness in Nursing and Health Care – An Introductory Text*, published in 2001 by Arnold.

Navneet Kapur is a Senior Lecturer and Honorary Consultant in Psychiatry at the Centre for Suicide Prevention, University of Manchester. His research interests include service provision for suicidal behaviour and the aetiology of illness behaviour.

Barry Lewis has been a GP Principal in the same teaching practice in Rochdale UK since 1979. He developed a specific interest in mental health during his junior doctor training and continued this into Primary Care. He has worked with alcohol and drug counselling services developing training packages applicable to UK Primary Care workers and extended this work during his appointment as RCGP Mental Health for North West England between 1994 and 1998. He has been involved in educational development work through the North West Mental Health Development. Involvement with two MRC sponsored research projects has allowed him to combine the development of training packages with educational research into their effectiveness in both improving clinical skills and patient outcomes. The STORM research project (suicide risk assessment) demonstrated the value of specific training targeted at clinicians across Primary and Secondary care in improving awareness, skills and safe practice. Barry has written extensively in GP educational journals and is currently editor of *Community Mental Health* (Hayward Publications).

Sarah Nelson has been with Samaritans for nearly two years as PR and Media Manager. Her role involves the strategic planning and implementation of campaigns aimed at raising awareness of Samaritans, its work and its vision among journalists and other relevant opinion formers such as academics, those working in health care provision and development and other voluntary sector organisations. Campaigns that she has overseen include the re-branding of Samaritans, the launch of an email emotional support service and Samaritans' 50th birthday celebrations. She is also responsible for managing Samaritans' busy press office and team of press officers, as well as working with journalists to encourage the responsible reporting of suicide.

Victoria Pallin is a clinical psychologist. Since qualifying she has worked in adult mental health with a particular interest in working psychotherapeutically with clients with a trauma history and long-standing mental health problems. Working within a Community Mental Health Team alongside a general hospital inpatient service she developed an interest in supervision and staff support. She has been active in promoting trust-wide training and multi-disciplinary support for staff working with suicidal clients. Pursuing her interest in training and supervision she has recently joined the University of Manchester doctoral Clinical Psychology training programme as a Clinical Tutor.

Anne Parry is a Trustee and the current Chair of PAPYRUS, and was formerly a secondary school science teacher and a co-ordinator of special educational needs. She has been instrumental in producing the booklets *Not Just a Cry for Help* and *Thinking of Ending it All?* and the teachers' resource notes that accompany the video. Anne has lost a child to suicide.

Jo Paton is Head of Research and Training Unit, Safer Custody Group, HM Prison Service. Originally a psychiatric social worker, Jo spent 10 years working at local and national level to improve mental health skills and services in general practice. She then moved to the Institute of Psychiatry, Kings College, where she co-edited the *WHO Guide to Mental Health in Primary Care* and *Mental Health Primary Care in Prison*. To inform the latter work, she surveyed prison health staff and interviewed Prison Officers about their mental health learning needs. Her current work includes leading work to improve how prisoners who are at risk of suicide and those who self-harm are assessed and cared for, including improving staff training.

Alison Pearsall is an experienced mental health practitioner who has worked in a variety of hospital and community settings ranging from acute inpatient, forensic, substance misuse and the community, since 1983. Alison works for Lancashire Care NHS Trust managing prison in-reach services and previously worked as a Clinical Nurse Specialist within the Access and Crisis Service in Bury. She also works as an Associate Consultant for the Health and Social Care Advisory Service, and has been involved with the co-ordination of the North West Suicide Prevention Network, a national project aiming to improve access for people with learning disabilities to mental health care and the reviewing of out-of-district placements for people with serious mental illness in the North West.

Rowan Purdy is a Programme Co-ordinator for NIMHE North West and leads on the Knowledge Management Programme. This programme aims to connect people, resources, projects and knowledge to support service improvement leading to better outcomes for people with mental health problems and their families in the North West. Rowan has successfully developed and leads a range of innovative and dynamic learning and knowledge-based work activities, from IT-based technical activity to people-based community building, communication and other activities that promote knowledge capture and knowledge sharing among the staff, networks and groups. He also plays an important role in delivering NIMHE Knowledge Community Project and will soon support the *Mental Health Today Magazine* collaborative between Pavilion and NIMHE. Rowan was previously the Resource Manager for the former North West Mental Health Development Centre. Rowan spends the rest of his life dedicated to his two amazing children, Bria and Evan, and his wonderful wife Tracy.

Richard Ramsay is a long-time professor of social work at the University of Calgary and previously worked in correctional after care and residential youth care programs. He is a co-founder of the telephone distress centres in Ottawa and Edmonton, charter member of Alberta's Suicide Prevention Provincial Advisory Committee, co-chair of the United Nations Interregional Meeting to develop guidelines for the formulation and implementation of national strategies for suicide prevention, co-founder of LivingWorks Education and the ASIST program, and recipient of the Dr John H. Read Award for outstanding achievement in the area of injury control.

Jo Robinson was the Senior Project Manager for the National Confidential Inquiry into Suicide and Homicide by People with Mental Illness and had been employed with the Inquiry since November 1999 until moving to Australia in January 2004. She was also recently seconded to the National Institute for Mental Health supporting the development and implementation of the national Suicide Prevention Strategy for England. Jo's background is in Applied Psychology and her interests are in mental health service development, with a specific interest in the prevention of suicide. Jo has authored several academic publications (currently in press) and has presented Inquiry findings at international conferences in Washington, Melbourne and Stockholm as well as at many academic meetings in the UK.

Tony Ryan works in research and service development for the Health and Social Care Advisory Service and Manchester University and previously for the North West Mental Health Development Centre. He worked for Turning Point for eight years developing and managing a range of mental health and alcohol services in Greater Manchester. Tony also spent 10 years working in the NHS as a mental health nurse in a variety of roles and in 1999 he edited the book *Managing Crisis and Risk in Mental Health Nursing*. Tony was awarded his PhD at Lancaster University on risk and mental health and has published on a wide range of topics including service development, mental health policy, nursing practice and research methodology. Tony is also co-editor of *Good Practice in Adult Mental Health* (with Jacki Pritchard) aslo published by Jessica Kingsley Publishers.

Pippa Sargent co-ordinates the Department of Health's Campaign Against Living Miserably (CALM), working across mental health, men's health and communications. Holding a BSc, and qualified in holistic therapies and counselling, she has worked for MIND in Manchester, and for 5 years both practised and chaired as a trustee, mental health advocacy projects. A freelance mental health trainer and facilitator, her work has also included developing the user-led anti-stigma focused Schizophrenia Media Agency, challenging the misrepresentation of mental health in the media. Since 1998 Pippa has established the CALM campaign on the ground in Manchester before taking a more strategic role as National Co-ordinator.

Hári Sewell is Director of Social Care and Substance Misuse Services in Camden and Islington Mental Health and Social Care Trust. He began his professional career as an Approved Social Worker. He has since held commissioning and strategic posts across social services and the NHS. Most recently Hári has worked at the previous NHS London Regional Office managing the implementation of the National Service Framework and in the Social Services Inspectorate assessing the performance of social services departments. He has also contributed to policy development within the Department of Health, from the genesis of the National Service Framework to recent implementation guidance. Outside of his substantive employment Hári teaches and presents on anti-discriminatory practice.

Clare Shaw has gained considerable knowledge around mental health from her experiences as a user/survivor of the psychiatric system. These experiences motivated her to become involved in the survivor movement, where she is still very active. This also informs her work in awareness raising around mental health. Clare went back into education in order to develop her understanding of women's mental health and graduated with an MA in Applied Women's Studies. She went on to begin PhD research around the diagnosis of borderline personality disorder, but is currently taking a break to focus on her poetry writing. Clare attends Survivor's Poetry in Manchester, performs regularly and is working towards her first collection.

Lester Sireling is an adult psychiatrist, working in a large and socially mixed catchment area in Barnet. Most of his research is on the topic of depression, and he has also researched and taught about bereavement. From the confluence of these subjects arises his interest in suicide. while still in training he proposed a survey of suicides, as this seemed to be the only clearly defined outcome in psychiatry. He was advised by the Medical Superintendent to wait until he became a consultant before attempting anything so radical…and so he did. Eighteen years later he wonders if perhaps the Medical Superintendent knew best.

Mike Smith is a freelance worker in mental health and has formerly held executive posts within the NHS and non-Government sector. He is the author of many publications in mental health including the workbooks *Working with Voices, Working with Self-harm, Working with Survivors of Sexual Abuse* and more recently *Psychiatric First Aid in Psychosis*. Mike has also contributed to and devised a number of national television and radio programmes on mental health. Mike was awarded the Bethlem and Maudsley 750th anniversary award for the advancement of mental health care and also is a former holder of the 'Nurse of the Year' title for the United Kingdom.

Jude Stansfield is a development worker for mental health promotion, social inclusion and suicide prevention at the National Institute for Mental Health in England (NIMHE) NW Development Centre. Her work is to support localities in implementing the health promotion requirements of the National Service Framework for Mental Health and to work with NW organisations and bodies in developing Mental Health Promotion policy and practice. She works closely with colleagues in NIMHE Equalities team and also with the GONW Public Health Team.

Gemma Trainor is a nurse consultant specialising in the treatment of young people who self-harm. She has to date over 20 years' experience of inpatient and outpatient work within the NHS. The intervention described in her paragraph 'developmental group psychotherapy' was submitted as her thesis and she was awarded her PhD in 2001. The pilot study showed positive results in reducing repetition of self-harming behaviour. As a result funding was secured and Gemma is currently one of the principle investigators of a large multi-centre randomised control trial looking at the effectiveness and transferability of the treatment.

Peter Walmsley is Manager of the Crisis Assessment and Rapid Domiciliary Support Team (CARDS) at Mersey Care NHS Trust. He was previously a Lecturer in Mental Health at Edge Hill University College. Peter has had many articles published within the nursing press and mental health press. He was born in Liverpool and trained as a general nurse before going on to train as a mental health nurse within the Merseyside area. Peter worked at Guys Hospital in London prior to moving to work in Southport and completed his MSc at Liverpool University. Peter was a finalist in the Florence Nightingale Travel Scholarship, travelling to the USA and Ireland to visit a range of services. He is married to Kate and lives with their two children, Emma and Holly.

Suzette Woodward is a qualified general and paediatric nurse who worked mostly in acute Trusts in London, and a year abroad in Bermuda, specialising in paediatric intensive care. She has a Postgraduate Diploma in Management Studies and an MSc in Clinical Risk Management. Prior to starting in January 2003 at the National Patient Safety Agency as an Assistant Director of Patient Safety (London), Suzette spent eight years at Great Ormond Street Hospital for Children, starting as a Clinical Risk Manager, progressing to Assistant Director, Clinical Governance in 1999. She has in-depth experience of undertaking inquiries and writing reports following high-profile serious incidents, complex risk assessments and creating a patient safety culture. During 2001 and 2002, Suzette was seconded to the Department of Health, Investigations and Inquiries Unit. During this secondment she assisted in the Government's response to the Bristol Royal Infirmary Inquiry Report.

Subject Index

Author Index